LEGACIES OF THE LEFT TURN IN LATIN AMERICA

LEGACIES OF THE LEFT TURN IN LATIN AMERICA

THE PROMISE OF INCLUSIVE CITIZENSHIP

EDITED BY
MANUEL BALÁN AND
FRANÇOISE MONTAMBEAULT

University of Notre Dame Press
Notre Dame, Indiana

Library of Congress Control Number: 2019952784

ISBN-13: 978-0-268-10657-7 (Hardback)
ISBN: 978-0-268-10659-1 (WebPDF)
ISBN: 978-0-268-10660-7 (Epub)

To our families

CONTENTS

FIGURES AND TABLES

FIGURES

TABLES

PREFACE

As we write these words, the Right turn in Latin America is no longer a possibility but a tangible and undeniable reality. The elections of Macri in Argentina, Duque in Colombia, Piñera in Chile, Kuczynski in Peru, and, most recently, Bolsonaro in Brazil are clear indications that the winds have shifted and that the Left turn is over. While some signs of the ebbing of the Left turn were apparent when we started this project, the context was significantly different from the one the region faces currently. As an example, during the 2016 conference that provided the starting point for this volume, many of the presenters made explicit references to Brazil's critical situation and Dilma's likely impeachment. For all the pessimism that surrounded those conversations, we do not think many of us foresaw that an extreme right-wing fringe candidate such as Bolsonaro would become the president only a couple of years later. Against this backdrop, the current context may lead us to ask what's left of the left in Latin America; a straightforward and simplistic answer is, not much.

However, and despite the changes in the political configuration in the region, our objective in putting forward this project in 2016 remains unchanged: we wanted to dig deeper and think about the significance of a decade and a half of self-identified left-of-center governments in the region. In doing so, we purposefully chose to embrace the complexity of the different cases under analysis, explicitly rejecting the categorization of presidencies across countries as moderate or radical or good or bad left governments. Rather, the analysis is organized across key issue areas, allowing for an assessment of different cases that can highlight their internal contradictions and tensions. As such, the study of the legacies of the Left turn entailed two central sets of questions. First, what has changed and what has remained the same after the Left turn? This question required an evaluation of both institutional and legal changes as well as of practices and realities on the ground in the region, and the contributors have done a fantastic job addressing this key issue. Second, what is the potential staying power of reforms and improvements—where there were any—that resulted from Left turn governments? This second question requires a complex assessment that is, by definition, uncertain and speculative. Many of the contributors engage explicitly this issue, which was always potentially important but has now become key in analyzing the potential backlash of this incipient Right turn. Therefore, this volume can help us understand not only the shortcomings and achievements of the different Left turn governments but also the potential for current right-wing governments to reverse the course, particularly in certain sectors and on certain issues.

Moreover, the complex and mosaic-like depiction of the Left turn provided in this volume is essential for shedding light not only on the value and legacies of the Left turn but also on the reasons for the current swing of the ideological pendulum to the right. While economic downturns and the punishment of incumbents seem to be at least part of the explanation for both the Left turn fifteen years ago and the current Right turn, the analyses provided by the contributors also point to some of the inherent tensions and shortcomings that defined the Left turn, which may also help explain its demise. In this sense, even when the explicit objective of the volume was not to analyze the end of the Left turn, the arguments and evidence presented provide a starting point for this analysis, which is likely a task that will shape the study of the region in the next few years.

This volume evaluates to what extent the Left turn managed to fulfill its promise to improve the lives of people, especially historically marginalized people, in the region. The overarching framework allows for a complex answer that highlights certain areas of progress and others of continuity or even regression. Now, as we collectively begin to think about questions related to the reasons for the current turn to the right and the potential for these governments to make substantial changes to policies and realities in the region, this volume identifies shortcomings

that may explain the left's fall from popular favor. Moreover, and perhaps most important, it also identifies the areas where the potential for
right-wing governments to push ahead with their agenda are the greatest. Our hope is that this volume will help inform not only our assess-
ments of the meanings of the Left turn over a decade and a half but also
future analyses of politics in the region.

ACKNOWLEDGMENTS

This book is the fruit of a collaborative effort at many levels, for which the support and work of our colleagues and institutions have been crucial. It reflects the dynamism of a collective endeavor started in 2014, when a group of Montreal-based colleagues working on Latin America in various disciplines of the social sciences met and created the Réseau d'études latino-américaines de Montréal (RÉLAM), a network of scholars and students who have since then engaged in an ongoing conversation about politics, society, history, and culture in the region. It is with this group of colleagues from the Université du Québec à Montréal (UQAM), McGill University, Université de Montréal, and Concordia University that the first seeds of the discussion that led to the book were planted: Cynthia Milton and Victor Armony, who were then codirectors of RÉLAM, and Jean-François Mayer, Nora Nagels, Julián Durazo Herrmann, Geneviève Dorais, and Tina Hilgers, who cofounded RÉLAM with us and have over time become our academic family here in Montreal.

It is with their support that we organized the international conference "What's Left?" sponsored by RÉLAM and held in Montreal on March 23 and 24, 2016, which was the beginning of the book project. We are grateful to the Social Sciences and Humanities Research Council of Canada (SSHRC); the Centre d'études et de recherches internationales de l'Université de Montréal (CÉRIUM); the Department of Political Science and Dean of Arts and Sciences at the Université de Montréal; the McGill Institute for the Study of International Development (ISID); the McGill Institute for the Study of Canada (MISC); the Department of Political Science and the Dean of Arts at McGill University; the Dean of Arts at Concordia University; the Department of

Political Science, Dean of Political Science and Law, Department of Sociology, and Dean of Humanities at UQAM; and the Chaire d'étude du Canada en histoire de l'Amérique latine for their financial support. We are very grateful to our graduate students, Geneva List and Annabelle Dias Felix, whose coordination work was impeccable, and to their team of volunteers who made sure the conference ran smoothly. We thank our colleagues from RÉLAM, who composed the conference scientific committee (Jean-François Mayer, Cynthia Milton, Kregg Hetherington, and Graciela Ducatenzeiler). We owe special thanks to Graciela Ducatenzeiler, who organized a groundbreaking international workshop at the Université de Montréal in 2006 as we were only starting to talk about the Pink Tide. She was involved in the initial conversations, the intellectual work, and all the organizational steps of the "What's Left?" conference, which was conceived as a way to take stock of this Pink Tide and go back to the earlier discussions about the scholarly community expectations, fifteen years after the election of the first leftist government in the region and ten years after the first conference was held in Montreal.

We are particularly grateful to all the contributors to this volume, whose enthusiasm for the project and dedication helped transform the project into an actual book. The minutiae and patience of Rose Chabot was much appreciated by us and by all the authors in the process of editing and preparing the manuscript for the press. Not all participants in the 2016 conference contributed a chapter to the volume, but their participation in panels and early discussions about the legacies of the left in the region strengthened our argument. They are Juan Pablo Luna, Tianna S. Paschel, Alberto Vergara, Tina Hilgers, Kregg Hetherington, Viviana Patroni, Mark Becker, Cynthia Milton, Rebecca Atencio, Claudio Barrientos, Alejandro Velasco, Jessica Stites-Mor, and Paulo Drinot. The discussants played an important part, too, as they asked questions that helped sharpen the reflections underlying the book and suggested improvements in the chapters that were first presented on this occasion. We would therefore like to thank Philip Oxhorn, Julián Durazo Herrmann, Jean-François Mayer, Carlos Figari, and Catherine LeGrand.

We are also grateful to our editor at the University of Notre Dame Press, Eli Bortz, who believed in the merits of our book project from the beginning and whose support and advice were key in moving forward with it. Working with him to bring the project to its final form has been a real pleasure. The anonymous reviewers' comments helped sharpen the book's overall focus and identified interesting avenues for improvements in all the chapters.

Finally, we want to thank Philippe Morin and Celina Van Dembroucke, our partners, whose support at all levels has once again been crucial throughout the process. We are extremely grateful to them and to our respective kids, Victor and Elsa and Teodoro and Elías, who once again bore with us as we were organizing a conference, attending innumerable meetings, and working to bring our project to life. This book is dedicated to them.

ABBREVIATIONS

AD	Acción Democrática (Democratic Action)
ANR	Asociación Nacional Republicana (Republican National Association)
APDH	Asamblea Permanente por los Derechos Humanos (Permanent Assembly for Human Rights)
APRA	Alianza Popular Revolucionaria Americana (American Popular Revolutionary Alliance)
BF	Bolsa Familia (conditional cash transfer program, Brazil)
BJA	Bono Juana Azurduy (conditional cash transfer program, Bolivia)
BJP	Bono Juancito Pinto (conditional cash transfer program, Bolivia)
CC	Consejo comunal (communal council)
CCTs	Conditional cash transfers
CELS	Centro de Estudios Legales y Sociales (Center of Legal and Social Studies)
CLAP	Comité Local de Abastecimiento y Producción (Local Supply and Production Committee)
CODENPE	Consejo de Nacionalidades y Pueblos del Ecuador (Council for the Development of Ecuadorean Nationalities and Peoples)
CONADEP	Comisión Nacional sobre la Desaparición de Personas (National Commission on the Disappearance of Persons)

CONADI	Corporación Nacional de Desarrollo Indígena (National Corporation for Indigenous Development)
CONAIE	Confederación de Nacionalidades Indígenas del Ecuador (Confederation of Indigenous Nationalities of Ecuador)
CONALCAM	Coordinadora Nacional por el Cambio (National Coordinator for Change)
CONLACTRAHO	Confederación Latinoamericana y del Caribe de Trabajadoras del Hogar (Latin American and Caribbean Confederation of Domestic Workers)
CSO	Civil society organization
CSUTCB	Confederación Sindical Única de Trabajadores Campesinos de Bolivia (Unique Confederation of Rural Laborers of Bolivia)
DINA	Dirección de Inteligencia Nacional (National Intelligence Directorate)
DINEIB	Dirección Nacional de Educación Intercultural Bilingüe (Directorate for Intercultural Bilingual Education)
ECLAC	Economic Commission for Latin America and the Caribbean
ELN	Ejército de Liberación Nacional (National Liberation Army)
EPL	Ejército Popular de Liberación (Popular Liberation Army)
ESMA	Escuela Militar de la Armada (Navy Petty Officers School of Mechanics)
EZLN	Ejército Zapatista de Liberación Nacional (Zapatista Army of National Liberation)
FA	Frente Amplio (Broad Front)
FARC-EP	Fuerzas Armadas Revolucionarias de Colombia—Ejército Popular (Revolutionary Armed Forces of Colombia—Popular Army)
FMLN	Frente Farabundo Martí de Liberación Nacional (Farabundo Martí National Liberation Front)

FPIC	Free, prior, and informed consent
FPV	Frente para la Victoria (Front for Victory)
FSLN	Frente Sandinista de Liberación Nacional (Sandinista Front for National Liberation)
GDP	Gross domestic product
HHRR	Human rights
H.I.J.O.S.	Hijos e Hijas por la Identidad y la Justicia contra el Olvido y el Silencio (Sons and Daughters for Identity and Justice against Oblivion and Silence)
IDP	Internally displaced persons
IIRSA	Iniciativa para la Integración de la Infraestructura Regional Sudamericana (Initiative for the Integration of the Regional Infrastructure of South America)
ILO	International Labor Organization
IMF	International Monetary Fund
INADI	Instituto Nacional contra la Discriminación, la Xenophobia y el Racismo (National Institute against Discrimination, Xenophobia, and Racism)
INDH	Instituto Nacional de Derechos Humanos (National Institute for Human Rights)
ISI	Import substitution industrialization
ITT	Ishpingo-Tambococha-Tiputini, Yasuní National Park
LAFTA	Latin American Free Trade Association
LPP	Ley de participación popular (Law of Popular Participation)
M-19	Movimiento 19 de abril (April 19th Movement)
MAB	Movimento dos Atingidos por Barragens (Movement of People Affected by Dams)
MAS	Movimiento al Socialismo (Movement toward Socialism)
MMA	Ministério do Meio Ambiente (Ministry of the Environment, Brazil)

MNR	Movimiento Nacionalista Revolucionario (Revolutionary Nationalist Movement)
MST	Movimento dos Trabalhadores Rurais Sem Terra (Landless Workers' Movement)
MUD	Mesa de la Unidad Democrática (Democratic Unity Roundtable)
MUPP-NP	Movimiento de Unidad Plurinacional Pachakutik—Nuevo País (Pachakutik Movement for Plurinational Unity—New Country)
MVR	Movimiento V República (Fifth Republic Movement)
NAFTA	North American Free Trade Agreement
NGO	Nongovernmental organization
PAC	Partido Acción Ciudadana (Citizens' Action Party)
PAC	Programas de Acceleración del Creciminento (Plans for Accelerated Growth)
PAIS Alliance	Movimiento Alianza Patria Altiva i Soberana (Proud and Sovereign Fatherland Alliance)
PAN	Partido Acción Nacional (National Action Party)
PC	Partido Colorado (Colorado Party)
PCCh	Partido Comunista de Chile (Communist Party of Chile)
PEEP	Plan de Erradicación de la Extrema Pobreza (Extreme Poverty Eradication Plan, Bolivia)
PJ	Partido Justicialista (Justicialist Party)
PLN	Partido de Liberación Nacional (National Liberation Party)
PLRA	Partido Liberal Radical Auténtico (Authentic Radical Liberal Party)
PMDB	Partido do Movimento Democrático Brasileiro (Brazilian Democratic Movement Party)
PND	Plan nacional de desarrollo: Bolivia digna soberana, productiva y democratica para Vivir Bien (National Development Plan: Bolivia Worthy, Sovereign, and Productive to Live Well)

PPG7	Pilot Programme for the Protection of Tropical Forests in Brazil
PRD	Partido de la Revolución Democrática (Party of the Democratic Revolution)
PRI	Partido Revolucionario Institucional (Institutional Revolutionary Party)
PRO	Propuesta Republicana (Republican Proposal)
PSCh	Partido Socialista de Chile (Chilean Socialist Party)
PSUV	Partido Socialista Unido de Venezuela (United Socialist Party of Venezuela)
PT	Partido dos Trabalhadores (Workers' Party)
REDD and REDD+	Reduced gas emissions from deforestation and forest degradation
SPF	São Paulo Forum
TIPNIS	Territorio Indígena y Parque Nacional Isiboro Sécure (Indigenous Territory and Isiboro Sécure National Park)
UCR	Unión Cívica Radical (Radical Civil Union)
UNDRIP	United Nations Declaration on the Rights of the Indigenous Peoples
UPP	Unidade de Polícia Pacificadora (Pacifying Police Unit)
VAW	Violence Against Women
VDEM	Variety of Democracy

Introduction

Manuel Balán and Françoise Montambeault

Before the Left turn that swept over Latin America in the late 1990s and early 2000s, leftist political parties and leaders in Latin America had rarely been able to win elections, much less govern on a leftist policy platform. It is perhaps this long history of the absence of sustained left- ist governments in the region that explains why the Left turn took most analysts by surprise. Few could imagine in the late 1990s that left- or center-left-leaning leaders would win elections, be reelected, and end up governing in most countries in the region for a period of roughly fifteen years. Conversely, the end of this Pink Tide seems to have been loom- ing at least since the 2008 economic crisis. In recent years, the electoral defeat of the Frente para la Victoria (Front for Victory, FPV) in Argen- tina in late 2015 and then again in mid-2017, the impeachment of the Partido dos Trabalhadores (Workers' Party, PT) president Dilma Rous- seff in Brazil in 2016 and the election of Jair Bolsonaro in 2018, and the breakdown of the Venezuelan economy and democratic institutions under Nicolás Maduro, among other developments, seems to signal that the Left turn is fading away. As the left recedes, it is time to take stock:

What were the effects of a decade and a half of left and center-left governments? The central purpose of this volume is to evaluate the effects of the Left turn in terms of the positive and negative changes—as well as the patterns of continuity—in state-society relations and inclusion. Arguably, promises of social inclusion and the expansion of citizenship rights were central to the center-left discourses upon their arrival to power in the late 1990s and early 2000s. This volume signifies a first step in understanding to what extent these initial promises were fulfilled or not, and why. In analyzing these issues, it is also paramount to think about the potential staying power of the changes Left turn governments managed to achieve.

The shift to the left in the late 1990s and early 2000s came with an array of more or less explicit promises that generated a set of expectations, both among populations and among—generally more skeptical—experts (Castañeda 2006). Existing research (Roberts 2014) has shown that there were important differences across cases in how leaders got to power and in the policy platforms of and promises made by each government (Levitsky and Roberts 2011b; Weyland, Madrid, and Hunter 2010). Moreover, in some cases these new expectations emerged during the electoral campaign that brought some of these leaders to power (Brazil, Venezuela, Bolivia), while in others the shift took place once the party or leader was in office (Argentina and, to some extent, Ecuador). Yet in all cases, leftist governments arrived in a region widely characterized by unparalleled levels of economic and social inequality, making the promise of redistribution and inclusion perhaps the strongest mandate and expectation behind the shift to the left (Huber and Stephens 2012). The governments that arrived to power in the late 1990s and early 2000s laid out the explicit or implicit promise to improve the living conditions of previously disadvantaged individual citizens and social groups, even if, as argued by Queirolo (2013), their election responded more to a rejection of incumbents than to an ideological shift in the electorate or to a backlash against neoliberalism. As it happens, there was massive room for improvement: after democratization and economic turmoil in the late 1980s, the initial stabilizing effect of market reforms in the 1990s was quickly followed by slow or even nonexistent growth, increased distributional problems (higher inequality), and dismal social consequences (Huber and Solt 2004; Lustig, Lopez-Calva, and Ortiz-Juarez 2013; Roberts 2008). The economic downturn of 1998–2002 worsened conditions further, even reversing any instances of lackluster growth that had taken place in previous years (ECLAC 2003). In fact, many analyses of the Left turn point to this economic situation as at least one of the main explanatory factors of its emergence, together with long-term structural factors such as inequality and the institutionalization of electoral competition (Levitsky and Roberts 2011a).

Before the recent Left turn, the historical governance record for leftist parties in Latin America was far from stellar: most previous political parties and leaders that promised to govern on the left were either swiftly defeated at the polls or forcefully removed from office before their terms were over or quickly shifted to the right after entering government (Stokes 2001). However, in the early 2000s, unlike previous left-leaning experiences, democracy—at least in a mostly procedural sense—appeared to be consolidated as the only game in town, and even deep challenges to presidential authority were now being channeled through institutional means (e.g., impeachments in Ecuador and Brazil and removal from office in Argentina; see Pérez Liñán 2007).

This context allowed, for the first time in Latin American history, for the arrival to government of an array of leftist and center-left political parties and leaders that had the realistic expectation that they would be able to complete their terms without fear of being removed from office. As it happened, the Left turn saw self-identified center-left and left political parties and leaders winning municipal, congressional, and, eventually, presidential elections and then getting reelected in competitive environments where victories were far from guaranteed. In this context, to what extent were these Left turn governments able to deliver on their promises and the expectations they generated? In other words, what's left in the region after a decade and a half of left-leaning governments? On the one hand, analyzing these questions can shed light on the empirical question regarding the performance and legacies of Left turn governments—an issue that has generated heated debates both in academic and in journalistic circles. On the other hand, given the lack of historical antecedents of sustained leftist governments in Latin America, answering these questions can help elucidate the actual impact that left and center-left governments can have on state-society relations.

While seemingly straightforward, the question of what's left after the Pink Tide is far from simple. There are several factors that add layers of complexity. First, as the literature that focused on the emergence of the Left turn pointed out, there is significant variation both across countries that turned to the left (Castañeda 2012; Flores-Macías 2012; Levitsky and Roberts 2011a; Weyland, Madrid, and Hunter 2010) and within countries through time (Cameron and Hershberg 2010), making it impossible to lump the region into a single category, or even two or three. In fact, many of the efforts to organize cases within the Left turn in a couple of broad categories, such as the good and the bad left, end up obscuring more than they illuminate the question (Cameron 2009). Second, the Left turn both coincided with and was triggered by an economic boom determined by the rise of China's economy and the spike in the price of and demand for commodities (Mazzuca 2012). This economic boom makes it difficult to disentangle the effects of external forces—demand for commodities—from domestic policies when it comes to explaining the causes of the economic growth we saw in the past decade and a half and the political and social possibilities this growth triggered. Finally, even the categorization of these governments as leftist is open for debate, as several authors have openly pointed out that countries considered part of the Pink Tide had in fact elements of continuity with the neoliberal model of the 1990s and autocratic tendencies that should not be associated with a "true" leftist ideological position (Dabène, this volume; Leiras 2016; Stefanoni 2016). These complications mean that a rigorous and systematic analysis of the consequences of the Left turn in Latin America requires an in-depth study that disentangles the variation across and within cases, looking at the patterns of change in different key institutions and policy issues in a way that resists simple blanket answers that provide a one-dimensional answer to a multilayered issue. This book advances such an analysis by focusing on key institutional reforms and policy areas that are linked by their importance for the potential creation of the expected inclusive citizenship regimes.

Of course, there is preliminary evidence pointing to some key conclusions, even if the causal effect of having left-leaning governments and policies is difficult to assess. What do we know? In terms of the economy, we know that there was economic growth in several countries governed by the left and that this growth was similar in countries governed by left and nonleft parties and leaders (IDB 2017; Leiras 2016). Yet countries governed by the left were more prone to both grow faster and suffer more from economic downturns, showing more sensitivity to external factors. And within countries that turned left, this tendency toward instability—higher highs and lower lows—was more acute in some cases (Ecuador, Bolivia, Venezuela) than others (Brazil, Chile, Uruguay) (Madrid, Hunter, and Weyland 2010). We know that inequality and poverty were reduced, albeit unevenly, across the region and that unemployment decreased throughout the period (Huber and Stephens 2012; Lustig, Lopez-Calva, and Ortiz-Juarez 2013). We also know that these advances started a quick process of reversal with the end of the commodity boom in the late 2000s (Leiras 2016). In broad terms, we know that there was a re-primarization of the economy in many countries in the region (Malamud 2016) and that the expectation of a new development model that departed from the extraction of natural resources was never met (Levitsky and Roberts 2011a). In terms of democratic electoral institutions, the rise of the left and the upswing in political polarization did not result in the breakdown of democracy, which would have been the expectation of many given the history of the left in the region (Malamud 2016). In addition, we know that there were important shifts in electoral competition patterns, with old political parties disappearing, new ones emerging, and others suffering important changes and adaptations that were required for their survival (Lupu 2016; Roberts 2014). These key general characteristics provide the backdrop for the analysis undertaken by our contributors.

OBJECTIVES AND ORGANIZATION OF THE BOOK

The objective of this volume is to assess the effects of the Left turn on state-society relations and on patterns of inclusion. In particular, we employ a theoretical framework anchored in the analysis of the citizenship regime, both in terms of formal policies and institutions and in terms of how these policies are implemented and changes in on-the-ground conditions. The focus on citizenship allows us to zoom in on the effects on societies, and especially on the historically disadvantaged or excluded sectors of the population. As argued in chapter 1 by Montambeault, Balán, and Oxhorn, citizenship regimes in the region have been historically characterized by persistent inequalities. Since democratization in the 1980s and 1990s, inclusive citizenship has been the subject of political claims by many actors in society, as states shifted to models of "citizenship as consumption" (Oxhorn 2011). It is in this context that leftist governments came to power in the early 2000s, promising to deepen democracy through different reforms and policies aimed at promoting more inclusive and meaningful citizenship regimes for all sectors of the population, especially the traditionally excluded. This volume starts from these promises and confronts them with the reality of nearly fifteen years of leftist governments in Latin America, looking specifically at the set of institutional reforms and public policies that have (or have not) been implemented by leftist governments and at their consequences for inclusion and citizenship from a comparative perspective.

This first chapter develops a theoretical framework that offers a conceptual lens for understanding the analyses presented later in the book, allowing for a cohesive interpretation of the range and scope of the legacies of the Left turn with regard to state-society relations and social inclusion. In short, the analysis proceeds on three main dimensions that relate to the development of a more inclusive and meaningful citizenship regime. First, the focus is on the boundaries of citizenship regimes through the lens of rights and formal rules established by policies or constitutional provisions. However, as Gargarella (2013) points out, guaranteeing rights in laws and constitutions is far different from actually guaranteeing the protection of these rights. Therefore, in the second dimension the analysis shifts to the practice of citizenship, shaped at least partly by the application of these formal changes on the ground, assessing the implementation of reforms and the creation and adaptation of informal practices that affect how citizenship is experienced by societies, particularly by the less well-off sectors of the population. Citizenship implies a sense of belonging to a political community, an aspect that is often overlooked (Yashar 2007). Third, therefore, the analysis focuses on this sense of belonging to a community anchored in both collective and intersectional identities as a key aspect of citizenship that is shaped and altered by state policies and their implementation. The focus is, in all cases, on inclusion and representation of historically marginalized groups.

In terms of specific areas of inquiry, the volume focuses on a set of key institutions and policy issues in the region. In chapter 2, Maxwell

A. Cameron analyzes liberalism and postliberalism as key notions in the study of the Left turn in Latin America. He traces the uses and misuses of liberalism in the region through time, detailing its past association with oligarchic forces and its transformation into neoliberalism in the early 1990s. However, despite this checkered past, Cameron argues that "liberalism has a future in Latin America," insofar as political forces position themselves as postliberal rather than antiliberal, emphasizing the emancipatory and empowering nature of liberalism, especially as it relates to citizenship regimes and citizenship rights.

Chapter 3, by Kenneth M. Roberts, looks at developments in the arena of political competition, providing a comparative analysis of how the years of New Left governments affected the composition of party systems and the specific party-voter linkages of left and nonleft political parties. The analysis proceeds both at the party system level and at the level of individual parties, and it focuses explicitly on the variations in the linkages between political parties and party systems with civil societies across the region. Roberts argues that the Left turn partially restructured programmatic competition, moving away from the convergence with the neoliberal model that characterized the previous decade. Yet he highlights how this new programmatic competition is unevenly and incompletely institutionalized, as the sociopolitical cleavages generated by the left only partially reconstructed national party systems. As the wave of the New Left ebbs, not only is it hard to see stable new alignments of partisan and electoral competition, but old alignments are still present and in some cases have been reinforced.

In chapter 4, Nathalia Sandoval-Rojas and Daniel M. Brinks focus on the constitutional changes that took place under the Left turn, analyzing whether the entrenchment of new rights and guarantees in national-level constitutions can help insulate the policy goals of these governments from reversal in the event of a turn to the right. The analysis is based on the cases of Colombia, Argentina, and Brazil, which allows an examination of what happens when the political pendulum shifts to the right or center right, as has happened recently in Brazil and Argentina. The conclusion of the chapter is nuanced and case specific, and the answer to their question is at least partially shaped by the role of the courts and their independence from political influence. However, the authors end up showing how social constitutionalism can in fact have at least midterm impacts on the stability and consolidation of acquired rights established in constitutions.

Benjamin Goldfrank, in chapter 5, studies an area in which there was a boom in experimentation during the decade and a half of the Left turn: participatory institutions. He documents the variation across left cases in their interest and willingness to engage in participatory reforms and shows a scenario in which even in countries where these initiatives were strongest, the end result is rather disappointing, as "participatory institutions of nearly all stripes are weak, stalled, disfigured, or in the process of being rolled back." Goldfrank explores different causes for this lackluster performance, such as the complexity of designing large-scale participatory institutions, the shifting social and political bases of support for these institutions, and the institutional incentives and constraints. Last, he highlights the impact of the neoextractivist development model employed to maintain power, which left key public policy decisions outside the scope of participatory institutions.

In chapter 6, Roberta Rice analyzes the improvement or lack thereof of Indigenous-state relations in the Andean region. In particular, she traces the impact of plurinational constitutionalism on how states and state policy deal with Indigenous peoples. Her analysis of Ecuador and Bolivia is anchored in two historical junctures, the unilateral and limited incorporation into the polity of Indigenous peoples in the mid twentieth century and constitutional recognition of plurinationality in the past decade, which has the potential to develop more equal relations between the state and Indigenous peoples. Ecuador and Bolivia represent cases where there have been concerted efforts to champion Indigenous rights, yet the results illuminate the manifold challenges in improving a relationship anchored in vast inequalities, neglect, and repression. The conclusion reached by Rice is that despite the importance of the constitutional changes of the past decade, relations between the state and Indigenous peoples are still characterized by a unidirectional logic that fails to empower the latter.

Chapter 7, by Elizabeth Jelin and Celina Van Dembroucke, looks at the shifting policies of human rights and memorialization of human rights violations in Argentina and Chile. In many ways, past human rights violations during dictatorships have been central to the construction of an active and engaged civil society, shaping the content and the practice of citizenship under democratic regimes. Jelin and Van Dembroucke trace the evolution over time of a growing consensus that condemns past violations, detailing the important impact that Left turn governments have had on this issue. They end their analysis with a look at how these consensuses have started to erode under post–Left turn governments, particularly in Argentina.

In chapter 8, Nora Nagels analyzes the impact of conditional cash transfers (CCTs), the main social policy design of recent decades in both Left turn and non–Left turn cases, on gender relations. While a vast body of literature analyzes the outcomes of CCTs in terms of poverty reduction, Nagels focuses on the effect of CCTs implemented in Bolivia on citizenship and more explicitly on gender inequalities and the reinforcement of maternalism. The chapter shows, on the one hand, that the universal character of Bolivian CCTs has signified a return to a redistributionist state, improving social inclusion; and, on the other, that CCTs have reduced the role of women to that of motherhood, limiting women's autonomy as full citizens. The insights of this case study are, according to Nagels, applicable to other cases, in Latin America as well as to other regions.

Merike Blofield, in chapter 9, zooms in on the issue of paid domestic workers in the region, who suffer from multiple disadvantages as an occupational group. This underprivileged position makes them a particularly good case to examine whether the Left has fulfilled its initial promise of deepening and widening citizenship regimes. Blofield uses a broad comparative lens to analyze whether Left turn governments, in comparison with nonleft governments both historically and contemporaneously, have promoted domestic workers' rights. Her findings reveal that Left turn governments, while neither a necessary nor a sufficient condition, improved the chances of equal rights reform and effective implementation, particularly after 2011.

In chapter 10, Jordi Díez also takes a wide comparative approach, in this case to analyze the expansion of sexual rights and the role of Left turn governments. While Latin America is nowadays at the forefront of the expansion of sexual citizenship, challenging the historical stereotypes of the region as conservative and *machista*, Díez's analysis reveals a far more complex image when it comes to the relationship between the Left and these advances. The chapter shows a rather mixed record, with countries on the left sitting on the ends of the spectrum: as both the most progressive and the most restrictive as regards sexual rights. Díez distinguishes among a variety of sexual rights and analyzes sixteen cases based on their record in sexual rights expansion. His central argument to explain the variation is that agency is a key part of the story: in most cases, the expansion of rights has been driven by gay and lesbian activism.

The last two issue-based chapters look at perhaps two of the main challenges and criticisms of the Left turn. In chapter 11, Eve Bratman looks at the politics of environmental protection and how it entered into tension with the developmentalist economic orientation during the Left turn, focusing on the Brazilian case in a comparative perspective. She shows how the revived developmentalist approach anchored in the exploitation of energy and infrastructure ended up sacrificing ecosystem health, often backtracking on the initial positions held by governments in Brazil, Ecuador, and Bolivia, to name a few. Bratman interrogates how Left turn governments approached deforestation, mining, and energy production in the Amazon region. She argues that the environmental legacy of the left should be assessed by looking both at the expansions of rights, which took place in many parts of the region, and at how, in practice, legal and political norms relating to environmental issues transformed social and ecological relationships.

In chapter 12, Gabriel Kessler delves into the other main challenge usually associated with the past decade and a half: the rise of urban crime as a main concern of the population. In the 1990s, urban crime rose in tandem with the increase in poverty, unemployment, and inequality, which led to an array of studies that made explicit causal linkages between social indicators and the rise of crime. However, Kessler shows that even though social indicators improved during the Left turn, crime either increased or did not decrease as expected. To shed light on the issue, the chapter first disentangles the different crime problems that are present in the region, showing areas of common concern as well as the specificities of certain areas and cases. Then it looks at whether there is common ground in security policies under Left turn governments but finds that here, too, there is quite a bit of variation. Kessler compares crime during the 1990s and crime during the Left turn, concluding that the main variation is the change in the forms of crime rather than intensity and that these transformations are based on mutations in the labor market and on the way in which deprivation, consumption, stigma, youth identities, peer groups, and the relationship with the police are experienced.

Finally, rather than a single concluding chapter, this volume offers two concluding chapters. The first, chapter 13 by Olivier Dabène, questions to what extent the Left turn was actually a turn to the "left." While recognizing the changes that took place in the region in the past fifteen years, he suggests we should be careful in our use of the "Left" as a descriptive or analytical category to accurately understand these recent evolutions. Dabène argues that the so-called Left turn failed to change the political offer available to voters and that, in fact, the left/right divide does not make much sense for Latin American voters. Moreover, he makes the point that the policy outcomes and realities on the ground did not substantially differ under leftist and nonleftist governments in the region. He finds that the "Left" turn did trigger moderate elite circulation that helped oxygenate democracy but closes on a note of distrust about the use of the "Left" category when it comes to Latin American politics.

Chapter 14, by Jared Abbott and Steven Levitsky, concludes the volume by comparatively assessing the extent to which citizenship regimes better reach the traditionally excluded after fifteen years of leftist governments in power in Latin America. Focusing on the extension of both liberal democratic rights and social rights and on the notion of access and belonging to citizenship regimes through the extension of participatory rights, their aggregate findings for the region are in line with those of the other contributors to the volume in that they are quite nuanced and modest. They find that while partisan ideology is an important factor in explaining the extension of citizenship regimes, it should not be overstated. Other factors such as economic constraints, state capacity, and social movement struggles should also be weighed to explain variation in institutional reforms and policy definition and implementation across and within countries. They conclude by saying that if leftist governments have contributed to laying the foundation for the construction of more inclusive and meaningful citizenship regimes, their sustainability over time remains questionable considering recent public opinion studies and political attitudes in the region.

Thus all the chapters in this volume explicitly look at the question of the legacies of the left for democratic institutions and public policy from the standpoint of the citizenship regimes framework we develop in chapter 1. In doing so, they implicitly (or in some cases explicitly) question different angles of our deliberately encompassing understanding of the otherwise multilayered and complex concept of democracy, sometimes looking at electoral democracy or at more substantive conceptions, participatory or social democracy. The chapters paint a detailed picture of specific issues in a set of different countries in the region, resulting in a mosaic that provides a nuanced assessment of the Left turn's legacies of inclusion for understanding both national and regional dynamics comparatively.

REFERENCES

Cameron, Maxwell A. 2009. "Latin America's Left Turns: Beyond Good and Bad." *Third World Quarterly* 30 (2): 331–48.

Cameron, Maxwell A., and Eric Hershberg. 2010. *Latin America's Left Turns: Politics, Policies, and Trajectories of Change.* Boulder, CO: Lynne Rienner.

Castañeda, Jorge G. 2006. "Latin America's Left Turn." *Foreign Affairs* 85.

———. 2012. *Utopia Unarmed: The Latin American Left after the Cold War.* New York: Vintage.

Flores-Macias, Gustavo A. 2012. *After Neoliberalism? The Left and Economic Reforms in Latin America.* Oxford: Oxford University Press.

Gargarella, Roberto. 2013. "Keeping the Promise: Rights and Realities in Latin America." *Boston Review*, January 1. www.bostonreview.net/world/keeping-promise.

Huber, Evelyne, and John D. Stephens. 2012. *Democracy and the Left: Social Policy and Inequality in Latin America.* Chicago: University of Chicago Press.

Huber, Evelyne, and Fred Solt. 2004. "Successes and Failures of Neoliberalism." *Latin American Research Review* 39 (3): 150–64.

Inter-American Development Bank (IDB). 2017. "LatinMacroWatch." www.iadb.org/en/databases/latin-macro-watch/latin-macro-watch-country-profiles%2C18579.html.

Leiras, Marcelo. 2016. "Economía y política en los gobiernos de izquierda de América Latina." Buenos Aires.

Levitsky, Steven, and Kenneth M. Roberts. 2011a. "Conclusion: Democracy, Development, and the Left." In Steven Levitsky and Kenneth M. Roberts, eds., *The Resurgence of the Latin American Left.* Baltimore, MD: Johns Hopkins University Press.

————, eds. 2011b. *The Resurgence of the Latin American Left*. Baltimore, MD: Johns Hopkins University Press.

Lupu, Noam. 2016. *Party Brands in Crisis: Partisanship, Brand Dilution, and the Breakdown of Political Parties in Latin America*. New York: Cambridge University Press.

Lustig, Nora, Luis F. Lopez-Calva, and Eduardo Ortiz-Juarez. 2013. "Declining Inequality in Latin America in the 2000s: The Cases of Argentina, Brazil, and Mexico." *World Development* 44: 129–41.

Madrid, Raúl, Wendy Hunter, and Kurt Weyland. 2010. "The Policies and Performance of the Contestatory and Moderate Left." In Kurt Weyland, Raúl Madrid, and Wendy Hunter, eds., *Leftist Governments in Latin America: Successes and Shortcomings*. New York: Cambridge University Press.

Malamud, Andrés. 2016. "¿Por qué retrocede la izquierda en América Latina?" In José Natanson and Martín Rodríguez, eds., ¿Por qué retrocede la izquierda? Buenos Aires: Capital Intelectual.

Mazzuca, Sebastián. 2012. "Commodity Boom and Institutional Poisoning: The New Political Economy of South America." In Jorge Dominguez and Michael Shifter, eds., *Democratic Governance in Latin America*. Baltimore, MD: Johns Hopkins University Press.

Oxhorn, Philip. 2011. *Sustaining Civil Society: Economic Change, Democracy, and the Social Construction of Citizenship in Latin America*. University Park: Pennsylvania State University Press.

Pérez Liñán, Anibal. 2007. *Presidential Impeachment and the New Political Instability in Latin America*. Cambridge: Cambridge University Press.

Queirolo, Rosario. 2013. *The Success of the Left in Latin America*. Notre Dame, IN: University of Notre Dame Press.

Roberts, Kenneth. 2008. "The Mobilization of Opposition to Economic Liberalization." *Annual Review of Political Science* 2: 327–49.

Roberts, Kenneth M. 2014. "Party Systems in the Neoliberal Era." In Kenneth M. Roberts, ed., *Changing Course in Latin America*. New York: Cambridge University Press.

Stefanoni, Pablo. 2016. "¿Alba o crepúsculo? Geografías y tensiones del 'socialismo del siglo XXI.'" In José Natanson and Martín Rodríguez, eds., ¿Por qué retrocede la izquierda? Buenos Aires: Capital Intelectual.

Stokes, Susan C. 2001. *Mandates and Democracy: Neoliberalism by Surprise in Latin America*. New York: Cambridge University Press.

United Nations Economic Commission for Latin America and the Caribbean (ECLAC). 2003. *Current Conditions and Outlook: Economic Survey of Latin America and the Caribbean 2002–2003*. Santiago: United Nations.

www.cepal.org/en/publications/1094-current-conditions-and-outlook-economic-survey-latin-america-and-caribbean-2002.

Weyland, Kurt, Raúl Madrid, and Wendy Hunter. 2010. *Leftist Governments In Latin America: Successes and Shortcomings*. New York: Cambridge University Press.

Yashar, Deborah. 2007. "Citizenship Regimes, the State and Ethnic Cleavages." In Joseph S. Tulchin and Meg Ruthenburg, eds., *Citizenship in Latin America*. Boulder, CO: Lynne Rienner.

PART 1

Theoretical Questions

ONE

Widening and Deepening Citizenship from the Left?

A Relational and Issue-Based Comparative Approach

FRANÇOISE MONTAMBEAULT, MANUEL BALÁN,
AND PHILIP OXHORN

Social, political, and economic inequalities have long been a defining feature of citizenship regimes in Latin America. Constructed on the premise of historically grounded social and political exclusion in the region, citizenship regimes changed dramatically under the neoliberal democratic regimes of the 1990s, as the backlash of economic austerity and ongoing democratic reforms contributed to the deepening of existing inequalities. If centuries of corporatism have resulted in what Oxhorn has called processes of controlled inclusion and "co-opted citizenship," with the turn to neoliberalism and neopluralism in the 1980s, access to citizenship remained essentially unequal as it shifted to a "citizenship as consumption" model (Oxhorn 2011). In this context, the redefinition of the boundaries and scope of citizenship, including both its institutional manifestations and its participants, became an important struggle for social movements and civil society actors, as they fought for inclusion, social justice, and the deepening of democracy in the 1990s (Dagnino 1998). Across Latin America, the language of citizenship resonated among activists and left-leaning political actors and translated into the discourses and proposals of the so-called New Left parties emerging in the electoral arena. It is in this context that the Left turn began in the late 1990s, with high popular expectations for substantively reducing inequalities and for the recognition of marginalized groups and traditionally excluded sectors' rights. Left turn governments thus came into power with the promise of deepening and widening citizenship regimes, for which a renewed relationship with traditionally excluded actors and civil society organizations was key. How have the governments of the Left turn performed in their efforts to deliver on this promise?

The objective of this introductory chapter is to offer a conceptual lens for understanding the analyses presented in this book and interpreting the range and scope of the legacies of the Left turn on citizenship in Latin America. However, because it is both theoretically contested and politically constructed, citizenship is not an easy concept to grapple with. Looking back at the way citizenship has been historically constructed and theoretically understood in Latin America, we argue that earlier approaches are inherently limited as they only provide a partial (and often overly optimistic) assessment of what citizenship means in practice, including its multiple layers and spaces. As Jelin emphasized, "Citizenship as well as rights are forever undergoing the process of construction and transformation" (1996, 104). And the interactions between groups in state and society at multiple levels are key to this process. It is of course through the definition and extension of formal rights that citizenship is defined; yet it is the everyday practices of an active citizenry that shape the extent and depth of citizenship regimes.

The implication is that in order to understand the breadth and depth of citizenship under the Left turn, it is not sufficient to look only at the nature of citizenship rights. We must also analyze who is included and who is not in *citizenship regimes*. We need to look at the level of inclusion, which is defined by formal access to these rights (the existence of institutional and social mechanisms for participation in the definition and exercise of these rights) and the population's sense of belonging to a community anchored in both collective and intersectional identities (collectively defined by their members and recognized as such). Throughout the volume, we thus propose a novel comparative approach to thinking about the ways the left has contributed to defining and redefining citizenship in Latin America. The book's first section looks at the boundaries of citizenship regimes through the lens of rights and formal rules established through policies or constitutional provisions. In the second section, the volume analyzes the practice of citizenship, as shaped at least partly by the changes and continuities in formal rules but also by social struggles. Looking at these aspects of citizenship regimes from a relational and intersectional perspective, we can disaggregate our empirical analysis of citizenship and develop both cross-country comparisons and comparisons of the different sectors of institutional and policy reforms adopted (or not) under the left in specific countries.

(RE)DEFINING CITIZENSHIP IN LATIN AMERICA

Citizenship has been a widely deployed concept in the literature on Latin America, particularly to understand the struggles of disadvantaged groups within society and their relation to the state; these define the nature of their incorporation in (or exclusion from) the processes of state formation and democratization during crucial moments in Latin American history. Despite (or perhaps because of) this, citizenship is a deeply contested concept in the social sciences. In Latin America alone, the notion of citizenship has been employed in significantly different ways over time. This raises important questions. Are existing conceptions of citizenship even relevant today? If so, which ones? Are they useful for understanding the legacies of the left in Latin America? We contend that, when defined appropriately, the concept of citizenship remains an insightful lens through which to understand Latin American state-society relations. To realize this potential, it is essential to redefine the concept to account for the fact not only that citizenship is relational but also that the historical development of citizenship has been uneven in the region, both across and within countries.

Most of the early literature on citizenship in Latin America has its origins in the work of T. H. Marshall, who delivered in his seminal

1949 Cambridge University Marshall Lecture one of the most influential speeches on the historical development of citizenship rights. For Marshall, citizenship is a status granted to all citizens that entails three categories of rights (Marshall 1964): civil rights, political rights, and social rights. By definition, citizenship is national, and the rights associated with it are guaranteed by a set of institutions (courts, parliaments, and social policies). According to him, the historical sequence for the acquisition of such rights (and the development of their associated institutions) in Britain (and more generally in Western Europe) has been quite linear over the course of three centuries. Civil rights were recognized in the eighteenth century, granting all free men the rights to justice, to work, and freedom of the press, among others. Political rights followed in the nineteenth century, as the right to vote became universal among male adults. Citizenship rights were then extended to the social realm with the development of welfare regimes in the twentieth century. For Marshall, citizenship was not only characterized by the (relative) universalism of the rights it created and granted, but also by its impact on social classes and social inequalities. In fact, according to Marshall, citizenship, as a status granted by the state, is functional by its very nature: it provides citizens with equal status in the face of material inequalities inherent to modern capitalist societies.

Although the Marshall-inspired perspective of rights has been dominant in the Latin American literature, it has not been exempt of criticism, mainly for being functionalist and reductionist in scope. First, for many critics, Marshall's functionalist teleology of rights based on the British case did not consider the fact that the acquisition of citizenship rights by citizens is not simply granted by the state and thus, for most societies, is far from linear. This has had an impact on the interaction between citizenship rights and inequalities, limiting social inclusion. In Latin America, for example, political rights came before basic civil rights were effectively guaranteed and universally granted (Oxhorn 2003). The transitions to democracy of the 1980s contributed to the expansion of political rights in Latin America and brought elected officials to power after years of authoritarianism. However, democracy did not imply democratic citizenship in a context characterized by socioeconomic inequalities and cultural pluralism (Hagopian 2007). In the 1990s, the new democratically elected Latin American governments did not focus on the extension and widening of citizenship rights. Quite to the contrary, during this decade, the various types of rights were unevenly distributed among different sectors of the population, leading to what Holston and Caldeira (1998) have called the emergence of "disjunctive" democracy. Although universal suffrage was no longer questioned, the depth of political rights was threatened by the so-called delegative democracies of the 1990s (O'Donnell 1994), where accountability mechanisms were weak and did not allow citizens to actively and meaningfully participate in democratic governance processes. Moreover, in the context of a weak rule of law (Méndez, O'Donnell, and Pinheiro 1999), evidenced by frequent cases of corrupt police forces, police misconduct, inefficient justice systems, and inaccessible courts, Latin Americans did not enjoy full access to civil rights. Social rights and welfare policies also remained limited and were under threat in the neoliberal era, which was characterized by the retreat of the state from the provision of social services. This trend coexisted with a persistent gender gap, rising economic inequalities, and the concentration of wealth in the hands of the few. In practice, then, democratically elected governments maintained the "modern-day identification of citizenship with rights and entitlements [that] underlies a version of citizenship that is 'passive' and 'thin'; and where citizens are denied the opportunity to exercise civic responsibility, a low intensity citizenship results" (Hagopian 2007, 28). If the idea of assessing citizenship as rights remained valid for some, the functionalist nature of Marshall's teleological logic did not hold, as Latin America's recent history has shown.

Second, the Marshallian conception of citizenship rights was also criticized for being incomplete, as it did not account for the heterogeneity inherent to societies and the citizenry's mobilized identities, such as gender, religion, and ethnicity, to name only a few (Beiner 1995; Tilly 1995; Turner 1997). For Marshall's critics, citizenship is not restricted to civil, political, and social rights, as the case of Latin America's complex social history dramatically exemplifies. For example, it became evident in the 1970s that not only were civil, social, and political rights in jeopardy, but basic human rights were also highly restricted under authoritarian governments throughout the region, threatening any meaningful sense of citizenship for the vast majority (Jelin 1996). More recently, the expansion of demands from Indigenous groups has challenged the classic conception of rights, emphasizing the importance of cultural rights (Yashar 2005). This became clear in the 1990s, when Indigenous and

Afro-descendant movements emerged with identity claims and demands for recognition and collective rights that went beyond the ethnocentric package of citizenship rights described by Marshall. Latin American democracies seemed plagued by what Hagopian has called the problem of "thin" citizenship, where "citizens do not participate fully in political life, [because] in many cases they are denied basic citizenship rights, and many, especially ethnic and racial minorities, are excluded from membership in national political communities" (2007, 21). Similarly, in the period following the transitions to democracy, as Yashar (2005) noted, neoliberal citizenship regimes not only reduced social expenditures and contributed to further dismantling social rights granted under the corporatist state but also denied collective and cultural rights. For many groups, including Indigenous, Afro-descendants, LGTBQ groups, women, and other minorities, cultural rights and "differentiated" citizenship was simply nonexistent in much of the region, resulting in a lack of access to full citizenship status.

In the late twentieth century, we saw the development of novel approaches to the study of citizenship in Latin America, which took stock of the aforementioned critiques and attempted to better understand the *variation* in citizenship models over time and across countries. Moving from a rights-based approach to a relational approach linked to the *social construction* of citizenship (and identities), these approaches focus on the relationships between the state and society and among society members, networks, and groups. For them, citizenship is not just a given bundle of rights universally granted by the state to those who possess the status of citizens, as defined by the formal rights entrenched in constitutions, laws, and institutions, as Marshall's conception entailed. For scholars like Yashar and Oxhorn, this approach has proven too narrow to assess the variation in citizens' capacity to effectively exercise their citizenship rights. Rights are an essential component of citizenship, but their breadth and depth are better defined by who is included, who is excluded, and why. Yashar insists that while the content of rights granted to citizens is an important dimension of the definition of citizenship, there are two other dimensions to what she calls *citizenship regimes* that are just as important: who has political membership to the community (belonging) and how interest intermediation is structured (access) (Yashar 2007).[1] Citizenship regimes thus vary according to the institutions and mechanisms that guarantee access to those rights, as well as the relational processes through which state actors and members of the political community are defined, interact, and struggle to demand access to those rights (Oxhorn 2003). As such, citizenship is the product of the struggle of social actors tied by their multiple identities and organized in groups and networks that demand access to this status (Tilly 1995). In other words, as Oxhorn puts it, citizenship is socially constructed.

Following this logic, scholars have shown that citizenship has traditionally been limited or granted through controlled-inclusion processes in Latin America (Oxhorn 2007), which set up and anchor patterns of social exclusion and partial incorporation that despite some changes end up enduring over time. Citizenship regimes thus remained exclusionary for most of the region's history.

In the 1980s, transitions to democratic rule raised expectations for extended and more inclusive citizenship regimes. However, as we have noted, these expectations fell short in the 1990s, and deeper conceptions of democratic citizenship emerged through social demands and social movements' struggles for inclusion, participation, and recognition. These demands came with a new conception of citizenship, one that in most cases recognized the importance of formal rights[2] but that stressed the importance of the lived experiences of citizens, including their struggles, and effective and active participation in the definition of the content and boundaries of inclusive citizenship. In Isin's words, the emphasis should be on norms, practices, meanings and identities as "citizenship must also be defined as a social process through which individuals and social groups engage in claiming, expanding, or losing rights" (2000, 8), a process in which citizens are being engaged politically and that produces differentiated citizenships, based on localized social struggles and practices that he calls acts of citizenship (Isin 2008). In Latin America, the idea of an active citizenry became the core of the public discourse on democracy and inclusion, where "the building of a new citizenship was to be seen as reaching far beyond the acquisition of legal rights, requiring the constitution of active social subjects, defining what they consider to be their rights, and struggling for their recognition" (Dagnino 2006, 19).

This new conception of citizenship also led to a radical and participatory political proposal that was championed by emerging and re-emerging left-leaning political parties in their discourses and promises, as analyzed in the following section. While the general frustration with the limits of political democracy in its "Third Wave" reincarnation meant that even conservative parties had to pay lip service to the importance of new mechanisms for citizen participation, such as the participatory budgeting processes implemented by Brazil's new-leftist Workers' Party beginning in the late 1980s (Oxhorn 2004), this participatory, constructivist dimension of citizenship was arguably the key distinguishing feature of leftist policy proposals since the turn of the century. This was true of both its more radical variants (e.g., Hugo Chávez in Venezuela) and its more moderate ones (e.g., Lula in Brazil and Michelle Bachelet in Chile).

The institutional and structural implications of adopting this type of citizenship regime also suggest that progress toward its effective implementation is a logical comparative lens for understanding the legacies of the left across the region. In fact, citizenship regimes are entrenched in historically constructed state-society relationships that create distinct patterns of inclusion or exclusion among countries and over time. However, because they tend to assess citizenship as a universalistic phenomenon, existing approaches remain limited when trying to account for the fact that citizenship is unevenly distributed both across countries and within them (O'Donnell 1993). First, citizenship rights have been and continue to be unevenly distributed across social sectors, given the variation in each sector's historically embedded relationship to the state. Second, institutional mechanisms that theoretically guarantee access to the state and to these rights in practice are unequally available to citizens across and within each social sector. Institutional reforms are often incomplete, and informal practices that circumvent access remain dominant in practice. The impact of participatory democracy mechanisms on citizenship regimes remains, for example, limited, as they do not necessarily contribute to equally furthering civil society's and individuals' autonomous capacity to organize and formulate collective demands (Montambeault 2015, 2016). Third, there is important variation in the way citizenship is defined and lived by individuals and groups within social sectors, at the individual level, across policy areas, and across levels of governments. Identities are intersectional, which means that citizens can have multiple identities, which should be simultaneously taken into consideration for the analysis of citizenship, even if some are brought to the forefront in given social struggles (Moreau 2015). The intersectional nature of identities can bring tensions within civil society organization and among groups over the definition of such identities (e.g., belonging). Moreover, citizenship can be understood as a multilayered construct (Yuval-Davis 1999), which means that "people are citizens simultaneously in more than one political community" (Yuval-Davis 2007, 562) and that "the nation-state is not the only locus of belonging" (Moreau 2015, 501). Thus, as Hagopian has suggested, "the demand for cultural rights and the right to different, tailored forms of citizenship opens the possibility that citizenship will not be identical for all, that the unit that holds rights will not necessarily be the individual, that there is not a fixed basket of rights that only the state will define and concede" (2007, 47).

Given these limits, and building on existing post-Marshallian approaches to understanding citizenship regimes in Latin America, we assess citizenship regimes from a *relational* perspective. Citizenship is thereby defined as rights but also "as a set of mutual, contested claims between agents of states and members of socially-constructed categories: genders, races, nationalities and others" (Tilly 1995, 5), which are entrenched in socially and historically constructed regimes. In fact, struggles for recognition and rights "play out at multiple, interrelated spatial scales" (Grundy and Smith 2005, 390), which means that citizenship as a practice is lived, expressed, and understood differently in different spaces (public/private, local/national) by citizens with complex and often intersectional identities (Isin 2008; Lister 2007; Moreau 2015). This understanding of citizenship in practice implies that broad analyses of citizenship at the national level gloss over important differences across sectors and issues and therefore becomes ill suited to understand the development of citizenship in the region. This book unpacks the transformations of citizenship regimes and the construction and redefinition of multiple citizenships under the left in Latin America during the past fifteen years by analyzing a variety of institutional and policy areas. In theory, participatory and identity politics transcend ideology. In practice, however, they have been closely associated with leftist parties that were elected in the early 2000s, embodying a new discourse and renewed hopes for citizenship, inclusion, and democracy, as we shall see next.

THE EMERGENCE OF A DISCOURSE FOR INCLUSIVE AND ACTIVE
CITIZENSHIP AND THE LEFT IN LATIN AMERICA

Once redefined to account for its relational and multilayered construction in different spaces, the concept of citizenship offers a useful lens to compare cases and to empirically make sense of the variation across and within countries concerning the legacies of the Left turn in Latin America. From a historical perspective, access to citizenship rights and the development of a shared and inclusive collective identity have been restricted by the exclusionary, unequal, and often privilege-based nature of state-society relations in Latin America (Oxhorn 2003). Since the 1980s, the question of citizenship has gained renewed importance in the public sphere across the region. On the one hand, political parties on the left and the right announced their intention to "govern for all citizens" and to renew otherwise exclusionary citizenship regimes. The neoliberal democracies that replaced authoritarian regimes in the 1990s fell short in meeting these expectations: the emerging neoliberal citizenship regimes were found to be elitist and exclusionary (Haber 2016; Oxhorn 2011; Yashar 2005). On the other hand, in the context of democratization, social movements and civil society organizations traditionally associated with the left increasingly claimed their "right to have rights" and sought a renewed and inclusive citizenship model (Foweraker 1995). As such, they have contributed to a transformation of the way citizenship was defined and articulated in the public sphere. This set the stage for the election of several presidents, governors, mayors, and representatives from the emerging New Left to which they are closely associated in the early 2000s in Latin America.

In fact, this evolution in how the concept of citizenship is understood made it almost inevitable that the left would adopt citizenship as a guiding principal for social change after the demise of the Soviet Union and the end of the Cold War. This is because the evolution of the left in many ways parallels, if not guides, how our changing conception of citizenship evolved over time. Like the Marshallian conception of citizenship, the left has historically been concerned about equality and structural change. The difference, of course, is the radical nature of the historical left's alternative to Marshall: a noncapitalist society that privileged social over political rights and circumscribed civic rights in order to legitimate the social system. Also like Marshall, the left historically focused on social class at the expense of other collective identities. This began to change even before the end of the Cold War. On the one hand, the left began to express a much more nuanced appreciation of other social identities and their concomitant implications for understanding socioeconomic marginalization and inequality in the 1970s. This often was the result of the same social movement mobilizations that led to a general reassessment of Marshall's economistic and class-based conceptualization of citizenship. On the other hand, political repression and the obvious corruption of the Soviet-style system led the left toward a new appreciation of basic political rights, including the importance of political democracy. As emphasized by Dagnino (2006) and Hochstetler (2000), citizenship became central to social movements' demands and mobilization cycles in the 1990s. The neoliberal democracies that had been established following the breakdown of authoritarian regimes in the region implied an important shift in citizenship regimes. Democracy formally extended political rights (the right to vote) and mechanisms for access to the state (through representative institutions). However, neoliberal policies considerably shrank social rights and transformed the nature of access to citizenship regimes in Latin America. In fact, as Oxhorn (2011) notes when talking about what he calls *citizenship as consumption*, market-based incentives and personal resources came to define social and political inclusion, as well as access to citizenship rights. These changes also transformed social movements' and civil society's struggles, widening the traditional range of actors from unions to emerging and heterogeneous social movements and identity-based groups (Grugel and Riggirozzi 2012). Although their concrete demands focused on specific (and often different) rights (social, cultural, political, civil) that varied across countries, the polysemic notion of citizenship was a powerful tool for these emerging social movements and civil society groups. It served as a rallying cry for the mobilization of different sectors of Latin American societies, articulating common struggles for equality, the extension of citizenship rights, and cultural recognition in the context of the deepening of democracy in the region. In fact, as Dagnino explains:

> Reference to citizenship often provided a common ground—and a connecting principle—for an immense diversity of social movements

that found in the language of rights a way of expressing their claims, helping them to escape fragmentation and isolation. Thus the building of citizenship was seen at the same time as a general struggle—for the broadening of democracy—which was able to incorporate a plurality of demands, and as a set of specific struggles for substantive rights (housing, education, health, etc.) whose success would deepen democracy in society. (2006, 17)

In addition to referring to the social, political, and economic exclusion of the marginalized and to claims for social justice, social movements and civil society organizations (CSOs) used the term "citizenship" to describe their own activities. Mobilization and participation within the frame of social movements was pictured as a way to construct citizenship from below, an active and effective citizenship extended to the unorganized and excluded sectors of Latin American societies (Hochstetler 2000).

There are several examples of this growing use of the inclusive citizenship language by social movements and CSOs in the context of the 1990s social struggles for democracy and against economic neoliberalism across the region. One particularly insightful example is the well-known case of the Movimento dos Trabalhadores Rurais Sem Terra (Landless Workers' Movement, MST) in Brazil, a peasant's movement that emerged in the mid-1980s and has become one of the largest and most durable social movements in Latin America. Born in the mobilization occupation of land by thousands of rural workers who challenged the highly concentrated structure of agrarian property in Brazil, the MST has played a very important role in Brazilian public debates about democracy and, in particular, citizenship (Carter 2010). In fact, the struggles of the MST soon became more than land occupations by landless peasants. The MST became politicized not only as a way to expand alternative spaces for land tenure and participation, but also to pursue effective forms of democratic citizenship (Wittman 2009) that located citizenship in everyday practices. These included how the land was used, civic education, and the articulation of concrete demands for agrarian and property reforms (Dagnino 2005). But they also included a wider struggle for human dignity and a broad social transformation in Brazil, which materialized at the national level on multiple political fronts (Wittman 2009). In fact, the MST demands that the state play an active role in "fostering an alternative model of development, one that seeks to rebalance the nation's social order and strengthen capabilities among its underprivileged" (Carter 2010, 188), emphasizing the role of the state in widening and deepening citizenship regimes.

The struggles by Indigenous peoples that emerged across the region in the 1990s provide further examples of the discursive use of the notion of inclusive citizenship, employed to widen the scope of social movements' claims, moving beyond claims for a specific minority group to include the marginalized more generally (Yashar 2005). Among them is certainly Subcomandante Marcos's Ejército Zapatista de Liberación Nacional (Zapatista Army of National Liberation, EZLN) in Mexico, or the so-called Zapatistas, which remains one of the most internationally recognized Indigenous movements of the region. On the eve of the implementation of the North American Free Trade Agreement (NAFTA) in January 1994, a group of Indigenous people led by Marcos emerged from the jungle and seized the city of San Cristobal de las Casas in Chiapas, rebelling against the seventy years of rule by the Partido Revolucionario Institucional (Institutional Revolutionary Party, PRI) and neoliberalism (Stephen and Collier 1997). Entrenched in historical struggles by Indigenous people for autonomy and cultural recognition, the movement was indigenous in essence, but in the longer run, as the initial uprising institutionalized itself into a demilitarized social movement,[3] its rhetoric had a wider scope, using the inclusive citizenship language to engage in the Mexican debate on democratization (Gilbreth and Otero 2011). As Marcos puts it in the EZLN's Fourth Declaration of the Lacandon Jungle, "In the world of the powerful there is no space for anyone but themselves and their servants. In the world we want everyone fits. The nation which we construct is one where all communities and languages fit, where all steps may walk, where all may have laughter, where all may see the dawn" (Subcomandante Marcos 1996). Thus, through Marcos's movement, the Indigenous peoples of Chiapas and Oaxaca fought for their collective rights for self-determination and autonomy but nonetheless saw their struggle for citizenship as part of the struggle of all the marginalized in Mexico and across the world (Kabeer 2005).

Other examples include the urban movements that emerged in the region, especially in slums and favelas. Based in civil society groups that locate their struggles for the expansion of social rights for popular sectors at the neighborhood level, these movements often resorted to an inclusive citizenship discourse that reached beyond their neighborhoods to mobilize and bring their voice to public debates on democratization and social justice (Guidry 2003). These include movements of the urban poor that emerged in the 1980s and early 1990s in Chile and Peru (Oxhorn 1995; Roberts 1998).

Similarly, broad references to citizenship can be found in the struggles for human rights that involved many local, national, and transnational movements that emerged during and after authoritarian periods in several countries. Raising the issue of societal memory and the victims of state repression, as the Madres and Abuelas de Plaza de Mayo did in Argentina, for example, they located this debate in the larger scheme of citizenship rights (Jelin 1994). On the one hand, the specific claims for truth, justice, and redress, although specifically related to the human right violations that had taken place during dictatorship, were not only demands about the past but also looked to the future, as the term "Nunca Más" (Never Again) makes clear. On the other hand, human rights claims went beyond the specific violations during authoritarian regimes, looking to construct "a new institutional apparatus to protect human rights more fully and determin[e] the content of the rights to be guaranteed" (Jelin 1994, 48). Here, human rights claims converged with claims for the expansion of citizenship, a process that took place not only in Argentina but in other countries in the region as well. As Pérez Esquivel points out, human rights refer not only to the person but also to "the rights of the people to education, to health, to housing, to political and trade union liberties, to the mass media" (quoted in Jelin 1994, 55). As time passed and human rights claims remained in the spotlight, the links to the citizenship regime deepened, and human rights became first and foremost a demand for a fuller and more democratic citizenship (Oxhorn 2001).

In these ways, by the end of the 1990s, the question of citizenship regimes—their breadth and depth—became a central issue on the political agenda throughout Latin America. As social movements occupied more space in the public sphere because of their contentious mobilization, they also often became more and more active in the political arena, often closely associated with the emerging (or reemerging) left political parties. It is in this context that the left came to power in many Latin American countries in the late 1990s, with the widening and deepening of citizenship regimes at the core of their political agendas. In fact, as Marxism eroded as an ideological underpinning of the socialist model of development, the left reinvented itself in Latin America and anchored its project in a wider social transformation aimed at "deepening democracy" and at "social inclusion" (Roberts 1998). Levitsky and Roberts defined the New Left as comprising those political actors who, while their political orientations and organizational features vary across countries, generally "seek, as their central programmatic objective, to reduce social and economic inequalities . . . *and* seek to use public authority to redistribute wealth and/or income, erode social hierarchies and strengthen the voice of disadvantaged groups in the political process" (2013, 5; original emphasis).

With this commitment to democratic deepening and social inclusion, the parties of the so-called New Left wave grew as an alternative for the poor, ethnic, or sexual minorities, as well as other traditionally marginalized sectors of Latin American societies. Left parties built support by nurturing close ties to social movements' and civil society's struggles while building electoral support (Brazil, Uruguay, and Bolivia, for example), or emerged in reaction to the incapacity of the neoliberal electoral democracies to incorporate and represent the traditionally marginalized (Venezuela and Ecuador) (see Roberts, this volume). Their discourse and programs were infused with the rhetoric of inclusive citizenship, raising expectations for an extension of the depth and breadth of citizenship regimes once they were elected. More specifically, the focus on equality and solidarity brought hope to their electors and some commentators for a deepening of social rights and a widening of the scope of citizenship rights to include cultural and human rights. These changes were to be accomplished through participatory and inclusive political processes with the potential of creating a postliberal alternative to neoliberal democracy (Arditi 2008; Cameron, this volume).

While they vary greatly across countries in their specific political orientations, the various experiences from Latin America tend to illustrate this observation. In Ecuador and Bolivia, for example, the recognition of cultural citizenship and the active participation of the traditionally exploited and excluded Indigenous peoples were central to both Rafael Correa's and Evo Morales's campaigns and early presidency discourses. In in both cases, this was articulated through the notion of *plurination-alism* (Escobar 2010), or the so-called plurinational states (Rice, this volume). In Brazil, Lula's Partido dos Trabalhadores was also elected on an inclusive citizenship platform. In 2002, the party campaigned on a government platform, *Um Brasil para Todos* (A Brazil for All), which had been developed with the PT think thank Instituto Cidadania and that was organized around the discourse of citizenship for all and social inclusion.[4] Many of the policy proposals included in the government program were tied to the idea of an inclusive citizenship that would reach the "marginalized" and the voiceless, those who did not have access to citizenship and were not recognized as citizens. Creating jobs, fighting poverty and hunger, making education better and more accessible, and strengthening and diversifying culture: all these proposals were legitimated as extensions of citizenship regimes to include those who were traditionally excluded on the basis of gender, sexual orientation, social class, ethnicity, and so on. The program actually stipulated the need to reach a new social contract between the state and Brazilian society, for which "civic mobilisation and large national agreements have to include and benefit the traditionally marginalized and voiceless of the Brazilian society. Only this way can we guarantee, in fact, the extension of citizenship to all Brazilians" (Partido dos Trabalhadores 2002, 2).

In sum, thus, the programs of the left rearticulated social movements and civil society organization's demands for inclusive citizenship regimes within an agenda of social redistribution, participation, and inclusion combined with growth and economic development strategies. Citizen expectations for change in citizenship regimes were raised as the left arrived to power or led the opposition in most Latin American countries in the early 2000s. How successful were the Left turn governments in meeting those expectations? Was citizenship (re)defined during the past fifteen years in the region, and if so, how? Are citizenship regimes now reaching the traditionally excluded? Have they become "active" citizens as a consequence? Now that the left is in retreat in many countries after exercising power for extended periods, are such changes part of the Left turn's legacy?

AN APPROACH TO UNDERSTANDING LEGACIES FROM THE LEFT: DIFFERENTIATED CITIZENSHIP(S)

As the current literature shows, and as the examples above illustrate, one should expect left discourses about citizenship and inclusion to differ from those coming from other ideological positions. Leftist legacies cannot, however, be assessed for the region as a whole. There is a high level of variation among Latin American countries, as different governments have distinct political and socioeconomic projects. Each of these governments emerged and evolved in very different countries, and as such there are significant differences in their relation to social movements and embeddedness in society (Cameron and Hershberg 2010; Levitsky and Roberts 2013). However, the "variety of lefts" argument, which explains different policy outcomes from a cross-national perspective by sketching differences among leftist parties and governments in Latin America (Weyland, Madrid, and Hunter 2012), is not able to capture the variety of legacies seen through the lens of citizenship (see Dabène, this volume). In fact, citizenship is a complex and multilayered social construct that is embedded in the multiple and dynamic linkages between the state (and the left hereafter) and society but also in society itself. Moreover, the trajectories of the left—and policy outcomes—not only vary across countries, but also over time and across sectors within single countries. Therefore, specific dimensions of citizenship regimes can be expanded and deepened for certain groups (and in certain areas), yet others may not benefit and may even be negatively affected by these changes.[5]

Were democratic institutions (re)designed during the Left turn in a way that transformed the nature of citizenship regimes in the countries in which the left came to power? To what extent did state and society actors who shaped the outcomes of citizenship struggles effectively appropriate these reforms? How have state-society relations evolved under the New Left? These are the questions that the following chapters address, understanding citizenship construction from a relational perspective. According to some analysts, this relationship, observed through the relation between social movements and the state, has changed positively across the region during the past fifteen years (Prevost, Campos, and Vanden 2012), becoming symbiotic under progressive leftist governments. Other authors are more critical, and consider the citizenship discourse of leftist parties to be universalizing and, as such, disempowering for the traditionally marginalized rather than empowering (Petras and Veltmeyer 2009; Veltmeyer 2013). The empirical reality, however, is more complex than these all-encompassing accounts allow for. A more nuanced approach to understanding variation among recent leftist governments is to move from a national and homogeneous understanding of society by introducing some complexity into our understanding of this empirically grounded concept. As Haber rightfully observed, "This situation is dynamic and fluid and it is important not to get locked into fixed a-historical position and to be sensitive to differences between national and sub-national experiences" (2016, 36). We would add that is not only important to be sensitive to variation in the levels and spaces where this relationship is defined, but also to variation across policy issues and societal sectors, where the intersectionality of identities can be observed and create otherwise overlooked tensions in state-society relations.

In fact, a focus on the reforms and on the relational dynamics that played out in different policy issue areas shows movement in complex and contradictory directions that bring nuances to the portrait of the legacies of the different left-leaning governments. For example, in the realm of social policies, usually conceived as a net positive, Nagels (this volume) shows that CCT reforms in Bolivia have also reinforced and redefined gender relationships, reifying maternal roles in unintended ways that limit the deepening of citizenship regimes. In terms of participatory institutions, Goldfrank (this volume) shows that initially promising advancements failed to produce actual policy changes, eventually undermining trust in both left leaders and the participatory mechanism themselves. Bratman (this volume) makes clear the tensions between two conflicting sides of a left-leaning discourse: a developmental strategy that allows for redistribution and the protection of the environment, with governments pivoting from one to the other, at least discursively. Then, a cross-issue analysis of any given country also portrays a complex picture, where advancements in some areas are accompanied by a lack of movement or even the worsening of conditions in other areas (Dabène and Levitsky, this volume).

The need to account for this multilayered level of complexity, where different sectors are affected in different ways by changes in formal rules and practices that operate at different levels of government and where individual policies can result in varying—and sometimes unintended—consequences for different actors, requires an approach that looks at citizenship regimes along different dimensions. The analysis of citizenship in this volume does this by disentangling three key and interrelated components that are explored in the different issues covered by the chapters. The first component of the analysis of citizenship questions the level of government at which institutional reforms affecting citizenship regimes are designed and implemented. The second component is located at the societal level, looking at the variation in how different groups and individuals deploy various identities and a differentiated way of defining the community(ies) to which they belong, which affects the type of demands advanced. The third and final component of the comparative analysis deals with the potential tension between claims cast in terms of individual or collective rights and in terms of the struggle for equality or the recognition of difference. With regard to the question of levels, it is important to assess the inclusiveness of leftist citizenship regimes as it plays out in more or less decentralized forms of governance. Institutional design and reforms play out at different scales (from national recognition of rights, often in constitutions, to policies designed and implemented at different levels—national, provincial, municipal), making it particularly difficult to assess and define access to citizenship regimes even at the level of formal rules. Moreover, key elements of citizenship regimes, such as representation rights, are shaped by rules and regulations in different issue areas, such as party systems (Roberts, this volume), nonelectoral and multilevel forms of participation (Goldfrank, this volume), and the constitutional protection of minorities (Brinks and Sandoval, this volume). Similarly, different actors and social movement struggles, such as indigenous, environmental, sexual rights, and human rights claims, also play out at different scales, many times simultaneously, from the local to the national level and in some cases even the transnational one. Second, demands vary across groups and individuals who deploy various identities and a differentiated way of defining the community or communities to which they belong. As discussed earlier, in Latin America, citizenship was redefined and appropriated by social movements, civil society groups, and the state alike as a common concept in the 1990s, during times of struggles for the deepening of democratic regimes. But debates about the meaning of membership and across the spectrum of claims for citizenship rights soon emerged, particularly given the reference to citizenship as a common concept underlying the various types of social struggles for inclusion. In fact, neither states nor civil societies are homogeneously permeated by progressive influences across and within countries. In fact, a view of civil society as the "social fabric formed by a multiplicity of self-constituted territorially and functionally based units, excluding families and business firms, which peacefully co-exist and collectively resist subordination by the state, at the same time as they demand inclusion into national [and local] political structures" (Oxhorn 2011, 9), implies an emphasis on power relationships both within a given society and in relation to the state. Civil society groups and social movements are plural by nature, and vary in terms of power resources and level of autonomy vis-à-vis the state and the political arena (Montambeault 2015), influencing their capacity to effectively organize and formulate demands for inclusion. Because they are plural, heterogeneous, and often composed of members with intersectional identities, civil society groups and social movements do not have a single definition of what inclusion means, of the boundaries of citizenship. Across groups, but also within groups, tensions can arise as members can have both complementary and competing demands. These tensions emerge, for example, in Nagels's chapter, where conditional cash transfer policies affect recipients as economically disadvantaged groups in society but also as women and as members of Indigenous communities. Different tensions also emerge within certain movements in their relationship to Left turn governments, for instance, in terms of the autonomy of Indigenous and environmentalist groups to make demands (see, e.g., Bratman, this volume, particularly in relation to the Brazilian case). Finally, there are inherent tensions for the Left turn governments between citizenship's universalistic claims and pluralism, between collective and individual rights (Kabeer 2005), between the quest for equality and the recognition of the right to difference (Jelin 2003). These tensions are often at the center of conflicts between civil society and the state under the Left turn and among actors within civil society. Examples of these are the emerging tensions between Indigenous rights and the pluralist state in Bolivia (Rice, this volume) and between human rights and environmentalist norms (Bratman 2014). Citizenship struggles are intimately linked with the economic model, as Yashar argued in the 1990s, and there is an inherent paradox in pursuing a neoliberal economic agenda while trying to extend the boundaries of citizenship through cultural recognition, formal inclusion, and participatory governance (see Rice, this volume).

More generally, it is important to unpack this relationship between the state, the political arena, and civil society groups to have a more accurate and differentiated understanding of the social construction of citizenship regimes in Latin America, particularly under the New Left. There are different ways to demand extension and access to rights across and within policy sectors, given the power relations between society that permeate groups, the multiple individual and collective identities that coexist and sometimes compete across and within movements, and the level of autonomy of groups vis-à-vis institutions and parties. Of course, the analysis of both change and stability across issues, sectors, and countries creates inherent methodological difficulties. Moreover, the focus on how these changes—or lack thereof—in rights and formal rules end up shaping the meaning of citizenship in practice complicates the assessment even more. The approach followed in this volume is to assess changes in formal rules as presented in constitutional provisions and key pieces of policy within each area of analysis. Each contributor has chosen a set of countries to analyze in depth, in order to provide a better sense of how the changes that shaped citizenship practices have evolved through time and across space. This analysis covers both how changes in formal rules came about through the way that they were negotiated by different groups within society and the effect these changes have in potentially raising tensions among different groups in society. The focus is, in all cases, on inclusion and representation of marginalized groups. This strategy results in a mosaic, where specific issues are covered in different countries and where each country is covered under different themes, providing a nuanced assessment of the legacies of the Left turn in terms of inclusion in order to understand both national and regional dynamics comparatively.

The theoretical perspective on inclusion and citizenship developed in this chapter and applied throughout the volume provides an important lens for understanding not only the Left turn's legacy but also the left in Latin America over time and across the region. Ironically, it does this by applying a classical political economy approach that Marx himself would feel comfortable with while at the same time expanding that political economy approach to include social formations other than class that

Marx—and the left in general until only relatively recently—tended to ignore (e.g., identity politics, including gender and Indigenous peoples in particular). The analysis of a temporally specific period—the twenty-first century's Left turn—is now situated in a historical framework that provides a comparative analysis of the evolution of both the "left" and the concept of citizenship over time within and across countries. The depth and breadth of citizenship rights becomes a mirror of the kind and extent of social change ushered in by the left—or the limits of such change.

The latter point exposes a second irony this theoretical framework reveals: a natural affinity between left ideologies and the concept of citizenship. As Marshall recognized over half a century ago, citizens by definition are equal. For Marshall, however, such "equality" was a legal construct intended to minimize the political consequences of the inequality inherent in market economies. For the left, such equality was historically seen as merely a facade intended to legitimate oppressive capitalist economies; citizenship inevitably was equated with "bourgeois democracy," obscuring this intrinsic compatibility between leftist ideologies and citizenship. True equality was possible only when capitalism had been destroyed by a dictatorship of the proletariat. The left's concern for equality and the need for structural change to achieve it remains one of its central pillars, even if its perspective on capitalism is more ambiguous after the collapse of the Soviet Union and the end of the Cold War. Such ambiguity, however, also reflects how the left has adopted a much broader perspective on equality, which now includes multiple dimensions in addition to its traditional concern with social class and is reflected in a similar expansion of the concept of citizenship itself.

NOTES

1. The concept of citizenship regimes is inspired by the literature developed in Europe and North America, including the work of Jane Jenson and her colleagues (Jenson 1997; Jenson and Papillon 2000; Jenson and Rousseau 2006).

2. The continued relevance of formal rights, particularly democratic ones, became problematic for some of the countries that turned left. This was particularly the case as harsh economic times loosened the government's grip on popular opinion, with some governments such as Maduro's resorting to increasingly authoritarian measures to maintain power. In fact, one possible

distinction among left parties in the region has become their acceptance of liberal democracy as an end in itself.

3. The Zapatistas are also unique in the post–Cold War period in Latin America because the movement began as an armed insurrection. This is in sharp contrast to other social movements and the New Left more generally, which rejected violence as a means toward the end of more just societies, and is more reminiscent of the more traditional left. The movement soon abandoned armed struggle, which is more consistent with the concept of inclusive citizenship, developed here.

4. The Instituto Cidadania was created in 1996 (Samuels 2004).

5. It is worth noting that differentiated citizenship has always been associated with the left, which made it threatening to middle- and upper-class groups who would pay the costs of the redistributive policies traditionally associated with the left.

REFERENCES

Arditi, Benjamin. 2008. "Arguments about the Left Turns in Latin America: Post-Liberal Politics?" *Latin American Research Review* 43 (3): 59–81.

Beiner, Ronald. 1995. *Theorizing Citizenship*. Albany: State University of New York Press.

Bratman, Eve Z. 2014. "Contradictions of Green Development: Human Rights and Environmental Norms in Light of Belo Monte Dam Activism." *Journal of Latin American Studies* 46 (2): 261–89.

Cameron, Maxwell A., and Eric Hershberg. 2010. *Latin America's Left Turns: Politics, Policies, and Trajectories of Change*. Boulder, CO: Lynne Rienner.

Carter, Miguel. 2010. "The Landless Rural Workers Movement and Democracy in Brazil." *Latin American Research Review* 45 (4): 186–217.

Dagnino, Evelina. 1998. "Culture, Citizenship and Democracy: Changing Discourses and Practices of the Latin American Left." In Evelina Dagnino and Arturo Escobar, eds., *Culture of Politics / Politics of Culture: Re-visioning Latin America Social Movements*. Boulder, CO: Westview Press.

———. 2005. "'We All Have Rights, But . . .': Contesting Concepts of Citizenship in Brazil." In Naila Kabeer, ed., *Inclusive Citizenship: Meanings and Expressions*. London: Zed Books.

———. 2006. "Meanings of Citizenship in Latin America." *Canadian Journal of Latin American and Caribbean Studies / Revue canadienne des études latino-américaines et caraïbes* 31 (62): 15–51.

Escobar, Arturo. 2010. "Latin America at the Crossroad." *Cultural Studies* 24 (1): 1–65.

Foweraker, Joe. 1995. *Theorizing Social Movements*. London: Pluto Press.

Gilbreth, Chris, and Gerardo Otero. 2011. "Democratization in Mexico: The Zapatista Uprising and Civil Society." *Latin American Perspectives* 28 (4): 7–29.

Grugel, Jean, and Pia Riggirozzi. 2012. "Post Neoliberalism in Latin America: Rebuilding and Reclaiming the State after Crisis." *Development and Change* 43 (1): 1–21.

Grundy, John, and Miriam Smith. 2005. "The Politics of Multiscalar Citizenship: The Case of Lesbian and Gay Organizing in Canada." *Citizenship Studies* 9 (4): 389–404.

Guidry, John. 2003. "Trial by Space: The Spatial Politcs of Citizenship and Social Movements in Urban Brazil." *Mobilization: An International Quarterly* 8 (2): 189–204.

Haber, Paul. 2016. "Pink Tide Governments, Radical Social Movements and the Practice of Citizenship in the Twenty-First Century Latin America." In Inbal Ofer and Tamar Groves, eds., *Performing Citizenship: Social Movements Across the Globe*. New York: Routledge.

Hagopian, Frances. 2007. "Latin America Citizenship and Democratic Theory." In Joseph S. Tulchin and Meg Ruthenburg, eds., *Citizenship in Latin America*. Boulder, CO: Lynne Rienner.

Hochstetler, Kathryn. 2000. "Democratizing Pressures from Below? Social Movements in the New Brazilian Democracy." In Peter Kingstone and Timothy J. Power, eds., *Democratic Brazil: Actors, Institutions and Processes*. Pittsburgh, PA: University of Pittsburgh Press.

Holston, James, and Teresa Caldeira. 1998. "Democracy, Law, and Violence: Disjunctions of Brazilian Citizenship." In Felipe Agüero and Jeffrey Stark, eds., *Fault Lines of Democracy in Post-Transition Latin America*. Boulder, CO: Lynne Rienner.

Isin, Engin F. 2000. "Introduction: Democracy, Citizenship, Sovereignty, Politics." In Engin F. Isin, ed., *Democracy, Citizenship, and the Global City*. London: Routledge.

———. 2008. "Theorizing Acts of Citizenship." In Engin F. Isin and Greg Marc Nielsen, eds., *Acts of Citizenship*. London: Zed Books.

Jelin, Elizabeth. 1994. "The Politics of Memory: The Human Rights Movement and the Construction of Democracy in Argentina." *Latin American Perspectives* 21 (2): 38–58.

———. 1996. "Citizenship Revisited: Solidarity, Responsibility and Rights." In Elizabeth Jelin and Eric Hershberg, eds., *Constructing Democracy:*

Human Rights, Citizenship and Society in Latin America. Boulder, CO: Westview Press.

————. 2003. "Citizenship and Alterity: Tensions and Dilemmas." *Latin American Perspectives* 30 (2): 101–17.

Jenson, Jane. 1997. "Fated to Live in Interesting Times: Canada's Changing Citizenship Regimes." *Canadian Journal of Political Science / Revue canadienne de science politique* 30 (4): 627–44.

Jenson, Jane, and Martin Papillon. 2000. "Challenging the Citizenship Regime: The James Bay Cree and Transnational Action." *Politics & Society* 28 (2): 245–64.

Jenson, Jane, and Stéphanie Rousseau. 2006. "Contesting the Boundaries of Citizenship: Politics and Policies in Contemporary Latin America." *Canadian Journal of Latin American and Caribbean Studies / Revue canadienne des études latino-américaines et caraïbes* 31 (62): 9–14.

Kabeer, Naila. 2005. *Inclusive Citizenship: Meanings and Expressions.* New York: Zed Books.

Levitsky, Steven, and Kenneth M. Roberts. 2013. *The Resurgence of the Latin American Left.* Baltimore, MD: Johns Hopkins University Press.

Lister, Ruth. 2007. "Inclusive Citizenship: Realizing the Potential." *Citizenship Studies* 11 (1): 49–61.

Marshall, Thomas H. 1964. *Class, Citizenship and Social Development: Essays by T. H. Marshall.* Westport, CT: Greenwood Press.

Méndez, Juan E., Guillermo A. O'Donnell, and Paulo Sérgio de Moraes Sarmento Pinheiro. 1999. *The (un)Rule of Law and the Underprivileged in Latin America.* Notre Dame, IN: University of Notre Dame Press.

Montambeault, Françoise. 2015. *The Politics of Local Participatory Democracy in Latin America: Institutions, Actors, and Interactions.* Palo Alto, CA: Stanford University Press.

————. 2016. "Participatory Citizenship in the Making? The Multiple Citizenship Trajectories of Participatory Budgeting Participants in Brazil." *Journal of Civil Society* 12 (3): 282–98.

Moreau, Julie. 2015. "Intersectional Citizenship, Violence and Lesbian Resistance in South Africa." *New Political Science* 37 (4): 494–508.

O'Donnell, Guillermo. 1993. "On the State, Democratization and Some Conceptual Problems: A Latin American View with Glances at Some Postcommunist Countries." *World Development* 21 (8): 1355–69.

————. 1994. "Delegative Democracy." *Journal of Democracy* 5 (1): 55–69.

Oxhorn, Philip. 1995. "From Controlled Inclusion to Coerced Marginalization: The Struggle for Civil Society in Latin America." In John Hall, ed., *Civil Society: Theory, History and Comparison.* Cambridge: Polity Press.

———. 2001. "From Human Rights to Citizenship Rights? Recent Trends in the Study of Latin American Social Movements." *Latin American Research Review* 36 (3): 163–82.

———. 2003. "Social Inequality, Civil Society and Limits of Citizenship in Latin America." In Susan Eckstein and Timothy Wickham-Crowley, eds., *What Justice? Whose Justice? Fighting for Fairness in Latin America.* Berkeley: University of California Press.

———. 2004. "Introduction: Unraveling the Puzzle of Decentralization." In Philip Oxhorn, Joseph S. Tulchin, and Andrew D. Selee, eds., *Decentralization, Civil Society, and Democratic Governance: Comparative Perspectives from Latin America, Africa, and Asia.* Washington, DC: Johns Hopkins University Press / Woodrow Wilson Center.

———. 2007. "Neopluralism and Citizenship in Latin America." In Joseph S. Tulchin and Meg Ruthenberg, eds., *Citizenship in Latin America.* Boulder, CO: Lynne Rienner.

———. 2011. *Sustaining Civil Society: Economic Change, Democracy, and the Social Construction of Citizenship in Latin America.* University Park: Pennsylvania State University Press.

Partido dos Trabalhadores. 2002. *Um Brasil para Todos: Programma de governo 2002.* Brasilia: Partido dos Trabalhadores.

Petras, James, and Henry Veltmeyer. 2009. *What's Left in Latin America? Regime Change in New Times.* Farnham: Ashgate.

Prevost, Gary, Carlos Oliva Campos, and Harry E. Vanden. 2012. *Social Movements and Leftist Governments in Latin America.* London: Zed Books.

Roberts, Kenneth. 1998. *Deepening Democracy? The Modern Left and Social Movements in Chile and Peru.* Palo Alto, CA: Stanford University Press.

Samuels, David. 2004. "From Socialism to Social Democracy: Party Organization and the Transformation of the Workers' Party in Brazil." *Comparative Political Studies* 37 (9): 999–1024.

Stephen, Lynn, and George A. Collier. 1997. "Reconfiguring Ethnicity, Identity and Citizenship in the Wake of the Zapatista Rebellion." *Journal of Latin American Anthropology* 3 (1): 2–13.

Subcomandante Marcos. 1996. "Fourth Declaration of the Lacandon Jungle." Mexico.

Tilly, Charles. 1995. "Citizenship, Identity, and Social History." In Charles Tilly, ed., *Citizenship, Identity and Social History.* Cambridge: Cambridge University Press.

Turner, Bryan S. 1997. "Citizenship Studies: A General Theory." *Citizenship Studies* 1 (1): 5–18.

Veltmeyer, Henry. 2013. "The Latin American Left in the Face of New Imperialism." In Jeffery R. Webber and Barry Carr, eds., *The New Latin American Left: Cracks in the Empire*. Lanham, MD: Rowman & Littlefield.

Weyland, Kurt, Raul L. Madrid, and Wendy Hunter. 2012. *Leftists Governments in Latin America: Successes and Shortcomings*. Cambridge: Cambridge University Press.

Wittman, Hannah. 2009. "Reframing Agrarian Citizenship: Land, Life and Power in Brazil." *Journal of Rural Studies* 25 (1): 120–30.

Yashar, Deborah. 2005. *Contesting Citizenship in Latin America: The Rise of Indigenous Movements and the Postliberal Challenge*. New York: Cambridge University Press.

———. 2007. "Citizenship Regimes, the State and Ethnic Cleavages." In Joseph S. Tulchin and Meg Ruthenberg, eds., *Citizenship in Latin America*. Boulder, CO: Lynne Rienner.

Yuval-Davis, Nira. 1999. "The 'Multi-Layered' Citizen." *Journal of Politics* 1 (1): 119–36.

———. 2007. "Intersectionality, Citizenship and Contemporary Politics of Belonging." *Critical Review of International Social and Political Philosophy* 10 (4): 561–74.

TWO

Liberalism and Its Competitors in Latin America

Oligarchy, Populism, and the Left

MAXWELL A. CAMERON

Hoy ser progresista es ser liberal, y viceversa.

—Guillermo O'Donnell

In recent decades Latin American social movements have struggled for inclusion by advocating grassroots and participatory forms of citizenship alongside traditional electoral and representative institutions (Montambeault, Balán, and Oxhorn, this volume). A number of scholars have described these struggles for inclusion as a postliberal challenge to contemporary democracies (Arditi 2008; Wolff 2013; Yashar 2005).[1] Others have claimed that the rhetoric of participation serves only to construct an electoral facade that masks authoritarian populism (Weyland 2013).

Still others have stressed the normalcy of populism given the persistence of both oligarchic and democratic elements in Latin American polities (Foweraker 2018, 124–26). Clearly, liberalism has powerful competitors. What are its insufficiencies in Latin America, why is it so feeble compared with populist and oligarchic modes of politics (Slater 2013), and what contribution can it make to progressive politics in the region?

I take as my point of departure the inherent tension between liberalism and democracy. Liberalism is at once a constraint on democracy and a condition of its smooth operation (Beetham 1993, 56). This tension is exacerbated by high levels of inequality, particularly when basic civil rights and freedoms are unevenly enforced in society. Put differently, although liberal notions of citizenship generate democratic outcomes in contexts of relative freedom and equality, liberalism without democracy tends toward oligarchy (Berman 2017). And populism is typically a reaction to the exclusion that accompanies high levels of inequality. In an era of neoliberal globalization this includes established as well as newer democracies.[2]

Moreover, Latin America did not follow the sequence outlined by T. H. Marshall (see Montambeault, Balán, and Oxhorn, this volume). Political and social rights were expanded even as the civil rights of citizenship were denied or unevenly enforced, leading to what Guillermo O'Donnell called "low intensity citizenship" (1993, 9). An aggressively liberal political agenda, such as O'Donnell advocated, would vigorously enforce equality before the law, guarantee access to justice, and, crucially, advance social inclusion by developing the capabilities of citizens to exercise their agency.

Finally, there is a disjuncture between liberalism and postcolonialism. The importation of liberalism in postcolonial contexts has often transformed the potentially emancipatory content of the doctrine into an instrument of discipline and exclusion. It may seem paradoxical that in Latin America liberalism has been tarnished by association with oligarchic states in the past and with neoliberal globalization today. But that is because liberalism itself is paradoxical. It is a doctrine with universal aspirations, yet it arose to make sense of politics in a specific historical context. Its prescriptions may be "addressed to the world" (Manning 1976, 60), but as Maurice Cranston observed many years ago, "to write about liberalism in more than a domestic context one must write about

liberalisms" (1954, 47; quoted in Manning 1976, 57). The tension between the universalistic aspirations of liberalism and the meanings it ac-
quires in particular contexts is what makes O'Donnell's statement—that
to be liberal is to be progressive and vice versa—so necessary to unpack.

Consider the specific context in which liberalism arose. Centuries
of religious warfare persuaded European liberal thinkers that the foundations of authority, sovereignty, and self-government must be found
outside the realm of the sacred and apart from substantive conceptions
of the good. Liberal skepticism and rationalism pointed to enlightened
self-interest and right reason as that foundation. In other words, arguments for a liberal society were believed to be, in principle, universally
applicable, but they were, in fact, the products of centuries of historical
experience. For political theorists like John Stuart Mill, citizenship concerned the rights and freedoms of individuals, as well as the limits of
what other citizens or the state could do to restrict these liberties. Mill
argued that individuals should be free from interference as long as they
do no harm to others; they should not be told what to think; and where
authority must restrain their conduct, it must be exercised with strict
impartiality. Yet this vision is only coherent under conditions of individual autonomy, where public and private spheres are clearly separated,
and in law-abiding states capable of enforcing the rights and duties of
the citizen.

Liberalism in Latin America—both historically and in the
present—has, in contrast, frequently run afoul of deep social, political,
and economic inequalities, long histories of oligarchic exclusion and
discrimination against Indigenous peoples, powerful redistributive pressures, and patrimonial states that lack the legal capacity or will to protect citizens from one another or from abuses by state authorities. Under
such adverse conditions it is conservative to insist on a *guachimán* (night
watchman) state that only protects the private property, liberal rights,
and freedoms of the individual against the encroachments of society, for
such a state will, in practice, uphold the interests of the powerful without
creating conditions for inclusive citizenship.

And yet the core principles of liberalism retain considerable emancipatory potential. Liberalism has a future in Latin America if it makes
a radical break with the oligarchic past and with contemporary neoliberalism. Liberals need progressive allies, just as progressives need liberals;

they must embrace a politics of democratic empowerment, the cultivation of collective capabilities, and the transformation of postcolonial states. They must also recognize postliberal demands for recognition and the rights of excluded groups and cultural minorities whose identity and sense of belonging are grounded in the life of the community, not in an abstract idea of society as agglomerations of autonomous individuals.[3]

What follows is an effort to situate liberalism in the context of Latin America's historical and social conditions. My aim is to show how liberalism produces perverse effects from the standpoint of its universalistic aspirations when it is applied in the context of extreme inequalities, weak state institutions, and postcolonial legacies. Only a radical reconstruction of liberalism can reclaim its progressive potential. The first section traces the history of liberalism in Latin America from the era of agro-exporting oligarchies through the rise of populism to the current neoliberal era. This leads to a discussion of three alternative ways of thinking about freedom, autonomy, and the state that arise from the unintended effects of liberalism. The chapter concludes by returning to the question of how a liberal politics can be progressive in Latin America today—especially now that the Pink Tide is receding.

OLIGARCHY, POPULISM, AND NEOLIBERALISM

Under colonialism, the Indigenous peoples of Latin America were not only denied a role in legislation; they were also largely denied the opportunity to develop even basic human capabilities such as reading and writing. Two centuries of republican government have not yet erased the legacy of three centuries of exclusion from access to written texts. Independence brought an end to Spanish colonialism but not exclusion of Indigenous peoples. After a period of anarchy—protracted and intense in some cases, briefer and milder in others—oligarchic states were established throughout the region, mostly on the basis of limited political representation (Isbester 2011, 36). The struggle between liberals and conservatives, which was the main cleavage in politics throughout much of the nineteenth century, was an intra-elite affair. Advocates of liberalism were often able to reconcile themselves to exclusion on the grounds that the masses were not ready for citizenship. In this respect they were not departing from classical liberalism: even Mill argued that despotism was a legitimate form of government in dealing with "barbarians," "provided the end be their improvement" (1968, 73). A review of the shifting constructions and interpretations of liberalism from the colonial era to the present suggests that such thinking is hardly a thing of the past.

Criollo Liberalism and the Oligarchic State (1820–1930)

Latin American liberalism was aptly described by the Peruvian socialist José Carlos Mariátegui (1971, 27) as a weak, *criollo* variant of European thought adapted to the circumstances and needs of New World oligarchies. Transplanted and grafted onto unequal societies, liberalism had very different effects in Latin America. A liberal polity based on the consent of the governed requires a society composed of relatively equal and autonomous citizens as agents capable of pursuing whatever ends they have good reasons to prefer. Such a polity, moreover, assumes the existence of state institutions that can impartially enforce and guarantee the rights of all citizens, not a patrimonial state based on personal relationships in which the distinction between public and private is blurred. Latin America presented neither such a society of equal agents nor a Weberian state. Two options were, therefore, available to Latin American rulers: either invest in promoting the conditions for full and inclusive citizenship or reinforce the exclusion of those presumed incapable of rational deliberation (such as illiterates), those who are trapped in dependency (servants or married women, for example), or those who cannot claim subjective rights assigned universally because of their particular circumstances (extreme poverty). The path of exclusion—or at least the indefinite postponement of inclusion—was chosen by Simón Bolívar.

We may take Bolívar as an exemplar of criollo liberalism. "It must be confessed," he said in his Angostura Discourse, "that most men are unaware of their best interests" (cited in Burns 1993, 54). This assumption led him to advocate, as he did for Bolivia in 1826, a mixed constitution with quasi-monarchical features and suffrage restricted to those who owned property and could read and write. Criollo liberals worried that, left to their own devices, the illiterate masses would deposit their trust in democratic caudillos, or strongmen. The Argentine liberal Juan Bautista Alberdi was one such skeptic; he argued that the will of the nation was best "expressed through the reason of educated men": "We are democrats with regard to the establishment of liberty in favor of national reason [but we oppose] the national will." He detested the "popular caudillo" who captures "the instincts and beliefs of the numeric majority" (quoted in Gargarella 2010, 170).

Seeking a middle ground between anarchy and caudillo rule, on the one hand, and tyranny or monarchy, on the other, criollo liberals of the nineteenth century upheld liberal principles of freedom, autonomy, and impartiality in a limited, restrictive, and discriminatory way. Like their European counterparts, they were averse to any imposition of specific conceptions of the good. Their commitment to moral autonomy meant that, in principle, every person "should be considered equally able to decide what was good or bad and should freely decide how to shape his or her own future" without "the use of the coercive powers of the state regarding 'personal' matters" (Gargarella 2010, 163–64). The role of the state should be limited to guaranteeing security and property and allowing the invisible hand of the market to operate freely. The vaunted impartiality of the oligarchic state became, however, a pretext to uphold the constituted power of the dominant classes: "In the end, the liberal approach, in actual practice, seems to be based on controversial elitist assumptions that fair or impartial decisions are better ensured through the debates of a small and enlightened or a technically efficient minority" (Gargarella 2010, 214). An impartial state could impose private property on Indigenous communities, thereby excluding them from their own ancestral lands; denying the franchise to women and illiterates; and limiting self-government to educated, property-owning, culturally European males.

Populism, the State, and Incorporation (1930–1980)

Populism emerged first as part of a reaction against liberal oligarchies. Populists mobilized "the people" not as citizens but as the excluded and downtrodden masses. As Ernesto Laclau puts it:

Liberalism had been the typical regime established by the ruling oligarchies in most Latin American countries following the period of anarchy and civil wars after independence. An electoral system controlled by local landowners in the rural districts, to which one has to add the incipient urban sectors equally controlled through clientelistic networks, was the political formula which presided over the economic development and integration of Latin America into the world market during the second half of the nineteenth century. (2005, 192)

Populism emerged first as an effort to reform—or overthrow—oligarchic states. Initially, at least, "democratic demands and liberalism were not opposed to each other" (Laclau 2005, 192). And in the more genuinely liberal republics, like Uruguay and Costa Rica, democratic reforms did not require radical populism. In those countries in which the oligarchic state was dominated by repressive caudillos, however, democratic reforms often required violent mobilization of the popular sectors. The populist leaders who led these movements were generally more paternalistic than liberal (Laclau 2005, 193).

Wherever populism was successful the popular sectors were incorporated not as citizens but as members of functional groups (workers, peasants, employees), and their forms of participation were controlled in a top-down and hierarchical manner through corporatist mechanisms (of either state-sponsored or party-based variants). Moreover, "the important thing to stress," wrote Laclau, "is that in all cases the 'people' constituted through the mobilizations associated with these regimes had a strong *statist* component. The construction of a strong *national* state in opposition to local oligarchical power was the trademark of this populism" (2005; original emphasis; see discussion in Beasley-Murray 2010, 54–61). Yet populism typically transformed the oligarchic state without creating a legal-rational instrument of industrial development: bureaucratic patrimonialism persisted and grew.

Neoliberalism and the Competitive Market (1980–Present)

The third major period in modern Latin American history is the current neoliberal era. Neoliberal globalization has imposed a new logic of competition that serves as a conditioning framework for the reconstruction of policy and governance (Grinspun and Kreklewich 1994). In Latin America, advocates of neoliberalism did not just oppose policies associated with import substitution industrialization (ISI) like tariffs, quotas, and subsidies; they also opposed the complementary policies of unionization, rising wages, and social benefits. Whereas the expansion of the local market under ISI contributed to rising incomes for an expanding working class and middle sectors that helped to sustain inward-oriented industrialization, under neoliberal globalization wages and benefits for workers and middle sectors were strictly a cost of doing business. Keeping wages down was critical to reducing production costs and achieving competitiveness. The expansion of the local market due to rising incomes and employment was not a policy goal; at best it would be a positive externality that would "trickle down" from improvements in competitiveness.

The essence of neoliberalism is not free trade—or even freedom to choose in Milton Friedman's argot—but competition. And competition does not happen naturally. Unlike the doctrine of laissez-faire, in which individuals pursue their natural or spontaneous tendency to barter and trade, neoliberalism recognizes that competitiveness must be actively promoted by the state in all spheres of life: not just the economy, but also education, health care, politics, culture, security (Brown 2015; Foucault 2004; Munck 2015, 369). Policy initiatives—whether social, political, or environmental—could be justified primarily in terms of competitiveness. Unions came to be seen as the source of labor market rigidities that undermined competitiveness, not as organizations crucial to ensuring the health, safety, and well-being of workers by protecting workers' rights and their share of improvements in productivity. For neoliberals, unions represented a limitation on the freedom of workers and a deadweight on the economy. In a globalized economy, the owners of capital were no longer limited by the capacity of the local market to expand. On the contrary, cheap labor was indispensable in the struggle to penetrate emerging markets.

In the neoliberal era, liberal principles—freedom, autonomy, impartiality—took on new meanings as they were integrated, retrodictively, into a new conceptual schema. Drawing on neoclassical economics, individuals were assumed to be competitive utility maximizers. Indeed, neoliberalism valued competition over all other goals precisely because it induces economic rationality and thereby undermines collectivism, which is seen as an expression of irrationalism. The value of autonomy lay in the destruction of constraints on individual choice. Impartiality was required to uphold predictable rules for investors, consumers, and producers. Democracy under neoliberalism has tended to be seen as a social choice mechanism: a system for aggregating preferences much like the marketplace. But the paradox of neoliberalism, like that of liberalism, is that the ostensibly universalistic aspirations of the doctrine function effectively only in specific historical contexts from whence they do not readily travel. The persistence of bureaucratic patrimonialism in Latin America virtually ensured that neoliberal reforms would have perverse consequences, among them the reassertion of oligarchic tendencies in politics as market reforms concentrated economic assets and weakened the organizational capacity of the popular sectors.

FREEDOM, AUTONOMY, AND THE STATE

Latin America's recent Left turns have not always entailed the rejection of progressive features of liberalism; on the contrary, many leftist governments have sought to advance goals necessary to create the conditions under which liberal citizenship might flourish. They have emphasized redistribution and shared prosperity, inclusive and active citizenship, and state reform—or republican refoundation (see Cameron and Hershberg 2010; Cannon and Kirby 2012; Ellner 2014; Levitsky and Roberts 2011; Montambeault, Balán, and Oxhorn, this volume; Panizza 2009). The agenda of the left is not necessarily incompatible with liberalism, but it requires a reworking or reinterpretation of liberal principles of freedom, autonomy, and impartiality to ensure their appropriateness in Latin American contexts. It also entails the revival of discourse on the public good. The notion of *buen vivir*—or living well, in harmony with nature and others—has been proposed to replace the implicit materialism and consumerism of the good life as understood in Eurocentric terms (see Rice, this volume).

Although the record of success of left-wing governments in achieving social and political inclusion has been at best mixed, and its record of upholding liberal rights and freedoms has been rightly criticized, as the chapters in this volume demonstrate, there is still much to be learned from these experiences, especially at a time when liberal democracy is under threat around the world. A central lesson is that democratic empowerment and the enhancement of human capabilities are necessary to overcome social structures and institutional arrangements that inhibit the possibility of human agency, and thus the role of the state must exceed impartially supervising existing relations of property and domination.

Freedom as Social and Political Empowerment

Latin American Left turn governments have tended to emphasize freedom understood in terms of political and social empowerment rather than noninterference. For example, Roberto Mangabeira Unger argues for an "empowered democracy," the goal of which, in his view, is "not chiefly to enlarge our field of choice but, rather, to imagine and defend a certain change in the quality of our experience of subjectivity and sociability and to describe the institutional conditions of this shift" (1987, 363). For Unger, it is not individual choice among set options that matters so much as expanding the capacity to be and do what we have reason to want. A politics of empowerment must continuously challenge the structures and roles that compel people to serve as mere placeholders for their class, gender, occupation, or other set categories, and to become fully free agents. Opening up institutions and enabling experimentation and change are essential to allow people to pursue the ends they have reason to value. Refusal to do this, to expand the sphere of freedom that allows for human creativity and change, is tantamount to insisting that institutions remain fetters upon improvements in the conditions of social existence.

The idea of freedom as empowerment is not new. As Philip Pettit (2014, xvi) has shown, the liberal ideal of freedom, understood as the absence of external constraints, contrasts with the Greco-Roman or republican idea of freedom as nondomination or mutual empowerment. Whereas the liberal idea of freedom emphasizes the isolated and asocial individual, the Greek- and Roman-inspired concept of freedom emphasizes collective action in the public sphere. The liberal idea is about constraining the state to ensure it does not trample on individual rights, or "negative liberty," in Isaiah Berlin's terms; the republican idea is about enabling collective action and exercising power to ensure the will of the people is, in fact, expressed and acted upon. Liberalism implies passive citizenship rather than the more demanding claims of republican citizenship.

The concept of politics that animates Latin America's Left turns—various manifestations of participatory democracy, for example—has, perhaps, closer affinity to classical conceptions of democracy and republicanism than to contemporary liberalism. For the Greeks the suffix *-kratos*, which is passed down to us through the etymology of the word *democracy*, implied the "collective capacity to effect change in the public realm" (Ober 2008, 7). By the same token, Latin America's progressives have emphasized active citizenship, popular sovereignty, and constituent power. Many of the contemporary liberal objections to the practice of democracy in Latin America—the abuses of power, the persecution of opponents, the arbitrary shifts in policy—are reminiscent of the objections to democracy expressed by elites in the classical era.

Liberalism extols the importance of freedom exercised in the private rather than in the public sphere. Freedom, in this view, means to be able to do as one pleases, provided one does not harm others. As long as citizens are not hurting anyone else, they should be free to pursue whatever activities they wish. This understanding of freedom privileges the private sphere as the domain of freedom left to us after we have eliminated all those activities—nearly all social activities—that pose potential harms to others. The liberal ideal, in which everyone cultivates their own garden, as Voltaire put it, is premised on an appreciation of the private sphere as the privileged space for the satisfaction of human wants and aspirations.

Liberals view the public sphere with wariness. When citizens combine they are constantly at risk of harming others: Émile Durkheim called this the ill effects of secondary associations. The formation of a union, for example, immediately alters the cost of labor to the entrepreneur and the costs of the final product to the consumer; to uphold the rights of those in the union may affect those who are not part of the union. For liberals, as long as public activity is benign and unobjectionable, it is permissible; as soon as it becomes disruptive, costly, or harmful to anyone, it becomes a problem. In this sense, the liberal conception of freedom is inevitably a constraint on progressive change understood in terms of mutual, collective empowerment. For progressives, differentials of power rooted in the private sphere—*dominium*, as opposed to *imperium*, or power in the public sphere (Pettit 2014, 110)—are sources of injustice that must be addressed, and this implies conflicts, costs, and harms.

In the European context, liberalism historically provided, at least in principle, the basis of democracy by imposing healthy constraints on its excesses; it was a relationship based on mutual necessity and tensions (Beetham 1993, 56). Liberalism allowed the inequalities associated with capitalism to coexist with the egalitarianism inherent in democracy. Capitalism generates inequalities that, in principle, threaten the stability of democracy. Liberalism promises to tame the excesses of both capitalism and democracy. For elites, it attenuates fear of the masses, typically expressed as a concern about the tyranny of the majority. For the masses, liberalism guarantees the basic rights and freedoms necessary to protect them against the market.

In Latin America, however, although the fears of elites are even more intense, the tyranny of minorities is a greater fetter on democracy. Since the early republics of the nineteenth century, minorities with immense de facto power have been a constant obstacle to democratization. After independence, landowners, the clergy, and military caudillos were perhaps the most significant de facto powers—and in some cases they became de jure powers through the creation of military and ecclesiastical *fueros* (courts) and other privileges. In any event, the problem for democracy lies in the deficiency, not excess, of the will of the people.

Some of the same de facto powers still exist today in the form of military courts and other privileges like special tax regimes for corporate groups. this is reflected in the extraordinary concentration of power by *grupos de poder económico* (often accompanied by control over the mass media), which has been exacerbated by neoliberal economic reforms and the atrophying (not the excess) of state power. An empowered democracy must be able to challenge these undemocratic sources of power, which, if unchecked, create the risk of effectively neutralizing democratic politics. Popular sovereignty is thwarted in a continuous and ongoing way by powerful minorities bent on preserving the status quo. These powers are largely invisible to contemporary criollo liberals, who see only the defense of legitimate interests grounded in private property and constituted power. Yet they create conditions that subject entire groups to low intensity citizenship.

In short, an "empowered democracy" necessarily embraces rather than eschews conflict; it is agonistic and contentious because nondomination cannot be achieved without challenging constituted powers. It cannot be achieved "unless the rich and powerful surrender their disproportionate portion of economic and political control" (Veltmeyer 2007, 104). Challenging structures of domination invites conflict, which invites objections that someone is hurting someone else. This generates a supply of complaints that can be taken up by liberals as evidence of the illiberalism of agents of change. Many of these objections may be entirely legitimate. But it is also important to recognize that conflict is inherent in an unjust status quo. Fights with de facto powers—including the media, powerful economic groups, the military, and the church— are inevitable in an empowered democracy. The failure to limit de facto powers is, however, or should be, every bit as problematic from a democratic perspective that defines freedom in terms of nondomination.

Autonomy as Enhanced Capabilities

There is a connection between the priority of empowerment over noninterference and a conception of autonomy that recognizes the need to overcome structural constraints that limit collective agency rather than individual freedom to choose. O'Donnell (2010) argued that agency implies subjects endowed with practical reason and moral autonomy, and he noted that its emergence is the product of lengthy historical processes. The conditions for the full exercise of agency must be recognized and guaranteed by legal and political institutions. Latin American Left turn governments have emphasized the need to promote conditions for expanding human agency, and challenging the structures that limit moral autonomy, rather than protecting individual autonomy under existing conditions of domination. Thus, in contrast to the liberal idea of autonomy—the notion that every *ego* knows his (or her) preferences and interests better than any *alter*, and ego alone is the best advocate of her (or his) rights—we may consider the idea of autonomy as a feature of agency. It involves a set of capabilities that are necessary in order to pursue the life plans ego has reason to value. Autonomy in this sense is not a given but an attribute of the individual that demands a socially constructed set of skills and abilities. These skills and abilities need to be cultivated, and this is an important justification for state intervention that classical liberalism neglected and contemporary neoliberalism disputes.

In her insightful book, Areli Valencia (2016) shows how the systematic denial of the freedom to develop human capabilities undermines fundamental rights in ways that are not well understood (and, indeed, *cannot* be well understood) within a liberal or negative rights framework. By showing how situations of systemic unfreedom or economic dependency can undermine the development of capacities for agency and rights assertion, Valencia explains why miners in the Peruvian smelting town of La Oroya, who are overwhelmingly victims of heavy metal poisoning, nevertheless deny their rights are being violated and instead seek to protect the very jobs that make them and their families sick.

Valencia challenges the "perpetrator-victim-remedy" model of human rights, in which rights violations are said to occur when a perpetrator victimizes someone. As she notes, this may ignore underlying or root causes of human rights abuses, particularly those arising from conditions that she describes in terms of systemic unfreedom. These situations cannot be redressed through the normal remedies for rights violations but instead require longer-term structural transformations. Valencia does a noteworthy job of explaining how we might actually make significant progress toward understanding systematic unfreedom in human rights terms by drawing on another intellectual tradition—the "capabilities approach" (Nussbaum 2011; Sen 1999).

The workers in La Oroya lack the information and awareness, the economic independence, and the social cohesion necessary to perform as fully functioning agents capable of transforming the resources available to them into outcomes that would enhance their well-being. This is the essence of their unfreedom, and it allows them to be ruthlessly exploited by the mining company in collusion with the state. In other words, violations of basic rights—and they are clearly documented—are only the tip of the iceberg. A structural condition of unfreedom enables these abuses and hinders the possibility of remedy. Small wonder then that the countries with the highest quality of democracy in Latin America today, like Uruguay and Costa Rica, lacking in abundant natural resources, have invested heavily in health care, education, social infrastructure, and political inclusion, while countries with extractivist economies, like Peru and Guatemala, have lagged in this respect, especially under neoliberal governments.

Public investments in social programs are unlikely to be sufficient to sustain democracy, however, unless opportunities are created to learn the habits and practices of citizenship. This is the foundation of what Barry Cannon and Peadar Kirby (2012, 189), drawing on Nancy Fraser, call "strong publics," whereby participation "brings the role of civil society beyond that of mere opinion formation and towards authoritative decision-making, implying that the liberal separation of state and civil society dissolves and is replaced by an inter-imbrication of these two spheres." Deepening democratization demands not only a set of human capabilities but also the experience of active participation. Yet liberal democracies generally offer few opportunities for active citizenship, and thus generate weak publics. This is why Latin America's Left turn countries have all experimented with new forms of popular participation, including participatory budgeting, Indigenous autonomies, municipal and community councils, various forms of decentralization, referendums, citizens' initiatives, and recall (see Cameron, Hershberg, and Sharpe 2012). Not all these institutions for direct participatory democracy serve equally well as spaces for the practice of citizenship (see Goldfrank, this volume), and some may simply reproduce clientelism. Much depends on the provision of genuine scope for autonomous collective decision making, investments in social policy, and the availability of resources.

It is, nonetheless, only through the practice of democratic self-government that the capacity for citizenship is acquired. Consistent with this, a major theme in the literature on social movements and participatory democracy is the need for autonomy (Oxhorn 2011, 2012). The Zapatistas created Juntas de Buen Gobierno, in which they put into practice a flexible, community-based model of collective autonomy (Stahler-Sholk 2007). The Bolivian government has invited Indigenous communities to create autonomy statutes to establish their own systems of self-rule based on customary practices (Rice 2015; Tockman 2016). Participatory budgeting has provided people in cities around the world with the chance to deliberate and decide on the allocation of municipal budgets, and these have been found to work best where civil society is given a wide margin of autonomy (Avritzer 2009; Goldfrank 2011; Montambeault 2012). Public policy conferences have given citizens in Brazil the chance to take an active part in public policy deliberation (Pogrebinschi 2012). The organization of community councils in Venezuela facilitated the coproduction of public goods (McCarthy 2012).

All these initiatives provide meaningful spaces for the development of the skills and know-how necessary for autonomous self-government. Yet a note of caution is necessary. Although democracy is made more meaningful by giving citizens a say in matters that affect them directly, participatory innovations are not a substitute for constitutional checks and balances, or horizontal accountability; nor can they guarantee that the spaces they provide will not be captured by clientelism, patronage politics, and partisan machinations. That these problems exist, however, ill justifies the rejection of participatory innovations as mere props for the perpetuation of illiberal democracies. Deficiencies of liberal democracy, and the low-intensity quality of its citizenship, must be addressed to ensure that participatory innovations live up to their potential.

Constituting a Good State

A central goal of many Latin American Left turn governments has been decolonizing, deprivatizing, or otherwise transforming the state (de Sousa Santos 2008, 266–67). As Unger notes, the state cannot be "neutral among all projects," or "among contrasting visions of the good" (1987, 363, 365). Although the state, through its ostensible neutrality or impartiality, seeks to make domination invisible, by providing a guarantee of order within the framework of a given set of structures and relationships it necessarily upholds whatever patterns of domination and exclusion are inherent in that framework. A progressive politics cannot afford to accept the illusion that the state is a neutral or impartial umpire of conflicts, since the most important conflicts in any social order arise from unequal relations and structures of domination. The reification of unjust arrangements promotes a false neutrality that prevents the state from being placed in the service of desirable social ends. As Gargarella (2010, 211) observed, nineteenth-century liberals failed to supply valid reasons for treating the existing state of affairs as either natural or defensible. The insistence that the state must have, as Bolívar put it, "a neutral body to protect the injured and disarm the offender" led him to advocate a hereditary senate. Who better than educated and privileged men could guarantee the neutrality of the social order?

There are different methods of transforming the state. One option is to exercise constituent power (Cameron 2013, 181–86; Ciccariello-Maher 2014; Colón-Ríos 2011), as Bolívar did. The idea has potentially radical implications: if democracy means the rule of the people (its etymological meaning), the people must surely have the right not only to choose their rulers, but the manner in which that choice is made. Democracy, in other words, implies the right to decide on what democracy means—the form it will take—as well as who the current incumbents should be. Rousseau captured this idea in the *Social Contract*. He suggested that each assembly should ask two questions before beginning its deliberations: "The first: 'Whether is pleases the sovereign to maintain the present form of government.' The second: 'Whether it pleases the people to leave the administration to those at present entrusted with it'" (Rousseau [1762] 1968, bk. 3, ch. 18).

If the idea of constituent power was always implicit in liberalism, it was crystallized during the French Revolution—specifically, in the thinking of Immanuel Joseph Sieyès. A key passage in *What Is the Third Estate* reads, "In each of its parts a constitution is not the work of a constituted power but a constituent power. No type of delegated power can modify the conditions of its delegation. It is in this sense, and in no other, that constitutional laws are *fundamental*" (Sieyès 2003, 136; original emphasis). In the spirit of Sieyès, the republican refounding in Latin America has taken the form of the introduction of constituent assemblies tasked with writing new constitutions. Generally, the process has begun with an election to secure a mandate to change the constitution followed by a referendum. Once the idea has been approved, a constituent assembly is elected to draft a new constitution, which is then subjected to another referendum before it enters into effect.

Advocates of constituent power promise to restore popular sovereignty to its central position in democratic theory and practice. Whereas neoliberalism places critical policy choices outside the reach of the democratic decision making in the interest of growth and competition, constituent power reaffirms the sovereign right of the people to determine the conditions of their self-government. Constituent power is a tonic against the conversion of liberalism into a dogma of constituted power. It reclaims the radical egalitarianism that accepts the proposition that all citizens are entitled to an equal share in the decisions that affect them. All constituted power is delegated power, and it owes its legitimacy to the same source: the sovereign will of the people.

The idea of popular sovereignty is, however, notoriously tricky. There is a danger that an "empowered democracy" will over-empower itself—leaving even its advocates dismayed by the abuses of power to which it gives rise, as seen most clearly in the case of *chavista* Venezuela. As Roberto Gargarella (2013) has noted, it is easy to write social rights into constitutions but much harder to organize power within the state in ways that guarantee those rights full protection. The notion of constituent power may serve only to mask the political ambitions of presidents acting in the name of the people (Bernal 2014). Many Latin American Left turn governments, in their haste to transform the state, have often reproduced the old vices of clientelism, paternalism, and bureaucratic patrimonialism and have governed in ways that undermine representative institutions and institutionalized opposition.

Another way to transform the state—more benign but not always feasible—is to guarantee the rights of citizens against the state and other citizens and empower citizens so that they are not the targets of paternalism, however well intentioned. Paternalism and patrimonialism are the inevitable corollaries of the lack of a lawful state capable of backing the rights and freedoms of citizens in a universalistic manner. O'Donnell called for recognition of the importance of the rule of law, horizontal accountability, and a lawful state based on citizenship as agency (2010, 93–113). This too is a progressive agenda—and, properly understood, it is a radical one. The risk with this strategy is that unless the insufficiencies of liberalism are recognized, its radical features will be neutralized.

O'Donnell was surely right to stress the evils of paternalism and the dire effects of states lacking the capacity to guarantee full rights of citizenship in Latin America (2010, 51–71, 145–66). Liberal principles of individual freedom, autonomy, and impartiality are radically at odds with the social habits and practices, such as clientelism and populism, that are endemic in contexts of inequality, social exclusion, and gross imbalances of power. The adoption of liberal reforms could address problems that have dogged successive Latin American efforts at reform. Liberalism is potentially transformative because other social changes are difficult or impossible without it. It is difficult if not impossible to achieve social justice without what Enrique Peruzzotti (2012) calls "a good state."

If I am right, and liberalism needs allies among progressives, then Latin America's current reversions to the right may constitute a setback for liberalism. After the October 2018 election in Brazil, the *Economist* ran a story under the title, "Jair Bolsonaro and the Perversion of Liberalism" (2018, 43–44, 46). True to its liberal creed, the magazine noted that the elected president of Brazil had recruited a free-market economist from the University of Chicago but that his rhetoric was "neither liberal nor democratic." Although the *Economist* recognized that the "combination of political authoritarianism and free-market economics is not new in Brazil or Latin America," it excused liberalism from any responsibility for this fateful association. Instead, the magazine blamed the French philosopher Auguste Comte for the region's failure to construct truly egalitarian societies and, bizarrely, suggested that corporatism "morphed" out of positivism.

The *Economist* refused to confront the limitations of what it called a "conception of society as . . . an agglomeration of free individuals." Yet it was precisely such a view of society that, placed in a postcolonial context, had perverse consequences for liberalism—and Latin America. Liberal notions of private property, for example, led to the displacement of Indigenous populations throughout the nineteenth century, and even into the twentieth century as the Zapatista uprising attests. The *Economist* blandly asserted that liberalism ended "the formal serfdom to which Indians [*sic*] were subjected in the Andes and Mexico." It forgot that liberal oligarchies imposed forced labor, poll taxes, voting restrictions, and the imposition of private property—often accompanied by fraud and violence—as a mechanism for the dispossession of Indigenous peoples from their lands. Neoliberal technocrats have pursued similar ends by more indirect but no less socially costly means.

Noting the brutal history of dictatorships in Chile and Peru, the *Economist* issued a stern warning: "Separating economic and political freedom may seem like a shortcut to development. But in Latin America it rarely is: the demand for strong government has vied with a persistent yearning for liberty." Yet it is precisely the meaning of liberty that is in question. Does liberty mean the freedom of autonomous individuals, or does it involve the empowerment of collectivities to participate in the decisions that directly affect their lives? Does it demand a minimal state that gets out of the way of private initiative or one that establishes the fiscal regime necessary to make social investment in areas like health and education? Bolsonaro called his victory a "celebration of freedom," but it was clear that he did not mean freedom as empowerment of the popular sectors. His rhetoric suggested that he was less committed to liberal values than the leaders of the Partido dos Trabalhadores (Workers' Party, PT), whose record in office not only included citizenship-enhancing investments in social policies, but these, moreover, were implemented in ways that were entirely compatible with the logic of markets (e.g., conditional cash transfer programs).

The *Economist* clearly identified Bolsonaro as illiberal but then repeated liberalism's gravest error, which is to fail to see how neoliberal globalization creates obstacles to the social and political reforms necessary for liberalism to achieve its progressive potential. An excessive faith in markets has meant that liberals too readily abandon their mission of "taming capitalism and holding economic power to democratic account" (Sandel 2018). It would not be the first time that the failure to balance liberalism with democracy reinforced the oligarchical tendencies inherent in unregulated capitalism. In every major historical period—from the construction of nineteenth-century oligarchic states to the twentieth-century politics of populism and in the current era of neoliberalism—aspects of liberalism have been in tension with the struggles of the popular sector for inclusion. The transcendence of *lo popular*, of paternalism, as well as its antitheses, oligarchy, exclusion, and repression, and the construction of good states based on citizenship, requires buttressing liberalism with a more inclusive, empowering, and participatory democracy. It demands the moral equivalent of a French Revolution, including the cultivation of capabilities and agency and the exercise of constituent power to refashion the state apparatus from an instrument of private power into a means of collective action toward just social ends. Liberalism in Latin America must become radical if it is to be progressive, or else it will be what it has mostly been in the region's past: another ideological weapon in the arsenal of the powerful.

NOTES

Presented at RÉLAM's First International Conference, "What's Left? The Left Turn in Latin America, 15 Years After," March 23–24, 2016, Bibliothèques et Archives Nationales du Québec, Montréal. I am grateful to Françoise Montambeault, Manuel Balán, Jon Beasley-Murray, Alec Dawson, and Phil Oxhorn for comments. Research funding was provided by the Social Sciences Research Council of Canada. None of the above are responsible for the argument of this chapter, much less errors or omissions.

1. For examples of postliberal critique in other contexts, see Schmitter 2006; Macpherson 1965.

2. Problems of democracy that have long characterized the Latin American region appear to be spreading globally. This was the consensus of a group of scholars who participated in the "Global Challenge to Democracy" workshop in San José, Costa Rica, May 4–6, 2017.

3. Citizenship refers to membership in the polis, a set of rights and duties, and the exercise of legitimate authority (see Montambeault, Balán, and Oxhorn, this volume; O'Donnell 2010; Yashar 2005). It also entails a set of capabilities necessary to exercise rights effectively (Nussbaum 2011; Sen 1999).

REFERENCES

Arditi, Benjamin. 2008. "Arguments about the Left Turns in Latin America: Post-Liberal Politics?" *Latin American Research Review* 43 (3): 59–81.

Avritzer, Leonardo. 2009. *Participatory Institutions in Democratic Brazil.* Baltimore, MD: Johns Hopkins University Press.

Beasley-Murray, Jon. 2010. *Posthegemony: Political Theory and Latin America.* Minneapolis: University of Minnesota Press.

Beetham, David. 1993. "Liberal Democracy and the Limits of Democratization." In David Held, ed., *Prospects for Democracy: North, South, East, West.* Stanford, CA: Stanford University Press.

Berman, Sheri. 2017. "The Pipe Dream of Undemocratic Liberalism." *Journal of Democracy* 28 (3): 29–38.

Bernal, Angélica M. 2014. "The Meaning and Perils of Presidential Refounding in Latin America." *Constellations* 21 (4): 440–56.

Brown, Wendy. 2015. *Undoing the Demos: Neoliberalism's Stealth Revolution.* New York: Zone Books.

Burns, E. Bradford. 1993. *Latin America: Conflict and Creation. A Historical Reader.* Atlantic Highlands, NJ: Prentice Hall.

Cameron, Maxwell A. 2013. *Strong Constitutions: Social-Cognitive Origins of the Separation of Powers.* New York: Oxford University Press.

Cameron, Maxwell A., and Eric Hershberg. 2010. *Latin America's Left Turns: Politics, Policies, and Trajectories of Change.* Boulder, CO: Lynne Rienner.

Cameron, Maxwell A., Eric Hershberg, and Kenneth E. Sharpe, eds. 2012. *New Institutions for Participatory Democracy in Latin America: Voice and Consequence*. New York: Palgrave Macmillan.

Cannon, Barry, and Peadar Kirby. 2012. "Civil Society–State Relations in Left-Led Latin America: Deepening Democratization?" In Barry Cannon and Peadar Kirby, eds., *Civil Society and the State in Left-Led Latin America: Challenges and Limitations to Democratization*, 189–202. London: Zed Books.

Ciccariello-Maher, George. 2014. "Constituent Moments, Constitutional Processes: Social Movements and the New Latin American Left." In Steve Ellner, ed., *Latin America's Radical Left in Power: Complexities and Challenges in the Twenty-First Century*, 227–48. Lanham, MD: Rowman & Littlefield.

Colón-Ríos, Joel I. 2011. "The Rights of Nature and the New Latin American Constitutionalism." *New Zealand Journal of Public and International Law* 13: 107.

Cranston, Maurice. 1954. *Freedom: A New Analysis*. London: Longmans, Green and Co.

de Sousa Santos, Boaventura. 2008. "Depolarised Pluralities. A Left with a Future." In Patrick Barrett, Daniel Chavez, and César Rodríguez-Garavito, eds., *The New Latin American Left: Utopia Reborn*, 255–72. London: Pluto Press.

Economist. 2018. "Jair Bolsonaro and the Perversion of Liberalism: Reviving Latin America's Unholy Marriage between Market Economics and Political Authoritarianism." www.economist.com/the-americas/2018/10/27/jair-bolsonaro-and-the-perversion-of-liberalism.

Ellner, Steve, ed. 2014. *Latin America's Radical Left in Power: Complexities and Challenges in the Twenty-First Century*. Lanham, MD: Rowman & Littlefield.

Foucault, Michel. 2004. *The Birth of Biopolitics: Lectures at the Collège de France 1978–1979*. New York: Palgrave Macmillan.

Foweraker, Joe. 2018. *Polity: Demystifying Democracy in Latin America and Beyond*. Boulder, CO: Lynne Rienner.

Gargarella, Roberto. 2010. *The Legal Foundations of Inequality: Constitutionalism in the Americas, 1776–1860*. Cambridge: Cambridge University Press.

———. 2013. "Keeping the Promise: Rights and Realities in Latin America." *Boston Review*. www.bostonreview.net/world/keeping-promise.

Goldfrank, Benjamin. 2011. *Deepening Local Democracy in Latin America: Participation, Decentralization, and the Left*. University Park: Pennsylvania State University Press.

Grinspun, Ricardo, and Robert Kreklewich. 1994. "Consolidating Neoliberal Reforms: 'Free Trade' as a Conditioning Framework." *Studies in Political Economy* 43 (1): 33–61.

Isbester, Katherine. 2011. "Democracy in Latin America: A Political History." In Katherine Isbester and Viviana Patroni, eds., *The Paradox of Democracy in Latin America: Ten Country Studies of Division and Resilience*. Toronto: University of Toronto Press.

Laclau, Ernesto. 2005. *On Populist Reason*. London: Verso.

Levitsky, Steven, and Kenneth M. Roberts. 2011. "Conclusion: Democracy, Development, and the Left." In Steven Levitsky and Kenneth M. Roberts, eds., *The Resurgence of the Latin American Left*. Baltimore, MD: Johns Hopkins University Press.

Macpherson, Crawford Brough. 1965. *The Real World of Democracy*. The Massey Lectures. Toronto: Canadian Broadcasting Corporation.

Manning, David John. 1976. *Liberalism*. London: J. M. Dent & Sons.

Mariátegui, José Carlos. 1971. *Seven Interpretive Essays on Peruvian Reality*. Austin: University of Texas Press.

McCarthy, Michael M. 2012. "The Possibilities and Limits of Politicized Participation: Community Councils, Coproduction, and Poder Popular in Chávez's Venezuela." In Maxwell A. Cameron, Eric Hershberg, and Kenneth E. Sharpe, eds., *New Institutions for Participatory Democracy in Latin America: Voice and Consequence*. New York: Palgrave Macmillan.

Mill, John Stuart. 1968. *Utilitarianism, Liberty, Representative Government*. London: Dent.

Montambeault, Françoise. 2012. "Learning to Be 'Better Democrats'? The Role of Informal Practices in Brazilian Participatory Budgeting Experiences." In Maxwell A. Cameron, Eric Hershberg, and Kenneth E. Sharpe, eds., *New Institutions for Participatory Democracy in Latin America: Voice and Consequence*. New York: Palgrave Macmillan.

Munck, Gerardo L. 2015. "Building Democracy . . . Which Democracy? Ideology and Models of Democracy in Post-Transition Latin America." *Government and Opposition* 50 (3): 364–93.

Nussbaum, Martha C. 2011. *Creating Capabilities: The Human Development Approach*. Cambridge, MA: Harvard University Press.

Ober, Josiah. 2008. "The Original Meaning of 'Democracy': Capacity to Do Things, not Majority Rule." *Constellations* 15 (1): 3–9.

O'Donnell, Guillermo. 1993. "On the State, Democratization and Some Conceptual Problems: A Latin American View with Glances at Some Post-communist Countries." *World Development* 21 (8): 1355–69.

———. 2010. *Democracy, Agency, and the State: Theory with Comparative Intent.* New York: Oxford University Press.

Oxhorn, Philip. 2011. *Sustaining Civil Society: Economic Change, Democracy, and the Social Construction of Citizenship in Latin America.* University Park: Pennsylvania State University Press.

———. 2012. "Understanding the Vagaries of Civil Society and Participation in Latin America." In Peter Kingstone and Deborah J. Yashar, eds., *Routledge Handbook of Latin American Politics.* London: Routledge.

Panizza, Francisco. 2009. *Contemporary Latin America: Development and Democracy beyond the Washington Consensus.* London: Zed Books.

Peruzzotti, Enrique. 2012. "El derecho a un buen estado." *Revista Temas y Debates* 6 (24): 74–83.

Pettit, Philip. 2014. *Just Freedom: A Moral Compass for a Complex World.* New York: Norton.

Pogrebinschi, Thamy. 2012. "Participation as Representation: Democratic Policymaking in Brazil." In *New Institutions for Participatory Democracy in Latin America: Voice and Consequence*, ed. Maxwell A. Cameron, Eric Hershberg, and Kenneth E. Sharpe. New York: Palgrave Macmillan. Quiroga, Hugo, and Osvaldo Iazzetta. 2005. "Guillermo O'Donnell: 'Hoy ser progresista es ser liberal, y viceversa.'" In Hugo Quiroga and Osvaldo Iazzetta, eds., *Hacia un nuevo consenso democrático: Conversaciones con la política.* Rosario: Homo Sapiens.

Rice, Roberta. 2015. "Indigenous Mobilization and Democracy in Latin America." In Richard L. Millett, Jennifer S. Holmes, and Orlando Pérez, eds., *Latin American Democracy: Emerging Reality or Endangered Species?* 2nd ed. New York: Routledge.

Rousseau, Jean-Jacques. [1762] 1968. *The Social Contract.* Trans. G. D. H. Cole. London: E. P. Dutton & Co.

Sandel, Michael J. 2018. "Populism, Trump, and the Future of Democracy." openDemocracy, May 9. www.opendemocracy.net/michael-j-sandel/populism-trump-and-future-of-democracy. Accessed January 2, 2019.

Schmitter, Philippe C. 2006. "A Sketch of What a 'Post-Liberal' Democracy Might Look Like." *Central European Political Science Review* 7 (23–24): 9–19.

Sen, Amartya. 1999. *Development as Freedom.* New York: Anchor.

Sieyès, Emmanuel Joseph. 2003. *Political Writings.* Indianapolis, IN: Hackett.

Slater, Dan. 2013. "Democratic Careening." *World Politics* 65 (4): 729–63.

Stahler-Sholk, Richard. 2007. "Resisting Neoliberal Homogenization: The Zapatista Autonomy Movement." *Latin American Perspectives* 34 (2): 48–63.

Tockman, Jason. 2016. "Decentralisation, Socio-Territoriality and the Exercise of Indigenous Self-Governance in Bolivia." *Third World Quarterly* 37 (1): 153–71.

Unger, Roberto Mangabeira. 1987. *False Necessity: Anti-Necessitarian Social Theory in the Service of Radical Democracy*. London: Verso.

Valencia, Areli. 2016. *Human Rights Trade-Offs in Times of Economic Growth: The Long-Term Capability Impacts of Extractive-Led Development*. New York: Palgrave Macmillan.

Veltmeyer, Henry. 2007. *On the Move: The Politics of Social Change in Latin America*. Peterborough, Ont.: Broadview Press.

Weyland, Kurt. 2013. "The Threat from the Populist Left." *Journal of Democracy* 24 (3): 18–32.

Wolff, Jonas. 2013. "Toward Post-Liberal Democracy in Latin America? A Conceptual Framework Applied to Bolivia" *Journal of Latin American Studies*, 45 (1): 31–59.

Yashar, Deborah. 2005. *Contesting Citizenship in Latin America: The Rise of Indigenous Movements and the Postliberal Challenge*. New York: Cambridge University Press.

PART 2

Deepening Democratic Institutions

THREE

Parties and Party Systems in Latin America's Left Turn

KENNETH M. ROBERTS

Latin America's post-1998 political shift to the left exerted significant, though widely varying, effects on political parties and party systems. Whereas some countries turned left by means of highly institutionalized alternations in office between established party organizations, others did so in contexts where mainstream parties had broken down and been displaced by populist outsiders or new "movement parties" on the left flanks of traditional party systems. In the latter cases the Left turn typically entailed significant processes of new party building, although rebuilding was often highly uneven (or asymmetrical) in systemic terms. Some of these leftist parties, both old and new, forged meaningful ties to social actors like labor and peasant unions or community associations, and the governments they led strengthened institutional channels for democratic representation, participation, and accountability. In so doing, they expanded the reach of democratic citizenship rights to previously excluded social and cultural groups, and they sometimes established new rights of social citizenship that were rarely before recognized in the region. Other leftist parties, however, had more distant or tenuous relationships with civil society, and the governments they led were less likely to transform citizenship regimes.

To understand this variation, it is essential to explain patterns of change and continuity at two different levels of analysis: individual party organizations and national party systems, which are constituted by rival party organizations and shaped by their competitive interaction. These two levels of analysis make it possible to identify the most important effects of the Left turn on partisan representation in Latin America: (1) a partial restructuring of programmatic competition across much of the region following the widespread convergence of mainstream parties around variants of market liberalism during the heyday of the "Washington Consensus" (Williamson 1990); and (2) the incomplete and asymmetrical institutionalization of this programmatic competition through durable and coherent party organizations. As explained below, in a number of cases the Left turn generated deep sociopolitical cleavages but only partially reconstructed national party systems around those societal divisions.

Consequently, as the Left turn entered into retreat—in some countries, at least—starting in 2015, Latin America continued to possess a diverse array of party systems with highly uneven patterns of institutionalization. The Left turn did not, in other words, systematically generate stable new alignments of partisan and electoral competition. Neither, however, did it consistently destroy the old ones. Indeed, in a number of countries it reinforced existing competitive alignments. Although party systems remained underinstitutionalized in much of the region, electoral competition became more consistently structured by left-right programmatic distinctions, even where voters' ideological identities remained ambiguous or where leftist parties in public office struggled to implement policy platforms that were a significant departure from inherited neoliberal prescriptions (see Dabène, this volume). The programmatic restructuring of electoral competition and at least a modest expansion of policy latitude in the social policy sphere were arguably the most important, and potentially the most durable, legacies of the region's political shift to the left.

Likewise, the Left turn spawned widely varying patterns of popular sector participation and interest representation through partisan channels. Although some governing leftist parties, in particular Bolivia's Movimiento al Socialismo (Movement toward Socialism, MAS) and Uruguay's Frente Amplio (Broad Front, FA), maintained strong linkages to organized popular constituencies (Anria 2019), others in countries like Chile and Ecuador were notable for their technocratic detachment from societal actors. These differences reflected the disparate formative experiences and development trajectories of leftist alternatives that emerged in Latin America in the aftermath of market liberalization in the 1980s and 1990s. This chapter explores how these path-dependent trajectories reshaped party systems in the region during the Left turn, and it analyzes their implications for democratic citizenship and the restructuring of programmatic competition following neoliberal reform.

MARKET REFORM, POLITICAL REINCORPORATION, AND THE PARTISAN CONFIGURATION OF LEFT TURNS

In many respects the Left turn in Latin America was a sequel to the "dual transitions" to political democracy and market liberalism in the 1980s and early 1990s (see Levitsky and Roberts 2011). Following a wave of military dictatorships in the 1960s and 1970s, democratic transitions led to the institutionalization of partisan and electoral competition and the restoration of basic civil rights and liberties. As such, they provided popular constituencies with newfound opportunities for political expression and representation. Regime transitions occurred, however, in a regionwide context of debt-fueled economic crisis and market-based structural adjustment that placed popular constituencies on the political defensive, largely postponing democratic responsiveness to their material demands (Haggard and Kaufman 1995). As hyperinflationary pressures and acute foreign exchange bottlenecks forced the region to converge on variants of the neoliberal model by the late 1980s and early 1990s (Edwards 1995), even traditional labor-based populist parties eschewed statist and redistributive policies in favor of orthodox austerity and adjustment measures (Stokes 2001).

The restoration of citizenship rights and democratic competition in the 1980s, therefore, entailed a very partial process of political reincorporation of popular constituencies (see Montambeault, Balán, and Oxhorn, this volume). Indeed, democratization was accompanied by widespread economic hardships and deepening socioeconomic inequalities, as well as steep declines in trade unionization and a temporary disarticulation and demobilization of popular constituencies (see Kurtz 2004; Roberts 2014). As such, Latin America's dual transitions largely decoupled the extension of democratic political rights from broader forms of social citizenship and popular sector representation.

In its most fundamental sense, then, the Left turn that got under way in the late 1990s—following the process of structural adjustment and the stabilization of inflationary pressures across the region—was aimed at a recoupling of social and political citizenship rights and a more thorough reincorporation of popular sectors in the democratic arena (Rossi 2017; Silva and Rossi 2017). It both reflected and encouraged a rearticulation of popular constituencies—albeit with organized labor in a diminished role—and a restructuring of democratic competition around program-matic alternatives to market orthodoxy.

This rearticulation of popular constituencies and restructuring of pro-grammatic competition helped to revive leftist alternatives across much of the region in the post-adjustment era. The partisan configuration of this revival, however, was heavily conditioned by political alignments during the earlier process of market liberalization, which I have elsewhere char-acterized as a "critical juncture" in Latin America's political development (Roberts 2014). Left turns unfolded as part of the "reactive sequences" (Mahoney 2001) to this critical juncture. In some cases—where conserva-tive actors led the process of market reform and a major party of the left was present to offer principled opposition—the critical juncture aligned and stabilized party systems along a left-right axis of programmatic competition. In others, however, bait-and-switch market reforms were imposed by center-left or labor-based populist parties, violating their tra-ditional platforms and dealigning partisan competition programmatically.

These different reform alignments did not strictly determine which type of left party would come to power in the aftermath period. Nevertheless, they weighed heavily on the reactive sequences of the post-adjustment era, when societal resistance to market orthodoxy intensified—as Polanyi (1944) would have expected—and the po-litical rearticulation of popular constituencies gathered force. Aligned and dealigned party systems varied dramatically in their capacity to institutionally channel and contain societal resistance to market insecurities. Programmatically aligned party systems contained a major leftist opposition party that provided an electoral outlet for this societal resistance, tempering social protest and ultimately helping to moderate the reactive sequences of the post-adjustment era. The Partido dos Trabalhadores (Workers' Party, PT) in Brazil, the Frente Amplio in Uruguay, the Partido Socialista de Chile (Socialist Party, PSCh) in Chile, the Frente Farabundo Martí de Liberación Nacional (Farabundo Martí National Liberation Front, FMLN) in El Salvador, and the Frente Sandinista de Liberación Nacional (Sandinista Front for National Liberation, FSLN) in Nicaragua all strengthened in the post-adjustment era and won national elections after 2000.[1]

With the partial exception of Nicaragua, Left turns in these countries took place with high levels of institutional continuity. Established political parties alternated in office, with incumbent centrist or conservative parties handing over power to leftist rivals. Party systems did not break down, as centrist or conservative parties remained major electoral contenders when they relinquished executive power and moved into opposition. These parties and their supporters maintained a strong presence in legislative and judicial branches of government, exercising significant institutional checks and balances on ruling leftist parties. Leftist parties, meanwhile, kept basic regime institutions intact and largely exercised power within the constraints of constitutional norms and procedures. Only in Nicaragua—where the conservative bloc split to allow the Sandinistas back into power, then weakened as Daniel Ortega consolidated personalistic authority—did leftist governments alter the rules of the democratic game in ways that tilted the playing field to their advantage. The reconstruction of Sandinista hegemonic-party rule thus contrasted with the consolidation of institutionalized pluralism in the other countries that turned left in the aftermath of aligning critical junctures.

The aftermath period was quite different where bait-and-switch market reforms adopted by traditional center-left or populist parties had dealigned party systems. In Venezuela, Bolivia, Ecuador, Argentina, and Costa Rica, all the major parties had supported the process of market liberalization, and no major opposition party of the left was available to channel societal dissent into formal institutional arenas. As Tarrow (2011, 7) suggests, the representational deficiencies associated with such forms of "neoliberal convergence" (Roberts 2014, 58) were conducive to contentious modes of collective action and demand articulation, including social protest by actors who lacked "regular access to representative institutions" and articulated "new or unaccepted claims." Societal dissent, therefore, was often channeled into extrainstitutional or even anti-institutional outlets, producing highly disruptive reactive sequences in the post-adjustment era. Anti-neoliberal social protest was widespread in all five of these cases (Almeida 2014, 31–64; Silva 2009; Spalding 2014; Yashar 2005), and major protest cycles led directly or indirectly to the impeachment or removal of elected presidents in Venezuela, Bolivia, Ecuador, and Argentina.

More important for our purposes, social protest served as a prelude to patterns of electoral protest that indelibly marked the Left turn in these countries. In all five countries, voters turned against all or part of the traditional party system and supported a diverse array of new alternatives on the left flank of the old order. The most important conservative party (or, in the Argentine case, the antipopulist Radical Party) weakened or collapsed in all five countries, as did the established populist or center-left parties that implemented neoliberal reforms in Venezuela, Ecuador, and Bolivia. In these latter three countries traditional party systems essentially collapsed as the Left turn got under way, sweeping aside Venezuela's highly institutionalized two-party system (Coppedge 1994), Bolivia's more recent three-party system (Slater and Simmons 2012), and Ecuador's more fluid and fragmented multiparty system. Consequently, new party systems were progressively reconstituted in these three countries during the Left turn, albeit in an asymmetrical manner and in highly polarized political environments. New governing leftist parties were built by the populist outsiders Hugo Chávez in Venezuela and Rafael Correa in Ecuador, while Evo Morales's new "movement party" (the MAS) rode the wave of social protest into state power in Bolivia (see Rice, this volume). Centrist and conservative actors bitterly opposed these new-leftist leaders, creating deep populist/antipopulist sociopolitical cleavages. Nevertheless, the conservative, antipopulist side of the cleavage struggled to rebuild solid party organizations, and it remained highly dependent on personalistic figures and fluid electoral fronts in all three countries.

The breakdown and reconstruction of national party systems during the Left turn was less thorough in Costa Rica and Argentina, but major transformations occurred nonetheless. In Costa Rica, the traditional center-left Partido de Liberación Nacional (National Liberation Party, PLN) survived after leading the process of market liberalization largely by displacing its main conservative rival on the right side of the programmatic spectrum. Leftist dissidents from the PLN helped form a new party, however, the Partido Acción Ciudadana (Citizens' Action Party, PAC), which won national elections in 2014 when Costa Rica joined (belatedly) the regional Left turn. Alone in the region, Argentina's historic labor-based populist party, the Peronist Partido Justicialista (Justicialist Party, PJ), not only led the process of market reform in the early 1990s but also spawned a new leftist current that channeled much of the social backlash against the neoliberal model following the financial crisis of 2001–2. This leftist current, known as the Frente para la Victoria (Front for Victory, FPV), was associated with Presidents Néstor Kirchner and Cristina Fernández de Kirchner. The FPV operated both inside and outside traditional Peronism, often assuming partylike attributes of its own (see Ostiguy and Schneider 2017).

Left turns in the aftermath of dealigning market reforms, therefore, were far more likely to entail new party formation on the left flank of traditional party systems. This can be seen in table 3.1 below, which locates the Left turn cases within four different categories determined by the leadership of the market reform process (by conservative actors or left/populist parties) and the leadership of the Left turn (by established or new party organizations, with new parties defined as those that were formed following neoliberal reform in each country). In the top left category are five countries with aligning critical junctures where conservative actors imposed market reforms and the Left turn was led by an institutionalized party of the left: Brazil, Chile, Uruguay, El Salvador, and Nicaragua. Only one country, Paraguay, occupies the bottom left category. Although the conservative Colorado Party led the process of market reform in Paraguay, there was no major party of the left in opposition. As such, when the country turned left in 2008, it did so under an independent leftist figure, Fernando Lugo, at the head of a fledgling party organization and a short-lived electoral alliance. Argentina is alone in the top right category as a singular case of a turn to the left under an established party following a dealigning, populist-led process of market reform. As mentioned above, however, the Argentine case has hybrid features that borrow from

TABLE 3.1. The Partisan Configuration of Market Reforms and the Left Turn

Party Leading the Left Turn	Conservative-Led Market Reform	Populist or Left-Led Market Reform
Established party organization	Brazil Chile Uruguay El Salvador Nicaragua	Argentina
New political party	Paraguay	Bolivia Costa Rica Ecuador Venezuela

Source: Roberts 2014, 113–14.

Note: See Roberts 2014 for an analysis of partisan alignments during the critical juncture of market reform.

the lower right category as well, since Kirchnerism brought together new political currents as well as elements from traditional Peronism. The other cases of dealigning, bait-and-switch reform—Venezuela, Bolivia, Ecuador, and Costa Rica—are all located in the lower right category, where the Left turn occurred under the leadership of new party organizations (or the populist figures who founded them, in several cases).[2]

Although political heterogeneity clearly exists in the top left and bottom right categories, where most of the cases are concentrated, some modal patterns are identifiable in each category. As mentioned above, the cases in the top left category are notable for their institutional continuity in both party-systemic and regime-level attributes, partially excepting Nicaragua. In Nicaragua, the Sandinistas chipped away at institutional checks and balances as the conservative bloc splintered and weakened, and the Ortega regime adopted increasingly authoritarian measures in response to social unrest. In the other four cases—Brazil, Chile, Uruguay, and El Salvador—established centrist and/or conservative parties remained viable competitors, and leftist parties that had progressively strengthened under new democratic regimes accepted the existing rules of the game and alternated in office within them. Left turns in these latter four countries did not transform party systems or alter regime institutions.

Cases in the bottom right category, by contrast, were notable for their institutional discontinuity during the Left turn. This was evident in the decline of traditional parties across the political spectrum, as well as the prevalence of new party formation on the left flank of party systems. With the exception of Costa Rica, discontinuity was also common in regime-level institutions. Where mass protest movements had forced presidents from office, weakened traditional parties, and challenged the legitimacy of existing democratic institutions, the new leftist leaders who captured the presidency in Venezuela, Ecuador, and Bolivia had all campaigned on pledges to convoke constituent assemblies and draft new constitutions. Following their election they moved quickly to implement these mandates and "refound" regime institutions, essentially making regime change a plebiscitary expression of popular sovereignty. They used popular referendums to convoke constituent assemblies and approve new constitutions, relying on mass appeal and the delegitimation of the political establishment to circumvent legislative and judicial constraints on institutional reform.

The rise of new-leftist parties in these countries and their plebiscitary transformation of regime institutions had mixed effects on democratic citizenship and practices. On the one hand, they created new channels and opportunities for popular participation in the democratic process (Anria 2016; Hawkins 2010; Madrid 2012, 165–70; Silva 2017). This was especially the case in Bolivia, where a social movement—the coca growers' peasant federation—had founded the MAS and other social actors retained a capacity for autonomous collective action (see Anria 2019). On the other hand, particularly in Venezuela, regime changes enhanced executive authority and allowed ruling leftist parties to weaken institutional checks and balances by asserting hegemonic control over legislative, judicial, and electoral bodies (De la Torre 2013; Levitsky and Loxton 2013). As such, the plebiscitary transformation of regime institutions sharply polarized the political arena, creating deep sociopolitical cleavages between dominant left-populist blocs and their politically fragmented and organizationally weakened conservative opponents.

Not surprisingly, ruling leftist parties in these three cases, along with the Kirchner and Fernández governments in Argentina, were also the most inclined to break with neoliberal orthodoxy by adopting statist and nationalist economic policies, including ambitious redistributive social reforms. As Flores-Macías (2012) suggests, ruling leftist parties operating within institutionalized party systems and facing strong conservative opponents were inclined toward policy moderation and pragmatism, and thus higher levels of continuity with the neoliberal models they inherited. Policy moderation, in short, was a correlate of institutional continuity. The range of heterodox policy options expanded, however, where conservative parties had collapsed, new movement or populist parties had risen to power, and institutional checks and balances had been eroded by plebiscitary regime transformations. Such conditions were found in Venezuela, Bolivia, and Ecuador, and to a partial extent in Argentina, loosening institutional constraints on heterodox policy experimentation. Indeed, these four cases had also experienced the most convulsive and politically consequential episodes of anti-neoliberal social protest in the region—the Venezuelan Caracazo (urban riots) in 1989, the series of indigenous and popular revolts that led to the downfall of Ecuadorean presidents in 1997, 2000, and 2005, the Bolivian water and gas "wars" in 2000 and 2003, and the Argentine *piquetero* (street picketer) movement and urban riots that brought down the de la Rúa government in 2001. As such, major policy reforms were in large part an endogenous, path-dependent output of the disruptive reactive sequences that unfolded in the aftermath of many dealigning critical junctures—reactive sequences in which mass social protest set the stage for widespread electoral protest, the partial or complete breakdown of traditional party systems, the refounding of regime institutions (other than in Argentina), and statist and redistributive policy reforms.

Particularly in the three so-called Bolivarian cases—Venezuela, Bolivia, and Ecuador—these reactive sequences created radically different formative experiences for the populist and movement left parties that took power in the post-adjustment era, in comparison to historical experiences that had shaped the institutionalized parties of the left in Chile, Brazil, Uruguay, and even El Salvador (see Madrid 2012). Although new populist and movement left parties in the Bolivarian cases did not necessarily have organizational roots in anti-neoliberal protest movements, they were politically shaped by the aforementioned popular revolts against democratic regimes that were tainted by severe representational deficiencies and highly technocratic forms of policy convergence. These parties' approaches to institutional and policy reform reflected this delegitimation of the old order, and of the political establishments that controlled it. By contrast, the institutionalized leftist parties in Chile, Brazil, Uruguay, and El Salvador had been seared by the political defeat and violent repression of radical left projects in the Cold War, and they were key players in democratic transitions that promised to restore basic civil and political rights following extended periods of authoritarian exclusion. These parties viewed the new democratic regimes of the 1980s and 1990s as popular conquests, whatever their institutional and policy limitations, and they moderated their earlier revolutionary and socialist aspirations in order to safeguard democratic advances, avoid political polarization, and prevent economic instability (Roberts 1998). As Panebianco (1988) suggests, such formative experiences can have durable political and organizational effects on parties.

PARTIES AND SOCIAL ACTORS

Although the two different pathways to power differentiated the multiple lefts that participated in Latin America's Left turn, they did not predetermine the nature of parties' ties to popular constituencies, the participatory opportunities they would open up, or the kinds of citizenship regimes they promoted. On these dimensions, considerable variation existed within (and not simply across) the different types of Left turns. Mass social protest may have weakened the old order and paved the way for electoral shifts to the left in Argentina, Bolivia, Ecuador, and Venezuela, but the leftist parties (or presidents, in the Argentine case)[3] that arose to power in these countries after 1998 had widely varying relationships to social movements and other organized popular constituencies. On one end of the spectrum, the Bolivian MAS was a paradigmatic case of a "movement-based party" (Anria 2019; Kitschelt 2006), or what I have elsewhere labeled an "organic" party of the left (Roberts 1998, 75–78)—that is, a party that is founded and directed by social movement actors as an electoral extension of the movement itself. In the Bolivian case, the core movement was the largely Indigenous coca growers' (*cocaleros*) union in the Chapare region of Cochabamba. Led by Evo Morales, the cocaleros became the dominant force in a broader peasant confederation, founded a series of quasi-partisan political "instruments" that culminated in the MAS, and participated in the groundswell of mass protests that rocked the political establishment between 2000 and 2005. These cycles of mass protest eventually toppled two presidents and transformed the MAS into an integrative partisan vehicle with organic linkages to a plethora of labor, peasant, Indigenous, and community-based movements (Madrid 2012, 49–68; Van Cott 2005). In office, tensions inevitably emerged between the MAS's charismatic authority, its partisan bureaucracy, and its movement bases, but the latter retained a capacity for independent political expression and exercised influence through a wide range of new participatory and consultative channels (Anria 2019).

At the other end of the spectrum, Ecuador also experienced a series of Indigenous uprisings and mass social protests that forced three presidents from office between 1997 and 2005, but the left-populist government of Rafael Correa had very limited—and often highly antagonistic—relations with the country's social movements. Ecuador's powerful national Indigenous confederation founded a movement party in the 1990s, Pachakutik (Van Cott 2005), but this party could not match the ability of the Bolivian MAS to incorporate diverse social actors and broaden its electoral appeal (Madrid 2012). Instead, Pachakutik provided tenuous electoral support for independent populist figures in presidential campaigns, including Lucio Gutiérrez in 2002 and the left-leaning economist Correa in 2006 (in the second round). Pachakutik quickly broke with these leaders, however, after being marginalized from effective participation in their administrations. Correa, then, did not govern with Ecuador's movement party; instead, he built a new party from scratch (Movimiento Alianza Patria Altiva i Soberana [Proud and Sovereign Fatherland Alliance], PAIS), drawing initially from his academic networks and activist circles, then using state resources and social programs to broaden the party's base. Blending populism, technocracy, and a state-led model of economic development based on resource extraction and ample commodity rents, the Correa administration won broad popular support but often clashed with labor, Indigenous, and other independently organized societal actors. As stated by Conaghan:

> Unlike Evo Morales, who built a political career on the basis of grassroots struggle, Correa regarded Ecuador's turbulent and intrusive civil society as an obstacle, not a building block, for his

revolution. He took a dim view of all organized interests, regardless of class, identity, or ideological leanings. Business organizations, labor unions, the Indigenous and environmental movements, all were dismissed as privileged interlocutors representing special interests, while his government was deemed the only legitimate guardian of the "national" interest. (2011, 274)

The Argentine and Venezuelan cases lie in between these two ends of the spectrum. In Argentina, the piquetero and other protest movements of the late 1990s and early 2000s did not form a new party of their own like the Bolivian MAS, but many of their activist networks and leaders were incorporated within the Kirchnerista current of Peronism, as were important sectors of the labor movement. Indeed, piquetero networks played an important role in the implementation of employment, public works, and social programs under the left Peronist governments (Etchemendy and Garay 2011, 286–87; Ostiguy and Schneider 2017; Wolff 2007). In Venezuela, Chávez's initial party, the Movimiento V República (Fifth Republic Movement, MVR), grew out of a dissident left nationalist current within the armed forces that failed to take power in a 1992 coup attempt. After serving time in prison for leading the failed coup, Chávez cultivated ties to activist networks and organized new civilian cadres, then founded the MVR to support his 1998 presidential campaign. In office, Chávez's "social missions" and various referendums and electoral campaigns created a wide range of opportunities for community-based forms of popular organization and participation, including "Bolivarian circles," communal councils, program committees, and electoral brigades (Hawkins 2010). These varied forms of grassroots Chavismo were partially, though not fully, integrated into the new party organ, the Partido Socialista Unido de Venezuela (United Socialist Party of Venezuela, PSUV), that Chávez founded in 2007 through a merger of the MVR with a number of small allied leftist parties.

Within the Left turn, the Paraguayan case stands out for the weakness of both party and social movement bases to support a leftist president. As a Catholic bishop influenced by liberation theology, Fernando Lugo had developed ties to peasant organizations and supported their land claims, but levels of social mobilization and protest in Paraguay lagged far behind those in the aforementioned cases.

Furthermore, Lugo was not involved in party politics until he cobbled together a loose coalition of parties and social actors—united primarily by their opposition to the long-ruling Partido Colorado (Colorado Party, ANR-PC)—to support his outsider bid for the presidency in 2008. The core of this alliance was the main centrist opposition party, the Partido Liberal Radical Auténtico (Authentic Radical Liberal Party, PLRA), whose abandonment of Lugo led to his abrupt impeachment by congress in 2012.

Variation in party-society linkages was less dramatic but still significant among the more institutionalized leftist parties that came to power in the post-adjustment era. The PT in Brazil was founded, like the MAS in Bolivia, as a classic movement party with roots in a wave of labor strikes and social protests that challenged the country's military dictatorship in the late 1970s (Keck 1992). Although the PT retained ties to labor unions, the Movimento dos Trabalhadores Rurais Sem Terra (Landless Workers' Movement, MST), and other civil society actors, over time the party apparatus asserted its autonomy from movement bases and became increasingly professional-electoral in orientation (see Hunter 2010; Panebianco 1988). The Chilean PSCh developed an even more pronounced professional-electoral orientation after distancing itself from the quasi-insurrectionary protest movement against the Pinochet dictatorship in the mid-1980s. Indeed, the PSCh's linkages to social actors withered during and after Chile's democratic transition, as the party leadership sought to stabilize the new regime and dampen political conflict by limiting social mobilization, adopting a highly technocratic approach to social policy reform, and maintaining the macroeconomic core of Pinochet's neoliberal model (Oxhorn 1995; Roberts 1998).

In comparison, professional-electoral tendencies in Uruguay's Frente Amplio were tempered by strong ties to organized labor and the student movement, as well as mechanisms for intraparty democratic representation and participation (Anria 2019; Pribble 2013). The FA also incorporated the remnants of the Tupamaros guerrilla movement into its ranks, creating some parallels to the leftist ruling parties in El Salvador and Nicaragua, which have their origins in mass-based revolutionary movements. In the latter two cases, revolutionary struggles created institutional legacies of strong territorial organizations, recognizable party brands, and relatively cohesive internal structures that were conducive to successful party building over time (Holland 2016; Levitsky, Loxton, and Van Dyck 2016).

ELECTIONS AND REELECTIONS: THE BREADTH
AND DEPTH OF THE LEFT TURN

With the Left turn in retreat after 2015, it is an opportune time to assess how the leftward shift transformed party politics in contemporary Latin America. In its breadth, depth, and duration, the post-1998 Left turn was without historical precedent in the region. Historically, electoral victories by well-defined leftist parties have been few and far between in most Latin American countries, and the rare leftist governments that they formed were typically short-lived. Military coups and/or U.S. intervention brought an abrupt halt to leftist experiments under Rómulo Betancourt in Venezuela (1945–48),[4] Jacobo Árbenz in Guatemala (1951–54), João Goulart in Brazil (1961–64), Juan Bosch in the Dominican Republic (1963), and Salvador Allende in Chile (1970–73), while hyperinflation ravaged the administration of Hernán Siles in Bolivia (1982–85). Not surprisingly, given the political pressures exerted by the armed forces, the United States, and business interests, as well as the structural constraints of domestic and international markets, many parties with populist or leftist origins gravitated toward centrist or even conservative positions in order to access or hold onto public office; examples included the Partido Revolucionario Institucional (Institutional Revolutionary Party, PRI) in Mexico, the Acción Democrática (Democratic Action, AD) in Venezuela, the Partido de Liberación Nacional (National Liberation Party, PLN) in Costa Rica, the Alianza Popular Revolucionaria Americana (American Popular Revolutionary Alliance, APRA) in Peru, and the Movimiento Nacionalista Revolucionario (Revolutionary Nationalist Movement, MNR) in Bolivia.

In short, Latin America has never before experienced leftist electoral victories in such quick succession in eleven different countries as occurred between 1998 and 2014 (table 3.2).[5] Furthermore, even where leftist presidents were not elected, leftist alternatives emerged, strengthened, or seriously contested national office in most of the remaining countries in the region after 2000, including Mexico, Colombia, Peru,

TABLE 3.2. Leftist Presidential Elections and Reelections in Latin America, 1998–2017

Initial Presidential Election	Presidential Reelections
Venezuela: Hugo Chávez 1998	Hugo Chávez 2000, 2006, 2012
	Nicolás Maduro 2013
Chile: Ricardo Lagos 2000	Michelle Bachelet 2006, 2013
	(nonsuccessive)
Brazil: Luiz Inácio Lula da Silva 2002	Luiz Inácio Lula da Silva 2006
	Dilma Rousseff 2010, 2014
Argentina: Néstor Kirchner 2003	Cristina Fernández de Kirchner 2007, 2011
Uruguay: Tabaré Vázquez 2004	José Mujica 2009
	Tabaré Vázquez 2014
Bolivia: Evo Morales 2005	Evo Morales 2009, 2014
Ecuador: Rafael Correa 2006	Rafael Correa 2009, 2013
	Lenín Moreno 2017
Nicaragua: Daniel Ortega 2006	Daniel Ortega 2011, 2016
Paraguay: Fernando Lugo 2008	—
El Salvador: Mauricio Funes 2009	Salvador Sánchez Cerén 2014
Costa Rica: Luis Guillermo Solís 2014	—

Source: Compiled by the author.

and Honduras. As such, the Washington Consensus of the 1990s progressively gave way to an enhanced left-right programmatic structuring of partisan and electoral competition in most of the region in the post-adjustment era. Recent empirical research demonstrates that this transformation has been associated with higher levels of class-based voting (Mainwaring, Torcal, and Somma 2015) and greater positional or issue-based voting behavior (Baker and Greene 2015).

Even more striking, perhaps, in light of the aforementioned historical record, was the remarkable reelection rate of leftist presidents and parties in the region from 1998 to 2015. Leftist presidents or parties were reelected, often multiple times, in Venezuela, Chile, Brazil, Argentina, Uruguay, Bolivia, Ecuador, Nicaragua, and El Salvador, producing a total of thirty-two presidential victories by leftist candidates between 1998 and 2017 (see table 3.2). Through mid-2017, incumbent leftist administrations only failed to achieve reelection in Chile in 2010, where the constitution prohibited Michelle Bachelet from running for reelection despite public approval ratings of over 80 percent (voters subsequently returned her to office in 2013); in Paraguay, where Fernando Lugo was abruptly removed from office by means of a presidential impeachment; and in Argentina, where the Peronist administration was defeated in the 2015 presidential elections after three consecutive victories.

Although the commodity export boom that lasted from 2003 to 2013 undoubtedly contributed to this successful rate of reelection—in the process, extending the Left turn—it does not fully account for it. Between 2000 and mid-2017, incumbent leftist parties were reelected 20 out of 23 times in the eleven countries included in table 3.2, an 87 percent reelection rate. Centrist and conservative parties throughout the region, on the other hand, achieved reelection only 11 out of 40 times during this period of relative prosperity, a 27.5 percent success rate. This difference in reelection rates suggests that, in comparison to their conservative rivals, governing leftist parties found ways to respond to popular demands at a time when fiscal and balance of payments constraints had been relaxed, creating new opportunities for experimentation with heterodox and redistributive policies.

Indeed, leftist parties in office after 2003 had greater latitude to "govern from the left" than their predecessors (Murillo, Oliveros, and Vaishnav 2011; Remmer 2012). This was in sharp contrast to the crisis-induced period of neoliberal convergence in the 1980s and 1990s, when populist and left-leaning parties routinely ignored their electoral mandates by imposing austerity and adjustment measures demanded by international creditors (Stokes 2001). Rising commodity prices and the resumption of steady economic growth in the early 2000s, however, led to an easing of debt service burdens as well as employment gains and higher wages. They also provided new revenues for targeted social assistance and a range of other social programs, allowing leftist governments to at least make a dent in pent-up social demands without provoking politically polarizing distributive conflicts.

Accordingly, poverty rates in Latin America fell sharply after 2000, and the region's notoriously high Gini index of inequality began to trend downward (see Cornia 2014; López-Calva and Lustig 2010). As seen in table 3.3, reductions in inequality were not limited to countries governed

TABLE 3.3. Changes in the Gini Index of Inequality in Latin America, 2000–2013

Countries That Experienced a Leftist Government	Initial Gini Index	Most Recent Gini Index	Change in Gini Index
Argentina (2000–2012)	54.4	47.5	−6.9
Bolivia (2000–2011)	64.3	47.2	−17.1
Brazil (2001–13)	63.9	55.3	−8.6
Chile (2000–2013)	56.4	50.9	−5.5
Ecuador (2000–2013)	55.9	47.7	−8.2
El Salvador (2000–2013)	53.1	45.3	−7.8
Nicaragua (2001–9)	57.9	47.8	−10.1
Paraguay (2001–13)	55.8	52.2	−3.6
Uruguay (2000–2013)	44.7	38.3	−6.4
Venezuela (2000–2013)	46.8	40.7	−6.1
Average	55.3	47.3	−8.0
Countries without a Leftist Government			
Colombia (2002–13)	56.7	53.6	−3.1
Costa Rica (2000–2013)	47.4	51.2	+3.8
Guatemala (2002–6)	54.2	58.5	+4.3
Honduras (2001–10)	57.7	57.3	−0.4
Mexico (2000–2012)	54.2	49.2	−5.0
Panama (2001–13)	55.5	52.7	−2.8
Peru (2001–13)	52.5	44.4	−8.1
Dominican Republic (2002–13)	53.7	54.4	+0.7
Average	54.0	52.7	−1.3

Source: ECLAC 2015, 68.

by the Left turn governments; significant improvements were made as well in a number of countries that remained under more conservative leadership, such as Peru and Mexico. The largest and most consistent declines in inequality, however, were registered in countries where leftist parties held national executive office at some point during the time period. The Gini index fell by an average of 8 points in countries that experienced a leftist government between 2000 and 2013, with Bolivia recording a stunning 17.1-point decline. Countries without a leftist government, by contrast, had an average decline in the Gini index of 1.3 points.

SHIFTING POLITICAL WINDS: NEW CHALLENGES TO LEFTIST PARTIES

In spite of these gains, Left turn governments encountered a series of new political and economic challenges in the region after 2013, many of which put leftist parties on the political defensive. First, as Latin America's historical record amply demonstrates, commodity booms eventually go bust, and such was the case after 2013. Plunging commodity prices in global export markets slowed growth across the region and—alongside economic mismanagement—contributed to serious recessions in three major countries with leftist governments by 2014–15: Argentina, Brazil, and Venezuela. In many countries, tighter fiscal and balance of payments constraints made it difficult to sustain forward momentum in social programs, and they heightened the risks of political polarization associated with redistributive policies. If anything, the commodity boom reinforced the region's historical dependence on resource extraction and commodity rents, demonstrating that leftist governments still struggled to identify more diversified and self-sustaining models of development.

Second, a number of ruling leftist parties were plagued by corruption scandals that not only inflamed conservative opposition but also eroded popular support for parties that had pledged to offer a qualitatively different mode of transparent and accountable governance. The Brazilian PT was hit especially hard, with the impeachment of President Dilma Rousseff in 2016 in response to a massive corruption scandal that involved kickbacks on government contracts and illegal campaign finance methods. Ruling parties in other countries like Argentina, Chile, and Ecuador were hardly immune from such challenges, however. Indeed, where leftist parties had governed for multiple terms across a decade or more, essentially being transformed into a new political establishment, a process of political attrition arguably began to whittle away at their support. No longer the "outsiders," leftist parties risked becoming the focal point for a plethora of societal grievances against which other political forces could mobilize.

Third, in this new political and economic context, conservative forces began to regroup, reorganize, and regain the initiative following extended periods of electoral weakness and organizational fragmentation. Traditional conservative parties moved to impeach Rousseff in Brazil and Lugo in Paraguay when these presidents became politically vulnerable and did not have a legislative majority to provide institutional protection. In Argentina, several small conservative groups formed an alliance in 2005 and then a new party organization, Propuesta Republicana (Republican Proposal, PRO), in 2010. The PRO provided an anchor for the anti-Peronist side of the political spectrum, which had lacked a major party following the demise of the historic Radical Party in the 2001–2 financial crisis. Conservative forces then rallied behind PRO candidate Mauricio Macri to defeat the Peronists in the 2015 elections. In Venezuela, both new and traditional political parties, mostly on the center and right, formed a new opposition coalition in 2008 known as the Mesa de la Unidad Democrática (Democratic Unity Roundtable, MUD) to challenge the increasingly autocratic rule of Hugo Chávez. The MUD earned 47.2 percent of the vote in the 2010 parliamentary elections, a mere percentage point behind Chávez's PSUV, and 44.3 percent of the vote in the presidential race against Chávez in 2012. Following the death of the populist leader the following year, the MUD narrowly lost to Chávez's designated successor, Nicolás Maduro, in the presidential election but then captured a two-thirds majority of seats in the national assembly as Venezuela descended into economic chaos and acute political polarization.

Fourth, cycles of social protest challenged leftist governments in several countries, most prominently Venezuela and Brazil but also in Chile. These protest movements, however, varied considerably in their political profiles. In Venezuela, centrist and conservative anti-Chavista sectors have mobilized street protests off and on since the early 2000s, intensifying in recent years as the country's political and economic crisis deepened. These protest cycles clearly nourished the growth of the MUD and precipitated a deepening crisis of the post-Chávez regime in 2016–17. In Brazil, mass protests began in 2013 around diverse claims for public goods like transportation and health care services but thereafter took a conservative turn and became more explicitly anti-PT. As Brazil's corruption scandal and economic crisis deepened in 2015–16, the protest movement increasingly called for the impeachment of Rousseff.

In Chile, on the other hand, social protest outflanked the party system on the left and frontally challenged the social pillars of the neoliberal economic model that a series of center-left governments left intact. In particular, protest focused on the highly privatized and class-stratified education system, as well labor, environmental, and Indigenous rights. A massive student rebellion that began under Socialist president Michelle Bachelet in 2006 and intensified under her conservative successor, Sebastián Piñera, induced Bachelet to incorporate the Partido Comunista de Chile (Chilean Communist Party, PCCh) into her center-left coalition when she returned to the campaign trail in 2013. Following her return to office, Bachelet imposed a tax hike to pay for social programs, reformed highly disproportional electoral institutions inherited from the Pinochet dictatorship, and initiated deeper reforms of the education system. Bachelet's reforms fell short of the students' demands, however, and movement activists eventually formed a new party vehicle on the left flank of the traditional party system. Ultimately, the Socialist Party that led Chile's Left turn lost much of its capacity to channel societal resistance to market orthodoxy, especially among a younger generation that was born after the country's regime transition and raised in a market society.

The Chilean case demonstrates that the pressures faced by governing leftist parties in Latin America do not emanate exclusively from the right. Indeed, the travails of Chile and Brazil together warn against facile assumptions that relatively moderate, institutionalized Left turns are necessarily more successful or enduring than the more radical Left turns that involved higher levels of institutional discontinuity in the Andean region—just as the Venezuelan debacle should warn against any romanticization of Bolivarian alternatives. The modal patterns identified in the top left and bottom right categories of table 3.1 (above) are, in fact, prone to quite different—perhaps even mirror opposite—types of degenerative effects over time. For the moderate, institutionalized left-ist parties in the top left quadrant, the challenge is to avoid becoming so thoroughly molded by the established order that they end up being indistinguishable from other mainstream actors. The Brazilian PT's gradual slide toward traditional forms of power-brokering and the Chilean Socialists' acquiescence to the neoliberal template not only diluted their historic "brands" (Lupu 2016), but ultimately divorced both parties from burgeoning societal demands—for governmental transparency and the rule of law in Brazil and for rights of social citizenship in Chile—that the parties themselves had once championed. In the other, lower right category where the Bolivarian cases are located, Venezuela illustrates the potentially tragic denouement of a hegemonic project that claims an exclusive right to define the contours of a new political and economic order.

Nevertheless, both quadrants also provide examples of ruling leftist parties that have, to date, tempered these degenerative effects and continued to govern in competitive environments with relatively broad bases of support. Uruguay's FA, in the top left category, has competed effectively against well-established conservative rivals, while the Bolivian MAS continues to dominate a political arena where conservative forces are slowly reorganizing partisan representation. Notably, these two parties retained the strongest ties to organized popular constituencies of any of the governing leftist parties in their respective modal categories. In so doing, they forged especially inclusive citizenship regimes and contained the most corrosive effects of the autocratic personalism, technocratic professionalism, and organizational rent-seeking that plagued their regional counterparts.

Given the robustness of leftist rule in these latter countries, along with the long-delayed, counter-cyclical rise and electoral victory of a major leftist alternative in Mexico, caution must be exercised in any sort of claim that Latin America is undergoing a new "Right turn" in the second decade of the twenty-first century. In much of the region, conservative forces remain dependent on broad electoral fronts or dominant personalities to compensate for the organizational deficiencies of their partisan vehicles. In countries like Bolivia, Venezuela, and Ecuador the Left turn generated a deep sociopolitical cleavage that should, in theory, have been conducive to party building on both sides of the populist divide (see Levitsky, Loxton, and Van Dyck 2016; Lipset and Rokkan 1967), but the rebuilding process on the right side of the cleavage has proceeded by fits and starts.

The regional experience thus demonstrates that the rebuilding of party systems after they have collapsed is often a slow and arduous process that is anything but automatic. The Peruvian case is paradigmatic, as new parties of the left and right have acquired only the most tenuous of footholds a quarter of a century after the collapse of the old order in the critical juncture of the early 1990s. Elsewhere, the reconstitution of party systems after their collapse has often proceeded in a highly asymmetrical manner, with one side of a cleavage reorganizing well in advance of the other, as seen in Bolivia, Ecuador, and Venezuela during the Left turn. In these countries charismatic leaders used state power and resources along with varied linkages to organized popular constituencies (at least in Bolivia and Venezuela) to construct formidable new governing parties.

Although conservative forces have lagged behind in the party rebuilding process, in much of the region they are able to draw from *poderes fácticos*—de facto power structures—such as the mass media, business elites, and military, professional, or technocratic networks to compensate for their organizational weaknesses. Indeed, they can erect "party surrogates" and contest the electoral arena with little in the way of a permanent partisan apparatus, and in a number of countries they have done so effectively. As such, ruling leftist parties are sure to encounter new electoral challenges in the years ahead, and some of them are likely to find themselves back in the opposition after extended periods of governance—something the Brazilian PT, the Argentine Peronists, and the Chilean Socialists have already experienced.

Such alternation in office, however, is the mainspring of electoral democracy, and it could well advance the institutionalization of the programmatic competition that the Left turn revived. Institutionalization requires the presence of relatively durable and well-defined electoral alternatives on both the left and right sides of the ideological spectrum. Until recently, very few party systems in the region—Chile being the most obvious exception—had sustained such patterns of programmatic structuration over an extended period. Competition between rival but ideologically undifferentiated patronage machines was more common historically in most of the region, while the debt crisis, bait-and-switch market reforms, and the political logic of the Washington Consensus largely dissolved what programmatic contestation existed following democratic transitions in the 1980s. By shattering the technocratic consensus around the neoliberal model, the Left turn made the restructuring of programmatic competition its hallmark, and it will likely prove to be its most enduring legacy (see Roberts 2014).

To understand that legacy, it is crucial to note that it does *not* require the indefinite continuation of leftist parties in power. Even if the Venezuelan PSUV, the Bolivian MAS, the Uruguayan FA, or other governing leftist parties follow the PT and the Peronists into opposition, these parties are highly likely to cleave the electorate and programmatically structure partisan competition for many years to come. That is especially the case where leftist parties maintained or built organic linkages to organized popular constituencies during their time in office. The Latin American experience suggests that such parties can generate remarkably durable sociopolitical cleavages that are reproduced—and perhaps even strengthened—by extended periods in opposition. The Argentine Peronists provide ample evidence of this resiliency and demonstrate that they can even survive the death of a charismatic founder and a series of organizational makeovers (Levitsky 2003).

Latin America, therefore, is unlikely to return to the days when two or more conservative parties could indefinitely dominate the electoral arena and manipulate patron-clientelist linkages to keep redistributive issues off the political agenda. Even in countries that retained nineteenth-century oligarchic party systems into the beginning of the twenty-first century—namely, Colombia, Honduras, and Paraguay—new-leftist alternatives are in gestation that appear likely to restructure partisan and programmatic competition in the years ahead. In short, social mobilization and democratic competition in the post-adjustment era have politicized Latin America's egregious social and economic inequalities, like much of the literature on democratization would predict (Acemoglu and Robinson 2006; Boix 2003). Leftist parties are both expressions and sources of that politicization, and they will structure partisan competition along programmatic lines so long as distributive conflicts shape political preferences.

In highly unequal societies, institutionalized forms of democratic contestation are prone to distributive conflicts that buttress left-leaning alternatives. Such alternatives in Latin America were sidelined or collapsed during the period of economic crisis and neoliberal reform in the 1980s and 1990s, but they reemerged and strengthened in the post-adjustment era, eventually taking power across much of the region. The partisan configuration of Left turns varied dramatically, however, depending in part on the alignment of actors around the process of market reform. Some countries turned left under the leadership of established leftist parties in highly competitive and relatively institutionalized party systems; others turned left when traditional party systems collapsed and radical new populist or movement-based alternatives emerged on their left flank.

These different trajectories shaped and constrained how leftist parties would govern, accounting for much of the variation in patterns of institutional and policy reform during the Left turn. They did not, however, dictate the nature of parties' ties to social actors, which were much stronger and deeper in some countries than others, under both new and established party organizations. Neither did these trajectories determine when and how Left turns would end. That latter story is still to be written in most of the region, and it will undoubtedly take some unforeseen paths before arriving at its destination.

If and when the Left turn ends, leftist parties in opposition are likely to structure electoral competition along programmatic lines in a more consistent manner than the region has seen in the past. Even though party systems remain weakly institutionalized along one pole or the other in a number of countries, social mobilization and electoral competition have repoliticized economic inequalities. In so doing, they shattered the technocratic consensus for market reforms that destructured and dealigned partisan competition during the heyday of the neoliberal model. The programmatic restructuring of partisan and electoral competition may thus be the most important and durable legacy of Latin America's Left turn. It is, in essence, the democratic expression of a Polanyian (1944) "double movement" of popular resistance to the creation of a market society. Such a legacy is surely an ironic sequel to Latin America's late twentieth-century market revolution.

NOTES

1. In Nicaragua, the return of the Sandinistas to power after a sixteen-year hiatus was attributable to the division of the center-right conservative bloc in the 2006 elections rather than a strengthening of the FSLN itself. This split within the anti-Sandinista bloc allowed Daniel Ortega to capture the presidency for the FSLN with a plurality of only 38 percent of the vote. From this modest baseline, Ortega's support swelled to 62.5 percent and 72.4 percent in his reelection bids in 2011 and 2016, respectively.

2. I am not including the ambiguous case of Peru under Ollanta Humala in table 3.2, since Humala made little effort to govern on the left after being elected on a leftist platform. If Peru were included, however, it would also be located in the lower right category of table 3.1 as a case of dealigning, bait-and-switch reform under Alberto Fujimori and an aborted turn to the left under a populist outsider, Humala, with minimal party organization.

3. In other words, the Peronist PJ in Argentina should not be considered a leftist *party*, either historically or in contemporary Argentine politics. As a complex and constantly shifting confluence of heterogeneous social, political, and ideological currents, the PJ has both a left and a right flank, either of which may be in ascendance in specific historical conjunctures. The PJ thus sponsored the conservative, neoliberal administration of Carlos Menem from 1989 to 1999 as well as the left-leaning, statist, and redistributive Kirchnerista administrations from 2003 to 2015.

4. Betancourt, the founder of Acción Democrática, took office following a military coup rather than a free election, in contrast to the other leftist presidents identified here.

5. That is leaving aside additional "questionable" cases such as the election of Hipólito Mejía in the Dominican Republic (2000), Álvaro Colom in Guatemala (2007), and Ollanta Humala in Peru (2011), all of whom had at least some leftist tendencies, or Manuel Zelaya in Honduras (2005), who was elected from a traditional conservative party but veered unexpectedly to the left after taking office (only to be deposed in a military coup in 2009). The election of Andrés Manuel López Obrador made Mexico a latecomer to the Left turn in 2018, albeit in a counter-cyclical fashion, given regional trends at the time.

REFERENCES

Acemoglu, Daron, and James A. Robinson. 2006. *Economic Origins of Dictatorship and Democracy*. New York: Cambridge University Press.

Almeida, Paul. 2014. *Mobilizing Democracy: Globalization and Citizen Protest*. Baltimore, MD: Johns Hopkins University Press.

Anria, Santiago. 2016. "Democratizing Democracy? Civil Society and Party Organization in Bolivia." *Comparative Politics* 48 (4): 459–78.

———. 2019. *When Movements Become Parties: The Bolivian MAS in Comparative Perspective*. New York: Cambridge University Press.

Baker, Andy, and Kenneth F. Greene. 2015. "Positional Issue Voting in Latin America." In Matthew M. Singer, Ryan E. Carlin, and Elizabeth J. Zechmeister, eds., *The Latin American Voter: Pursuing Representation and Accountability in Challenging Contexts*. Ann Arbor: University of Michigan Press.

Boix, Carles. 2003. *Democracy and Redistribution*. New York: Cambridge University Press.

Conaghan, Catherine. 2011. "Ecuador: Rafael Correa and the Citizens' Revolution." In Steven Levitsky and Kenneth M. Roberts, eds., *The Resurgence of the Latin American Left*. Baltimore, MD: Johns Hopkins University Press.

Coppedge, Michael. 1994. *Strong Parties and Lame Ducks: Presidential Partyarchy and Factionalism in Venezuela*. Palo Alto, CA: Stanford University Press.

Cornia, Giovanni Andrea. 2014. *Falling Inequality in Latin America: Policy Changes and Lessons*. Oxford: Oxford University Press.

De la Torre, Carlos. 2013. "Technocratic Populism in Ecuador." *Journal of Democracy* 24 (3): 33–46.

Edwards, Sebastian. 1995. *Crisis and Reform in Latin America: From Despair to Hope*. Oxford: Oxford University Press.

Etchemendy, Sebastián, and Candelaria Garay. 2011. "Argentina: Left Populism in Comparative Perspective, 2003–2009." In Steven Levitsky and Kenneth M. Roberts, eds., *The Resurgence of the Latin American Left*. Baltimore, MD: Johns Hopkins University Press.

Flores-Macias, Gustavo A. 2012. *After Neoliberalism? The Left and Economic Reforms in Latin America*. Oxford: Oxford University Press.

Haggard, Stephan, and Robert R. Kaufman. 1995. *The Political Economy of Democratic Transitions*. Princeton, NJ: Princeton University Press.

Hawkins, Kirk A. 2010. "Who Mobilizes? Participatory Democracy in Chávez's Bolivarian Revolution." *Latin American Politics and Society* 52 (3): 31–66.

Holland, Alisha C. 2016. "Forbearance." *American Political Science Review* 110 (2): 232–46.

Hunter, Wendy. 2010. *The Transformation of the Workers' Party in Brazil, 1989–2009*. New York: Cambridge University Press.

Keck, Margaret. 1992. *The Workers' Party and Democratization in Brazil*. New Haven, CT: Yale University Press.

Kitschelt, Herbert. 2006. "Movement Parties." In Richard S. Katz and William Crotty, eds., *Handbook of Party Politics*. Thousand Oaks, CA: Sage.

Kurtz, Marcus J. 2004. "The Dilemmas of Democracy in the Open Economy: Lessons from Latin America." *World Politics* 56 (2): 262–302.

Levitsky, Steven. 2003. *Transforming Labor-Based Parties in Latin America: Argentine Peronism in Comparative Perspective*. New York: Cambridge University Press.

Levitsky, Steven, and James Loxton. 2013. "Populism and Competitive Authoritarianism in the Andes." *Democratization* 20 (1): 107–36.

Levitsky, Steven, James Loxton, and Brandon Van Dyck. 2016. "Introduction: Challenges of Party-Building in Latin America." In James Loxton, Steven Levitsky, Brandon Van Dyck, and Jorge I. Domínguez, eds., *Challenges of Party-Building in Latin America*. New York: Cambridge University Press.

Levitsky, Steven, and Kenneth M. Roberts. 2011. "Conclusion: Democracy, Development, and the Left." In Steven Levitsky and Kenneth M. Roberts, eds., *The Resurgence of the Latin American Left*. Baltimore, MD: Johns Hopkins University Press.

Lipset, Seymour Martin, and Stein Rokkan. 1967. "Cleavage Structures, Party Systems, and Voter Alignments: An Introduction." In Seymour Martin Lipset and Stein Rokkan, eds., *Party Systems and Voter Alignments: Cross-National Perspectives*. New York: Free Press.

López-Calva, Luis Felipe, and Nora Claudia Lustig. 2010. *Declining Inequality in Latin America: A Decade of Progress?* New York and Washington, DC: United Nations Development Programme and Brookings Institution Press.

Lupu, Noam. 2016. *Party Brands in Crisis: Partisanship, Brand Dilution, and the Breakdown of Political Parties in Latin America*. New York: Cambridge University Press.

Madrid, Raúl L. 2012. *The Rise of Ethnic Politics in Latin America*. New York: Cambridge University Press.

Mahoney, James. 2001. *The Legacies of Liberalism: Path Dependence and Political Regimes in Central America*. Baltimore, MD: Johns Hopkins University Press.

Mainwaring, Scott, Mariano Torcal, and Nicolás M Somma. 2015. "The Left and the Mobilization of Class Voting in Latin America." In Matthew M. Singer, Ryan E. Carlin, and Elizabeth J. Zechmeister, eds., *The Latin*

American Voter: Pursuing Representation and Accountability in Challenging Contexts. Ann Arbor: University of Michigan Press.

Murillo, María Victoria, Virginia Oliveros, and Milan Vaishnav. 2011. "Economic Constraints and Presidential Agency." In Steven Levitsky and Kenneth M. Roberts, eds., *The Resurgence of the Latin American Left*. Baltimore, MD: Johns Hopkins University Press.

Ostiguy, Pierre, and Aaron Schneider. 2017. "The Politics of Incorporation: Party Systems, Political Leaders and the State in Argentina and Brazil." In Eduardo Silva and Federico Rossi, eds., *Reshaping the Political Arena in Latin America: From Resisting Neoliberalism to the Second Incorporation*. Pittsburgh, PA: University of Pittsburgh Press.

Oxhorn, Philip. 1995. *Organising Civil Society: The Popular Sectors and the Struggle for Democracy in Chile*. University Park: Pennsylvania State University Press.

Panebianco, Angelo. 1988. *Political Parties: Organization and Power*. New York: Cambridge University Press.

Polanyi, Karl. 1944. *The Great Transformation*. New York: Farrar and Rinehart.

Pribble, Jennifer. 2013. *Welfare and Party Politics in Latin America*. New York: Cambridge University Press.

Remmer, Karen L. 2012. "The Rise of Leftist-Populist Governance in Latin America: The Roots for Electoral Change." *Comparative Political Studies* 45 (8): 947–72.

Roberts, Kenneth M. 1998. *Deepening Democracy? The Modern Left and Social Movements in Chile and Peru*. Palo Alto, CA: Stanford University Press.

———. 2014. "Party Systems in the Neoliberal Era." In Kenneth M. Roberts, ed., *Changing Course in Latin America*. New York: Cambridge University Press.

Rossi, Federico M. 2017. *The Poor's Struggle for Political Incorporation: The Piquetero Movement in Argentina*. New York: Cambridge University Press.

Silva, Eduardo. 2009. *Challenging Neoliberalism in Latin America*. New York: Cambridge University Press.

———. 2017. "Reorganizing Popular Sector Incorporation: Propositions from Bolivia, Ecuador, and Venezuela." *Politics & Society* 45 (1): 91–122.

Silva, Eduardo, and Federico M. Rossi, eds. 2017. *Reshaping the Political Arena in Latin America: From Resisting Neoliberalism to the Second Incorporation*. Pittsburgh, PA: University of Pittsburgh Press.

Slater, Dan, and Erica Simmons. 2012. "Coping by Colluding: Political Uncertainty and Promiscuous Powersharing in Indonesia and Bolivia." *Comparative Political Studies* 46 (11): 1366–93.

Spalding, Rose J. 2014. *Contesting Trade in Central America: Market Reform and Resistance.* Austin: University of Texas Press.

Stokes, Susan C. 2001. *Mandates and Democracy: Neoliberalism by Surprise in Latin America.* New York: Cambridge University Press.

Tarrow, Sidney G. 2011. *Power in Movement: Social Movements and Contentious Politics.* New York: Cambridge University Press.

United Nations Economic Commission for Latin America and the Caribbean (ECLAC). 2015. *Statistical Yearbook for Latin America and the Caribbean.* Santiago de Chile: ECLAC.

Van Cott, Donna Lee. 2005. *From Movements to Parties in Latin America: The Evolution of Ethnic Politics.* New York: Cambridge University Press.

Williamson, John. 1990. "What Washington Means by Policy Reform." In John Williamson, *Latin American Adjustment: How Much Has Happened.* Washington, DC: Institute for International Economics.

Wolff, Jonas. 2007. "(De-)Mobilising the Marginalised: A Comparison of the Argentine Piqueteros and Ecuador's Indigenous Movement." *Journal of Latin American Studies* 39 (1): 1–29.

Yashar, Deborah. 2005. *Contesting Citizenship in Latin America: The Rise of Indigenous Movements and the Postliberal Challenge.* New York: Cambridge University Press.

FOUR

Entrenching Social Constitutionalism?

Contributions and Challenges of the Left in Latin American Constitutionalism

NATHALIA SANDOVAL-ROJAS AND DANIEL M. BRINKS

In this chapter, we explore the question whether the investment by the left in social constitutionalism over the last decades will serve to insulate the Left turn policy goals from reversal even in the event of a "turn to the right." Since the 1970s—initially simply as participants in constituent assemblies and later abetted by their electoral successes in the Left turn of the late 1990s—the Latin American left has invested considerable political capital and energy in securing the constitutional rights that would underpin later claims for social and economic citizenship. Blind faith in constitutions and the power of law would suggest that these constitutional rights are now cemented into the very notion of citizenship, and therefore locked away from the hazards of ordinary politics. A more realistic view of how constitutions, rights, and courts work counsels a more complex forecast. Evidence shows that social rights constitutionalism has provided an important platform for resistance to retrenchment but only in countries with independent courts responsive to social goals. Moreover, it seems a left-oriented constitutionalism has primarily been useful in resisting or mitigating an initial abrupt turn away from social guarantees.

Even when elected governments are against policies that enforce social and economic rights, we expect that a politics anchored in the principles and institutions of constitutional justice can, at times, push back. Theoretically informed models of constitutionalism and judicial politics offer reasons for expecting that the politics of constitutional justice will yield somewhat different consequences for economic and social rights than ordinary politics. The left's participation in constitutional origin moments yielded a quite substantial constitutionalization of the Left turn's policy goals, long before the Pink Tide. Therefore, social rights constitutionalism can potentially serve as a platform to contest the extent of the so-called turns to the right and the more traditional right wing's backsliding.

Despite its many internal differences, the Latin American Left turn is defined by its advocacy of greater social provision (Gargarella 2010; Hillebrand and Lanzaro 2007; Uprimny 2011), a key component of extending the citizenship regime. There are several other issues related to citizenship that we could also identify as left-progressive in the region, which different left movements and parties have embraced to different degrees: environmental protection, Indigenous rights, and economic nationalism, for example. In the past century, when governments attempted land reform, the creation of a welfare state, or any of the other markers of social citizenship—to the extent they pursued these goals at all—they did so in the realm of ordinary politics, through legislation and centralized executive branch decision making (Brinks 2017; Brinks and Blass 2018). Left social and political movements similarly pursued these goals with the tools and in the spaces of ordinary politics—from elections to lobbying to protest.

Over the past four decades, the participation of left-of-center governments, parties, and social movements in constitutional origin moments yielded a quite substantial constitutionalization of the Left turn's policy goals, and the subsequent transformation of the politics of social provision and citizenship in many countries, as we will show in figure

4.1 below. This is one consequence of changes in the region such as the wave of transitions to democracy (Mainwaring and Pérez-Liñán 2014) and then the so-called turn to the left (Levitsky and Roberts 2011; Weyland, Madrid, and Hunter 2010). Debates about health, education, housing, food, and workers' conditions, about the environment and living conditions, autonomy and territorial control of Indigenous peoples, about access to water and basic economic goods, have increasingly been framed as a matter of rights and thus amenable to the tools and spaces of constitutional justice (see, e.g., Brinks, Gauri, and Shen 2015). Also in this period, Latin America experienced an increase in rights-based social mobilization, often but not only using explicitly legal constitutional means, and courts in various countries have, at one time or another, intervened quite substantially in the design and implementation of social policies.

In addition to its protagonism in legal mobilization and in various constitutional originating coalitions, the incumbent left in Latin America has aimed since the late 1990s to contribute directly to the satisfaction of social needs and the extension of citizenship rights. Helped along by a commodity-driven boom, the budget allocation for social provision had its most significant increase in 2003, when left governments were flourishing (ECLAC 2016). Indeed, these governments implemented social programs that actually reduced poverty and inequality (Arnson, Jara, and Escobar 2009). The turn toward left governments, however, shows clear signs of exhaustion.

Recent elections and other political events, in fact, have replaced left or center-left governments with a number of new governments that range from the center right to the extreme right, to the point where it clearly makes sense to speak of a "Right turn." The list includes the election of Mauricio Macri in Argentina in 2015, the Temer and Bolsonaro governments that followed Rousseff's 2016 impeachment in Brazil, and the short-lived rule of Pedro Pablo Kuczynksi, followed by his vice president, Vizcarra, in Peru. In Chile, Bachelet's Socialist government was replaced by the center-right Piñera. In Central America, the governments that succeeded the coup against the left-of-center Zelaya in Honduras in 2009 were both on the right, while the center-left government of Colom in Guatemala was succeeded by two governments that were clearly right of center, especially the government of Jimmy Morales. Further losses might be in the offing for the left following the significant electoral gains by the opposition in Venezuela's legislature in 2015, although Mexico is bucking the trend with the election of Andrés Manuel López Obrador, El Salvador remains in the left column, and Correa's handpicked successor in Ecuador narrowly avoided losing in 2017.

Whether this turn to the right is a true and growing trend or not, the ordinary swing of the political pendulum suggests that, sooner or later, more market-oriented governments will undoubtedly succeed the more statist, social welfare–oriented governments that prevailed in the region in recent years.

Clearly, many of these new governments will prefer to roll back extensive social rights protections, especially if this policy decision is coupled with an economic crisis. This has prompted many to suggest that this most recent trend portends a sharp swing away from the policy agenda of the progressive left and a new moment of neoliberal state retrenchment. In effect, we have already seen some such attempts, such as the bills to reduce social expenditure and the constitutional amendment capping social spending for twenty years, advanced by Temer's government in 2016 and the dramatic reduction in utility subsidies proposed by Macri in Argentina. Indeed, as the contributions by Eve Bratman and Roberta Rice in this volume attest, faced with sharp resource constraints, even leftist governments such as those in Bolivia and Ecuador have increasingly pursued extractive projects despite the strenuous objections of their Indigenous erstwhile allies (Burchardt and Dietz 2014; Riofrancos 2015). Much earlier, of course, in Colombia, a constituent assembly that was strongly marked by the presence of a progressive left gave way to the much more market-oriented governments of Uribe and Santos. Because it predates many of the other reversals of fortune for the left and thus gives us a longer time frame, this latter case should prove particularly useful for understanding the potential and the limits of constitutional justice to carve out a space for progressive politics in a neoliberal context.

Whether we subscribe to the idea that there has been a regionwide turn to the right or whether we anticipate a less dramatic shift in the politics of the region, this is a good time to explore the possible effect of the left's investment in constitutions and rights. There is enough evidence now already to explore the extent to which the constitutionalization of the left's agenda and policy priorities will lead to the protection of its policy gains, and even to the possibility of continuing to pursue progressive politics through constitutional justice even in the face of a rightward turn in ordinary politics. Might social constitutionalism have a sort of ratchet effect that prevents rolling back social advances in a neoliberal political environment, no matter what might happen in the electoral arena?

We begin this chapter with a theoretical framework that accounts for the shift of the social question from ordinary politics to the constitutional justice sphere. Using this foundation, we explore the history of leftist ideas related to social issues and explore how the left contributed to the entrenchment of social constitutionalism in a series of constitutions beginning in the mid-1980s and ending with the constitutions of Ecuador and Bolivia in the first decade of this century. In this chapter, "the left" in Latin America refers to the broad set of political ideas and actors whose central objective is to promote equality among individuals and groups (Bobbio 1995). There is a huge variation in leftist strategies and ideologies across time and territory; still, it is possible to group actors who share meaningful ideological commitments together under the umbrella of leftism.

Next, we explore the possible ratchet effect of social constitutionalism, using some of the most salient cases in which a center-right and right government seeks to roll back social benefits while opponents attempt to resist using the courts: the cases of the *tarifazo*, which is the popular name for the sudden, unexpected, and dramatic hike in utility rates that took place under President Macri in 2016 in Argentina and its attendant social consequences, the "fiscal ceiling" in Brazil, and "fiscal sustainability" in Colombia. We use these cases to bring to light the possibilities and limits of social rights constitutionalism to push back against a government's conflicting agenda. The sudden cut of utility subsidies in Argentina and the cut in social spending coupled with a constitutional amendment that caps government expenditures in Brazil raise the question we posed here quite clearly. In each of these cases a new government came in and sought a fairly dramatic change in social policies; opponents resisted using the tools of constitutional justice. We will see that in both of these cases the courts took the side of social rights over the indisputable economic exigency that led to the policies in the first place.

Similarly, the debate over fiscal sustainability in Colombia is a particularly challenging case to illustrate the potential of social constitutionalism and its possible limits. Despite the generous rights provisions in the 1991 Constitution, in 2011 the Colombian government passed a constitutional amendment to challenge the implementation of social rulings. The amendment allowed the government to object to compliance with any social ruling if there were macroeconomic risks. What makes this case a difficult one is that it poses a clash between social constitutionalism and a subsequent, equally constitutional, rule. The Constitutional Court, however, interpreted the constitutional amendment to mean that, nevertheless, neither it nor the government can use economic arguments to deny compliance with social rights rulings.

All three cases occurred in countries where the left played a significant role in the adoption of social constitutionalism (Brazil 1988, Colombia 1991, and Argentina 1994). Also, all three cases developed as a response to right-wing policies or constitutional changes, following a weakening of the left's influence. Therefore, they are useful for studying the potential and the limits of social constitutionalism in a broad sense. The sudden rate hike known as the tarifazo in Argentina and the "fiscal ceiling" in Brazil took place after the turn to the right. The case of "fiscal sustainability" in Colombia did not involve any regime change, but we included it because the change was a major backslide from the leftist legacies of the original 1991 Constitution. In fact, in Colombia, the influence of the left began to fade as soon as the constitution was concluded. Our argument is that the influence of the left on constitutional frameworks can sometimes persist even after the right becomes dominant in ordinary politics. If this is true we should be able to see it even in those cases where the left never really got the chance to govern beyond the constitutional moment.

We should be clear that we do not, in this piece, take a position on the wisdom of these judicial actions. It may well be that the courts' insistence on protecting social rights in the face of economic contractions, as in Brazil, or increasing demands, as in Colombia, is foolhardy and ruinous. The point is to illustrate cases in which constitutional rights *and* constitutional justice have provided a space to give initial responses to abrupt cuts to social provision fostered by both right-turn and traditional center-right and right governments.

FROM SOCIAL ISSUES TO SOCIAL CONSTITUTIONALISM

Our theoretical expectation for the effectiveness of social rights constitutionalism to resist a turn to the right is not obvious. Much of the literature on constitutions and judicial review is based on the assumption that constitutions and judicial review provide a "credible commitment" device by locking certain issues—property rights, democratic processes—away from the reach of ordinary politics (Ginsburg 2003; North and Weingast 1989). This model implicitly assumes a fairly sharp separation between constitutional enforcement and contemporary politics. An extreme, perhaps naive, version of this would simply expect that the constitutionally favored ends will prevail regardless of the politics of the moment.

At the opposite end of the spectrum, rights, and social and economic rights in particular, have come under considerable criticism lately for being ineffective. There are calls in the popular press by prominent academics to abandon human rights as a paradigm,[1] as well as empirical analyses that show that substantive rights appear ineffective and that social and economic rights appear not to have any impact on spending (Chilton and Versteeg 2015, 2016). As if that were not enough, we know that courts are creatures of their political context and depend on it for their effectiveness, so we should be skeptical that they would be interested in (see, e.g., Hirschl 2004), much less capable of (see, e.g., Rosenberg 2008), mounting a strong challenge to an ascendant neoliberal regime on behalf of social rights.

Still, a theoretically informed understanding of the relationship between constitutional justice and politics might lead us to hold out some—however qualified—hope for its effectiveness, under the right conditions. We know, for example, that human rights treaties are effective conditional on the presence of civil society actors who can engage with them and advocate for them (Simmons 2009). Case studies also show that domestic social rights can be effective in some cases, again conditional on political activity to make them so (Gauri and Brinks 2008; Rodríguez-Garavito 2009, 2011a), and that judicial decisions that seek to enforce them can produce compliance and therefore have some impact, once again, so long as there is a politics of compliance and follow-up (Botero 2018; Langford, Rodríguez-Garavito, and Rossi 2016). The effects may be limited to particular areas, may involve more

rearranging than growing of infrastructure, and may not have the consequences people expected, but certainly there is enough in the literature
to suggest that rights-based mobilization can be politically efficacious.
These observations fit neither a "lock box" model, in which rights are
locked away from ordinary politics and placed under the care of apo-
litical institutions for enforcement in a technocratic sort of way, nor a
"parchment barriers" model, in which rights are simply words on paper.

This common refrain—that rights of whatever nature are effective insofar as there is supportive social and political mobilization behind them—
prompts a somewhat different model of constitutional effectiveness. We
expect a system of constitutional justice to configure an alternative space
with two characteristics that distinguish it from the space of ordinary politics. First, it identifies certain goals—in constitutional texts and subsequent
judicial interpretations—that deserve special consideration and higher priority. Second, it establishes a set of procedures and decision criteria, and
privileges a set of social and institutional actors, that are conceptually distinct from the ones that prevail in ordinary politics. Without attempting to
catalog all the differences between the two spaces, we can identify some of
the most distinctive features of the space of constitutional justice, in contrast to that of ordinary politics: additional veto players and the possibility
of delaying or multiplying the decision points by appealing to judges at all
levels; agenda setting in the hands of litigants, whether individual citizens
or organized civil society, rather than in the hands of elected officials; judicial rather than majoritarian decisions; and an indirect role at best for the
winners of the most recent elections. All of this might lead us to expect
that having a robust alternative space for constitutional justice might serve
to temper some of the swings in electoral politics.

But have Latin American constitutions really incorporated a substantial portion of the left's agenda into the space of constitutional justice? By almost any measure, Latin America has witnessed a marked
turn toward what we might call social rights constitutionalism, which
is much more congruent with a social democratic model than with a
stripped-down neoliberal model (Brinks and Blass 2017). Figure 4.1
shows the movement toward social rights constitutionalism in Latin
America from 1975 to 2009. Movement upward, as an empirical matter,
means the additional incorporation of social and economic rights, as
well as more accessible and effective mechanisms for claiming rights.

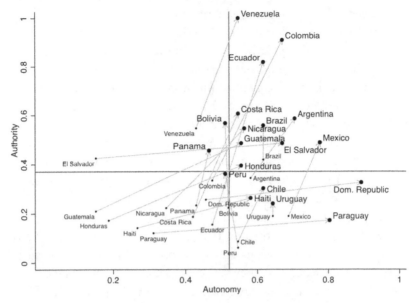

FIGURE 4.1. Movement in Latin American Systems of Constitutional Justice along Autonomy and Authority Dimensions. *Source*: Brinks and Blass 2018.

Movement rightward indicates the expansion of the number of actors who have influence within the sphere of constitutional justice, beyond the winners of the latest election (see Brinks and Blass 2017 for a detailed explanation of the two dimensions).

The turn to the right, thus far at least, is mostly limited to the space of ordinary politics, although the constitutional amendments that took place in two of our cases suggest that constitutional justice might soon be affected as well. If the left's agenda had not been moved into the sphere of constitutional justice, we might expect a relatively quick reversal of their policies. The U.S. Constitution and recent swings in electoral politics give us a prominent example of how this might work when the social question is relegated entirely to the sphere of ordinary politics. The U.S. document does not contain social rights clauses or amendments. Social welfare is a permissible but not required end of the federal government, and the scope of welfare protection depends heavily on the presidential agenda and Congress's decisions. As a result, the New Deal measures, perhaps the most consequential transformation of the U.S. state, were approved through the ordinary political process, and the Supreme Court intervened only to prohibit certain measures—until it eventually stepped aside in favor of the ruling coalition. In theory at least, these measures are all open to reversal. Similarly, advances in the public provision of health care by the Obama administration were potentially subject to reversal in the short term, by a subsequent administration hostile to the policy.

In contrast, in Latin America, it is conceivable at least that legal mobilization using the tools, concepts, and spaces of constitutional justice might be able to challenge, delay, and even block such a reversal. In the constitutional sphere, constitutional judges have the power to use social rights to block measures they deem harmful to constitutional ends. In fact, we know that courts are better at blocking legislative initiatives than building new policy, so it is exactly in the context of a retrenchment that we would expect to see them at their most powerful. This power does not entail that their decisions on issues contained in the constitutional justice sphere are univocal or even final (see Dahl 1957 for evidence that courts that run against the current of their political context cannot hold out for long). It is common to observe struggles and negotiations around the content of issues contained in the constitutional justice sphere. But time and again we have seen courts veto new policies and constrain choices around matters that are included in the constitution.

In short, it seems entirely possible that the social rights constitutionalism that now characterizes Latin America will make it more difficult for the right's success in electoral politics to translate into a quick and dramatic policy reversal. In principle, social assistance programs are no longer merely public policies that can expand and contract in response to elections, they are constitutionally protected components of everyone's bundle of basic citizenship rights—however unevenly and weakly they are extended in practice. Next, we show that this movement to social rights constitutionalism was a left project that came to fruition in recent decades.

THE ENTRENCHMENT OF SOCIAL CONSTITUTIONALISM IN LATIN AMERICA

The debates about the place of the social question in political debates began soon after independence. But it was only when the constitutional design coalitions became more diverse that social issues were included in the constitutional sphere. In Latin America, political diversity is directly related to the inclusion of the left, for it has been the political actor with less participation in government, as we discuss below. Moreover, the left is associated with the struggle for better material conditions and the elimination of economic and social inequalities. Thus, the more the left participates in the constitutional coalition, the broader the inclusion of social issues in the constitutional sphere.

Initially, the nascent Latin American republics opted for classical liberal constitutions and located social issues in the sphere of ordinary politics. Nonetheless, Gargarella (2010) posits that one of the main topics in the nascent Latin American republics was the overcoming of inequalities left by the colonial hierarchies. Liberals and conservatives were interested in the social question, but the main demands came from early nationalists (e.g., Martí, Ingenieros, and Haya de la Torre) and socialists (e.g., Recabarren and Mariátegui). Nationalists and socialists mixed social concerns with demands related to the deepening of majority rule, the end of oligarchies, and economic independence from the United States (Félix Godio 1981). Liberals and conservatives saw these interests as radical and dangerous for the new democracies. Therefore, apparently ideologically opposite groups formed an elite alliance that excluded the left and the social question from constitutions (García Lema 1994; Gargarella 2010).

A remarkable exception was the 1917 Mexican Constitution, which opened the path for the inclusion of social rights in Latin American constitutions. At the end of the Mexican Revolution, the victorious faction called a constitutional congress. The conformation of the assembly was diverse in terms of the political tendencies,[2] professions, and varied social backgrounds of the elected representatives (Murray 2015). The 1917 original constitutional coalition, without abandoning a liberal democratic framework, introduced the social function of property— meant to subordinate property rights to the pursuit of the common good—and a mandate for land reform. Moreover, they succeeded in including the famous Article 123, a lengthy article that entitled workers to social rights (De la Madrid Hurtado 1977).[3] Similar experiences occurred later in the adoption of the 1949 Argentine Constitution and the 1945 Guatemalan Constitution. They included a large list of social rights but combined them with the exercise of a centralized political authority, especially marked in the populist Peronist regime in Argentina (Brinks and Blass 2017; Gargarella 2010).

In the rest of Latin America, workers and European immigrants reinforced leftist movements and parties. The left linked its aim to improve social conditions and promote social rights with an alternative model to development, a Socialist Marxist one. In the ideological and political context of the Cold War fostered by U.S. hegemony in the region, they were marginalized and violently repelled (Castañeda 1993). The exception was the 1959 Cuban Constitution, adopted after a revolution that led to a Communist regime. The 1960s and 1970s authoritarian regimes in Chile, Argentina, Brazil, the Dominican Republic, and Uruguay suspended constitutions, repressed parties and political movements, and limited the guarantees of rights. Countries such as Venezuela and Colombia did not have military authoritarian regimes, but this did not prevent the government from suppressing leftist groups (Levitsky and Way 2011). The left was generally excluded from the design of the constitutions of that period.

Beginning mostly in the 1980s, however, the region experienced a new wave of constitutionalism. After the breakdown of authoritarian regimes or the signing of peace agreements, some governments drafted new constitutional texts (i.e., the 1988 Brazilian Constitution, the 1982 Honduran Constitution, and the 1978 Ecuadorean Constitution, as well as El Salvador in 1982, Guatemala in 1985, and Nicaragua in 1987). Other countries, such as Bolivia, Peru, and Uruguay, reinstated constitutions that had been suspended during military rule. In addition, the past four decades have produced an average of ten constitutional reforms per country in Latin America (Brinks and Blass 2017). All this change produced the remarkable expansion of the systems of constitutional justice we documented in the previous section.

To understand the broad inclusion of the social issue in recent constitutions, it is necessary to examine the role of the left. In the 1990s, the left experienced significant changes (Roberts 2013; Rodríguez-Garavito 2005). It abandoned its commitment to a revolutionary socialist model. Instead, Communist movements and former guerrillas[4] decided to demand social transformations through democratic methods, questioning to different degrees the neoliberal doctrine in local or national government positions (Castañeda 1993; Weyland, Madrid, and Hunter

2010). More important, leftist parties decided to adopt the framework of rights as a political strategy to pursue the reduction of inequalities (Brinks and Forbath 2014; Yashar 2011). Although the implementation of neoliberal policies in the 1980s resulted in the undermining of leftist parties and unions (Rovira Kaltwasser 2010), new mobilization structures arose to oppose neoliberal measures (Castañeda 1993; Seoane, Taddei, and Algranati 2005).

In this context, partisan pluralism in the constitutional design moment opened the opportunity for social constitutionalism. Coalitions included the persistent liberal-conservative alliance, but they also introduced representatives that came from social movements, political minorities (i.e., Indigenous people and peasants), former guerrillas, and leftist parties. This pluralistic composition promoted the inclusion of usually excluded topics such as social rights.

Political mobilization supporting social and judicial reforms also turned into an opportunity for the adoption of activist judicial decisions to protect social rights. Many nongovernmental organizations (NGOs), civil movements, and transnational antiglobalization movements close to the left embraced the possibility to demand through legal and political venues the fulfillment of social needs, now framed as rights (Yamin and Gloppen 2011). In Latin America, more organizations incorporated constitutional mobilization in their contentious repertoire. High courts in countries such as Colombia, Argentina, Costa Rica, and, to a lesser extent, Guatemala responded, producing decisions that broadly protect social rights and, more recently, have included structural remedies and follow-up measures.

In the 2000s some of the leftist governments in the "Left turn" also expanded the constitutional sphere to include social issues, although they did not grant enough autonomy to the courts. Venezuela, Ecuador, and Bolivia changed their constitutions[5] and increased their social commitments with rights related to basic needs such as the right to health and to education. Constitutional texts explicitly included social rights that are still controversial in other countries such as the right to water, to food sovereignty, and to practice sports. Moreover, the Ecuadorean Constitution added a right to living well, linked with Indigenous conceptions of welfare.[6] Besides, these new constitutions authorized constitutional tribunals and judicial review. Nonetheless, requirements for serving as judges and removal rules have taken away courts' autonomy.

In this sense, the expansion of the social rights under leftist governments is consequential, but it did not imply necessarily an expansion of social constitutionalism.

A deeper look into the constitutional changes in Colombia (1991) and Argentina (1994) illustrates the role of the left in the expansion of social constitutionalism.

Argentina

Argentina's constitutional justice system shifted from the elitist liberalism of the 1853 Constitution to a more inclusive social constitutionalism in 1994. The original document set up a tutelary regime, run by a small elite of immigrants over a vast territory (García Lema 1994). The constitution gave significant powers to the executive and adopted a laissez-faire orientation in the economy. Furthermore, the Argentine Supreme Court did not have the explicit power of constitutional review, although it quickly adopted it by judicial interpretation. This constitutional document contained the basic set of rights characteristic of liberal constitutions (due process, right to a fair trial, right to property, freedom of religion, etc.), but it did not contain social guarantees except for the right to work (art. 14).

In 1949, the populist regime of Perón endorsed a new constitution that combined a new social orientation with more executive powers. As soon as 1957, however, the subsequent military regime called for a constituent assembly to reinstate the original 1853 text. Their plan largely succeeded, although the Unión Cívica Radical (Radical Civil Union, UCR) and the Partido Socialista (Socialist Party, PS) managed to include labor rights in one article.[7] It was not until 1994, one decade after the end of the last military regime, that a pact between elites opened the opportunity for the expansion of the constitutional justice sphere. Neoliberal president Menem from the Partido Justicialista (Justicialist Party, PJ) agreed with Raúl Alfonsín, leader of the opposition liberal party UCR, to a constitutional reform that authorized the president's reelection in exchange for taking away some of the presidential powers (Brinks and Blass 2018, ch. 5). An initial elite agreement called the "Pacto de Olivos" prioritized institutional stability and sought to limit the scope of the reform that could come out of the constituent assembly.

The pluralistic composition of the convention and some looseness in that initial agreement provided the legal and political opportunity for the inclusion of social guarantees in the constitution. Unlike earlier Argentine conventions, this time a center-left coalition called the Frente Grande emerged as the third largest party.[8] While the traditional parties, the PJ and the UCR, won the majority of the votes in the convention (37.7 percent and 19.9 percent, respectively), the Frente Grande won nearly 13 percent of the seats, and about 5 percent was won by smaller parties. The traditional parties, the UCR and the PJ, for a variety of reasons, felt compelled to accept proposals from the new members of the originating coalition. Alfonsín envisioned pluralism as the way to achieve legitimacy (Alfonsín 2004, 197). The PJ upheld a conservative view in terms of the rights that should be included but also felt the need to be more inclusive and agreed to update Argentina in accordance with the "social constitutionalism fashion" (García Lema 1994, 241).

The center-left coalition known as Frente Grande played a starring role in the expansion of clauses that included more rights. The party headed the commissions of social rights (Juan Terzaghi) and constitutional order (Francisco Fuster). Moreover, members of the Frente Grande such as Eugenio Zaffaroni and the socialist Guillermo Estévez Boero advocated together with the UCR member Elisa Carrió for an article to grant constitutional status to human rights treaties. The debate on social rights generated the largest number of proposals, more than one hundred from members of the constituent assembly and members of the public (Brinks and Blass 2018, ch. 6). Some representatives of the Socialist Party participated in the debates, but they mostly believed that social rights were not strong enough to produce revolutionary transformations. The PJ argued against including a large list of social rights but accepted the inclusion of international human rights treaties as enforceable constitutional commitments (García Lema 1994, 240).

As a result, the 1994 amendment added social rights to the 1853 Constitution. "Chapter Two, New Rights and Guarantees" (*Capítulo Segundo, Nuevos Derechos y Garantías*), introduced the right to a healthy, balanced environment (art. 41) and protection for consumers (art. 42). Ambiguously, the constitution lists, in the attributes of Congress, the power to "recognize the cultural and ethnic preexistence of Argentine indigenous peoples" and to "guarantee respect for their identity" (art. 75

(17)). More important, the constitution granted constitutional status to a series of human rights treaties such as the American Declaration on the Rights and Duties of Man, the Universal Declaration on Human Rights, the American Convention on Human Rights, and the International Pact on Economic, Social and Cultural Rights that widen the list of social rights.

This inclusion of rights was accompanied with provisions that enhanced judicial leverage to enforce rights. Article 42 incorporated the right—for the first time in the constitutional text, although it had existed before as a matter of judicial interpretation and legislation—to bring an *amparo* (writ of protection) any time a constitutional right is violated. The norm authorizes directly affected citizens, the national ombudsman,[9] and any associations organized to protect these rights to file claims. This mechanism can also be used to protect diffuse and collective rights. Likewise, the requirement for the election of Supreme Court judges moved from a simple majority to a two-thirds senatorial consent. The change increased the role of the opposition in the Senate in the selection of justices, and, in consequence, the court's autonomy from the party in power (República Argentina 1994).

The set of social rights, international treaties, and judicial enforcement mechanisms transformed the politics of social provision in Argentina. Civil society and prominent NGOs increased public litigation to ensure the enforceability of social rights. Catalina Smulovitz (2008) finds that between 1992 and 2004 the number of social rights cases filed in the national and provincial judicial systems increased by 111.6 percent. According to Paola Bergallo (2011, 52), between 1998 and 2007, the number of right-to-health claims went from 449 to 1159, with a success rate of approximately 80 percent.

In spite of subsequent swings in policy from the neoliberal Menem to the more statist-populist Kirchner and Fernández administrations to the more recent conservative Macri administration, the Argentine Supreme Court has consistently intervened in the protection of social rights. To mention some of the most acclaimed cases, the court protected the right to public health (*Viceconte* case), to health of HIV patients (*Benghalensis Association* case), to a clean environment (*Matanza Riachuelo* case), to fair retirement payments (*Badaro* case), and the right of prisoners to decent living conditions (*Verbitsky* case). While before

1994 social rights decisions were left entirely to the hazards of electoral politics, social constitutionalism has given civil society and courts a major role in challenging the reach and implementation of social provision. Social rights protection had become an enforceable citizen's entitlement.

The Macri administration is relatively recent, and it is unclear to what extent the Supreme Court will be able to continue this trajectory. Already some judicial replacements trend in a more restrictive direction. Carlos Rosenkrantz—one of the justices appointed by the Macri administration—is known to be somewhat skeptical of the judicial enforcement of social and economic rights. The question is to what extent more progressive social movements will be able to capitalize on the work of the Frente Grande during the constituent assembly to resist movements away from a robust welfare state and extensive social programs.

Colombia

Colombia has had twelve national constitutions since its independence from Spain in 1819.[10] The number is larger than the Argentine tally, but the form of addressing the social question follows the same pattern as in that country. The traditional Liberal and Conservative Parties dominated the originating coalitions for all previous constitutions until the 1990 Constitutional Assembly. It was not until the 1990 Constitutional Assembly that the left, including a variety of leftist political actors and former guerrilla members, was able to have meaningful input into Colombia's charter.

In 1990 the intensification of political violence, the economic opening, and the war against drugs combined to create demand for a solution that included a new, more inclusive constitution. Violence and poverty posed significant challenges. Several guerrilla groups disputed territorial power.[11] Armed forces fought against both drug trafficking groups and the "Communist threat," in many cases violating human rights. The so-called dirty war entailed the first paramilitary alliances and the near-disappearance of the Patriotic Union party. Prominent politicians and presidential candidates were murdered. Along with that, 65 percent of the national population lived in poverty, 80 percent of them in rural areas, and the national extreme poverty rate was 29 percent (World

Bank 2002). Civil society realized then that this crisis would not be solved with an exclusionary agreement that would simply repeat what had probably been one of its causes (Dugas 1993).

Broad sectors of society converged in the 1990 National Constitutional Assembly. Seventy delegates included members of left parties, representatives of Indigenous peoples, Protestant church leaders, students, the demobilized guerrilla M-19, and a member of the demobilized guerrilla Ejército Popular de Liberación (Popular Liberation Army, EPL). The three presidents of the assembly represented the Liberal Party, the Alianza Democrática M-19 (Democratic Alliance M-19), and a dissident faction of the Conservative Party. Ordinary citizens submitted proposals to the commissions. Angelino Garzón, from the Democratic Alliance M-19, and Iván Marulanda Gómez, from the Liberal Party, were the most active constituent members in including social rights.[12] As in Argentina, the internal dynamic of the Constitutional Assembly was marked by the presence of a strong left coalition that had more influence within the assembly than in electoral politics at any time before or after it.

The 1991 Constitution thoroughly expanded the sphere of constitutional politics. In the first articles the new national regime is defined as based in a "Social and Democratic Rule of Law." The text includes a chapter with a full list of social rights (art. 42–art. 77), collective and environmental rights (art. 78–art. 82), and includes a clause for the internal incorporation of international human right treaties that scholars call *bloque de constitucionalidad* (Uprimny 2008). Articles 83 to 94 ordered rights protection and created the writ of protection (*acción de tutela* or *tutela*) as an easy and direct judicial mechanism to individually enforce rights that could be filed before any judge and could be reviewed by a high court—the Constitutional Court. Unlike the other existent high courts,[13] this new Constitutional Court was more open to ordinary politics because the government and high courts nominate candidates that the Senate finally elects. Yet the court has large judicial review powers, and it can determine the content of social rights through the revision of tutelas, even when reviewing a decision coming from another high court.

There is no question that social rights constitutionalism judicialized social provision in Colombia. The number of writs of protection filed in Colombia grew from 3.2 tutelas annually for every ten thousand inhabitants in 1992 to 104.54 tutelas for every ten thousand inhabitants in 2014. The right to health was the second most protected right (23.74 percent), and other social rights were the third most protected rights (16.05 percent) in 2014 (Defensoría del Pueblo 2014). Moreover, policy reform around the public health system and internally displaced people's rights to housing and other basic services has been predominantly driven by prominent structural decisions such as the T-760 on the right to health and the T-025 on internally displaced persons' (IDP) rights. Scholars tend to see in this explosion of individual protection a regressive outcome and find more value in structural cases (Gloppen 2011; Lamprea Montealegre 2015; Uprimny and Durán 2014). Still, both the individual and collective cases show how consequential the expansion of the constitutional sphere has been (Gauri and Brinks 2008).

SOCIAL CONSTITUTIONALISM UNDER NEOLIBERAL ENVIRONMENTS

In this section we briefly review some cases that might prefigure the fate of social rights constitutionalism after a possible turn to the right. It is clearly premature to propose definitive conclusions about the legacies of social constitutionalism at the end of the Left turn. If there is a Right turn, it is still getting under way. At the same time, it is possible to identify some early examples that give us some hints and plausible hypotheses about the potential for social constitutionalism even in the event of a neoliberal shift.

A clear "turn to the right" case is Argentina, where Mauricio Macri, from the center-right party Propuesta Republicana (PRO), defeated the populist-left Justicialist Party governments that ran the country from 2003 to 2015. The incumbent government had implemented utility subsidies and frozen services tariffs after the 2001 economic crisis to offset its negative effects on households' real purchasing power. Yet as these subsidies steadily increased they became quite inefficient (Lakner et al. 2016). As a result, as soon as he assumed office, Macri designed a reorganization plan arguing economic stagnation, chronic inflation, and unreliable macroeconomic information. The reform package entailed a sudden cut in utility subsidies for basic commodities such as natural gas, water, electricity, and other public services such as transportation. The measure caused an increase of almost 400 percent in many people's utility bills.

Even though scholars recognize the fiscal burden of the subsidies, the sudden increase of prices—the tarifazo—affected vulnerable people who could not continue paying. Along with large protests (El Clarín 2016; La Nación 2016), multiple judicial decisions followed. At first, judges in trial courts in places such as Chubut, Mendoza, and San Luis decided individual amparos ordering the continuation of subsidies in water bills. Likewise, the Federal Tribunals of La Plata and Córdoba ordered the subsidies maintained—temporarily in the former case and permanently in the latter case. The Supreme Court intervened, requesting that the government provide a detailed justification of the measures, including compliance with the principle of progressive realization and nonregression in social rights. Later, the Court voided the increase in the price of gas. In these decisions the Supreme Court protected the right to housing and to participation, and ordered the government to consult with civil society on any modification of prices in utilities that satisfy social rights (CSJN 2016).

While there is no question that the subsidy policies will change, the inclusion of this issue in the sphere of constitutional justice did exactly what we would expect. New decision points appeared in the political landscape, beyond the legislature and executive. Additional actors, beyond the majoritarian ruling coalition, became relevant actors in the decision-making process; these included not only courts but also organizations acting on behalf of consumers and those most affected by the change. New arguments beyond simple economic efficiency became important to the decision-making process as well: the government was forced to justify its actions and to consider their impact on the interests protected by social rights constitutionalism. In short, the system worked exactly the way our model of constitutional governance would expect—not as a technical-legal judicial veto but as a space for constitutional politics.

Another recent turn occurred in Brazil, where Michel Temer, a center-right politician, took office in 2016 after Dilma Rousseff's impeachment. The leftist PT that governed Brazil from 2002 to 2016 had increased public expenditure in social goods (OECD 2016) and implemented cash transfer programs to ameliorate poverty (Hunter and

Sugiyama 2014; Soares, Ribas, and Osório 2007). When the Temer government took power, however, the economic recession had harshly affected the national economy. To revert the economic cycle, the National Congress included an amendment that freezes public expenditures over twenty years, and local governments such as the Rio de Janeiro Assembly passed bills reducing public servants' salaries. Moreover, Temer passed a constitutional amendment to repeal the federal duty to expend minimum percentages in health and education over the next twenty-five years (Adamo Idoeta 2016). Another attempt to reduce social expenditure is the proposal to modify the regime of retirement provisions (Soto, Flynn, and Hay 2016).

Responses to the austerity measures that could imply a setback in social provision included both court interventions and protests. The Rio de Janeiro court intervened to interrupt the decision that authorized a reduction of public servants' salaries or pensions of 30 percent of their total wages (RCL 24438) (Superior Tribunal Federal de Justiça 2016). NGOs, parties, and civil organizations framed their criticisms of the measures as social rights violations (Conectas 2016; Trevisani 2016). International NGOs are joining the struggle under the banner of social and economic rights.[14] The case has now been brought to the attention of the Interamerican Commission on Human Rights.[15] This is salient because civil society used the language of social rights to evaluate an economic policy, and also because civil society considered social rights mandatory even when the contraction was included in the constitution. The results of the amendment that freezes social expenditure and the impact of the legal actions that have protected the social rights of specific groups are not definitive. Still, unlike the market liberalization reforms at the end of the 1980s, current neoliberal reforms need a justification that may include the satisfaction of social rights entrenched in the constitution.

Earlier events in Colombia also showcase some of the observable impacts of social constitutionalism. In 2011, center-right president Juan Manuel Santos promoted a constitutional amendment to include "fiscal sustainability" as guidance for the economic performance of all organs of government. The measure was meant to address perceived excesses in social expenditures in the face of recessive cycles.[16] It entitled the government to request a financial impact assessment for discussing the implementation of judgments adopted by any supreme judicial body, although it also provides that "in no case shall the essential core of a fundamental right be affected." A citizen challenged the amendment in the Constitutional Court, arguing that it replaced the social aspect of the constitution by placing budgetary concerns above the satisfaction of people's rights and limited judicial autonomy by allowing the government to question judicial orders.

The Constitutional Court gave the "fiscal sustainability" amendment an interpretation that privileges social constitutionalism. In decisions C-288 of 2012 and C-870 of 2014 the court set fulfillment of rights and material equality as part of the very nature of the 1991 Constitution (Constitutional Court of Colombia 2012, 2014). Thus the court prohibited including any kind of norms that go against these basic objectives. Congress disputed whether fiscal sustainability would be a constitutional principle, a right, or a duty of citizenship. The High Court answered by positing that fiscal sustainability does not have any of these salient statuses; rather it is one among other economically useful guidelines to develop constitutional principles and rights. Moreover, the Court ruled that the challenge based on sustainability could not modify the content of the orders. Instead, it held that while the government can expose concerns about the financial requirements to comply with a judicial order, it is the Court itself that still decides whether to modify its own orders.

The ruling deterred the government from filing challenges based on a lack of fiscal sustainability. For instance, the Court denied the ancillary procedure based on fiscal sustainability aimed at stopping a recall referendum of the mayor of Bogotá in 2015 and also denied a similar procedure in cases mandating compliance with the law governing public health care provision. It was not until five years after the incorporation of the provision that the Constitutional Court used the question of fiscal sustainability to modulate the effects of a judicial decision that limited the amount of taxed income to protect the social right to a basic income. The Court approved postponing the implementation of its decision after the government argued that the cut in taxes would harm the national budget (Auto 184; Constitutional Court of Colombia 2016). The "fiscal sustainability" clause will continue to be a crucial argument in debates on social expenditure. What is different is that the Court and potential plaintiffs will be able to intervene in the scope of those changes, and, when they do, they will frame their opposition as a matter of constitutional rights.

Two additional cases suggest some of the limits of social rights constitutionalism. The most recent left-ruling coalitions placed "the social question" at the center of constitutional justice. At the same time, however, some governments of the Left turn have been criticized for pursuing revenue increases through oil exploitation and mining in national parks at the expense of the issues we have identified as part of both a progressive Left agenda and social rights constitutionalism. Rafael Correa in Ecuador ordered oil extraction in the Yasuní National Park (Martínez 2009; Pastor and Donati 2008), and Evo Morales in Bolivia advocated the construction of a road crossing the Isiboro Sécure National Park (TIPNIS) (Perreault 2008). Whether we should consider oil extraction a left or right project is an open question. While some scholars and popular movements advocate for the protection of the environment (Robbins 2004), some left governments and their supporters consider this resistance "eco-imperialism," because environmentalists impose high eco-standards in Latin America while countries in the North continue polluting (Driessen 2003). But in any event, it is undisputed that these projects endanger the social and economic rights of Indigenous and peasant communities, such as the right to housing and the right to food (Rodríguez-Garavito 2011b). Therefore, these policies allow us to see to what extent the constitutional legacy of the left will prevent the erosion of social protection in the face of the extractivist market policies of any government, left or right.

Unfortunately, it is possible that in neither of these cases will social rights constitutionalism prevail over the contrary policies of a sitting government. Despite an initial win in 2011, in which protests by Indigenous communities put a stop to the construction of the highway through the TIPNIS, the conflict continues, and it now appears the highway will be reauthorized. Similarly, Ecuador is forging ahead with oil extraction in the Yasuní Park. Judicial interventions have not been significant elements in the struggle to determine whose rights, and whose vision of development, should prevail in these two cases. As we saw, these are precisely the countries in which the constitution fails to provide the sphere of constitutional justice with sufficient autonomy from the ruling coalition. Without some degree of autonomy, constitutional justice becomes no more than a mechanism for legitimizing and clearing the way for the ruling coalition's governing agenda. At the same time, the many protests around these issues using the language of social, economic, and cultural rights, with temporary wins, delays, and frequent setbacks, suggests the new constitutionalism can also transform the politics of an issue even without recourse to courts. At this writing, the TIPNIS highway has still not been constructed, due to the national and international resistance to it on behalf of Indigenous and environmental rights.

Read together, we can find evidence in these cases that social constitutionalism has transformed the initial phases of the politics of retrenchment even in the face of strong financial constraints, so long as the system of constitutional justice has some autonomy from the ruling party. To a lesser degree, the discursive effects of the hegemony of social rights discourse in the region might also influence public policy, even in the sphere of ordinary politics. In the cases of Argentina and Brazil, the changes in policy arose directly from concerns about the economic crises that the countries faced at the end of their left governments. In Argentina, the court blocked an initial retrenchment and imposed significant procedural requirements. In Brazil, the changes had to be legitimized in constitutional language, through a formal amendment, and they remain deeply contested as inconsistent with the social rights guarantees of the 1988 Constitution, although the drastic change in that country's politics augurs poorly for those guarantees. In Colombia, concerns arose from recent economic crises in the region and the fear that structural judicial decisions would entail expenditures as large as those in nearby countries, but the court has refused to back down from vigorous enforcement of social and economic rights. In all three cases, center-right presidents fostered the reforms and social rights constitutionalism played a crucial role in shaping the politics and strategies of resistance.

We can see the influence of social rights constitutionalism in a variety of places. First, social constitutionalism made the design and implementation of responses to the crises more deliberative, invoking a specific discourse of rights and empowering specific actors such as courts. Only in Argentina was the government decision adopted in ordinary politics. In Brazil and Colombia, both reforms required constitutional amendments, that is, higher majorities and special procedures. And yet in all three cases, civil society actors felt entitled and empowered to challenge the decision. More important, the rights discourse compelled states to justify their decisions to the legislature, the courts, and public opinion, requiring consideration of and a degree of protection for social rights. In the best of cases, these constraints and the requirement to give reasons and explain the effect on vulnerable populations might make economic decision making more inclusive and transparent.

Social constitutionalism showed two normative features that allowed courts to constrain governments. The first one is that social rights are justiciable legal norms (Abramovich and Courtis 2002). Thus, even though the exigencies of economic crises pushed social issues to the background in the initial proposals to cut subsidies, pursue fiscal sustainability, and establish expenditure ceilings, the governments were eventually forced to consider and comply with minimum social legal duties. The second feature is the principle of nonregression or nonsocial decline. This principle forbids public authorities from adopting measures or regulations that reduce the level attained by the country in the satisfaction of a specific social right (González-Bertomeu and Gargarella 2016). As a consequence of this principle, the Argentine court decided that cuts required further deliberation, and the Colombian court highlighted that fiscal sustainability could not harm the already achieved level of protection. These two legal constraints may have deterred the expected outburst of challenges on fiscal sustainability grounds in Colombia and stopped the sudden impact of the austerity measures in Argentina.

The contribution of social constitutionalism may also be relevant from a strategic perspective. The enforcement of normative commitments in Argentina and Colombia depended on courts. In contrast to these two countries, the easy amendability of the constitution and the relatively weaker judicial structure of Brazil will make it difficult to reverse measures embodied in constitutional amendments. Similarly, in the cases of Bolivia and Ecuador, the courts have not found the requisite autonomy from the government to ban extractive projects.[17] Even without the support of strong courts, however, rights have leverage because they are central to the region's current political discourse. The increasing number of protests in Brazil and the massive political actions that Indigenous and environmental NGOs have undertaken at the national and international levels are grounded in the language of rights. One of the major impacts of social rulings may well be to provide social movements and vulnerable populations with legal arguments to support otherwise silent claims.

Governments may address social provision issues related to citizenship in several different ways. In Latin America, after a long history of political exclusion and inclusion of "the social question," leftist and social democratic support has entrenched social provision in the sphere of constitutional justice. Social constitutionalism in the region has expanded the formal boundaries of citizenship and has provided—with notable variations across the region—institutions and mechanisms that guarantee access to those rights. The left played a significant role in this entrenchment, although it is not the "owner" of the constitutional social project, as we see in the cases of Bolivia and Ecuador. Social movements can make use of the space of constitutional justice in ways that challenge even former allies in the government. Our discussion here makes it clear that on its own social rights constitutionalism does not advance a social agenda that can avoid the reemergence of a neoliberal economic model. And yet it can provide a platform for a mobilized civil citizenry to challenge the dominant project of the ruling coalition, on behalf of the interests and principles it protects. It does so by adding new spaces for deliberation and decision, by empowering alternative actors who may not find their voices heard in ordinary politics, and by requiring the consideration of basic social protections even in the face of acute crises. What its limits might be and to what extent it might prevail in the face of a prolonged turn to the right remains to be seen. But we can see some glimpses of a potential for social rights constitutionalism, and a formal expanded citizenship, to limit some of the more drastic swings of the political pendulum.

NOTES

1. See, e.g., Posner 2014.

2. There were members of the winning moderate factions (led by President Carranza) and different left radical factions and representatives of the Catholic Church and the right.

3. Article 123 contained clauses to protect the working class. De la Madrid Hurtado (1977) summarizes it as follows: (a) individual worker

guarantees and nondiscrimination clause; (b) guarantees for women and children workers; (c) guarantees to unions; (d) labor justice; (e) social security (retirement assignments and health) provisions; and (f) guarantees in the employment relationship.

4. Except for the Colombian guerrilla FARC and some remnants of the Shining Path in Peru.

5. Venezuela changed its constitution in 1999, Ecuador in 1997 and then in 2007, and Bolivia in 2009.

6. Article 14: "The right of the population to live in a healthy and ecologically balanced environment that guarantees sustainability and the good way of living (*sumak kawsay*), is recognized" (República del Ecuador 2008).

7. Article 14 includes workers' rights, labor unions' rights, and social security rights. Although the endurance of these rights is not trivial, in the end they remain mostly symbolic because of the lack of enforcement mechanisms (República del Ecuador 2008).

8. This coalition was formed in 1990 by a dissenting group of representatives affiliated with the PJ. Later, members of other leftist groups such as the Movements for Democracy and Social Justice, the Intransigent Party, the Popular Progressist Movement, the Popular Democracy, the Humanist Party, and the Communist Party joined the coalition.

9. The constitution refers to the *defensor del pueblo*, another of the rights-protecting institutions included in the 1994 reform.

10. Colombia has had the following constitutions: 1821, 1828, and 1830 Gran Colombia Constitutions; 1831, 1832, 1843, and 1853 New Granada Constitutions; 1858, 1861, and 1863 Federal Constitutions; 1886 and 1991 Constitutions of the Republic of Colombia.

11. The groups included the FARC-EP, ELN, M-19, EPL, and Quintín Lame.

12. Both Angelino Garzón and Iván Marulanda belonged to the Fifth Commission on economic aspects. Garzón presented drafts of the chapter on social and economic rights, agrarian rights, and labor rights. Marulanda discussed drafts on the rights of people with disabilities, the economic model, and the rights to education and housing (Banco de la República 2017).

13. The 1991 Constitution maintained the previous scheme of multiple high courts: the Supreme Court, which decides civil and criminal cases; the Council of State, which decides administrative law appeals; and the Superior Council of Judicature, which decides disciplinary cases involving lawyers.

14. See, e.g., the discussion by the Center for Economic and Social Rights (CESR 2016), available at www.cesr.org/brazils-austerity-cap-stunting -rights-food-health-and-education.

15. See the discussion of the collaboration among multiple NGOs and their efforts to use the language and mechanisms of rights to affect the politics of social spending in Brazil (Global Alliance for Tax Justice 2018), available at www.globaltaxjustice.org/en/latest/brazil%E2%80%99s-austerity-cap -stunting-rights-food-health-and-education.

16. Legislative Act 3 of 2011 reads in part: "Fiscal sustainability shall provide guidance to the branches and organs of government, within their competences, in a framework of harmonious collaboration. When a judgment has been handed down by any of the supreme judicial bodies, the General Prosecutor of the Nation or one of the government ministries may request the initiation of a Financial Impact Assessment, the holding of which shall be obligatory. The explanations of the supporters on the consequences of the judgment on the public finances shall be heard, as well as the concrete plan for its execution, and a decision shall be taken whether to modulate, modify or postpone the effects of the judgment with the objective of preventing serious disturbances to fiscal sustainability. In no case shall the essential core of a fundamental right be affected."

17. The story may not be over yet. Instead of continuing to press their claims before the national courts, both the Bolivian and Ecuadorean peoples have taken their cases to the Inter-American system for protection. Many of the principles we have identified with social rights constitutionalism are also present in the Inter-American system, although the Interamerican Court of Human Rights has been more reluctant to enforce social and economic rights, with the possible exception of Indigenous peoples' rights.

REFERENCES

Abramovich, Víctor, and Christian Courtis. 2002. *Los derechos sociales como derechos exigibles*. Madrid: Trotta.

Adamo Idoeta, Paula. 2016. "Proposta do PMDB traz riscos ao orçamento da educação, diz especialista cotado para ministério." BBC Brazil, May. São Paolo. www.bbc.com/portuguese/brasil/2016/05/160516_entrevista _educacao_mozart_pai.

Alfonsín, Raúl Ricardo. 2004. *Memoria política: Transición a la democracia y derechos humanos*. Buenos Aires: Fondo de Cultura Económica de Argentina.

Arnson, Cynthia J., José Jara, and Natalia Escobar. 2009. "Gobernabilidad democrática y la Nueva Izquierda." Santiago de Chile/Washington, DC. http://dx.doi.org/10.1007/bf02900345.

Banco de la República. 2017. *Miembros de la Asamblea Nacional Constituyente de 1991.* Buenos Aires: Archive Virtual Library Luis Angel Arango. www.banrepcultural.org/asamblea-nacional-constituyente/miembros #Marulanda.

Bergallo, Paola. 2011. "Courts and the Right to Health: Achieving Fairness Despite 'Routinization' in Individual Coverage Cases?" In Alicia Yamin and Siri Gloppen, eds., *Litigating Health Rights: Can Courts Bring More Justice to Health?* Cambridge, MA: Harvard University Press.

Bobbio, Norberto. 1995. *Derecha e izquierda: Razones y significados de una distinción política.* São Paulo: Fundação Editora Unesp.

Botero, Sandra. 2018. "Judges, Litigants, and the Politics of Rights Enforcement in Argentina." *Comparative Politics* 50 (2): 169–87.

Brinks, Daniel M. 2017. "La justicia constitucional en América Latina: Nuevos modelos, viejos desafíos." In Catherine Andrews, ed., *Un siglo de constitucionalismo en América Latina (1917–2017)*, vol. 1. Mexico City: Editorial CIDE.

Brinks, Daniel M., and Abby Blass. 2017. "Rethinking Judicial Empowerment: The New Foundations of Constitutional Justice." *International Journal of Constitutional Law* 15 (2): 296–331.

———. 2018. *The DNA of Constitutional Justice in Latin America: Politics, Governance and Judicial Design.* New York: Cambridge University Press.

Brinks, Daniel M., and William Forbath. 2014. "The Role of Courts and Constitutions in the New Politics of Welfare in Latin America." In Randall Peerenboom and Tom Ginsburg, eds., *Law and Development of Middle-Income Countries: Avoiding the Middle-Income Trap.* New York: Cambridge University Press.

Brinks, Daniel M., Varun Gauri, and Kyle Shen. 2015. "Social Rights Constitutionalism: Negotiating the Tension between the Universal and the Particular." *Annual Review of Law and Social Science* 11 (1): 289–308.

Burchardt, Hans-Jürgen, and Kristina Dietz. 2014. "(Neo-)extractivism—A New Challenge for Development Theory from Latin America." *Third World Quarterly* 35 (3): 468–86.

Castañeda, Jorge G. 1993. *Utopia Unarmed: The Latin American Left after the Cold War.* New York: Vintage.

Center for Economic and Social Rights (CERS). 2016. "Brazil's Austerity Cap Stunting Rights to Food, Health and Education." Brasilia/New York. www.cesr.org/brazils-austerity-cap-stunting-rights-food-health -and-education.

Chilton, Adam S., and Mila Versteeg. 2015. "Do Constitutional Rights Make a Difference?" *American Journal of Political Science* 60 (3): 575–89.

————. 2016. *Rights without Resources: The Impact of Constitutional Social Rights on Social Spending*. Charlottesville: University of Virginia School of Law.

El Clarín. 2016. "Protestas en distintos puntos del país contra los tarifazos." El Clarín (Buenos Aires). www.clarin.com/politica/Protestas-distintos -puntos-pais-tarifazos_0_1625837584.html.

Conectas. 2016. *Violação continuada: Dois anos da crise em Pedrinhas*. São Paulo: Conectas Direitos Humanos. www.conectas.org/publicacoes/download /violacao-continuada-dois-anos-da-crise-em-pedrinhas.

Corte Constitucional de Colombia. 2012. Sentencia C-288. Bogotá: República de Colombia. www.corteconstitucional.gov.co/relatoria/2012/C -288-12.htm.

————. 2014. Sentencia C-870. Bogotá: República de Colombia. www .alcaldiabogota.gov.co/sisjur/normas/Norma1.jsp?i=63743.

————. 2016. Auto 184: Escrito de subsanación. Incidente de impacto fiscal. Sentencia C-492 de 2015. Bogotá: República de Colombia. www .corteconstitucional.gov.co/relatoria/autos/2016/A184-16.htm.

Corte Suprema de Justicia Nacional (CSJN). 2016. *Centro de Estudios para la Promoción de la Igualdad y la Solidaridad y otros c/ Ministerio de Energía y Minería s/ amparo colectivo*. Buenos Aires. http://sjconsulta.csjn .gov.ar/sjconsulta/documentos/verDocumentoById.html?idDocumento =7327885&cache=1520035320001.

Dahl, Robert A. 1957. "Decision-Making in a Democracy: The Supreme Court as a National Policy-Maker." *Journal of Public Law* 6: 279.

De la Madrid Hurtado, Miguel. 1977. *Estudios de derecho constitucional*. Mexico City: Universidad Nacional Autónoma de México (UNAM), Instituto de Investigaciones Jurídicas.

Defensoría del Pueblo. 2014. *La tutela y los derechos a la salud y a la seguridad social*. Bogotá: Defensoría del Pueblo.

Driessen, Paul. 2003. *Eco-Imperialism: Green Power Black Death*. New Delhi: Academic Foundation.

Dugas, John. 1993. "El desarrollo de la Asamblea Nacional Constituyente." In John Dugas, ed., *La Constitución de 1991: ¿Un pacto político viable?* Bogotá: Universidad de los Andes.

Félix Godio, Julio. 1981. "Nacionalismo y socialismo en America Latina, 1918–1930." *Desarrollo Indoamericano* 16 (3): 37–39.

García Lema, Alberto Manuel. 1994. *La reforma por dentro: La difícil construcción del consenso constitucional*. Buenos Aires: Planeta.

Gargarella, Roberto. 2010. *The Legal Foundations of Inequality: Constitutionalism in the Americas, 1776–1860*. New York: Cambridge University Press.

Gauri, Varun, and Daniel M. Brinks. 2008. *Courting Social Justice: Judicial Enforcement of Social and Economic Rights in the Developing World*. New York: Cambridge University Press.

Ginsburg, Tom. 2003. *Judicial Review in New Democracies: Constitutional Courts in Asian Cases*. New York: Cambridge University Press.

Global Alliance for Tax Justice. 2018. "Brazil's Austerity Cap Stunting Rights to Food, Health and Education." Global Alliance for Tax Justice. www.globaltaxjustice.org/en/latest/brazil%E2%80%99s-austerity-cap -stunting-rights-food-health-and-education.

Gloppen, Siri. 2011. "Litigating Health Rights: Framing the Analysis." In Alicia Yamin and Siri Gloppen, eds., *Litigating Health Rights: Can Courts Bring More Justice to Health*. Cambridge, MA: Harvard University Press.

González-Bertomeu, Juan F., and Roberto Gargarella. 2016. *The Latin American Casebook: Courts, Constitutions, and Rights*. London: Routledge.

Hillebrand, Ernst, and Jorge Lanzaro. 2007. *La izquierda en América Latina y Europa: Nuevos procesos, nuevos dilemas*. Montevideo: Friedrich Ebert Stiftung.

Hirschl, Ran. 2004. *Towards Juristocracy: The Origins and Consequences of the New Constitutionalism*. Cambridge, MA: Harvard University Press.

Hunter, Wendy, and Natasha Borges Sugiyama. 2014. *Transforming Subjects into Citizens: Insights from Brazil's Bolsa Família*. New York: Cambridge University Press.

Lakner, Christoph, Maria Ana Lugo, Jorge Puig, Leandro Salinardi, and Martha Viveros. 2016. *The Incidence of Subsidies to Residential Public Services in Argentina*. La Plata: Universidad Nacional de la Plata. http://dx .doi.org/10.1596/24987.

Lamprea Montealegre, Everaldo. 2015. *Derechos en la práctica: Jueces, litigantes y operadores de políticas de salud en Colombia (1991–2014)*. Bogotá: Universidad de los Andes, Facultad de Derecho.

Langford, Malcolm, César A. Rodríguez-Garavito, and Julieta Rossi. 2016. *Compliance with Socio-Economic Rights Judgments: Making It Stick*. New York: Cambridge University Press.

Levitsky, Steven, and Kenneth M. Roberts, eds. 2011. *The Resurgence of the Latin American Left*. Baltimore, MD: Johns Hopkins University Press.

Levitsky, Steven, and Lucan Way. 2011. "Introduction: Latin America's 'Left Turn': A Framework for Analysis." In Steven Levitsky and Kenneth M. Roberts, eds., *The Resurgence of the Latin American Left*. Baltimore, MD: Johns Hopkins University Press.

Mainwaring, Scott, and Aníbal Pérez-Liñán. 2014. *Democracies and Dictatorships in Latin America: Emergence, Survival, and Fall*. New York: Cambridge University Press.

Martínez, Martínez Yánez. 2009. *Yasuní: El tortuoso camino de Kioto a Quito*. Quito: Abya Yala.

Murray, Thomas. 2015. "Socio-Economic Rights versus Social Revolution? Constitution Making in Germany, Mexico and Ireland, 1917–1923." *Social & Legal Studies* 24 (4): 487–508.

La Nación. 2016. "Protestas contra el aumento de tarifas en distintos puntos de la Ciudad." *La Nación*, Buenos Aires. www.lanacion.com.ar/1918519 -comenzaron-las-protestas-contra-el-tarifazo-en-distintos-puntos-de-la -ciudad.

North, Douglass C., and Barry R. Weingast. 1989. "Constitutions and Commitment: The Evolution of Institutions Governing Public Choice in 17th-Century England." *Journal of Economic History* 49 (4): 803–32.

Organisation for Economic Co-operation and Development (OECD). 2016. "Education at a Glance: Educational Finance Indicators." www.oecd -ilibrary.org/education/data/oecd-education-statistics/education-at-a -glance-educational-finance-indicators-edition-2017_6cad591a-en.

Pastor, Ginés Haro, and Georgina Donati. 2008. *Yasuní Green Gold: The Amazon Fight to Keep Oil Underground*. Oxford: New Internationalist.

Perreault, Thomas. 2008. *Extracting Justice: Natural Gas, Indigenous Mobilization, and the Bolivian State*. Geneva: United Nations Research Institute for Social Development.

Posner, Eric. 2014. "The Case Against Human Rights." *The Guardian*, New York. www.theguardian.com/news/2014/dec/04/-sp-case-against-human -rights?CMP=fb_gu.

República Argentina. 1994. *Constitución Nacional de la Nación Argentina*. Buenos Aires: Poder Legislativo Nacional. www.casarosada.gob.ar /nuestro-pais/constitucion-nacional.

República del Ecuador. 2008. *Constitución de la República del Ecuador*. Quito: Asamblea Constituyente del Ecuador. http://pdba.georgetown.edu /Constitutions/Ecuador/english08.html.

Riofrancos, Thea. 2015. "Beyond the Petrostate: Ecuador's Left Dilemma." *Dissent Magazine*. www.dissentmagazine.org/article/riofrancos-beyond -petrostate-ecuador-left-dilemma.

Robbins, Paul. 2004. *Political Ecology: A Critical Introduction*. Malden, MA: Blackwell.

Roberts, Kenneth M. 2013. "Market Reform, Programmatic (De)Alignment, and Party System Stability in Latin America." *Comparative Political Studies* 46 (11): 1422–52.

Rodríguez-Garavito, César. 2005. "Global Governance and Labor Rights: Codes of Conduct and Anti-Sweatshop Struggles in Global Apparel Factories in Mexico and Guatemala." *Politics & Society* 33 (2): 203–33.

———. 2009. "Assessing the Impact and Promoting the Implementation of Structural Judgments: A Comparative Case Study of ESCR Rulings in Colombia." www.escr-net.org/usr_doc/Rodriguez_-_Colombia.pdf.

———. 2011a. "Beyond the Courtroom: The Impact of Judicial Activism on Socioeconomic Rights in Latin America." *Texas Law Review* 89: 1669.

———. 2011b. "Ethnicity.gov: Global Governance, Indigenous Peoples, and the Right to Prior Consultation in Social Minefields." *Indiana Journal of Global Legal Studies* 18 (1): 263–305.

Rosenberg, Gerald N. 2008. *The Hollow Hope: Can Courts Bring about Social Change?* Chicago: University of Chicago Press.

Rovira Kaltwasser, Cristóbal. 2010. "Moving beyond the Washington Consensus: The Resurgence of the Left in Latin America." *Internationale Politik und Gesellschaft / International Politics and Society* 3: 52–62.

Seoane, José, Emilio Taddei, and Clara Algranati. 2005. "The New Configurations of Popular Movements in Latin America." In Atilio Boron and Gladys Lechini, eds., *Politics and Social Movements in an Hegemonic World.* Buenos Aires: CLACSO.

Simmons, Beth A. 2009. *Mobilizing for Human Rights: International Law in Domestic Politics.* New York: Cambridge University Press.

Smulovitz, Catalina. 2008. "La política por otros medios: Judicialización y movilización legal en la Argentina." *Desarrollo Económico* 48 (190–91): 287–305.

Soares, Fábio Veras, Rafael Perez Ribas, and Rafael Guerreiro Osório. 2007. *Evaluating the Impact of Brazil's Bolsa Familia: Cash Transfer Programs in Comparative Perspective.* New York: United Nations Development Programme (UNDP).

Soto, Alonso, Daniel Flynn, and Andrew Hay. 2016. "Brazil Says Can Pass Pension Reform in 2016 Despite Headwinds." Reuters, June. London. www.reuters.com/article/us-brazil-politics-idUSKCN0ZE2P6.

Supremo Tribunal Federal de Justiça do Brasil. 2016. AG.REG. Na Medida Cautelar Na Reclamação (RCL) 24438. Brasília: Supremo Tribunal Federal de Justiça. www.stf.jus.br/portal/cms/verNoticiaDetalhe.asp?idConteudo=328308.

Trevisani, Paolo. 2016. "Brazil Senators Rail against Austerity Measures." *Wall Street Journal.* New York. www.wsj.com/articles/brazils-goldfajn-restoring-confidence-is-key-to-rekindling-growth-1475592692.

Tribunal de Justiça do Rio de Janeiro. 2016. Reclamação (RCL 24438). Rio de Janeiro: Tribunal de Justiça do Estado do Rio de Janeiro.

United Nations Economic Commission for Latin America and the Caribbean (ECLAC). 2016. *Social Panorama of Latin America 2015*. Santiago de Chile: ECLAC. www.cepal.org/en/publications/39964-social-panorama -latin-america-2015.

Uprimny, Rodrigo. 2008. *Bloque de constitucionalidad, derechos humanos y proceso penal*. Bogotá: Consejo Superior de la Judicatura, Sala Administrativa. www.cejamericas.org/BoletinNexos/publicaciones/Dia1Impactodelcon troldeconvencionalidadLibroBloquedeConstitucionalidadyProcesoPenal .pdf.

———. 2011. "Las transformaciones constitucionales recientes en América Latina: Tendencias y desafíos." In César Rodríguez-Garavito, ed., *El derecho en América Latina: Un mapa para el pensamiento jurídico del siglo XXI*. Buenos Aires: Siglo Veintiuno Editores.

Uprimny, Rodrigo, and Juanita Durán. 2014. *Equidad y protección judicial del derecho a la salud en Colombia*. Bogotá: ECLAC. https://repositorio.cepal .org/handle/11362/36758.

Weyland, Kurt, Raúl Madrid, and Wendy Hunter. 2010. *Leftist Governments in Latin America: Successes and Shortcomings*. New York: Cambridge University Press.

World Bank. 2002. *The World Bank Annual Report 2002*. Washington, DC: World Bank Publications. http://documents.worldbank.org/curated/en /379051468163155729/Main-report.

Yamin, Alicia Ely, and Siri Gloppen. 2011. *Litigating Health Rights: Can Courts Bring More Justice to Health?* Cambridge, MA: Harvard University Press.

Yashar, Deborah. 2011. "The Left and Citizenship Rights." In Steven Levitsky and Kenneth M. Roberts, eds., *The Resurgence of the Latin American Left*. Baltimore, MD: Johns Hopkins University Press.

FIVE

Participatory Democracy in Latin America?

Limited Legacies of the Left Turn

Benjamin Goldfrank

Latin America's Left turn included a boom of experimentation with participatory institutions, first at the local level in many cases and later at the national level. While discursively, Left turn governments aimed at widening and deepening citizenship, in practice there was substantial variation in their efforts to experiment, the institutions they created or revitalized, and the outcomes in terms of citizenship. It may be true that the extent of experimentation with participatory institutions has been greater in Latin America than in other world regions, yet on the whole, as the political tides begin to shift, it is increasingly apparent that a historic opportunity to fundamentally transform citizenship regimes in Latin America has been missed.[1] Throughout the region, even in the most celebrated case of participatory democracy—Brazil—the legacy of the left is limited. Participatory institutions of nearly all stripes are weak, stalled, disfigured, or in the process of being rolled back. How can we account for the great variation of efforts, forms, and fates of participatory democracy under the Left turn? And why is the Left turn's legacy so limited?

This chapter explores several factors that help explain the Left turn's varied but limited legacy for participatory democracy. These include the sheer complexity of designing ideal large-scale participatory institutions, the social bases and ideological preferences regarding participatory democracy of governing parties, institutional opportunities and constraints stemming from constitutions and party systems, and, for most countries, the neoextractivist development model employed to maintain power. Without a clear blueprint for establishing participatory democracy, facing resistance from defenders of representative institutions, and relying on natural resource extraction to fund social programs, create jobs, and deliver economic growth, left governments experimented to different degrees with a variety of participatory institutions but failed to consolidate mechanisms that were simultaneously open, transparent, inclusive, and powerful. This is not to negate some advances in several facets of citizenship, including interesting experiences at the local, state, and national levels in different time periods, especially early on in the Left turn and in the cases where a more participatory ideology predominated. Yet, in recognizing variation across time, scale, and country, this chapter emphasizes a common theme: the advances in citizenship mostly did not extend to important public policy decisions, particularly regarding economic policy and especially the reliance on natural resource extraction and exploitation (see chapters by Rice and by Bratman, this volume).

This chapter proceeds by outlining the debates over the Left turn governments' implementation of participatory institutions and then describing the extraordinary variety of these institutions and highlighting achievements and shortcomings of several of them at the municipal, provincial, and national levels. Achievements include the increase in formal opportunities for citizens to express their preferences and to influence public policies and budgets and, in some cases, improvements in public services and social indicators as well as the prioritizing of the needs of disadvantaged social groups. The rest of the chapter focuses on attempting to explain both the variety of institutions and their limitations, underscoring the inherent challenges of designing ideal participatory institutions, especially taking into account the complexities and inequalities of twenty-first-century Latin American societies, the differences in the ruling parties and corresponding political systems, and neoextractivism. The conclusion considers the future of participatory institutions in the region.

COMPETING PERSPECTIVES ON PARTICIPATORY INSTITUTIONS AND THE LEFT

The literature on Latin America's Left turn, whether celebratory or disparaging, often associates it with the increasing prevalence of participatory institutions (Cameron and Hershberg 2010; De la Torre 2013; Pogrebinschi 2013; Sandbrook 2014; Weyland, Madrid, and Hunter 2010). While some degree of correlation exists between these two trends, it is important to acknowledge that the *participatory* turn did not always start at the national level but at the subnational level, that it was and still is apparent in countries governed by various political ideologies, and that, even within the left, there are many who reject the notion of participatory democracy as an appropriate strategy or goal (Goldfrank 2015). This latter position is one of several interpretations in the multisided and wide-ranging scholarly discussion regarding the left and participatory democracy, in which even the key terms themselves are under debate. To Gargarella (2014), for example, most of the governments reviewed in this volume should not be considered "left" given their continuation of private property and market relations and their sometimes questionable adherence to democracy. For others, what this chapter refers to as participatory institutions are better understood as "contested spaces" (Wilde 2017) or as vehicles either for clientelism (García-Guadilla 2018) or for taming popular movements and integrating them within the state (Machado and Zibechi 2016). Leaving the definitional questions aside, this section briefly presents the main positions in the debate. They range from the notion that the Latin American left's participatory experiments are leading the way to deepening democracy to the ideas that the left's experiments have failed or that national-level participatory democracy is simply infeasible, and they include disputes over which country serves as the best model.

One prominent position is that of authors like Richard Sand-brook (2014) and Thamy Pogrebinschi (2013), who see the left in Latin America as the vanguard of participatory innovations that can serve as beacons for the rest of the world. Deploring the decline of the left in the "Global North" for its lack of answers to current political and economic problems, Sandbrook hails "the moral and intellectual leadership of the left" in the Global South, "most notably in Latin America" (2014, 3-4). Pogrebinschi (2013) views the spread of participatory experiments in the region as improving the democracies resulting from the third wave of democratization. She argues that the left's rise facilitated this participatory turn. Importantly, Pogrebinschi understands the participatory turn as neither substituting representative institutions nor hindering them but as an "attempt to *correct* some of the alleged failures of representative institutions with participatory and deliberative innovations." Further, she claims these participatory innovations by leftist local and national governments in countries across the region have "expanded the delivery of public services, increased the distribution of public goods and ensured the enactment of social policies and rights, in addition to strengthening the voice of disadvantaged groups in the political process" (2013, 4; original emphasis).

Other scholars who share the view that participatory and representative institutions can fruitfully combine to strengthen democracy point to Brazil as exemplary for the region and even the world. According to Cameron and Sharpe, with its combination of local- and national-level participatory institutions, Brazil "has emerged as a leader in the hemisphere in terms of direct democracy, and it has managed to reconcile new forms of institutionalized voice with robust representative institutions." They call Brazil a "model for the region's democracies" (2012, 244). Similarly, the democratic theorist Archon Fung sees in Brazil "an epicenter of democratic revitalization and institutional invention" where innovations "fuse participatory and representative democracy" (2011, 857–58). Reviewing local-level participatory reforms in Brazil, he concludes that there "are simply no analogs of similar scale or depth in North America, Europe, Asia or Africa" (2011, 868). And Pogrebinschi and Samuels go further, declaring that Brazil's public policy conferences "are by far the world's largest experiment with such practices [of participatory democracy] in terms of number of participants, policy scope, and potential impact" (2014, 321). They view representative and participatory democracy as complementary, even at the national level, arguing that "participatory practices can deepen actually existing democratic regimes by opening the doors for extensive civil society influence over national governance" (Pogrebinschi and Samuels 2014, 314).

This suggestion by Pogrebinschi and Samuels (2014, 313–17) directly targets traditional political science arguments against participatory democracy. Though it may be compatible with representative democracy at the local level (which is considered essentially irrelevant for macropolitics), at the national level participatory democracy is infeasible and/or incompatible with representative democracy. In his explanation of the left's limitations with participatory democracy, Mainwaring summarizes why scaling up and institutionalizing participation to the national level faces "severe, largely insurmountable" constraints: "The scale of the polity and the great complexity of aggregating individual preferences at the national level; the huge information asymmetries between politicians and experts, on the one hand, and citizens on the other; the need for expertise to make many decisions; time limits of citizens; the need to protect minority rights; and the influence of moneyed interests all conspire against participatory democracy at the national level" (2012, 961). Mainwaring thus represents a third, and widely held, perspective. This view considers that in countries governed by moderate leftist parties, countries like Brazil and Uruguay, local-level participatory institutions may help strengthen liberal, representative democracy. However, in countries governed by radical left parties like Venezuela, as well as Bolivia, Ecuador, and Nicaragua, participatory institutions are used to mobilize followers in ways that undermine and erode representative democracy and civil society, leading to "participatory competitive authoritarianism" (Balderacchi 2015; see also De la Torre 2013; Mainwaring 2012, 961–63).

By contrast, some scholars with more favorable views of these so-called radical left parties seem to view participatory democracy as superseding representative democracy. For Webber and Carr, and many of the contributors to their book, the "radical Left sees liberal capitalist democracy as a limited expression of popular sovereignty and seeks instead to expand democratic rule through all political, social, economic, and private spheres of life" (2013, 6), which entails community control over neighborhoods. Rather than hold up Brazil as a model democracy, Katz, for example, admonishes the Partido dos Trabalhadores (Workers' Party, PT) for "governing on behalf of the dominant classes" (2013, 44) after moderating its political program and calling for responsibility. Instead, this perspective views Venezuela—with its referendums, communal councils, and worker cooperatives—as coming closest to the radical left ideal by "gradually and partially transforming . . . into a socialist economy and a participatory democratic polity" (Wilpert 2013, 208; see also Webber and Carr 2013, 6, 22).

A final perspective, closest to my own, dispenses with the dichotomization of the left into moderate and radical (see also Dabène, this volume). Recognizing wide variation in the meaning and importance of participatory institutions in the region, this perspective emphasizes the "fading of participatory democracy" across the spectrum of Left turn governments (Dagnino 2016, 161). One of the leading scholars of participatory democracy, Evelina Dagnino (2016, 159), stresses that, while not always effective, the initial spread of participatory institutions in the 1990s allowed for experimentation with new models of state-society relations by providing additional channels of interaction and representation, especially for previously excluded voices from popular sectors. The promise of these new models heightened with the Left turn, yet Dagnino (2016, 161) argues that a central factor in the dashing of this promise was the left's common embrace of the "new developmental state" as a reaction against neoliberalism's notion of a minimal state. The problem is that new developmentalism's proponents see representative democracy as the only channel of participation. With their emphasis on a strong state playing the protagonist's role in development, "there is no role of society's participation in the formulation of public policies" (Dagnino 2016, 163).

This literature offers many insights. However, there remains more to learn about the extent of variation across the region and the reasons behind it. Rather than hold up one or another country as a model for the rest, this chapter seeks to understand, like Dagnino, why, despite their various forms, none of the models of participatory democracy lived up to their potential and expectations to transform citizenship regimes. While new developmentalism played a limiting role in several cases (particularly Argentina, Brazil, Chile, Ecuador, and Uruguay), it does not help explain the wide variety in the degree and type of left experimentation with participatory institutions. Moreover, if new developmentalism ever held influence in Venezuela, it soon was overtaken by the notion of twenty-first-century socialism, which seeks an even stronger protagonistic role for the state but also, simultaneously, promotes partisan civil society institutions outside of traditional state channels and representative democracy. These include worker cooperatives and communes eventually intended to supplant the state and representative democracy. In this regard, Venezuela stands out from the rest. In other countries, the left's desired relationship between participatory and representative institutions may have been ambiguous (Goldfrank 2011), but only in Venezuela was there—eventually—an explicit drive to replace existing state and representative institutions.

VARIETIES OF PARTICIPATION: EFFORTS, TYPES, FEATS, AND FLAWS

Since the start of the new millennium, the Left turn at the national level has often but not always been accompanied by the creation of new participatory institutions, the writing of new constitutions promising yet more participation, and the rebirth of several older participatory mechanisms as well. This participatory boom has varied widely depending on the country, attaining political significance in some more than others and emphasizing different levels of government and policy sectors. Even mechanisms bearing the same name can be designed quite differently by country. Participatory budgeting as practiced in most Andean and Southern Cone municipalities, for example, is not the same as that practiced in Brazil, and the differences lead to divergent outcomes (Goldfrank 2013). Within the spectrum of leftist governments in South America, the presidencies of Lagos and Bachelet in Chile and those of the Kirchners in Argentina stand out for the lack of efforts to institutionalize citizen participation beyond electoral politics. The most experimentation with participatory institutions and the largest numbers of participants can be found in Brazil and Venezuela, followed by Uruguay, Bolivia, and, much further down, Ecuador.

Brazil

The PT in Brazil is perhaps the political party that is best known for its efforts to implement participatory institutions. It was the foremost promoter of participatory budgeting at the municipal and state levels, most famously in the city of Porto Alegre. After winning the presidency in 2002, the PT initially tried to implement a version of a nationwide, multiyear participatory budgeting process, but it placed more emphasis on the expansion and re-creation of older forms of participation, such as policy councils at the municipal, state, and federal levels. The new national-level Economic and Social Development Council, for instance, had a neocorporatist bent, including representatives of private firms, unions, and nongovernmental organizations. Perhaps most interesting are the public policy conferences, which are organized at the municipal, provincial, and national levels and include both state and civil society actors. Though not PT creations, they have been used much more by PT governments than by prior governments, have more participants than in the past (millions of citizens have attended at least one), and have covered more policy sectors than any previous government. There were more national public policy conferences held in Brazil during the first eight years of the PT government—fifty-eight in total—than in all the previous governments since 1941 combined (Pogrebinschi and Samuels 2014, 320–21).[2] Dilma Rousseff continued with the conferences and the expansion of the number of policy councils.

In terms of the new institutions' effects, let us first focus on participatory budgeting. The majority of studies in a now vast literature examine a few cases or only one, and generally show varied though often positive citizenship outcomes, especially with respect to strengthening or expansion of civil society organizations, improvements in transparency, inclusion of previously excluded groups, and more and better public services for disadvantaged sectors of the population (Fung 2011). Two recent analyses of participatory budgeting in Brazil show interesting and similar outcomes, though they use different econometric methodologies and take into account multiple control variables. These studies demonstrate that cities that use participatory budgeting increase public spending on health care and sanitation infrastructure, and they achieve larger reductions of child mortality rates compared to cities that do not use participatory budgeting (Gonçalves 2014; Touchton and Wampler 2014). In addition, cities that use participatory budgeting for longer time periods have stronger results.

In Rio Grande do Sul, the effects have been similarly positive. Rio Grande do Sul is the Brazilian state that has most used participatory budgeting, starting in 1999 under the PT's Olívio Dutra, the former mayor of Porto Alegre who had introduced participatory budgeting there in the early 1990s. Dutra's copartisan, Tarso Genro, expanded participatory budgeting as governor between 2011 and 2014 and added new mechanisms, including online ones. In addition to the creation of a new provincial university, participatory budgeting in Rio Grande do Sul was associated with an increase in efficiency of public expenditures, an increased percentage of spending on social services, and an equality-enhancing distribution of public spending such that less developed municipalities received more projects and programs (Goldfrank 2014; Goldfrank and Schneider 2006).

Despite the positive results generated by participatory budgeting in a few hundred cities, most of the more than five thousand municipal governments have not adopted the process, and many of those that adopt it later abandon it when a new mayor is elected (Spada 2010). As of 2010, only twenty-six Brazilian cities had maintained participatory budgeting for three consecutive administrations (Costa 2010, 12). There is also evidence that the PT, which had been the most important adopter and promoter of participatory budgeting in the 1990s, changed emphases once it reached national power and no longer champions the process as it had in the past. Before, the PT insisted that their mayors adopt it, even sending teams abroad to help others implement participatory budgeting. During the 1997–2000 period, 96 percent of Brazilian PT-ruled municipalities with more than fifty thousand inhabitants implemented participatory budgeting; by the 2005–8 period, that figure had decreased to 73 percent (Goldfrank 2012, 2).

With respect to other participatory institutions, relevant studies of the national public policy conferences have focused on their impact on the federal government, both the executive and legislative branches. In a study of six national conferences, for example, Pettinelli and Silva (2014) found that 78 percent of the approved proposals in the conferences were incorporated in the programs of the respective agencies or federal ministries. Pogrebinschi and Santos (2013) examined eighty conferences in a period of more than twenty years and verified that 26 percent of the proposals in the national conferences later appeared in government public policy proposals. And according to Pogrebinschi and Samuels (2014), almost half of the legislated or decreed public policies regarding women's issues are congruent with the proposals in the national conferences, including Brazil's first domestic violence law (known as the Maria da Penha Law).

Nonetheless, even though the national public policy conferences are deliberative and transparent, and they treat a broad spectrum of important issues, they are not especially socially inclusive (Cunha 2012), the number of participants is small considering the size of Brazil's population, and, in the end, many observers and social movement activists question their degree of influence (Dagnino and Teixeira 2014, 55; Goldfrank 2011, 171–74; Silva 2016, 17). Even Pogrebinschi and Samuels (2014, 330) recognize that few of the hundreds of proposals in the national conferences eventually become influential. One of the key intellectual champions of participatory institutions on the left, Boaventura de Sousa Santos (2014), argues that under President Rousseff, "the tools of participatory democracy that were the hallmark of popular government (participatory budgeting, sectoral policy councils, national conferences) have been worn down, losing the capacity for renovation, and above all, they were relegated more and more to deciding over less and less important issues. The major investments and large public works projects were left out of the reach of participatory democracy." And many observers would agree that the widespread public protests in 2013 were a testament to the "insufficiency of existing mechanisms of participation" (Dagnino and Teixeira 2014, 59).

Venezuela

Venezuela is notable both for the quantity of different participatory initiatives and for the number of participants involved in them. A nonexhaustive list of initiatives, most of them promoted by the national government but some beginning prior to the election of Hugo Chávez, includes Bolivarian circles, the Constituent Assembly, referendums, water planning boards, land use committees, local public planning councils, self-managed communal organizations, cooperatives, and dozens of "missions." The missions are included here because many of them have their own local committees, such as Barrio Adentro, with its community-run health clinics. The most popular participatory innovations in terms of the number of participants are the communal councils (CCs), which began in 2005 and gradually absorbed other local-level initiatives. The CCs can be formed by between 150 and 400 families in urban areas and by smaller numbers of families in rural and indigenous areas, and their main purposes are proposing, planning, implementing, and monitoring community projects and programs. A census of the CCs in 2013 indicated that more than forty thousand CCs existed in the country and that millions of Venezuelans had attended at least one CC assembly (Canache 2014, 31); more recently, government sources have referred to forty-six thousand CCs (AVN 2015). By the late 2000s, the CCs had received well over US$4 billion in order to carry out thousands of mostly small infrastructure projects (Azzellini 2016, 102–3). Before and especially after the 2010 Law of Communes, some CCs began joining together to form communes, and by 2015, the government had registered 1,195 communes (Azzellini 2016, 243–45). Under President Nicolás Maduro, the most recent addition to this list is the Comités Locales de Abastecimiento y Producción (Local Supply and Production Committees, or CLAPs), which are linked to the CCs and distribute subsidized food baskets.

What have the CCs and other initiatives meant for widening and deepening citizenship? Some early studies showed that many of them could work as "schools of citizenship"—teaching citizens to organize, run meetings, and make collective decisions—and were relatively politically pluralistic (Hawkins et al. 2008; Machado 2008, 2009). They also suggested that the CCs served to include and empower previously excluded groups, particularly women and people living in poverty (Hawkins 2010; Lalander 2016). While some observers continue to see "subaltern self-empowerment," social transformation, autonomy, and "highly efficient management of resources and projects" in the CCs as they build twenty-first-century socialist communities (e.g., Azzellini 2016, 269), many observers now conclude that problems initially identified in the CCs have become worse, and infect the CLAPs as well (e.g., García-Guadilla 2017).[3] Several scholars, even some sympathetic to the idea of participatory democracy, recognize that most CCs suffer from clientelism, corruption, inefficiency, lack of transparency, co-optation and subordination of previously autonomous social movements, exclusion of those not aligned with the ruling party, and even reinforcement of gendered inequality (García-Guadilla 2018; Goldfrank 2011; Rhodes-Purdy 2015; Wilde 2017). Furthermore, governing party politicians have repeatedly attempted to use the CCs in electoral campaigns, and the government itself has even placed voting polls within CC headquarters (Briceño 2014). Using the CCs electorally clearly hinders inclusionary citizenship. More generally, the overlapping roles of the CCs means that they mix society, the ruling political party, and the state in a way that is damaging for democracy overall by giving the appearance (and likely often the reality) that access to participation in decision making on public goods is conditioned by partisanship.

Comparing Venezuela to Brazil, let us highlight three main differences. First, unlike in Brazil, the main participatory initiatives in Venezuela are meant to supplant rather than complement representative institutions; while CCs received extensive funding, local and provincial governments were starved of resources and responsibilities (Balderacchi 2015, 8; Eaton 2013, 433–35). Second, the focus in Venezuela is territorial and local rather than sectoral and national as in Brazil. After Venezuela's Constituent Assembly of 1999, in which autonomous social organizations participated actively through various forums and succeeded in attaining incorporation of more than half of their 624 sectoral proposals in the constitution (García-Guadilla 2003, 186), opportunities for sector-based and nonelectoral national-level participation diminished as the CCs became the primary participatory vehicles and provincial- and national-level councils never materialized. The one major exception is the referendum of 2007, in which Chávez asked citizens to approve dozens of constitutional changes; when the majority rejected those changes, many of the same reforms were made through Congress anyway (Welp 2015, 11). Third, a considerably larger percentage of the Venezuelan population was involved in participatory initiatives than was true in Brazil, even in the state of Rio Grande do Sul (table 5.1).

TABLE 5.1. Number of Participants, Selected Countries, and Mechanisms

Brazil Public Policy Conferences	~7 million participants total 2003–11 ~5% of the adult population
Brazil Participatory Budgeting	~2011 ~3% of the adult population
Rio Grande do Sul State-Level Participatory Budgeting	~1.1 million participants annually, 2011–14 ~15% of the adult population
Venezuela Communal Councils	~6–8 million participants annually, 2007–12 ~29%–36% of the adult population

Sources: For Brazil, see Pogrebinschi and Samuels 2014; Avritzer 2012; for Rio Grande do Sul, see Goldfrank 2014; for Venezuela, see Canache 2014; Hawkins 2008; Briceño 2014.

Uruguay

The national governments of the Frente Amplio (Broad Front, FA), in power since 2005, are also known for their participatory institutions. Some of these are similar to those in Brazil, including the neocorporatist National Economic Council and national policy conferences called dialogues. It might be said that there was less creativity in the Uruguayan case and more recovery of prior participatory practices, such as the continued use of referendums and the reinstallation of salary councils. The salary councils have been perhaps the most studied and best evaluated "innovation." They are not so innovative in the sense that they had existed in the past, but there is some novelty to them in that they were extended to include rural workers as well as domestic service workers. According to two exemplary studies, the salary councils had significant effects, leading to increases in real wages and to more stable and more legitimate labor mediation (Chasquetti 2007; Pucci, Nión, and Ciapessoni 2014). What is indeed new in Uruguay is the establishment of a municipal level of government following the Decentralization and Citizen Participation Law of 2010 (previously, Uruguay only had two levels of government, national and provincial). This law, which created new representative institutions, was promoted as a way to redistribute power to citizens. Though nearly three quarters of the newly elected mayors decided to implement some type of local-level participatory institutions, such as public audiences and thematic committees, their significance is limited, in part because they have neither the resources nor the substantive responsibilities to carry out important tasks (Freigedo 2015, 18, 111–16). In a country of just three million inhabitants, moreover, the FA government has not attempted to launch a national participatory budgeting process, though it has continued to use it in Montevideo and has introduced it in a few other departments.

Bolivia

Participatory institutions under Evo Morales differ from those of other countries within the Left turn. Like in Ecuador and Venezuela, considerable civil society participation in constitution making occurred early on, the constitution granted citizens new rights and broad roles in public policy making at all levels, and citizens did participate in referendums. In Bolivia alone, however, at the local level, Indigenous communities were granted authority to create their own mechanisms of self-governance distinct from other communities (Haber 2016, 38–40). At the same time, a key participatory institution that existed previously in all municipalities—the monitoring committees (*comités de vigilancia*)—was abolished (Zuazo 2017, 100). Other participatory institutions mentioned in the constitution have not been implemented, including the ostensibly most important one—the National Mechanism for Participation and Social Control (Zuazo 2017, 108). Members of social movements aligned with the ruling party have played a role in the public policy process through meetings of their members at all levels of government and with Morales himself, first through the Unity Pact and later through the CONALCAM (National Coordinator for Change). Scholars of participation in Bolivia emphasize these informal alliances between the ruling party and social movements, with some stressing movement autonomy, others their subordination to Morales and eventual dissolution (Balderacchi 2015; De la Torre 2013; Zuazo 2017). Most important, unlike in the other cases, these informal alliances were separate from the state and closed to most citizens.

Ecuador

Despite Rafael Correa explicitly calling for a "citizens' revolution," after the participatory process for the constitution in 2008, participatory institutions under his administrations were scarce. Many of the local-level institutions endorsed in the constitution have not been promoted, like participatory budgeting, or, like the *silla vacía* (empty chair), which gives a representative of civil society the right to participate in municipal council decisions, are used sporadically in certain municipalities and lack effectiveness (Welp 2015, 8). At the national level, the main "participatory" institution is the Council of Citizen Participation and Social Control, yet it consists of a small group of professionals selected by means of a competition that includes a written exam and mostly serves to appoint the members of other state institutions such as the National Electoral Council (Balderacchi 2015, 12). As De la Torre (2013, 36) writes, "Participation under Correa is mainly reduced to voting in elections." Correa implemented neither formal participatory institutions like those in Brazil and Venezuela, nor neocorporatist institutions like those in Brazil and Uruguay, nor informal alliances with social movements for policy making like those in Bolivia.

EXPLAINING VARIATIONS AND LIMITATIONS

This panoramic view of only the most well known initiatives shows that the progress of participatory democracy is varied but limited overall. With no government creating new participatory institutions that are simultaneously broad-based, inclusive, transparent, deliberative, and influential over important decisions regarding public policy or spending, advances in citizenship through these mechanisms have been restricted. The limitations emerged even before the drop in primary commodity prices and corresponding economic difficulties in the region, and thus the reasons for the Left turn's failure to advance further with participatory institutions must lie elsewhere. This section offers four reasons for both variation and limitations: the intrinsic complications of designing participatory institutions, the varying ideological inclinations and constituencies of leftist leaders, the different constitutional and party system contexts, and the unwavering commitment to a neoextractivist development model.

Innate Problems of Participation

Participatory democrats holding elected office face the fundamental problem that designing ideal institutions is difficult if not insurmountable. This is especially the case in societies with several types of profound inequalities and many diverse identities, in societies that are full of individuals with little free time, and at a time when governments confront complex, divisive questions. For any participatory democrat, similar challenges always emerge regarding how to convince busy people to participate, how to ensure that the inequalities in society are not reproduced within the participatory mechanisms, how to guarantee high-quality deliberation, how to include political rivals without letting them sabotage the process, and how to combine new participatory institutions with existing representative institutions and the state. At the same time, participatory democrats continue to debate whether or not participation should be open to individuals or designated for civil society organizations or social movements; whether participation should be face-to-face or internet facilitated; whether it should be based on issues, geography, or identity; and whether decisions reached should be binding, if those decisions should be reached by consensus or by vote, and, if the latter, whether the voters should include only those who participated in the deliberation or the citizenry in general. There are no simple recipes or obvious answers for all these questions, and left parties answered them differently in different countries.

The ruling parties, furthermore, have a relatively short term before the next elections to try to respond at the same time that they struggle with a variety of urgent political problems. Participatory processes—and especially more deliberative ones—necessarily take time. They also require skilled facilitators with experience, patience, and a willingness to listen to, tolerate, and respect opposing opinions. Facilitators with such gifts are not particularly numerous within political parties regardless of their ideology, and finding a sufficient number of talented facilitators is difficult, especially if one wants to scale up participatory institutions to higher levels of government. Unlike representative institutions, which have long histories with clear models (regular elections, legislatures) and choices (majoritarian vs. proportional, presidential vs. parliamentary), participatory institutions are incredibly varied, and the few viable historical precedents, like New England's town hall meetings, do not offer blueprints for scaling up. Indeed, scaling up local-level participatory institutions, especially to the national level, opens another set of challenges, including those listed by Mainwaring (2012) together with a key challenge he misses: the reaction of those holding power in representative institutions. Without a clear model, left leaders experimented with different participatory institutions according to their ideological proclivities and constituent pressures as well as strategic concerns stemming from the political and economic context.

The Left's Ideological Preferences and Social Bases

While all the Left turn leaders included promises of enhanced citizen participation in their electoral campaigns, only for some were these promises historically grounded and held by significant swaths of their political parties and social constituencies. Historical ideological commitment to participatory democracy was weakest with the Kirchners in Argentina, the Partido Socialista (Socialist Party, PSCh) in Chile (at least in the 1990s), and Correa's personal political vehicle, PAIS Alliance, in Ecuador. It was strongest with the PT in Brazil and the FA in Uruguay, which had both implemented participatory experiments at the local level for over a dozen years prior to winning national power and had ties to social movements espousing participatory ideals. Some of the political parties allied with Hugo Chávez in Venezuela also historically had advocated and practiced participatory democracy (García-Guadilla 2003; Goldfrank 2011), though Chávez was obviously best known for attempting a military coup d'état. In Bolivia, the historical focus of Morales and his Movimiento al Socialismo (Movement Toward Socialism, MAS) was on Indigenous rights to communal democracy and autonomy.

These basic ideological commitment differences match up fairly well with the different degrees of effort leftist parties exerted toward establishing new participatory institutions but do not explain the different types of institutions they developed, which are linked at least in part to their social bases. The emphasis on neocorporatist participatory mechanisms in Brazil and Uruguay, for example, stems from the strong trade union and partial business sector support for the PT and the FA, which were both absent for Chávez in Venezuela (Goldfrank 2011). Similarly, the stress on local Indigenous self-governance and informal alliances with social movements in Bolivia is clearly linked to the history of the MAS, while Correa's lack of ties to Indigenous movements and to unions helps explain the dearth of the kinds of participatory institutions that allow collective actors to mobilize in Ecuador. The solitary "empty chair" mechanism is the alternative. As Becker observes, Correa "emerged out of a liberal framework that emphasized individual rights" and called for a "citizens' revolution[,] . . . not one built by social movements" (2011, 48).

Political Opportunities and Constraints

Not only did Left turn leaders vary in their commitment to participatory democracy and their social bases. They governed in strikingly different political systems that allowed for more or less experimentation. It is by now commonplace to point out that Chávez, Correa, and Morales came to power amidst the collapse of party systems as leaders of new political parties, while Lula and Rousseff, Vázquez and Mujica, Lagos and Bachelet, and the Kirchners were elected as leaders of established parties (PT, FA, PSCh, and the Partido Justicialista [PJ], respectively) within relatively institutionalized party systems. The former leaders took advantage of popular support to rewrite constitutions that enshrined new rights and participatory mechanisms; the latter were constrained in their participatory institution building both by the existing constitutions and by the strength of rival political parties threatened by new participatory institutions. That the FA and particularly the PT experimented more with participatory institution building than did the PSCh and PJ reflects both the ideological inclinations of the different parties and the fact that the existing Uruguayan and especially Brazilian constitutions already included or allowed participatory mechanisms, such as referendums in Uruguay and policy councils in Brazil.

The FA and especially the PT and the PSCh were also constrained by the alliances they needed with centrist political parties in order to gain power. While Bachelet's PSCh remained hamstrung throughout both her terms, the FA and the PT attempted to navigate their political alliances by reintroducing or expanding existing participatory mechanisms or accommodating their coalition partners. The FA's participatory efforts, for example, renewed older forms that other parties had used in the past, such as the salary councils, or were explicitly designed to include representatives from multiple political parties, such as the creation of municipal governments, which required official elections for new city councilors and mayors. And when Lula's coalition became fragile in 2005, he replaced his copartisan, Olívio Dutra, with a right-wing cabinet minister, effectively ending the most advanced participatory institution of his term, which Dutra had led as minister of cities (Goldfrank 2011, 171–74). More recently, in 2014, Rousseff failed to convince her coalition partners to even hold a vote when she submitted a decree to institute a National System of Social Participation that would regulate the relationship between the public policy conferences and policy councils and the government. According to opposition legislators and a good part of the press (especially the major weekly, *Veja*), Rousseff's "Bolivarian" decree aimed at creating "soviets" and posed a threat to representative democracy. In his attack on the decree, one journalist perfectly summed up a common idea among the left's opponents: "The leftists always sneakily speak about 'bettering democracy' in order to avoid saying 'implanting socialism or communism'" (Dias Viana 2014).

Neoextractivism

The most striking failure of the Left turn governments is their unwillingness to adopt effective participatory mechanisms for addressing the nexus between the environment and economic development, and particularly the use of natural resources for energy and export. Even where commitment to participatory democracy was supposedly strong, where Indigenous groups gained new rights to participation, where opposition from rival parties was weak, and where clear models existed—such as free, prior, informed consent—leftist leaders consistently ignored or overruled citizen participants (see chapters by Rice and by Bratman, this volume). The strongest limitation on participatory democracy is the left's continued reliance on the so-called neoextractivist development model. Neoextractivism entails a strong state role in resource extraction and the use of the resulting rents to fund social spending; it was crucial to the left governments' ability to stoke economic growth, employment, and decreases in poverty during the recent primary commodity price boom and thus maintain popularity (Haber 2016; Siegel 2016). However, neoextractivism has produced opposition as well because it reinforces dependence on primary products and, most importantly, damages the environment.

Despite pronouncements in favor of combating climate change and protecting nature, Left turn leaders across the spectrum routinely prioritize potentially harmful development projects, even over citizen objections. Well-known examples of Left turn leaders ignoring local citizen preferences regarding environmentally destructive development projects include Correa allowing oil wells in the Ishpingo-Tambococha-Tiputini (ITT) section of Yasuní National Park; the decision by Lula and Rousseff to proceed with the Belo Monte hydroelectric dam (see Bratman, this volume); and Morales's insistence on building a highway through the Territorio Indígena y Parque Nacional Isiboro Sécure (Indigenous Territory and Isiboro Sécure National Park, TIPNIS) after initially conceding in the face of massive protests. Less recognized is Maduro's decree in 2016 that allows mining for gold and other precious metals and minerals in a strategic development zone around the Orinoco River of over 112,000 square kilometers, or 12 percent of Venezuelan territory (Lander 2016, 14). According to Lander, this decree will cause "irreversible social and environmental destruction of a large area of the country and the ethnocide of the indigenous peoples who live there. . . . All this will happen as a result of a decision taken by the president, with no public debate whatsoever in a country whose constitution defines society as 'democratic, participatory[,] . . . multiethnic and pluricultural', and with none of the environmental impact studies required by law" (2016, 14). Moreover, the decree not only violates constitutionally—and internationally—recognized Indigenous rights to informed prior consent, it overtly suspends civil and political rights within this "Arco Minero del Orinoco"—effectively outlawing protest (2016, 15–17).

The broad overview of the Left turn's experiments with participatory institutions offered here is consistent with the volume editors' argument, as it suggests that while advances in the quality of citizenship occurred, they were limited to certain groups at certain times and certain places rather than generalized. A significant opportunity to transform citizenship through building robust participatory institutions has been lost. In Argentina and Chile, left-leaning presidents never committed to participatory democracy. For Brazil, local-level participatory budgeting gradually lost importance in the PT, while the national public policy conferences had limited effectiveness and reach, and the subsequent president, Michel Temer, after helping to oust Rousseff in 2016, implemented austerity measures that rendered the few remaining national councils and public policy conferences meaningless. Participatory initiatives in Uruguay remain in place for now. In Bolivia and Ecuador, participatory mechanisms listed in the constitutions were barely implemented if at all. And in Venezuela, participatory institutions have devolved into clientelism and important rights have now been revoked in parts of the country.

In sum, the left has bequeathed a rather dim future for participatory institutions in the region. With promises of expanding citizen participation unmet or distorted, trust in both Left turn leaders and in participatory institutions is likely to continue to erode. As rival political parties on the right begin winning elections, as in Argentina and Chile, or removing the left from office, as in Brazil and possibly Venezuela, they are unlikely to expand or upgrade existing participatory institutions or to develop new ones. One of the left's legacies in Latin America is that discourse around participatory democracy appears now more than ever as empty rhetoric or as threatening to representative democracy. Ultimately, there is no doubt that contemporary polities continue to suffer from exclusion, inequality, and the overwhelming power of economic elites. For the most part, the left's efforts to combat these maladies in Latin America through participatory institutions have failed.

NOTES

1. This chapter draws from Goldfrank 2015, which presented a somewhat more optimistic perspective.

2. Avritzer (2012, 7–8), using a broader definition, counts 115 national conferences in total up until 2011, with 74 held during the Lula da Silva government.

3. The CLAPs have their own website (www.clapsoficial.com.ve) and a magazine, titled *Todo el Poder para los CLAP* (All Power to the CLAPs), and President Maduro is on the editorial board.

REFERENCES

Agencia Venezolana de Noticias (AVN). 2015. "46.000 consejos comunales convocados a postular jueces de paz." www.avn.info.ve/contenido/46000 -consejos-comunales-convocados-postular-jueces-paz.

Avritzer, Leonardo. 2012. "Conferências nacionais: Ampliando e redefinindo os padrões de participação social no Brasil." IPEA Texto para Discussão 1739, Rio de Janeiro.

Azzellini, Dario. 2016. *Communes and Workers' Control in Venezuela*. Leiden: Brill.

Balderacchi, Claudio. 2015. "Participatory Mechanisms in Bolivia, Ecuador and Venezuela: Deepening or Undermining Democracy?" *Government and Opposition* 52 (1): 131–61.

Becker, Marc. 2011. *Pachakutik: Indigenous Movements and Electoral Politics in Ecuador*. Lanham, MD: Rowman & Littlefield.

Briceño, Héctor. 2014. "Los consejos comunales y la democracia participativa en Venezuela." In A. Sakaguchi, ed., *Venezuela under Chavez's Administration*. Tokyo: IDE.

Cameron, Maxwell A., and Eric Hershberg. 2010. *Latin America's Left Turns: Politics, Policies, and Trajectories of Change*. Boulder, CO: Lynne Rienner.

Cameron, Maxwell A., and Kenneth E. Sharpe. 2012. "Institutionalized Voice in Latin American Democracies." In Maxwell A. Cameron, Eric Hershberg, and Kenneth E. Sharpe, eds., *New Institutions for Participatory Democracy in Latin America: Voice and Consequence*. New York: Palgrave Macmillan.

Canache, Damarys. 2014. "Political Trust and Polarization in the Post-Chavista Venezuela." LACC Working Paper, No. 1. Latin American and Caribbean Center, Florida International University, Miami.

Chasquetti, Daniel. 2007. "Uruguay 2006: Éxitos y dilemas del gobierno de izquierda." *Revista de Ciencia Política (Santiago)* 27 (Esp): 249–63.

Costa, Danielle Martins Duarte. 2010. "Vinte anos de orçamento participativo: Análise das experiências em municípios brasileiros." *Cadernos Gestão Pública e Cidadania* 15 (56): 8–28.

Cunha, Eleonora Schettini. 2012. "Conferências de políticas públicas e inclusão participativa." IPEA Texto para Discussão 1733, Rio de Janeiro.

Dagnino, Evelina. 2016. "State-Society Relations and the Dilemmas of the New Developmentalist State." *IDS Bulletin* 47 (2A): 157–67.

Dagnino, Evelina, and Ana Claudia Chaves Teixeira. 2014. "The Participation of Civil Society in Lula's Government." *Journal of Politics in Latin America* 6 (3): 39–66.

De la Torre, Carlos. 2013. "In the Name of the People: Democratization, Popular Organizations, and Populism in Venezuela, Bolivia, and Ecuador." *European Review of Latin American and Caribbean Studies* 95 (October 2013): 27.

De Sousa Santos, Boaventura. 2014. "O Brasil na hora das decisões." *Le Monde Diplomatique Brasil*. www.diplomatique.org.br/artigo.php?id=1715.

Dias Viana, Helio. 2014. "O Decreto 8243 e a sovietização do Brasil." *Epoch Times*. www.epochtimes.com.br/decreto-8243-sovietizacao-brasil/#.VOp4P3vR-ws.

Eaton, Kent. 2013. "The Centralism of 'Twenty-First-Century Socialism': Recentralising Politics in Venezuela, Ecuador and Bolivia." *Journal of Latin American Studies* 45 (03): 421–50.

Freigedo, Martín. 2015. "¿Por qué unos más y otros menos? Los incentivos para crear mecanismos de innovación democrática en los municipios uruguayos." PhD dissertation, FLACSO, Mexico City.

Fung, Archon. 2011. "Reinventing Democracy in Latin America." *Perspectives on Politics* 9 (4): 857–71.

García-Guadilla, María Pilar. 2003. "Civil Society: Institutionalization, Fragmentation, Autonomy." In Steve Ellner and D. Hellinger, eds., *Venezuelan Politics in the Chávez Era*. Boulder, CO: Lynne Rienner.

———. 2017. "El socialismo petrolero venezolano en la encrucijada por su supervivencia: El soberano unívoco, la inclusión neoliberal y la participación leninista." *LASA Forum* 48 (1): 43–47.

———. 2018. "Exclusionary Inclusion: Post-Neoliberal Incorporation of Popular Sectors and Social Movements in New Left 21st Century Socialism: The Experience of Venezuela." In Eduardo Silva and Federico M. Rossi, eds., *Reshaping the Political Arena in Latin America: From Resisting Neoliberalism to the Second Incorporation*. Pittsburgh, PA: University of Pittsburgh Press.

Gargarella, Roberto. 2014. "The Left That Is Not: On the Concept of 'Left' in *The Resurgence of the American Left*." *Política y Gobierno* 21 (2): 443–77.

Goldfrank, Benjamin. 2011. "The Left and Participatory Democracy: Brazil, Uruguay and Venezuela." In Steven Levitsky and Kenneth M. Roberts, eds., *The Resurgence of the Latin American Left*. Baltimore, MD: Johns Hopkins University Press.

———. 2012. "The World Bank and the Globalization of Participatory Budgeting." *Journal of Public Deliberation* 8 (2). 18 pp.

———. 2013. "Participatory Budgeting and Urban Sustainability: Reviewing Lessons from Latin America." In Harald A. Mieg and Klaus Töpfer, eds., *Institutional and Social Innovation for Sustainable Urban Development*. New York: Routledge.

———. 2014. "Participation, Distribution, and the Left: The Return of PB in Rio Grande do Sul." Paper presented at the conference "A New Critical Juncture? Changing Patterns of Representation and Regime Politics in Contemporary Latin America," Kellogg Institute, University of Notre Dame, April 24–26.

————. 2015. "Democracia participativa e izquierdas: Logros, contradic-
ciones y desafíos." In Anja Minnaert and Gustavo Endara, eds., *Democracia participativa e izquierdas: Logros, contradiccione, y desafíos*. Quito:
Friedrich-Ebert-Stiftung.

Goldfrank, Benjamin, and Aaron Schneider. 2006. "Competitive Institution
Building: The PT and Participatory Budgeting in Rio Grande do Sul."
Latin American Politics and Society 48 (3): 1–31.

Gonçalves, Sónia. 2014. "The Effects of Participatory Budgeting on Municipal
Expenditures and Infant Mortality in Brazil." *World Development* 53 (1):
94–110.

Haber, Paul. 2016. "Pink Tide Governments, Radical Social Movements and
the Practice of Citizenship in the Twenty-First Century Latin America."
In Inbal Ofer and Tamar Groves, eds., *Performing Citizenship: Social
Movements across the Globe*. New York: Routledge.

Hawkins, Kirk A. 2010. "Who Mobilizes? Participatory Democracy in
Chávez's Bolivarian Revolution." *Latin American Politics and Society* 52
(3): 31–66.

Hawkins, Kirk, Adam Anguiano, Jane Ann Patch, and Mitchell Seligson.
2008. *Political Culture of Democracy in Venezuela: 2007*. Nashville, TN:
Vanderbilt University.

Katz, Claudio. 2013. "Socialist Strategies in Latin America." In Jeffery R.
Webber and Barry Carr, eds., *The New Latin American Left: Cracks in the
Empire*. Lanham, MD: Rowman & Littlefield.

Lalander, Rickard. 2016. "Gendering Popular Participation: Identity-Politics
and Radical Democracy in Bolivarian Venezuela." In H. Kettunen and
A. Korpisaari, eds., *Multidisciplinary Latin American Studies: Festschrift in
Honor of Martti Pärssinen*. Helsinki: University of Helsinki.

Lander, Edgardo. 2016. *The Implosion of Venezuela's Rentier State*. Amsterdam:
Transnational Institute's Public Alternatives Project. www.tni.org.

Machado, Decio, and Raúl Zibechi. 2016. *Cambiar el mundo desde arriba: Los
límites del progresismo*. La Paz: CEDLA.

Machado, Jesús E. 2008. *Estudio de los consejos comunales en Venezuela*. Caracas:
Fundación Centro Gumilla.

————. 2009. "Participación social y consejos comunales en Venezuela." *Revista Venezolana de Economía y Ciencias Sociales* 15 (1): 173–85.

Mainwaring, Scott. 2012. "From Representative Democracy to Participatory
Competitive Authoritarianism: Hugo Chávez and Venezuelan Politics."
Perspectives on Politics 10 (4): 955–67.

Pogrebinschi, Thamy. 2013. *The Pragmatic Turn of Democracy in Latin America*.
Berlin: Friedrich-Ebert-Stiftung.

Pogrebinschi, Thamy, and David Samuels. 2014. "The Impact of Participatory Democracy: Evidence from Brazil's National Public Policy Conferences." *Comparative Politics* 46 (3): 313–32.

Pogrebinschi, Thamy, and Fabiano Santos. 2013. "Where Participation Matters: The Impact of a National Level Democratic Innovation on Policymaking in Brazil." In A. Römmele and H. Schober, eds., *The Governance of Large-Scale Projects*. Baden-Baden: Nomos Verlagsgesellschaft.

Pucci, Francisco, Soledad Nión, and Fiorella Ciapessoni. 2014. "La negociación colectiva en el primer gobierno de izquierda del Uruguay." *Latin American Research Review* 49 (2): 3–23.

Rhodes-Purdy, Matthew. 2015. "Participatory Populism: Theory and Evidence from Bolivarian Venezuela." *Political Research Quarterly* 68 (3): 415–27.

Sandbrook, Richard. 2014. *Reinventing the Left in the Global South: The Politics of the Possible*. Cambridge: Cambridge University Press.

Siegel, Karen M. 2016. "Fulfilling Promises of More Substantive Democracy? Post-Neoliberalism and Natural Resource Governance in South America." *Development and Change* 47 (3): 495–516.

Silva, Fabricio Pereira da. 2016. "Padrões de participação em governos de esquerda na América Latina: Brasil e Venezuela em perspectiva comparada." *Dados* 59 (3): 651–81.

Spada, Paolo. 2010. "Political Competition and the Diffusion of Policy Innovations in local Government: The Case of Participatory Budgeting in Brazil." Paper presented at the Latin American Studies Association Congress, Toronto, October 6–9.

Touchton, Michael, and Brian Wampler. 2014. "Improving Social Well-Being through New Democratic Institutions." *Comparative Political Studies* 47 (10): 1442–69.

Webber, Jeffery R., and Barry Carr. 2013. "Introduction: The Latin American Left in Theory and Practice." In Jeffery Webber and Barry Carr, eds., *The New Latin American Left: Cracks in the Empire*. Lanham, MD: Rowman & Littlefield.

Welp, Yanina. 2015. "¿Era cuestión de piel? Reflexiones sobre el future de la participación ciudadana en tiempos de cambio." Paper delivered at the Conferencia RedGob, Quito, December 8–9.

Weyland, Kurt, Raúl L. Madrid, and Wendy Hunter. 2010. *Leftist Governments in Latin America: Successes and Shortcomings*. New York: Cambridge University Press.

Wilde, Matt. 2017. "The Communal Councils and Participatory Democracy in Chávez's Venezuela." *Latin American Perspectives* 44 (1): 140–58.

Wilpert, Gregory. 2013. "Venezuela: An Electoral Road to Twenty-First Century Socialism." In Jeffery Webber and Barry Carr, eds., *The New Latin American Left: Cracks in the Empire*. Lanham, MD: Rowman & Littlefield.

Zuazo, Moira. 2017. "Bolivia: 'Social Control' as the Fourth State Power 1994–2015." In G. Zaremberg, V. Guarneros-Mesa, and A. G. Lavalle, eds., *Intermediation and Representation in Latin America*. London: Palgrave Macmillan.

SIX

Indigenous Autonomies under the New Left in the Andes

ROBERTA RICE

Latin America has long suffered from exclusionary state structures. The failures to incorporate, represent, and respond to large segments of the population led to increasing conflicts between state and society during the 1990s. The crisis of deteriorating state-society relations was especially acute in the Andes, where a broadly mobilized Indigenous sector felt increasingly alienated from a monocultural, distant, and repressive state (Burt and Mauceri 2004; Drake and Hershberg 2006; Mainwaring, Bejarano, and Pizarro Leongómez 2006). Throughout the 1990s, mass pressures for socioeconomic and political inclusion by Indigenous and popular sector groups began to pry open spaces in the region's governing structures and redefine citizenship rights. The broad wave of leftist governments that swept Latin America by the end of the 1990s promised to address socioeconomic inequalities and promote democratic participation and inclusion for Indigenous peoples and other marginalized sectors of society. Constitutional reforms in the 1990s sought to repair the relationship between Indigenous peoples and the state by legally recognizing and affirming cultural rights in society as well as the multicultural character of the state (Nolte and Schilling-Vacaflor 2012; Van Cott 2000). The constitutions developed under Left turn regimes in Bolivia (2009) and Ecuador (2008), however, have advanced Indigenous agendas a step further by establishing the plurinational basis of their respective states, thereby formally acknowledging distinct legal and political orders within them. Indigenous autonomies in the central Andes may be a means to transform Indigenous-state relations on the basis of a differentiated citizenship regime.

The central question taken up by this chapter is, are Indigenous-state relations improving in the Andes with Left turn governments in power? More specifically, to what extent has plurinational constitutionalism meant a change in state policy and practice with regard to Indigenous peoples? In light of this question, the study analyzes the changing dynamics of Indigenous-state relations in the exceptional cases of Bolivia and Ecuador based on two historic junctures. Indigenous peoples were first incorporated into the polity in the mid-twentieth century through corporatist measures that imposed a unidirectional or top-down relationship between the state and Indigenous groups. The constitutional recognition of plurinationality in Bolivia and Ecuador represents a second phase of Indigenous incorporation, with the potential to develop a bilateral, or government-to-government relationship between the state and Indigenous peoples. The Bolivian and Ecuadorian cases highlight the left's best efforts at championing Indigenous rights, yet they also reveal the challenges or limits to reconciling postneoliberal democracies with Indigenous peoples' demands and expectations. The analysis shows that while the constitutional reconfiguration of the state along plurinational lines has resulted in a partial break with the previous model of Indigenous-state relations, in practice the Left turn governments in Bolivia and Ecuador continue to operate under a unidirectional logic.

The chapter opens with an overview of the crisis in Indigenous-state relations experienced by the Andean countries in the twentieth century. Attempts to contain and control Indigenous populations through state corporatism and, later, state-sponsored multiculturalism fell short of addressing Indigenous demands. The chapter explores the emergence of autonomous forms of organizing and mobilizing on the part of Indigenous groups that challenged existing models of citizenship, democracy, and the state in Latin America (Walsh 2009; Yashar 2005). Indigenous calls for autonomy strike at the heart of state power. Indigenous autonomy questions the character of the uninational and monocultural state and proposes new structures and institutions that recognize and respect political and cultural diversity. This process demands a refounding of the state and its relationship to society. The chapter then assesses the gap between government rhetoric and reform under the administrations of Evo Morales (2006–) in Bolivia and Rafael Correa (2007–17) in Ecuador, with particular attention to the inherent tension between Indigenous political and territorial autonomy, on the one hand, and heightened state control over land and natural resource management, on the other. The chapter suggests that while the recognition of a plurinational state is an important first step in improving Indigenous-state relations in a country, it is insufficient until such constitutional reforms dramatically alter state practices and priorities.

THE CRISIS OF INDIGENOUS-STATE RELATIONS IN THE ANDES

Indigenous peoples in the central Andes are a marginalized majority (Gustafson 2009). Given that Indigenous demands have been historically oppressed, ignored, and silenced, it is little wonder that the central Andean states are weak and democracy is unconsolidated. National attempts to link this long-excluded segment of the population to the state have generally followed on the heels of major crises. According to Drake and Hershberg (2006), Latin America has faced two such crises in the twentieth century, both precipitated by economic disruptions that upset the existing contract between state and society. The first of the major crises occurred in the 1930s with the Great Depression, the impact of which was felt worldwide, and the second in the 1980s owing to the international debt crisis. In both instances, economic dislocations opened the door to new models of development, growth, distribution, participation, and inclusion in the region. The 1930s crisis led to inward-looking development, redistribution, and import-substitution industrialization (ISI) as a means to decrease Latin America's economic dependency. The state-led development model was accompanied by

TABLE 6.1. Models of Indigenous Incorporation in the Andes, 1960s–2000s

	Timing	*Direction*	*Target*
State corporatism	1960s	Unilateral	Indigenous peasants
Neoliberal multiculturalism	1980s	Unilateral	Indigenous citizens
Plurinational constitutionalism	2000s	Bilateral	State structures and institutions

Source: Compiled by the author.

corporatist measures that offered a modicum of popular inclusion in national life, though according to the terms set out by the state. The 1980s crisis led to free-market reforms as part of the general shift to the neoliberal economic model. The multicultural polices that accompanied the market-led development model privileged policies of recognition over those of redistribution as a means of managing difference (Hale 2002). Although state-sponsored corporatism and neoliberal multiculturalism proposed distinct models of state-society relations, both targeted Indigenous peoples as the problem in need of change (table 6.1).

Latin American states promoted assimilation into the dominant mestizo (mixed-race) culture by reconstituting Indigenous peoples as national peasants as part of the corporatist project of the mid-twentieth century. State corporatism served as an important means for the state to structure group representation and regulate official channels for demand making (Collier 1995). It was through agrarian reform that the rural masses in Latin America were first incorporated into the polity. Land reforms were billed as progressive measures to emancipate Indigenous communities from repressive and exploitative forms of labor control in the countryside. Throughout much of Latin American history, the Indigenous peasantry was largely under the social control of the rural elite and remained beyond the reach of urban politics. However, by the 1960s and 1970s, as a result of dramatic social mobilizations and the proliferation of leftist alternatives in the region, the peasantry had begun to emerge as a powerful new political force and one that had few ties to the state or political parties. In return for access to land, credit, and services from the state, Indigenous peoples were obliged to organize and define themselves as peasants. While Indigenous peoples assumed peasant status before the state, they continued to express their Indigenous identity within their communities (Yashar 2005).

One of the immediate consequences of the adoption of the neoliberal economic model in the 1980s was the weakening of state corporatist institutions (Oxhorn 1998). Neoliberal discourse advocates the shift from corporatist, class-based integration to more atomized or individuated state-society relations. As the corporate organizations of the peasantry lost their social and political standing, the primary mode of interest intermediation between the state and Indigenous communities was severed. In response to this changing economic and political context, Indigenous groups in Latin America increasingly mobilized on the basis of their ethnic identities (Rice 2012). A pressing concern for governing elites during this second crisis of state-society relations was how to deal with popular sector actors that were never fully incorporated into the system (Drake and Hershberg 2006, 9). Neoliberal multiculturalism became the preferred policy option to address Indigenous demands for citizenship throughout the 1980s and 1990s. "Neoliberal multiculturalism" refers to state-sponsored constitutional and legislative efforts to accept and embrace ethnic differences and the free-market philosophies that underpin them (Postero 2007; Van Cott 2000). Hale (2002) has suggested that policies of neoliberal multiculturalism in Latin America purposively promoted a limited set of cultural and political rights for Indigenous peoples as a means of defusing more radical demands for economic redistribution. Much like state corporatism of the previous era, neoliberal multiculturalism did not sufficiently address Indigenous demands for autonomy. In the cases of Bolivia and Ecuador, organized and mobilized Indigenous groups were able to take advantage of these initial institutional openings to foster greater reform.

Latin America's postcorporatist period has witnessed the emergence of new social actors, promoting new types of claims and demands. In the Andean region, the second phase or wave of incorporation is attached to the rise of Indigenous actors. According to Rossi, "The 'second wave of incorporation' means the second major redefinition of the sociopolitical arena ... caused by the broad and selective inclusion of the popular sectors in the polity after being excluded or disincorporated by military authoritarian regimes and democratic neoliberal reforms"

(2015, 2). Contemporary Indigenous rights struggles represent an opportunity to address the Indigenous question in much the same way that worker organization and labor protests in early twentieth-century Latin America prompted ruling elites to respond to the social question (Collier and Collier 1991). The "Indigenous question" refers to the debate over the special rights that Indigenous peoples should be granted as citizens of democratic nation-states (Postero and Zamosc 2004, 5). As Oxhorn (2011) notes, struggles over citizenship have profound consequences for state-society relations. The model of citizenship underpinning the first period of Indigenous incorporation via state corporatism, as well as subsequent efforts at state-sponsored multiculturalism, was based on "citizenship as co-optation." Whereas citizenship as co-optation serves to curb popular sector pressures for structural change and inclusion, "citizenship as agency" involves the active participation of disadvantaged groups in the social construction of citizenship (Oxhorn 2011, 30).

The plurinational constitutionalism of the 2000s represents a second, more meaningful chance at Indigenous incorporation, one predicated on a model of citizenship as agency. "Plurinational constitutionalism" refers to constitutional reform or replacement in an attempt to change the balance of power and transform the political system to advance Indigenous and popular sector interests by including new institutions, elements of direct and participatory democracy, new citizenship rights, and new conceptualizations of the state (Schilling-Vacaflor and Kuppe 2012). In contrast to state corporatism and neoliberal multiculturalism, plurinational constitutionalism focuses on transforming the state to better serve and reflect the interests of Indigenous peoples. The new constitutional texts of Ecuador (República del Ecuador 2008) and Bolivia (Estado Plurinacional de Bolivia 2009), which were heavily influenced by the United Nations Declaration on the Rights of the Indigenous Peoples (UNDRIP) (2007), exemplify this approach. Without question, this historic accomplishment has been the result of the independent organizing and mobilizing efforts of Indigenous movements in the two countries and their capacity to represent their own interests in the public sphere in the negotiations that define the boundaries of citizenship (discussed below). Plurinational constitutionalism challenges previous governmental attempts to divide Indigenous peoples, to categorize them in ways that obscure their ethnicity, to discount them from national policy debates, and to denigrate them as obstacles to development. A plurinational state recognizes the plurality of cultural, legal, and political systems that exist within a territory and places them on an equal footing (Becker 2011; Walsh 2009). It seeks to end the unidirectional system of domination and replace it with relations of mutual respect and consideration.

Repairing and rebuilding Indigenous-state relations on a more just and equal footing requires recognition and respect for the Indigenous right to autonomy. The demand for autonomy centers on the call for greater self-determination and self-government within Indigenous territories (Aparicio Wilhelmi 2007; UNGA 2007). However, autonomy is more than just another demand. It is the foundational claim of Indigenous peoples. Autonomy is "the demand that allows for the realization of all other demands" (Díaz Polanco 1998, 218). According to Article 5 of the UNDRIP, "Indigenous peoples have the right to maintain and strengthen their distinct political, legal, economic, social and cultural institutions, while retaining their right to participate fully, if they so choose, in the political, economic, social and cultural life of the State" (UNGA 2007, 5). The practice of Indigenous autonomy means redefining the boundaries and scope of citizenship to incorporate Indigenous peoples as equal, yet different citizens. Stated differently, Indigenous peoples can only enjoy full citizenship status through a differentiated citizenship regime (Montambeault, Balán, and Oxhorn, this volume). In sum, plurinational constitutionalism has the potential to reset Indigenous-state relations in Latin America.

SHIFTING INDIGENOUS-STATE RELATIONS IN BOLIVIA

In Bolivia, Evo Morales of the Indigenous and popular-backed Movimiento al Socialismo (Movement Toward Socialism, MAS) party made history on January 22, 2006, when he became the country's first Indigenous head of state and joined the ranks of Latin America's Left turn governments.[1] The national rise of the MAS took place in the context of a severe crisis of democratic representation. The victorious water war of Cochabamba in 2000 against the privatization of that city's water supply marked the first in a series of massive civic uprisings that led to a rupture in the national political system and the dissolution of the neoliberal consensus (Arce and Rice 2009; Crabtree 2005; Dangl 2007; Kohl and Farthing 2006). The period of social mobilization reached its peak with the gas war in the capital city of La Paz in October 2003 that led to the ouster of President Sánchez de Lozada, an architect of neoliberalism in Bolivia. A sense of marginalization and frustration over failed neoliberal economic policies and a political system that produced strong barriers to genuine participation contributed to the resurgence of protest politics in the country and the search for an alternative political and economic project (Bonifaz 2004; Suárez 2003). The crisis highlighted the complete disconnect between the state and society and ultimately opened the door to the presidential election of Morales. As Levitsky and Roberts (2011, 408) note, not only was Morales a political outsider, but he was also a regime outsider who won on a pledge to abolish the established political order and refound the country along more inclusive, participatory lines.

In the bid to promote a more inclusive polity, Morales made Indigenous rights the cornerstone of his administration. The newly drafted 2009 Constitution is central to this agenda. According to the constitution's preamble, Bolivia has left behind the colonial, republican, and neoliberal state of the past.[2] In its place is a plurinational state that rests on Indigenous autonomy. The new constitution goes further than any previous legislation in the country, indeed in Latin America, in securing representation and participation for the nation's Indigenous peoples, including, for example, the recognition of all thirty-six Indigenous languages of Bolivia as official languages of the state (art. 5) and the guaranteed right to proportional representation of Indigenous peoples in the national legislature (art. 147). The constitution explicitly identifies a new political subject: First Peoples Indigenous Peasants (Estado Plurinacional de Bolivia 2009). This hybrid term is inclusive of the first peoples of the highland plateau, the Indigenous peasants of the highland valley region, and the Indigenous peoples of the Bolivian lowlands. Canessa (2012) has suggested that the country is witnessing a new form of Indigenous citizenship, one in which the model citizen in Bolivia today is an Indigenous person. This differentiated citizenship regime moves beyond the circumscribed notion of citizenship for Indigenous peoples as part of the neoliberal multicultural policies of the 1990s to promote the Indigenous demand for autonomy. The constitution also redefined

Bolivian democracy as "intercultural." An intercultural democracy is a new form of democracy that is direct and participatory, representative, and communitarian. Some of the new mechanisms for direct citizen participation include recall referendums, town councils, citizen-led legislative initiatives, and the legal-political recognition of citizens' associations and Indigenous groups to contest elections (Exeni Rodríguez 2012).

The Morales administration has committed itself to deepening the decentralization process that began in the mid-1990s as part of a package of neoliberal multicultural policies designed to draw in excluded sectors of society. The 1994 Law of Popular Participation (LPP) created over three hundred municipal governments with widespread administrative powers, direct citizen oversight, and dedicated resources as a means to bring government closer to increasingly mobilized rural and Indigenous communities (Arce and Rice 2009; Postero 2007). The reforms opened the door to the electoral participation of a new generation of Indigenous leaders, including Evo Morales. Now that the MAS is the governing party, it has instituted additional reforms that grant a substantial degree of autonomy to departmental, regional, municipal, and Indigenous governments (Centellas 2010; Faguet 2014). The 2010 Framework Law of Autonomy and Decentralization regulates the new territorial organization of the state as defined in the 2009 Constitution. In addition to the recognition of the three hierarchical levels of government in Bolivia (i.e., departmental, regional, and municipal), the constitution also identifies Indigenous autonomies as a separate and distinct order of government, one that is not directly subordinate to the other levels (CIPCA 2009). Under current provisions, existing Indigenous territories as well as municipalities and regions with a substantial Indigenous presence may convert themselves into self-governing entities based on cultural norms, customs, institutions, and authorities in keeping with the rights and guarantees in the new constitution (Faguet 2014, 6). Bolivia's experiment with Indigenous autonomies aims to improve citizen engagement and government responsiveness, and ultimately to make democracy more meaningful for Indigenous citizens.

Bolivia's 2009 Constitution (alongside Ecuador's 2008 Constitution) makes an explicit commitment to the rights of nature and to the Andean Indigenous principle of Living Well (*buen vivir/vivir bien* in Spanish; *sumac kawsay* in Quechua; *suma qamaña* in Aymara) as an

TABLE 6.2. Bolivia's National Development Priorities, 2016–2020

Stated Priority	Word Count
Development	401
Living Well	91
Economy	81
Natural resources	69
Human rights	68
Environment	18
Autonomy	10

Source: Ministerio de Planificación del Desarrollo 2016.

alternative model of development around which the state and its policies are now organized (Bretón, Cortez, and García 2014; Vega Ugalde 2014). An examination of Bolivia's National Development Plan (2016–20) reveals the gap between the government's official discourse on Living Well, for instance, and its conventional strategy for economic development on the basis of natural resource wealth. The term "development" appears four times more frequently in the government's planning document than does the term "Living Well" and forty times more frequently than the reference to Indigenous autonomy (table 6.2). The Living Well principle is based on the values of harmony, consensus, and respect, the redistribution of wealth, and the elimination of discrimination all within a framework that values diversity, community, and the environment (Fisher and Fasol 2013). It represents an alternative to Western conceptualizations of development based on higher material standards of living. The concept of Living Well plays an important role in building consensus among Indigenous and environmental activists, as well as the broader public, for the government's agenda for change. The National Development Plan utilizes Bolivia's inferior position in the global economy as well as the capture of the state by elites to justify the government's incursion into Indigenous territories to extract natural resource wealth in order to achieve the long-term goal of Living Well for all citizens (Ministerio de Planificación del Desarrollo 2016, 1).

The governance innovations of the MAS have brought about important changes to the structure of the state, the practice of democracy, and the model of citizenship in Bolivia. Yet tensions and contradictions within the new constitution itself have limited the construction of the plurinational state in practice. Bolivia's new constitution concentrates state power while expanding Indigenous rights. According to the constitutional scholar Roberto Gargarella (2013), a highly centralized organization of power tends to work against the application of Indigenous rights in practice. For instance, the Morales government's commitment to Indigenous autonomies is at odds with its resource-dependent, state-led model of development. The constitutional provision that all non-renewable resources remain under state control places firm limits on the right to self-government and self-determination within Indigenous territories (Tockman and Cameron 2014). Bolivia's Constitution (art. 30.15) establishes the right of Indigenous peoples to free, prior, and informed consultation, not consent, concerning planned measures affecting them, such as mining and oil or gas exploration. The constitution does stipulate that the prior consultation process by the state must be conducted in good faith and in a concerted fashion and that it should respect local Indigenous norms and procedures. Nevertheless, Indigenous groups cannot veto state-sponsored development and resource extraction projects in their territories (Schilling-Vacaflor and Kuppe 2012; Wolff 2012). It is clear that the new constitution has not yet fully changed power relations between the state and Indigenous communities.

The practice of communitarian democracy is also heavily circumscribed, despite its equal standing in the new constitution. Communitarian democracy is based on Indigenous customs and traditions. The constitutional recognition of communitarian democracy holds considerable promise as a means to strengthen democratic governance by constructively linking state and Indigenous institutions (Retolaza Eguren 2008). In other words, it institutionalizes Indigenous forms of governance as part of the state. The creation of self-governing Indigenous communities is the key to fostering communitarian democracy. According to Cameron and Sharpe, "The cumulative effect of these innovations is to use direct institutionalized voice to transform and democratize the state as a whole—not by scaling up but by devolving more democratic power to small-scale self-governing communities everywhere" (2012, 246). Under the current constitutional configuration, communitarian democracy is relegated to lower-level governments and is to be exercised within the Indigenous autonomies through the election or selection of governing authorities using traditional methods. However, the election methods and governance structures at the local level do not inform practices at the national level. Nonetheless, these constitutional gains represent an important first step toward building a plurinational state and healing Indigenous-state relations in the country.

SHIFTING INDIGENOUS-STATE RELATIONS IN ECUADOR

Ecuador's Indigenous movement was once widely regarded as Latin America's strongest social movement. Under the direction of the Confederation of Indigenous Nationalities of Ecuador (CONAIE), the movement managed to disrupt the implementation of neoliberal economic reforms throughout the 1990s. In contrast to other countries with a significant Indigenous population, such as Bolivia, Ecuador's Indigenous movement has been able, at least until quite recently, to avoid extensive interethnic conflict and unite diverse interests from the coastal, highland, and Amazonian regions (Lucero 2008; Van Cott 2005; Yashar 2005). Since 2003, however, CONAIE and the Indigenous movement have lost much of their power to convoke the masses both in the streets and in the electoral arena. A complex set of factors contributed to the decline of the movement's power to mobilize, including its participation in a military-supported coup, its ill-fated electoral alliances, and its perceived shift to a more radical, ethnicist stance. Nonetheless, Indigenous activism in the country has paved the way for an alternative economic and political model, though under the leadership of left-leaning, populist president Rafael Correa (2007–17).[3] Ecuador's recent Left turn government has introduced a number of important policy measures to address Indigenous demands in the country, albeit without meaningfully including Indigenous peoples in the policy deliberations.

The young and charismatic former minister of the economy, Rafael Correa, of the PAIS Alliance, was elected president in the 2006 elections on a strong anti-neoliberal campaign platform. Correa's administration has since taken up most of the political space formerly occupied by the Indigenous-based political party Movimiento de Unidad Plurinacional Pachakutik–Nuevo País (Pachakutik Movement for Plurinational

Unity–New Country, MUPP-NP). His so-called citizen's revolution, which is based on the mobilization of the citizenry and the redistribution of political power, has eclipsed autonomous organizing efforts in the country (Conaghan 2008). Paradoxically, the assumption of power of President Correa institutionalized the Indigenous movement's political project while marginalizing the movement itself. There are strong areas of convergence between Correa's and Pachakutik's governing proposals. Both projects are nationalistic and emphasize investment in domestic industries, and both emphasize direct democracy as a corrective to the limits of representative democracy in advancing popular sector interests (Jameson 2008). During his presidential inauguration, Correa declared the end of Ecuador's neoliberal era. The president immediately convened a constituent assembly to redraft the constitution, a process over which he dominated. The passage of the 2008 Constitution marked a rare moment of unity between the Indigenous movement and the Correa administration. In addition to its stance against neoliberalism and the strengthened role for the state in the economy, the new constitution officially proclaimed Ecuador a plurinational state, the historic objective of the nation's Indigenous peoples.[4]

Ecuador's model of plurinational constitutionalism is quite limited in comparison to Bolivia's. For instance, Spanish remains Ecuador's official language (art. 2), with Indigenous languages recognized only in the realm of intercultural relations (Schilling-Vacaflor and Kuppe 2012, 360). In addition, while both countries recognize Indigenous or customary law, the Bolivian constitution places ordinary and customary legal systems on an equal footing (art. 179), whereas the Ecuadorean constitution does not (Wolff 2012, 192). Ecuador's new constitution does recognize Indigenous territories as jurisdictions that may take on the same responsibilities as those of local governments, yet falls silent on the matter of the guaranteed proportional representation for Indigenous peoples in the legislature and on the explicit recognition of the right to self-determination and self-government (Radcliffe 2012, 243). It also fails to open up participatory spaces for Indigenous actors within the structures of the state. Perhaps most telling, in Ecuador, as in Bolivia, the state retains control over the exploitation of nonrenewable resources in Indigenous territories. In Ecuador, this discrepancy has translated into escalating conflicts between Indigenous groups and the state. In particular, Correa's vision of a socially

TABLE 6.3. Ecuador's National Development Priorities, 2013–2017

Stated Priority	Word Count
Development	720
Human rights	526
Natural resources	443
Economy	338
Living Well	266
Environment	97
Autonomy	40

Source: Secretaría Nacional de Planificación y Desarrollo 2013.

responsible mining sector as the backbone of the country's development has drawn protests from Indigenous groups whose territories stand in his way (Dosh and Kligerman 2009).

Ecuador's National Development Plan (2013–17) envisions sustainable development and the equitable distribution of wealth and resources as the route to attaining the principle of Living Well, the government's new policy guidepost. A textual review of the government's planning document reveals the top three priorities of Correa's administration to be the pursuit of development, human rights, and natural resource wealth (table 6.3). The term "development" is used three times more frequently than the term "Living Well" and eighteen times more often than the concept of Indigenous autonomy. To advance the long-term goal of Living Well, the government assumes responsibility for the defense of the right to live in a healthy environment and to respect the rights of nature (Secretaría Nacional de Planificación y Desarrollo 2013, 16). According to the National Plan for Living Well (Secretaría Nacional de Planificación y Desarrollo 2013, 14), the principle of Living Well cannot be improvised from below by community groups but must be planned and managed from above by the government. This state-led approach to Living Well is completely at odds with Indigenous peoples' conceptualizations and expectations. Ecuador's development plan, in conjunction with the new constitution, places nature and natural resource management under strict state control. Instead of displacing conventional notions of development based on economic growth, the Correa government's use of the concept of Living Well has broadened the definition of economic development to include a more balanced relationship between nature and society that can only be brought about by state actions (Arsel 2012).

In contrast to Bolivia, where many of the cultural and political gains made under neoliberal multicultural policies have been deepened and extended, Ecuador has witnessed a reversal of fortune for Indigenous peoples in a number of key areas. In the late 1980s and early 1990s, Ecuador was home to the region's most successful programs in Indigenous co-management and administration of state funds targeting Indigenous health, education, and welfare. Ecuador's Directorate for Intercultural Bilingual Education (DINEIB), for instance, was the first public education institution in Latin America that was headed, staffed, and run by Indigenous peoples (Chartock 2013). In the 1990s, the Council for the Development of Ecuadorean Nationalities and Peoples (CODENPE) was formed as a semiautonomous ministry tasked with implementing Indigenous-targeted social funds and development projects (Van Cott 2000; Yashar 2005). Since taking office in 2007, President Correa has sought to centralize state authority over social policy by bringing both DINEIB and CODENPE under greater presidential control and oversight. Following the massive Indigenous-led protests of January 2009 against the government's Mining Law and its related water reform bill, Correa revoked the legal status of the vocal nongovernmental organization Acción Ecológica and announced the closure of several Indigenous-run government offices, including CODENPE. DINEIB was then placed under the control of the Ministry of Education (Dosh and Kligerman 2009). Gaining authority over these two offices had been one of the Indigenous movement's most significant achievements of the past twenty years (Lucero 2009, 75). Most recently, Correa had attempted to eject CONAIE from its national headquarters (Becker 2013). Ecuador's plurinational state, at least for the time being, appears to be stuck at the level of rhetoric.

The central task of this chapter has been to assess the extent to which Indigenous-state relations have improved under Latin America's Left Turn governments. I have found that they have improved, at least in the case of Bolivia, and to a lesser extent in the case of Ecuador, though the results remain partial and uneven. The governments of Evo Morales in Bolivia and Rafael Correa in Ecuador extended the boundaries of citizenship in their respective countries through cultural recognition, formal inclusion, and participatory governance. Yet it remains unclear if Indigenous communities can maintain meaningful democratic control over these newly strengthened states (Arsel 2012). The constitutional recognition of plurinationality in the two countries marks a watershed moment in Indigenous-state relations in Latin America. This new, potential period of Indigenous incorporation represents an opportunity for governments to reconceptualize their political relationship with Indigenous peoples as sovereign and self-determining peoples or nations. Underpinning this shift in Indigenous-state relations is a model of differentiated citizenship, one that privileges Indigenous ways of knowing and being. The Andean Indigenous principle of Living Well is touted by the governments of Bolivia and Ecuador as the central objective of public policy. If governments in the Andes are serious about their commitments to advancing the Indigenous rights agenda, they must be willing to work with Indigenous communities, in all stages of development planning and practice and in a bottom-up fashion.

Significant challenges remain in bringing to fruition the promises contained in the Bolivian and Ecuadorean constitutions. First, the process is heavily dependent on the political will of the president to support reforms to enhance the plurinational state. President Correa, a populist leader who pursued top-down policy initiatives, has been more reluctant to cede authority to Indigenous groups than President Morales, whose governing party is organically linked to social movement organizations and prides itself on its efforts to "lead by obeying" (Quispe et al. 2011, 243). Nevertheless, the concentration of executive power in both cases is at odds with the exercise of local power by Indigenous autonomies (Gargarella 2013; Schilling-Vacaflor and Kuppe 2012; Wolff 2012). Second, the dismantling of previous state structures, institutions, and practices and their replacement with a new order is fraught with difficulties. The situation is more precarious in Ecuador, where the plurinational nature of its constitution is weak compared to that of Bolivia. Finally, there are serious tensions between Indigenous autonomies and the resource-dependent, state-led model of development pursued by Left turn governments. Indigenous autonomy is the cornerstone of plurinationality, a new way of doing government. The experiences of Bolivia and Ecuador reviewed in this chapter indicate that while the rise to power of leftist forces represents a rupture with previous models of Indigenous-state relations, it has yet to transform state power.

NOTES

Fieldwork for this paper was carried out by the author in La Paz, Bolivia, in August 2014 and Quito, Ecuador, in August 2012 under the auspices of a standard research grant from the Social Sciences and Humanities Research Council of Canada (SSHRC).

1. The Movement Toward Socialism (MAS) captured 54 percent of the total national vote in the 2005 presidential elections, the only party to win an absolute majority since the country's democratic transition. In 2009, Morales was reelected to a second term in office with 64 percent of the vote. In 2014, he was elected to a third term (technically the second term under the rules of the new constitution) with 61 percent of the vote.

2. The 2009 Bolivian Constitution can be downloaded at http://pdba .georgetown.edu/constitutions/bolivia/bolivia.html.

3. Correa was first elected in the 2006 presidential elections with 57 percent of the vote. He was reelected as leader of the Movimiento Alianza Patria Altiva i Soberana (Proud and Sovereign Fatherland Alliance, PAIS) party with 52 percent of the vote in the 2009 elections. In 2013, Correa was elected to a third term (technically the second term under the rules of the new constitution) with 57 percent of the total national vote. In 2017, Correa's hand-picked successor, Lenín Moreno, won the presidency with 51 percent of the vote.

4. The 2008 Ecuadorean Constitution can be downloaded at http://pdba .georgetown.edu/Constitutions/Ecuador/english08.html.

REFERENCES

Aparicio Wilhelmi, Marco. 2007. "La construcción de la autonomía indígena: Hacia el estado intercultural como nueva forma de estado." In Salvador Martí i Puig, ed., *Pueblos indígenas y política en América Latina: El reconocimiento de sus derechos*. Barcelona: Fundacio Cidob.

Arce, Moisés, and Roberta Rice. 2009. "Societal Protest in Post-Stabilization Bolivia." *Latin American Research Review* 44 (1): 88–101.

Arsel, Murat. 2012. "Between 'Marx and Markets'? The State, the 'Left Turn' and Nature in Ecuador." *Tijdschrift voor Economische en Sociale Geografie* 103 (2): 150–63.

Becker, Marc. 2011. *Pachakutik: Indigenous Movements and Electoral Politics in Ecuador.* Lanham, MD: Rowman & Littlefield.

———. 2013. "The Stormy Relations between Rafael Correa and Social Movements in Ecuador." *Latin American Perspectives* 40 (3): 43–62.

Bonifaz, Carlos Romero. 2004. "Las jornadas de octubre: Levantamiento popular en Bolivia." *Artículo Primero* (16): 21.

Bretón, Víctor, David Cortez, and Fernando García. 2014. "En busca del Sumak Kawsay: Presentación del dossier." Íconos: Revista de Ciencias Sociales 48 (January 2014): 9–24.

Burt, Jo-Marie, and Philip Mauceri. 2004. *Politics in the Andes: Identity, Conflict, Reform.* Pittsburgh, PA: University of Pittsburgh Press.

Cameron, Maxwell A., and Kenneth E. Sharpe. 2012. "Institutionalized Voice in Latin American Democracies." In Maxwell A. Cameron, Eric Hershberg, and Kenneth E. Sharpe, eds., *New Institutions for Participatory Democracy in Latin America: Voice and Consequence.* New York: Palgrave Macmillan.

Canessa, Andrew. 2012. "Conflict, Claim and Contradiction in the New 'Indigenous' State of Bolivia." Working Paper Series No. 22.

Centellas, Miguel. 2010. "Bolivia's Regional Elections: A Setback for Evo Morales." *Americas Quarterly*. Online. www.americasquarterly.org/bolivia -regional-elections-april2010.

Centro de Investigación y Promoción del Campesinado (CIPCA). 2009. *Posibles caminos hacia las autonomías indígena originario campesinas.* La Paz: CIPCA.

Chartock, Sarah. 2013. "'Corporatism with Adjectives'? Conceptualizing Civil Society Incorporation and Indigenous Participation in Latin America." *Latin American Politics and Society* 55 (2): 52–76.

Collier, David. 1995. "Trajectory of a Concept: 'Corporatism' in the Study of Latin American Politics." In Peter H. Smith, ed., *Latin America in Comparative Perspective.* Boulder, CO: Westview Press.

Collier, Ruth Berins, and David Collier. 1991. *Shaping the Political Arena: Critical Junctures, the Labor Movement, and Regime Dynamics in Latin America.* Princeton, NJ: Princeton University Press.

Conaghan, Catherine 2008. "Ecuador: Correa's Plebiscitary Presidency." *Journal of Democracy* 19 (2): 46–60.

Crabtree, John. 2005. *Patterns of Protest: Politics and Social Movements in Bolivia.* London: Latin America Bureau.

Dangl, Benjamin. 2007. *The Price of Fire: Resource Wars and Social Movements in Bolivia*. Chico, CA: AK Press.

Díaz Polanco, Héctor 1998. "La autonomía, demanda central de los pueblos indígenas: Significados e implicaciones." In D. Iturralde, M. A. López-Bassols, and V. Alta, eds., *Pueblos indígenas e estado en América Latina*. Quito: Editorial Abya-Yala.

Dosh, Paul, and Nicole Kligerman. 2009. "Correa vs. Social Movements: Showdown in Ecuador." *NACLA Report on the Americas* 42 (5): 21–24.

Drake, Paul W., and Eric Hershberg. 2006. *State and Society in Conflict: Comparative Perspectives on Andean Crises*. Pittsburgh, PA: University of Pittsburgh Press.

Estado Plurinacional de Bolivia. 2009. *Constitución política del Estado boliviano*. La Paz: Asamblea Constituyente and Honorable Congreso Nacional. http://pdba.georgetown.edu/constitutions/bolivia/bolivia.html.

Exeni Rodríguez, José Luis. 2012. *Elusive Demodiversity in Bolivia: Between Representation, Participation, and Self-Government. New Institutions for Participatory Democracy in Latin America*. Berlin: Springer.

Faguet, Jean-Paul. 2014. "Can Subnational Autonomy Strengthen Democracy in Bolivia?" *Publius: Journal of Federalism* 44 (1): 51–81.

Fisher, Valdi, and Marc Fasol. 2013. *Las semillas del Buen vivir: La respuesta de los pueblos indígenas del Abya Yala a la deriva del modelo de desarrollo occidental*. La Paz: Fondo Indígena.

Gargarella, Roberto. 2013. *Latin American Constitutionalism, 1810–2010: The Engine Room of the Constitution*. Oxford: Oxford University Press.

Gustafson, Bret. 2009. "Manipulating Cartographies: Plurinationalism, Autonomy, and Indigenous Resurgence in Bolivia." *Anthropological Quarterly* 82 (4): 985–1016.

Hale, Charles R. 2002. "Does Multiculturalism Menace? Governance, Cultural Rights and the Politics of Identity in Guatemala." *Journal of Latin American Studies* 34 (3): 485–524.

Jameson, Kenneth P. 2008. "The Indigenous Movement and the Economic Trajectory of Ecuador." Working Paper, University of Utah, Department of Economics.

Kohl, Benjamin, and Linda C. Farthing. 2006. *Impasse in Bolivia: Neoliberal Hegemony and Popular Resistance*. London: Zed Books.

Levitsky, Steven, and Kenneth M. Roberts. 2011. "Conclusion: Democracy, Development, and the Left." In Steven Levitsky and Kenneth M. Roberts, eds., *The Resurgence of the Latin American Left*. Baltimore, MD: Johns Hopkins University Press.

Lucero, José Antonio. 2008. *Struggles of Voice: The Politics of Indigenous Representation in the Andes*. Pittsburgh, PA: University of Pittsburgh Press.

————. 2009. "Decades Lost and Won: Indigenous Movements and Multicultural Neoliberalism in the Andes." In Philip Oxhorn John Burdick, and Kenneth M. Roberts, eds., *Beyond Neoliberalism in Latin America?* New York: Palgrave Macmillan.

Mainwaring, Scott, Ana María Bejarano, and Eduardo Pizarro Leongómez. 2006. *The Crisis of Democratic Representation in the Andes*. Stanford, CA: Stanford University Press.

Ministerio de Planificación del Desarrollo. 2016. *Plan de desarrollo económico y social 2016–2020: En el marco del desarrollo integral para Vivir Bien*. La Paz: Estado Plurinacional de Bolivia.

Nolte, Detlef, and Almut Schilling-Vacaflor. 2012. *New Constitutionalism in Latin America: Promises and Practices*. Burlington, VT: Ashgate.

Oxhorn, Philip. 1998. "Is the Century of Corporativism Over? Neoliberalism and the Rise of Neopluralism." In Philip Oxhorn and Graciela Ducatenzeiler, eds., *What Kind of Democracy? What Kind of Market?* University Park: Pennsylvania State University Press.

————. 2011. *Sustaining Civil Society: Economic Change, Democracy and the Social Construction of Citizenship in Latin America*. University Park: Pennsylvania State University Press.

Postero, Nancy Grey. 2007. *Now We Are Citizens: Indigenous Politics in Postmulticultural Bolivia*. Stanford, CA: Stanford University Press.

Postero, Nancy Grey, and Leon Zamosc. 2004. *The Struggle for Indigenous Rights in Latin America*. Portland: Sussex Academic Press.

Quispe, Alber, María Tereza Zegada, Claudia Arce, and Gabriela Canedo. 2011. *La democracia desde los márgenes: Transformaciones en el campo político boliviano*. La Paz: Muela del Diablo Editores and Consejo Latinoamericano de Ciencias Sociales.

Radcliffe, Sarah A. 2012. "Development for a Postneoliberal Era? Sumak Kawsay, Living Well and the Limits to Decolonisation in Ecuador." *Geoforum* 43 (2): 240–49.

República del Ecuador. 2008. *Constitución de la República del Ecuador*. Quito: Asamblea Constituyente del Ecuador. http://pdba.georgetown.edu /Constitutions/Ecuador/english08.html.

Retolaza Eguren, Iñigo. 2008. "Moving Up and Down the Ladder: Community-Based Participation in Public Dialogue and Deliberation in Bolivia and Guatemala." *Community Development Journal* 43 (3): 312–28.

Rice, Roberta. 2012. *The New Politics of Protest: Indigenous Mobilization in Latin America's Neoliberal Era*. Tucson: University of Arizona Press.

Rossi, Federico M. 2015. "The Second Wave of Incorporation in Latin America: A Conceptualization of the Quest for Inclusion Applied to Argentina." *Latin American Politics and Society* 57 (1): 1–28.

Schilling-Vacaflor, Almut, and René Kuppe. 2012. "Plurinational Constitutionalism: A New Era of Indigenous-State Relations?" In Detlef Nolte and Almut Schilling-Vacaflor, eds., *New Constitutionalism in Latin America: Promises and Practices.* Burlington, VT: Ashgate.

Secretaría Nacional de Planificación y Desarrollo. 2013. *Plan nacional para el Buen Vivir 2013–2017.* Quito: República del Ecuador.

Suárez, Hugo José. 2003. *Una semana fundamental: 10–18 Octubre 2003.* La Paz: Muela del Diablo.

Tockman, Jason, and John Cameron. 2014. "Indigenous Autonomy and the Contradictions of Plurinationalism in Bolivia." *Latin American Politics and Society* 56 (3): 46–69.

United Nations General Assembly (UNGA). 2007. *United Nations Declaration on the Rights of Indigenous Peoples.* New York: United Nations Press.

Van Cott, Donna Lee. 2000. *The Friendly Liquidation of the Past: The Politics of Diversity in Latin America.* Pittsburgh, PA: University of Pittsburgh Press.

———. 2005. *From Movements to Parties in Latin America: The Evolution of Ethnic Politics.* New York: Cambridge University Press.

Vega Ugalde, Silvia. 2014. "El orden de género en el Sumak Kawsay y el Suma Qamaña: Un vistazo a los debates actuales en Bolivia y Ecuador." *Íconos: Revista de Ciencias Sociales* (48): 73–91.

Walsh, Catherine. 2009. "Estado plurinacional e intercultural: Complementariedad y complicidad hacia el 'Buen Vivir.'" In Alberto Acosta and Esperanza Martínez, eds., *Plurinacionalidad: Democracia en la diversidad.* Quito: Ediciones Abya-Yala.

Wolff, Jonas. 2012. "New Constitutions and the Transformation of Democracy in Bolivia and Ecuador." In Detlef Nolte and Almut Schilling-Vacaflor, eds., *New Constitutionalism in Latin America: Promises and Practices.* Burlington, VT: Ashgate.

Yashar, Deborah. 2005. *Contesting Citizenship in Latin America: The Rise of Indigenous Movements and the Postliberal Challenge.* New York: Cambridge University Press.

PART 3

The Multiple Struggles for Inclusive Citizenship Rights

SEVEN

Human Rights and Memory Politics under Shifting Political Orientations

ELIZABETH JELIN AND CELINA VAN DEMBROUCKE

Coping with recent past violence and state terrorism was one of the challenges that transitional governments in South America had to face after dictatorship. They did so by means of a series of institutional processes: truth commissions, trials, official reparations, and memorialization policies. Besides constant demands for specific policies, the human rights movements, as well as other societal actors, developed a variety of cultural and symbolic initiatives. Rather than being interpreted in terms of winners and losers of violent confrontations and war, these demands fell under the "human rights violations" framework, which gained salience and legitimacy since the 1970s (Sikkink 2017).

As the Left turn swept through the region, one of the issues where many expected to see progress was on human rights claims, both about justice regarding violations during the years of dictatorship and about current problems that can be cast as human rights concerns. In this context, and after fifteen years of Left turn governments in the region, this chapter poses two key questions, both explicitly related to the main objectives of this volume. First, to what extent are institutional arrangements regarding the violent recent past long-lasting or, alternatively, dependent on the leanings of governments and therefore subject to the shifts that reflect changing political situations. In this sense, what has been the impact of Left turn governments on human rights when it comes to dealing with acts of state repression committed during dictatorships? Second, to what extent has the human rights framework expanded from a concern for the civic and political rights violations of dictatorship to a broader and more encompassing understanding of the notion of human rights—one that includes economic, social, and cultural rights, both at the individual and collective level. In other words, have Left turn governments moved to adopt a broader view of human rights that moves beyond past state repressions? And, if they did, how have they implemented this agenda?

Before going into the subject, a short analytic detour is needed. Analytically, the human rights framework seems not to fit with the notion of citizenship and citizenship regimes. The latter are anchored at the nation-state level, while human rights pertain to the human condition, irrespective of where people are born or reside. Yet the two levels (or even more, if regional or subnational units are taken into consideration) are not independent, and a multiscalar approach would be needed to disentangle their links. Political struggles to accept or enlarge the human rights framework take place at the international level; yet it is nation-states' representatives who confront these matters. And they have to do so at both levels, in a movement that goes in both directions. At times, actors in the national, regional, and local political scenes struggle at these levels, using the international human rights framework as part of their tool kit for state recognition of rights, whether as formal rules or in policies and forms of implementation. It is in these struggles and confrontations, in collective action and in claims for recognition, that the sense of belonging to a (political) community is fostered, in the multiplicity of layers and identities that this entails (as conceptualized in chapter 1 of this book). The bottom line is that both citizenship and human rights refer to the recognition, promotion, and protection of rights—not as a given crystallized set of positive rights, but as the recognition of the "right to have rights."

This chapter offers a comparative analysis of the ways Argentina and Chile incorporated the human rights framework to deal with their recent violent past as well as with broader issues, looking at the different specific processes and results during the period starting from around the turn of the century. We chose these two countries for several reasons. Both experienced bloody dictatorships in the 1970s and 1980s, with military rulers who followed similar strategies in their repressive practices. In both cases, human rights movements emerged as internal opposition to the regimes, backed by the international human rights solidarity community. Furthermore, their transition processes entailed a strong commitment to strengthen democratic institutions and practices, including the expansion of citizenship rights, yet with slightly diverging power and ideological configurations, institutional practices, and social mobilization traditions.

In order to carry out this comparative exercise, we provide a brief historical account of how both countries initially adopted the human rights (HHRR) framework in the transitional years. We quickly move to analyze how this agenda ended up taking shape once democracies were well established and how it was—or was not—challenged by changes in the ideological leanings of the democratically elected governments since the turn of the century.

In a nutshell, in Argentina, from 2003 until 2015, the governments of Néstor Kirchner and Cristina Fernández de Kirchner incorporated the discourse of human rights organizations into official discourse, giving unprecedented recognition to human rights associations—particularly those related to the crimes committed during the last dictatorship (1976–83), such as Madres and Abuelas de Plaza de Mayo, which were ostracized during the 1990s, after a brief spring in the transitional years. Centered on the figure of the victim, and with a relatively narrow definition focused only on the last dictatorship, the human rights framework endorsed by the Argentine state promoted human rights associations' symbolic victories but also disavowed (yet never censored) memories that did not fit the official definition of victimhood, which were not recognized as valuable testimony holders. With the changing political scenario marked by the election of the center-right president Mauricio Macri in 2015, the links between the state and these human rights associations were weakened or even severed, and questions arise as to possible changes in state policies in this respect.

In Chile, the issue is to what extent policies regarding the dictatorial past that have been institutionalized during the transition and afterward are subject to political whims, taking into consideration the shifts in political orientation of the various presidencies: Ricardo Lagos (2000–2006), the first tenure of Michelle Bachelet (2006–10), followed by a center-right period during the presidency of Sebastián Piñera (2010–14), the reelection of Michelle Bachelet (2014–18), and the reelection of Sebastián Piñera, installed in 2018.

ARGENTINA'S AND CHILE'S ADOPTION OF THE HHRR FRAMEWORK: TWO DIFFERENT CASES

After experiencing periods of state violence, societies take different paths in their transition to democratic regimes. In the context of Latin American democratization processes, political scientists usually define these transitions as either "by collapse" or "by transaction" (O'Donnell and Schmitter 1986), signaling either a rapid transition to democracy after the collapse of the military regime or a protracted process of negotiation that leads to democratization after years of transition. The cases of Argentina and Chile present contrasting paths in this regard: Chile's transition was made possible by a pact whereby the military preserved its position of power—including the fact that General Pinochet remained as commander in chief of the armed forces—while Argentina's transition was marked by a strongly explicit concern for human rights that emerged after the rapid collapse of the military regime following the Malvinas/Falklands War. The first transitional president in Argentina, Raúl Alfonsín, was the vice president of one of the most important human rights organizations, Asamblea Permanente por los Derechos Humanos (Permanent Assembly for Human Rights, APDH) and committed himself to the human rights agenda (his presidential campaign motto was "Somos la vida"). Yet in both cases the incorporation of the human rights framework proved to be a rich arena for reflecting the contested meanings and negotiations after a dictatorial period characterized by violence and repression. The Argentine and Chilean cases have both similarities and differences, but if one were to point to the contrasts, two different institutional approaches to deal with the past stand out.

Whereas during its transition into democracy Argentina focused on the judiciary as a means to promote justice, Chile was reluctant to point fingers and promote trials and instead intended to avoid triggering the reenactment of past conflicts that ended in political violence, by replacing the *confrontación* (confrontation) with a *concertación,* a coalition of different parties founded in 1988 (Jelin 1994, 8). In what follows, we present the two cases, with succinct accounts of the transitional periods and of developments since the turn of the century.

ARGENTINA

In the case of Argentina, Raúl Alfonsín, who was elected in 1983 after the military resigned from power, put into motion a series of initiatives to deal with the country's recent violent past. Among his first decisions was to create a commission that would carry out research in order to establish a record of the number and identity of those who were kidnapped and killed during that period. Because of the clandestine nature of most executions, the Comisión Nacional sobre la Desaparición de Personas (National Commission on the Disappearance of Persons, CONADEP), whose members included several notable public figures and intellectuals, based its investigations on oral testimonies of the relatives of disappeared people and survivors, that is, those who had been disappeared but managed to survive. As is well known, the research carried out by the CONADEP led to the publication of the *Nunca más* (Never Again, 1984), which provides a list of close to nine thousand victims and a careful account of the modalities in which the military carried out its repressive endeavor (the usual ways in which they would move around in mob squads, or *patotas,* torture techniques, etc.). This commission was the most significant antecedent to the by now widespread practice of establishing truth commissions in order to gather information about the crimes committed by states (Sikkink 2008).

Along with the *Nunca más,* the most important initiative to settle accounts with the past was the trial of the members of the military juntas (Juicio a las Juntas) in 1985. It was arguably one of the most impactful moments in the context of the struggle for human rights, since nine members of the three military juntas were put on the stand as responsible for the crimes committed. In that way, "victims turned into witnesses, perpetrators into the 'accused', and political actors had to transform themselves into 'observers' to the judges' decisions, as they were supposed to be a 'neutral' authority" (Jelin 2008, 185). This was a breakthrough moment, and in time, trials of perpetrators became a significant practice in many countries (and internationally, by establishing the International Criminal Court) as a way to deal with the violent past (Sikkink 2011). The Argentine trials were held to stop impunity and to prove that, regardless of opinions, the state was recognizing the fact that clandestine detention camps, kidnappings, torture, and executions were part of a systematic plan orchestrated by the highest state authorities.

Yet the result of this and other efforts, far from resting the case of the crimes committed during that period and allowing society to "move on," encouraged the reactivation of further trials, and, with them, the conflicts that existed between different societal actors came to take center stage in the public debate, even triggering additional indictments (Acuña and Smulovitz 1995, 58; Acuña and Smulovitz 1996, 17; Jelin and Kaufman 2000, 4). Later on, in a turn of events that only demonstrated the considerable power still held by the military under the new democratic regime, in December 1986 Congress passed the Full Stop Law (Ley de Punto Final) and the next year, in June 1987, the Law of Due Obedience (Ley de Obediencia Debida). The Full Stop Law was an effort to stop the growing number of indictments and prosecutions against the military by establishing that indictments would be received only during a sixty-day period—the deadline was February 23, 1987—whereas the Law of Due Obedience absolved all those who had committed crimes while carrying out orders from their superiors. This law was passed amid a rebellion from a section of the military that demanded a "political solution" to the "problem" of the trials. The government's intention was to soften the discontent within the armed forces, but it did not accomplish this. Even when punishments were being lessened for low-ranking officers, they still had to admit that they had committed crimes, not really justifying the actions of the military on a symbolic level (Acuña and Smulovitz 1995, 65).

Later, in October 1989, during the presidency of Carlos Menem, the democratic government again favored the military by issuing a number of pardons to convicted military men, only to issue a second round of pardons the next year, which ended up releasing the heads of the Juntas—as well as others who were in jail for their participation in guerrilla actions (Acuña and Smulovitz 1995, 89).

Far from being a smooth process, the incorporation of the human rights framework involved continuous tensions both with the military and with the human rights movement from the outset, ultimately acting as a constant reminder that the accounts with the dictatorial past were far from settled. After the amnesty laws were enacted, the Argentine state closed all institutional channels to judge crimes against humanity committed during the dictatorship. If in the initial transitional years there was a clear sense of the pursuit of justice on the part of the state, this sense vanished by the beginning of Menem's first government, generating profound discontent among human rights associations. Unsurprisingly, Menem's pardons were a blow to the human rights movement, and massive rallies protested the decisions. However, shortly after the movement entered a period of retreat—in part due to the participation of some of its leaders in the assault on a military barracks in early 1989. After the hyperinflation of 1989, economic issues became paramount, and human rights issues lost their salience.

However, this state of affairs was only transitory, and by the mid-1990s, the public scene was again occupied by HHRR issues. Perhaps the most important measure implemented by Menem's government was a policy of individualized economic reparations for victims and their relatives: in 1991, for political detainees; in 1994, for relatives of disappeared persons. This move renewed tensions inside the human rights movement, since some (especially Hebe de Bonafini, head of the Asociación Madres de Plaza de Mayo) considered that accepting money was a form of prostitution.

If the government's goal was to move on, several events made evident that far from being forgotten, the problem of the disappeared, and the lack of justice surrounding it, was not nearly closed. Just to mention a few events, in 1995, a former navy officer named Adolfo Scilingo described at length one of the horrible procedures the military carried out to get rid of the detainees: the "death flights" (Verbitsky 1996).[1] His confession shook the public, the church—as Scilingo clearly described that many priests were involved in this practice—and other military men who were compelled to confess their involvement. This led to a self-critical and apologetic declaration by the chief of staff of the armed forces, General Martín Balza, in which he recognized the responsibility of the armed forces in the violation of human rights during the dictatorship.

The second half of the decade witnessed an important development in the human rights movement: the emergence of Hijos e Hijas por la Identidad y la Justicia contra el Olvido y el Silencio (Sons and Daughters for Identity and Justice against Oblivion and Silence, H.I.J.O.S.), the organization of children of the disappeared, with their own ways to voice their demands (Bonaldi 2006) and to reinvigorate the human rights movement. The year 1996 marked the twentieth anniversary of the military coup. Public attention to the past, through commemorations, street mobilization, and cultural events, was intense. From that moment, the issue of human rights violations during the dictatorship returned to the forefront of public attention. Part of this public attention was focused on the developments in international prosecutions: in addition to France and Italy, where prosecutions and trials were somewhat earlier, in April 1996, the Spanish judge Baltasar Garzón began procedures to prosecute Argentine military members who served during the dictatorship (Anguita 2001). Subsequent developments in the Spanish justice system extended to the Chilean case and led to the arrest of Augusto Pinochet in London in 1998.

At the national level, after apparent government apathy was dispelled by a profound sense of injustice, human rights organizations found a loophole in the immunity laws and presidential pardons and went after those who had illegally adopted, or "appropriated" in the local jargon, children of the disappeared. In 1998, former general Videla, former admiral Massera, and other senior military commanders were arrested and prosecuted for their responsibility for these crimes. In 1998, based on the ruling of the Inter-American Court of Human Rights, a new form of trials developed, "truth trials." These trials were based on the recognized demand that even when punishment is not possible because of amnesty laws, relatives of victims and the society at large have a "right to truth"; that is, courts have a duty to investigate and communicate the fate of each and every victim (Andriotti Romanin 2013). The truth trials once again placed the country at the forefront of innovations in ways of dealing with the past.

On March 6, 2001, federal judge Gabriel Cavallo declared the "un-constitutionality and invalidity" of the Full Stop and Due Obedience Laws that came into force in 1986 and 1987. Judge Cavallo's ruling applied to a particular case. Yet his ruling went beyond the individual case being tried and had an immediate and lasting political impact, which was added to the symbolic impact of the twenty-fifth anniversary of the March 24 coup, a few days later. Two lines developed over those twenty-five years converged: memory and institutional justice. Justice, truth, and memory met in one and the same motto: *Memoria, Verdad, Justicia.*

The Twenty-First Century

In Argentina, the onset of the twenty-first century was filled with crises and far from auspicious or promising. Economic conditions were worsening quickly, the ranks of the poor and the indigent were growing throughout the country, and the government was unable to handle the internal economic situation and the pressures of the foreign debt. The peak of the crisis occurred at the end of 2001, with popular mobilizations, violent repression that resulted in the deaths of several dozen people, and the resignation of the president. Interim succession mechanisms led to new elections and the installation of Néstor Kirchner as president in May 2003. Already in his inaugural speech, Kirchner suggested that he would follow a different approach to the recent past: "We arrive [to power] without resentment but with memory" (quoted in Granovsky 2003). Only a couple of months later, he stated his intention to make Congress consider nullifying both the Full Stop and Due Obedience Laws. Indeed, Congress repealed both amnesty laws that same year. Yet the repeal could not be retroactive, and thus the handling of the trials dealing with the dictatorship had to wait for some time before the judiciary could act.

The turning point was in 2005, when the Supreme Court ruled that the impunity laws were unconstitutional. In this way, based on the principles established by international human rights law, the Court indicated that the legal barriers erected to block justice in cases related to crimes committed during the dictatorship had to be removed. After this decision, trials for human rights violations committed during the dictatorship could reopen.

What happened since has to be put into a longer-term perspective. As the report prepared by the Procuraduría de Crímenes contra la Humanidad (Prosecutor for Crimes against Humanity) shows, trials and sentences multiplied: in the period 2006–15, there were 592 persons convicted and 53 acquitted (Ministerio Público Fiscal 2016).[2] One of the significant features of this wave of trials is the increasing number of *megacausas*, that is, trials that deal with the actions of a group of indicted persons, all of them involved in a single detention center or linked to the same specific case. These trials and the resulting sentences have received a great deal of media coverage and stir public opinion and especially the human rights movement.[3]

Furthermore, a significant new feature developed during this period: the prosecution of civilians bearing responsibility for crimes against humanity. This involves members of the judiciary, big entrepreneurs and chief executive officers of major firms, and Catholic clergy (CELS 2017).[4] Although it is very hard to legally prove civilian participation and complicity during the dictatorship, growing research has collected evidence of this complicity (Basualdo et al. 2016; Verbitsky and Bohoslavsky 2013).

In terms of memory policies, 2004 marked a shift in terms of how the Argentine state dealt with the crimes committed during the dictatorship. On March 24, the anniversary of the coup d'état, President Kirchner held a ceremony at the Escuela Militar de la Armada (Navy Petty Officers School of Mechanics, ESMA)—a former concentration camp, which was to be transformed into a cultural center and *lieu de mémoire*—sharing the stage with members of several HHRR associations such as H.I.J.O.S., Abuelas, and Madres.[5] That same day, another symbolic gesture was made: removal of the portraits of former military generals Jorge Rafael Videla and Reynaldo Bignone—first and last heads of the military Junta during the dictatorship, respectively—from the walls of the most important military academy, Colegio Militar de la Nación. In turn, Madres and Abuelas were received in the Casa Rosada (the presidential palace) and even participated in several public functions. In January 2006, the Madres decided to cancel their Thursday marches in front of the Casa Rosada.

All in all, from 2003 to 2015, a period covering the administrations of both Néstor Kirchner and Cristina Fernández de Kirchner, the state took a public stance on the crimes committed by the military dictatorship by making the human rights associations' discourse their own. Centered on the figure of the victim and focused only on the most recent dictatorship, the human rights framework endorsed by the state promoted human rights associations' symbolic conquests, silencing other memories in an attempt to construct a dominant or even hegemonic interpretation of the recent past. The preparation and public launching of a new preface to the *Nunca más* report in 2006—presenting an alternative interpretation and replacing the narrative of the "two demons"—reflects this official policy. Other interpretations with a lesser voice were present: the self-definition of "victims" of the perpetrators and their organization, Memoria Completa (Complete Memory) (Salvi 2012), reflexive discussions about armed struggle (Ediciones La Intemperie 2007), and those questioning the association of the state with some of the human rights organizations or the emphasis on judicial proceedings.

With the changing political scenario marked by the election of center-right president Mauricio Macri in 2015, the links between the state and human rights associations deteriorated, and state policies began to head in the opposite direction. This did not come as a shock, since as early as his election campaign in 2015, Macri famously promised that with him "the human rights racket ends" (Rosemberg 2015), a phrase that appeared on the facade of the former detention center known as Mansión Seré the very same day he won the presidential election. But this paradigm change also materialized in concrete actions. At the executive level, the government dismantled agencies related to human rights abuses during the dictatorship, such as the Human Rights Office—Dirección Nacional de Derechos Humanos—at the National Ministry of Security, while budgets and personnel of governmental agencies dealing with human rights issues experienced significant cuts. Convicted military men got special privileges, notably, a new regulation that called for moving those convicted of crimes against humanity from regular prisons to a special military facility in Campo de Mayo. At the same time, the Supreme Court ruled in the direction of decreasing time served by those convicted for crimes against humanity (the application of the "2x1" law), a move that prompted immediate social repudiation and social mobilization and was eventually withdrawn. Several gestures set the tone of the new administration regarding human rights and the last dictatorship, such as Macri's own declarations, refusing to meet with the leader of Abuelas de Plaza de Mayo when elected, or Minister of Justice Germán Garavano meeting in April 2016 with relatives of detained military officers (such as Cecilia Pando, leader of a group known to protest against the trials), among many others.

It seems clear that state officials and powerful economic, political, and intellectual forces are on the offensive, challenging previously enacted policies and even the human rights framework itself. In fact, dominant media are influencing public opinion in the same direction. For instance, a day after Macri's electoral victory, the national newspaper *La Nación* published an op-ed asking for the end of former repressors' trials, virtually inaugurating a political atmosphere largely hostile to human rights organizations and demands. Indeed, voices challenging the trajectory and legitimacy of the claims of the human rights movement gained resonance, with accusations that the HHRR movement had overstated the numbers of victims.[6]

Even when the notion of human rights works as a comprehensive category emcompassing economic and reproductive rights, freedom of expression, and protection against violence, among others, in Argentina the commonsense meaning largely refers to the crimes committed during the last dictatorship. This is partly because during the democratic transition and afterward, the human rights framework was invoked time and again to denounce the abuses by the military but also because the wider legal sense of the notion circulated almost exclusively in legal circles and did not penetrate the public consciousness. For some people, the human rights discourse—a signature of the Left turn—is seen as a symbol of the division in the country, promoting rancor against those who participated in the last dictatorship. The agenda on human rights has become an arena for political and symbolical confrontation, a way for the state to express leniency—or the opposite—toward the recent past and military involvement.

In December 2017, Macri launched the "First National Human Rights Action Plan" (*Primer plan nacional de acción en derechos humanos*), making explicit that his was a "comprehensive" plan that included not only the "human rights of the past" but also those "of the present." The statement triggered instant disapproval among human rights organizations, not only for the wink to those who disliked the previous official stance toward the dictatorship, but also for the government's disdain for human rights in the present. For example, the administration disregarded Inter-American Court rulings regarding the imprisonment of Milagro Sala, a social and political leader being held without trial, and various cases of violence on the part of security forces. Unfortunately, the promise of tackling central human rights in the present—whether civil rights regarding state violence or concerns such as living conditions and poverty—has been derailed by the rampant increase in unemployment and inequality and lack of access to housing, eroding the exercise of basic economic and social rights of citizenship (CELS 2017).

THE CHILEAN TRANSITION

After seventeen years of the Pinochet dictatorship in Chile, the incoming elected government in 1990 had to face societal demands to deal with the violent crimes of the dictatorship. Right after taking office, President Patricio Aylwin established the Comisión Nacional de Verdad y Reconciliación (Truth and Reconciliation Commission), whose mandate was to prepare a report on human rights abuses that resulted in deaths and disappearances during the dictatorship; to install a memorial in the cemetery in Santiago; and to undertake some administrative measures to aid in the return of exiles. Ever since those early steps, the way to settle accounts with the past has been a constant concern of Chile's people and government. However, it has rarely, if ever, made it to the top of the governmental agenda or received widespread media coverage.

Contrary to Argentina, Chile did not follow a judicial path. Since the very moment of the military coup, when detentions, executions, and disappearances started, relatives began presenting habeas corpus requests, which were usually rejected by the judiciary. Early on, after the 1978 Amnesty Law,[7] the Chilean judiciary took the position that there was no need to conduct investigations or searches. Since the transition in 1990, different organizations and actors have demanded the repeal of the 1978 amnesty. More than twenty-five years later, this amnesty is still in force, and the demands for its repeal are still active (INDH 2015).

In fact, during the first years of the transition to democracy, the judiciary acted in an ambivalent way. In some cases, as in a 1993 case of a disappearance, it argued that the crime persists in time until the person or the body appears and thus is not covered by the Amnesty Law, which deals with crimes committed during a specific period of time. Occasionally at the beginning and gradually later on, the judiciary started to follow international norms regarding human rights violations, as in the case of the convictions of General Contreras and Brigadier Pedro Espinoza in the early 1990s for the assassination of Orlando Letelier in Washington, DC, in 1976.[8]

A major political turning point was the shift in the position and in the actual power of Augusto Pinochet, who went from being commander in chief of the armed forces during the first years of the transition to a life senator in 1998, until his detention in London later that year. After the moorings of his power were dismantled, the accounts with the dictatorial past could be handled with more ease. Nonetheless, one should remember that societal support for Pinochet and the dictatorial policies did not dwindle immediately in Chile, nor were the fear and silences lifted instantaneously.[9]

The Twenty-First Century

The 1990 Truth and Reconciliation Commission report on human rights abuses dealt only with the worst violations, namely, cases of execution and disappearances. Demands that other forms of abuses should also be recognized and dealt with emerged immediately, yet it took two presidential terms and a shift in the political climate—from Christian Democrat to Socialist presidents—to see a governmental response. In 2003, President Ricardo Lagos established a new investigative commission, the National Commission on Political Imprisonment and Torture (known as the Valech Commission), with a mandate to record abuses committed in Chile between 1973 and 1990 by agents of the military regime. The report was released in 2004, registering around 38,000 cases of denunciations of persons imprisoned for political reasons, most of whom had been tortured. It also added 30 disappeared or executed persons to those recorded by the earlier Rettig Report (about 3,000). A few years later, under the first presidency of Michelle Bachelet (2006–10), the commission was reopened, and in this new round it certified close to 10,000 new cases of torture. The new report was presented in August 2011 and delivered to the incoming president, Sebastián Piñera, a member of a center-right coalition.[10]

Legally, testimony given to the commissions is considered confidential, and Rettig Report testimony can only be accessed through court requests. Further limitations exist for testimonies collected by the Valech Commission: they are to be kept secret for fifty years. Demands to open these archives for judicial purposes have been constant. In 2016, a proposed law to open the archives was defeated in Congress, yet new demands continue relentlessly. Human rights activists debate the scope of the opening—whether to lift completely the legal secrecy imposed on the historical records of the National Commission on Political Imprisonment and Torture or to make them available to the judiciary if victims agree, based on right to privacy concerns. Neither Congress nor the executive has responded to this demand, and it is one of the most significant pending issues in Chile, as the annual human rights reports of the Instituto Nacional de Derechos Humanos (National Institute for Human Rights, INDH) and the Universidad Diego Portales attest.

Perhaps the most significant institutional innovation in Chile during the period is the creation of a public policy institution to deal with issues related to human rights broadly understood to include the promotion and protection of civil, political, economic, social, and cultural rights, both at the individual and collective levels. Although this was already a recommendation of the Rettig Commission in 1991, it took more than a decade for the Chilean government to take steps in that direction. Only in 2005 did President Lagos propose the creation of the INDH, which got its final Senate approval in 2009, under the presidency of Michelle Bachelet. The INDH is an autonomous organization, with its own budget and governing board, and its mandate is to monitor the state of human rights in Chile, thus going well beyond the legacies of the dictatorial past. Its annual reports constitute an important diagnosis of advances and reversals in human rights policies, as well as a discussion of "pending issues." A further significant step in the direction of institutionalizing human rights policies was the incorporation in the Ministry of Justice of an undersecretary of human rights, a move that took place only in 2016.

Pinochet's detention in London in 1998 was a crucial moment for how the Chilean judiciary handled the crimes of the dictatorship. From then on, many lawsuits were filed, and while the judiciary has been active since, it has done so at a very slow pace. In fact, in 2013, the Inter-American Court of Human Rights declared the Chilean state responsible for the unjustified slowness in the initiation of investigations of documented cases of torture; and in another 2016 case, issues of torture during the dictatorship in Chile were also brought to the fore.

Condemned military men keep all the benefits attached to their military status. Moreover, they usually receive very lenient sentences and often are released early. These special privileged conditions are denounced time and again by human rights watchdogs such as victims associations and the INDH. To summarize, one can quote a public declaration of the INDH Council: "We carry a set of debts in these issues that still hinder the search for more truth, more justice and more reparations for victims of human rights violations during dictatorship" (Public Declaration of the INDH Council, August 21, 2015).

A highly significant symbolic and cultural landmark came into being during the first presidency of Michelle Bachelet, the Museo de la Memoria y de los Derechos Humanos (Museum of Memory and Human Rights). President Bachelet personally wanted to establish the museum and to leave office with the project completed. The date chosen for the opening ceremony was December 10, 2008, the sixtieth anniversary of the Universal Declaration of Human Rights. In her speech, the president insisted on the commitment to defend human rights as a basic principle beyond political and ideological differences. And the references to the dictatorship were in the tone of *Nunca más*.[11] The permanent exhibition of the museum covers a strictly defined time period: violations committed between September 11, 1973, and March 10, 1990, the date of the inauguration of President Aylwin. In the entry hall, an important inscription indicates that the script of the museum is based on the reports of the official Rettig and Valech Commissions. The clearly specified time period and the statement about the official sources have, no doubt, the political aim of legitimation. Given the high degree of polarization in Chilean society regarding dictatorship, the museum organizers tried to avoid disputes and controversies about its origins, meanings, and legacies. However, the actual exhibits include information and objects that go beyond the official reports, and the Documentation Center includes documents of various types and origins.

The personal will and power of President Bachelet was the driving force behind the museum. The project was carried out by a small group of people involved in human rights issues, in whom the president could confide. Open competitions for the design of the building and the museum script were carried out. Yet there was no major public debate about it. The decision was to limit controversy and open opposition as much as possible, based on the conviction that if it were open to public participation and debate, the museum would not exist (María Luisa Ortiz, interview, October 2016). Thus President Bachelet could inaugurate the museum before leaving office, on January 11, 2010.

The presidency of Sebastián Piñera (2010–14) did not affect the functioning of the museum. President Piñera himself, who had not visited the museum before taking office, paid an unpublicized visit. Since its opening in 2010, the museum has become an undisputed landmark in the urban landscape of Santiago. There seems to be no controversy about its presence and its survival. Its budget and its board and directors are solidly established and institutionalized. School visits have increased, and it has become an official script for framing the memories of dictatorship—its human rights violations, the resistance and reaction of the human rights movement, and the patterns of international solidarity of victims.

Initiatives stemming from societal organizations and groups have followed a different pattern, both in terms of their participatory nature and in the content of their demands and mandate. Londres 38 Espacio de Memorias (London 38 Space of Memories) is the result of struggles on the part of victims, relatives, and social activists to recover the building located in that central Santiago site, namely, Londres 38. For several years before the military coup of 1973, the building housed offices of the Partido Socialista de Chile (Socialist Party of Chile, PSCh). It was taken over by the military and turned into a clandestine detention and torture site, which functioned from 1973 through 1975. After that, the military government turned the building into the premises of the Instituto O'Higginiano, a historical institution linked to the military. Finally, in 2005, after years of demands and collective action, the government declared it a historic monument and halted the attempts to sell the building. Many rallies took place in front of the building throughout the years, and after negotiations regarding the its future, activists were able to enter the building in August 2007, and a memorial (blocks with names of disappeared persons replacing cobblestones on the sidewalk and street) was built in 2008.

For some time, the building remained empty, with only occasional openings linked to commemorations. The government wanted to turn the building into the premises of the INDH, while survivors and human rights activists wanted it as a memorial site. After negotiations, the government agreed to this demand and committed itself to provide permanent financial resources that would allow the Colectivo Londres 38 (Collective London 38) to manage the site autonomously. Since 2010, the national budget includes funds for this objective, yet special funds for restoration and building maintenance have to be negotiated, and only in 2016 were they forthcoming. Other local community-based memorials have been developed, following the Londres 38 pattern, such as the Memorial Detenidos-Desaparecidos de Paine (Detained-Disappeared Memorial of Paine), inaugurated in 2008. In that line, the government grants official recognition to sites of memory, usually at the request of social organizations linked to victims and survivors.

The agenda of these organizations tends to be very broad, encompassing a wider understanding of the defense of human rights. For instance, on the occasion of the fortieth anniversary of the military coup (in 2013), together with other organizations, Londres 38 organized a series of participatory activities in which issues related to the past were linked to current violations of human rights.[12] Similarly, in January 2017, the new director of the Museo de la Memoria, Francisco Estevez, expressed his intention to link the *Nunca más* (Never Again) with *Ahora más que nunca* (Now More than Ever):

> Today, more than ever, there is a need to fight for the rights of Indigenous peoples, the rights of migrants, the rights of children, young people, and women, and against gender-based violence, the rights of people with disabilities and for social inclusion, the rights of sexual diversity, and the rights of workers. (Estevez 2017; authors' translation)[13]

BEYOND SETTLING ACCOUNTS WITH THE DICTATORSHIP: HUMAN RIGHTS IN THE TWENTY-FIRST CENTURY

In the struggles to expand and deepen respect for human rights, different approaches intersect to gauge advances, stalemates, and regressions. Even when sharing a common ethical stand vis-à-vis the human condition, there are both optimists and pessimists among activists, scholars, the state, and international officers of diverse backgrounds and parts of the world. There are those who see progress and change and those who count defeats or paralysis—even questioning the human rights paradigm itself (Sikkink 2017). In part, as Sikkink claims, these diverse attitudes can be explained by the diverse yardsticks used to measure what is going on and by the different markers taken as points for comparison.

Both scholars and practitioners tend to use two different types of comparisons to conceptualize effectiveness of human rights policies: on the one hand, comparison to the ideal and, on the other, empirical comparisons. Depending on the metric of choice, one can arrive at very different conclusions about the legitimacy, effectiveness, and progress of human rights through time (Sikkink 2017, 17).

In fact, in the various scenarios in which the issues are discussed and decisions are taken, both yardsticks are used in conjunction, and controversies arise as to which one is to prevail. When comparing the current situation to the past, one can measure change. Yet in most cases, change is slow and nonlinear. Moreover, any measurement or comparison based on the ideal of full respect for human rights shows that the distance between reality and the ideal scenario is indeed very large. Perhaps this distance is not only large but constantly growing, insofar as the ideal is not a fixed and predetermined point of eventual arrival but a moving target based on the premise that the fundamental right is "the right to have rights" and that the specific content of struggles shifts and broadens. One always wants more.

It is undeniable that the conception of human rights that prevails in both Argentina and Chile is limited primarily to violations committed during dictatorship. The adoption of an integral human rights framework, broader than violations of the physical integrity of persons during dictatorship, is still to be implemented. Political, economic, social, and cultural rights, both individual and collective, are at stake. The question emerges as to whether the contrast and comparison between Chile and Argentina regarding human rights abuses during dictatorship also holds for other issues related to human rights as a whole. Although dealing with the vast range of issues involved in Argentina and Chile since the turn of the century goes beyond the scope of this chapter, we argue that the dilemmas posed by measuring rods, as discussed by Sikkink, are valid for the whole range of rights and responsibilities at stake.

To illustrate this matter, we take up briefly the recognition of rights of Indigenous peoples, a subject that has become highly visible and controversial during the period in both countries. Using this case, we want to show the paradoxical and always unfinished nature of the struggles to enlarge and deepen active citizenship and the rights involved in such struggles. Analogously, one could take up other subjects, such as the struggles for gender equality that include the redefinition of gender roles, gender self-identification, and sexual rights, among others.

Both in Argentina and in Chile, in the changing international context where rights of Indigenous peoples are increasingly being recognized, and after centuries-old conflicts and confrontations, state violence, cultural genocidal practices, and land dispossession, the incoming elected authorities have had to face the challenge of dealing with cultural diversity and with long-held claims.

In postdictatorial Chile, the initial recognition of the existence of various Indigenous ethnic groups took place through the 1993 Indigenous Law.[14] Based on the recognition of linguistic, territorial, and cultural diversity, the law called for the creation of a special state office—Corporación Nacional de Desarrollo Indígena (National Corporation for Indigenous Development, CONADI)—in charge of the promotion, coordination, and execution of development plans for the Indigenous peoples of Chile. Other governmental initiatives, such as the Comisión de Verdad Histórica y Nuevo Trato hacia los Pueblos Indígenas (Historical Truth and New Deal with Indigenous Peoples Commission), established in 2001, followed. Yet only in 2008 did the Chilean government ratify the International Labor Organization (ILO) Convention 169, and despite constant demands and several proposals, the Chilean Constitution was not amended to include an explicit reference to Indigenous peoples' rights. In spite of progressive governments (the "Left turn"), it is still a constitution reflecting a single unified nation; it does not recognize cultural diversity.

Through CONADI and other agencies, governmental action during the period included intercultural education programs, special scholarship programs, and some recognition of property titles. From a historical perspective, then, there is no doubt that there have been advances in the recognition of Indigenous peoples, their individual and collective rights. Yet state action has not been sufficient to respond to demands, and it has not resolved or eased the multiple conflicts between Indigenous peoples, the state, and various economic agents and interests active in the areas of the country where Indigenous groups claim their rights to land, to water, and to resources. Violent conflicts in the southern part of the country have been constant. And here is where the contrast between the reality and the ideals and international standards becomes more salient.

The shortcomings of Chilean policies have been the object of several critical international reports by UN rapporteurs and the Inter-American Court of Human Rights. Special attention has been placed on the use of an antiterrorist law of 1984 for the prosecution of Mapuche militants. In fact, since 2001 this law has only been invoked in cases involving Mapuches. Clearly, it has not had a deterrence effect, and according to experts, it is discriminatory and inefficient.

In 2017, President Bachelet announced the *Plan Araucanía*, with some symbolic measures such as establishing a National Day of Indigenous Peoples and the proposal to make Mapudungún an official language in the southern part of the country. Institutionally, the plan calls for the creation of a Ministry of Indigenous Peoples, a Council of Indigenous Peoples, and an interministerial commission that will consider the territorial claims of the Mapuche people against farmers and forestry companies. The objective is to gather in a participatory and transparent way the information that will allow for concrete solutions to the existing demands in this area, through short-, medium-, and long-term actions. Bachelet also announced policies to promote regional development and policies to protect victims of violence in the region.

Analysts and activists agree that there has been some state action geared to the recognition of Indigenous rights. From the perspective of international norms and ideals—which include the protection of ancestral territories, the right to self-determination, the mechanisms of participation and prior consultation, and equality and nondiscrimination before the law—however, real achievements seem to lie far in the future. The paradox is that as the state recognizes rights and promotes certain policies, populations become aware of the deficiencies in their citizenship rights, and this leads to redefinition of frameworks and to more claims.

The Argentine story is somewhat different. The 1994 Constitution recognized the ethnic and cultural preexistence of the Indigenous peoples of Argentina, specifying—among others—their right to bilingual and intercultural education, to ownership of the land they have traditionally occupied, and to their participation in the management of their natural resources and other issues that affect their interests. The mechanisms to assure these rights, however, have not been fully implemented, and thus, more than twenty years after constitutional recognition of rights, there has been little action. In fact, Indigenous communities are subject to institutional violence on the part of state agents, to criminal prosecutions, and to displacements linked to new extractive industries (open-air mining, fracking, lithium) and the advancement of the agricultural frontier for soy production (Amnesty International 2017). Most conflicts have remained localized, with Indigenous groups subject to arbitrary powerful local bosses and repression on the part of police and military forces. Some of these conflicts have reached national attention, when the claims led to action in the capital city of Buenos Aires. This was the case with the Qom protest that lasted for months in the center of Buenos Aires in 2014–15 and the rallies protesting repression of Mapuche communities in the province of Chubut during 2017, which gained national attention due to the disappearance and death of Santiago Maldonado, an activist supporting the Mapuche claim for their ancestral territory.[15]

One clear indication of the inequality of and discrimination against Indigenous peoples is that they are among the poorest sectors of the population of Argentina and Chile. In both countries, it seems to be relatively easy for progressive governments to recognize identities and cultural diversity and implement measures having to do with identity politics. However, when the claims affect valuable economic resources—ownership of ancestral territories, access to water sources, and free traditional passageways, for instance—the conflicts are more acute and recognition of rights is systematically suspended or delayed. Rights may be recognized on paper but not in actual practice.

In fact, the HHRR framework is so vast and comprises such a varied range of issues that a serious evaluation should be conducted singling out the rights at stake. The Left turn certainly amplified a broad notion of citizenship throughout the region, yet it was not able to face and find an answer to the condition of the Indigenous peoples and their rights, which remain relegated to the bottom of any political platform so far. In both Argentina and Chile, the Left turn left a bittersweet taste regarding an improvement in Indigenous living conditions and rights to landownership and water access, leaving many efforts unmaterialized.

When circumscribed to the dictatorship, the contrast and comparison between the postdictatorial processes in Chile and Argentina in the twenty-first century shows differences in the way the state has handled the legacies of the past. In Chile, powerful forces linked to dictatorship have blocked or hindered measures of redress—such as the repeal of the Amnesty Law of 1978, still in force, or the privileges of convicted military men. Processes of institutionalization are very slow and gradual in Chile. In contrast, given the type of transition, it was easier to change normative and institutional matters in Argentina, with more upfront and abrupt measures, creating and re-creating oppositions and confrontations—between the transition government and the military, between state authorities and the human rights movement. The process looks more like cycles than a straight road. Once established, actual policies, including operating budgets and the implementation of new laws and decrees, are kept in place in Chile, while in Argentina there is more room for periodic shifts in state policy. Yet, even when state officials would rather go in a different direction, the existence of a strong human rights movement and insistence of human rights activists keeps the issue open and active in Argentina.

In sum, the stories of the two countries show how issues related to human rights have been conceived and the struggles they engendered. In the struggles to enlarge and deepen the conception of human rights, interests and ideologies confront each other time and again. There cannot be a *punto final*, since the very notion of what constitutes the core of human rights is a historical and cultural construction. To paraphrase Norbert Lechner (1986), the construction of the ideal and desired social order is a conflicting and never ending endeavor.

NOTES

1. Adolfo Scilingo is now serving time in a prison in Spain. He stood trial in 2005 under Spain's universal jurisdiction law and was charged with crimes against humanity.

2. The report gives specific information about the number of lawsuits (458, of which 31 percent reached sentencing, with the remainder, as of the end of 2015, in different stages of the judicial process). There were 2,051 persons charged; 29 percent were convicted, 43 percent are still in process, and the remainder were acquitted (2 percent), died (10 percent), or in other stages of the legal process.

3. The annual Human Rights Report prepared by CELS gives detailed information regarding the actions of the judiciary each year of the period (CELS 2017).

4. The most renowned case is that of Christian von Wernick, chaplain of the Province of Buenos Aires Police Force, who was sentenced to life imprisonment in 2007.

5. For an analysis of Néstor Kirchner's speech, see Jelin 2017.

6. In an interview with a U.S.-based site, President Mauricio Macri referred to what happened during the last dictatorship as a "dirty war." When asked if 30,000 persons were missing, the president replied, "It is a debate I will not go into. I have no idea if it was 9,000 or 30,000. If they are registered on a wall or there are many more. It is an argument that does not make sense" (La Política Online 2016).

7. The 1978 Amnesty Law applies to all persons who took part in politically motivated criminal acts while the state of siege was in effect between 1973 and 1978. It provides a legal pretext for the courts to close investigations into deaths and disappearances, thereby ensuring impunity for those responsible. Thus the law closes the possibilities for many relatives of victims to at least discover the truth about the crimes committed.

8. When the first guilty verdicts resulted in prison sentences for high-ranking military officers—in particular, General Manuel Contreras, former head of the intelligence agency (Dirección de Inteligencia Nacional, DINA), for his responsibility in the murder of Orlando Letelier in Washington, DC—the Chilean government decided to build special prison facilities for them. In these facilities (Punta Peuco in 1995, under the presidency of Eduardo Frei Ruiz-Tagle; Penal Cordillera in 2004, under the presidency of Ricardo Lagos), prisoners have had access to amenities and services that place them in a highly privileged regime. Since then, the authorities have dismissed constant societal demands for eliminating these privileges and closing down such special facilities. The Penal Cordillera was closed during the first presidency of Sebastián Piñera, since it held just ten prisoners. They were transferred to the other special prison, Punta Peuco.

9. The description, analysis, and interpretations offered here regarding the Chilean developments, demands, and governmental action on human

rights issues are based on the annual human rights reports produced by the INDH since 2010 and the reports of the Center for Human Rights of the Universidad Diego Portales (published since 2003), complemented by scholarly publications and information in the media.

10. Just to indicate the change in positions vis-à-vis dictatorship, one should mention that the 2004 Valech I report and the list of victims (delivered during the Lagos presidency) were published online on the Ministry of Interior webpage. These documents stayed there until they were eliminated when President Piñera took office. Public protest, especially by the organization of relatives of detained and disappeared people, led to their reinstatement a week later.

11. "We will remember all the victims of violence. Our 'Nunca más' will be heard louder than ever. . . . Let us reaffirm today our commitment to the consistent defense of human rights at all times and in all places, regardless of the affiliation of the victims or of the perpetrators. I believe that this is the great lesson we must pass on to the next generations" (Museo de la Memoria).

12. Available on the organization's website, www.londres38.cl.

13. "Hoy más que nunca es necesario luchar por los derechos de los pueblos indígenas, los derechos de las y los migrantes, los derechos de las y los niños, de las y los jóvenes, de las mujeres y contra la violencia de género, de las personas en situación de discapacidad y por la inclusión social, los derechos de la diversidad sexual, los derechos de las y los trabajadores."

14. The sources of information about the way the Chilean government and the international organizations are handling indigenous rights are primarily the annual HHRR reports of the INDH and the Center for Human Rights of the Universidad Diego Portales, complemented by press reports.

15. This highly visible case followed many other less publicized yet locally important repressive policies and action, such as the repressive acts in the same region in January 2017 (Dandan 2017). The Maldonado case preceded the assassination of Rafael Nahuel, a young Mapuche man, by security agents in September 2017, again in a situation in which a Mapuche community was claiming its land.

REFERENCES

Acuña, Carlos, and Catalina Smulovitz. 1995. "Militares en la transición argentina: Del gobierno a la subordinación constitucional." In Carlos Acuña, ed., *Juicio, castigos y memorias: Derechos humanos y justicia en la política argentina*. Buenos Aires: Nueva Visión.

————. 1996. "Adjusting the Armed Forces to Democracy: Successes, Failures, and Ambiguities in the Southern Cone." In Elizabeth Jelin and Eric Hershberg, eds., *Constructing Democracy: Human Rights, Citizenship and Society in Latin America.* Boulder, CO: Westview Press.

Amnesty International. 2017. "Argentina 2017/2018." www.amnesty.org/es /countries/americas/argentina/report-argentina/.

Andriotti Romanin, Enrique Salvador. 2013. "Decir la verdad, hacer justicia: Los Juicios por la Verdad en Argentina." *European Review of Latin American and Caribbean Studies* 94 (April): 5-23.

Anguita, Eduardo. 2001. *Sano juicio: Baltasar Garzón, algunos sobrevivientes y la lucha contra la impunidad en Latinoamérica.* Buenos Aires: Sudamericana.

Basualdo, E. M., J. E. Santarcángelo, A. Wainer, C. Russo, and G. Perrone. 2016. *El Banco de la Nación Argentina y la dictadura: El impacto de las transformaciones económicas y financieras en la política crediticia (1976–1983).* Buenos Aires: Siglo Veintiuno.

Bonaldi, Pablo. 2006. "Hijos de desaparecidos: Entre la construcción de la política y la construcción de la memoria." *El pasado en el futuro: Los movimientos juveniles* 21 (1): 143–84.

Center for Legal and Social Studies (CELS). 2017. *Human Rights in Argentina: 2017 Report.* Buenos Aires: CELS.

Comisión Nacional sobre la Desaparición de Personas (CONADEP). 1984. *Nunca más.* Buenos Aires: CONADEP.

Dandan, Alegranda. 2017. "Para que la investigación no quede en la nada." *Página12.* Buenos Aires. www.pagina12.com.ar/71962-para-que-la -investigacion-no-quede-en-la-nada.

Ediciones La Intemperie. 2007. *No matar: Sobre la responsabilidad.* Córdoba: Ediciones La Intemperie.

Estevez, Francisco. 2017. "Opinión: Derechos humanos." Cooperativa 93.3 FM, Buenos Aires.

Granovsky, Martín. 2003. "Llegamos sin rencores y con memoria." *Página12.* Buenos Aires. www.pagina12.com.ar/diario/elpais/1-20614-2003-05-26 .html.

Instituto Nacional de Derechos Humanos (INDH). 2015. *La situación de derechos humanos en Chile.* Santiago de Chile: INDH.

Jelin, Elizabeth. 1994. "The Politics of Memory: The Human Rights Movement and the Construction of Democracy in Argentina." *Latin American Perspectives* 21 (2): 38–58.

————. 2008. "Victims, Relatives, and Citizens in Argentina: Whose Voice Is Legitimate Enough?" In Richard Ashby Wilson and Richard D. Brown, eds., *Humanitarianism and Suffering: The Mobilization of Empathy*. New York: Cambridge University Press.

———. 2017. *The Battle for the Past: How We Construct Social Memory*. Buenos Aires: Siglo Veintiuno.

Jelin, Elizabeth, and Susana G. Kaufman. 2000. "Layers of Memories: Twenty Years after in Argentina." In T. G. Ashplant, Graham Dawson, and Michael Roper, eds., *Studies in Memory and Narrative: The Politics of War Memory and Commemoration*. London: Routledge.

Lechner, Norbert. 1986. *La conflictiva y nunca acabada construcción del orden deseado*. Santiago de Chile: FLACSO.

Ministerio Público Fiscal. 2016. "Lesa humanidad: Procuraduría de Crímenes contra la Humanidad." www.mpf.gob.ar/lesa/.

O'Donnell, Guillermo, and Philippe C Schmitter. 1986. *Transitions from Authoritarian Rule: Tentative Conclusions about Uncertain Democracies*. Baltimore, MD: Johns Hopkins University Press.

La Política Online. 2016. "Macri: 'No tengo idea si fueron 9 o 30 mil desaparecidos, no tiene sentido la discusión.'" *La Política Online*. Buenos Aires. www.lapoliticaonline.com/nota/99512/.

Rosemberg, Jaime. 2015. "Mauricio Macri: 'Conmigo se acaban los curros en derechos humanos.'" *La Nación*. Buenos Aires. www.lanacion.com.ar /1750419-mauricio-macri-conmigo-se-acaban-los-curros-en-derechos -humanos.

Salvi, Valentina. 2012. "Sobre 'memorias parciales' y 'Memoria Completa': Prácticas conmemorativas y narrativas cívico-militares sobre el pasado reciente en Argentina." In Anne Huffschmid and Valeria Durán, eds., *Topografías conflictivas: Memorias, espacios y ciudades en disputa*. Buenos Aires: Nueva Trilce.

Sikkink, Kathryn. 2008. "From Pariah State to Global Protagonist: Argentina and the Struggle for International Human Rights." *Latin American Politics and Society* 50 (1): 1–29.

———. 2011. *The Justice Cascade: How Human Rights Prosecutions Are Changing World Politics*. Norton Series in World Politics. New York: Norton.

———. 2017. *Evidence for Hope: Making Human Rights Work in the 21st Century*. Princeton, NJ: Princeton University Press.

Verbitsky, Horacio. 1996. *The Flight: Confessions of an Argentine Dirty Warrior*. New York: New Press.

Verbitsky, Horacio, and Juan Pablo Bohoslavsky. 2013. *Cuentas pendientes: Los cómplices económicos de la dictadura*. Buenos Aires: Siglo Veintiuno.

EIGHT

Gender and Conditional Cash Transfers

Shifting the Citizenship Regime in Bolivia?

Nora Nagels

Conditional cash transfer (CCT) programs have spread across Latin America since the late 1990s. The development of CCT programs as the principal instrument of social assistance constitutes one of the major changes in social policy in Latin America over the past twenty years (Barrientos 2012). This chapter documents the development of these programs and analyzes their effect on state-society relations in Bolivia. In particular, it identifies the consequences of these changes as they pertain to gender relations from a citizenship regime perspective (Jenson 1997). As underlined in chapter 1, "'Citizenship regimes' refer to (1) the level of inclusion, which is defined by formal access to these rights (the existence of institutional and social mechanisms for participation in the definition and appropriation of these rights); and (2) the population's sense of belonging to a community anchored in both collective and intersectional identities (collectively defined by its members and recognized as such)" (Montambeault,

Balán, and Oxhorn, this volume). CCT programs aim to reduce the intergenerational cycle of poverty by transferring subsidies to poor families, on the condition that mothers send their children to school and that they send them for health checkups. They are among the most prominent policy innovations that coincided with the Left turn, even though they were not implemented by leftist governments alone (Huber and Stephens 2012, 142–46). As highlighted by Fenwick, "In the world's perception, the fame, success and sheer size of BF [Bolsa Familia] have forever tied CCTs to Brazil" (2013, 149). Almost all Latin American governments implemented CCTs, however, although the implicit purposes of the programs arguably changed according to their ideological inclinations (see Nagels 2014 for a comparison of Peru [right] and Bolivia [left]; and Tomazini 2013, for Mexico [right] and Brazil [left]). While left-leaning governments emphasized the redistributive role of CCTs, governments on the right used them as a tool to control low-income people.

This chapter looks at the CCT programs in Bolivia, the 2006 Bono Juancito Pinto (BJP) and the 2009 Bono Juana Azurduy (BJA), and their effect on gender relations during the Evo Morales administration. Bolivia is an interesting case because the shift from a neoliberal regime to an "Indigenous and postneoliberal" regime is among the most extreme in Latin America; in 2006, the Evo Morales New Left government explicitly announced it would tackle deep poverty—among other persistent issues faced by Indigenous peoples in particular—by way of large redistributive social policies. Moreover, gender inequalities were among the most pronounced in the region. As a result, the Bolivian case provides insights for the analysis of other countries in the region, as it questions the legacies of the Left turn in terms of challenging the deep intersectional and structural social, ethnic, and gender inequalities. The main argument of this chapter is that Bolivian CCTs—as the main social policies of the new plurinational state—have had mixed results in terms of citizenship. On the one hand, they have improved the material conditions of the poor and their sense of national belonging; on the other, they have not addressed gender inequalities and have in fact reinforced maternalism. This argument is divided into two sections. The first section articulates how the universal character of Bolivian CCTs has meant a return to a redistributionist state, improving social inclusion. Yet the analysis also shows that they have not sufficiently built universal social rights based on a broad understanding of citizenship. The second section looks at the effects of the Bonos on gender; although they improved recipients' sense of belonging, the Bonos remain maternalist. Maternalism is based on the reduction of women's role to that of motherhood, and is linked to moral values such as sacrifice and altruism (Jelin 1990). Maternalist Bolivian CCTs limit women's autonomy as "full citizens." In fact, women are depicted in Bolivian CCT programs as "mothers" rather than as individuals "having rights to have rights." Therefore, although the universal feature of the Bonos signifies an improvement to the Bolivian citizenship regime, their maternalist features detract from these advances. Most research on gender and Latin American CCTs depict the latter as maternalist, regardless of the government's ideological leanings (Gil-García 2015; Lavinas 2015; Molyneux 2007; Nagels 2016; Tabbush 2010). This is also the case in other regions. The majority of unconditional cash transfers and CCTs in Asia and Africa have been instrumental in singling out women as responsible for increasing their children's well-being. The evidence shows that these programs have enhanced women's role in the household, increased the use of contraception, improved education for girls, and reduced the incidence of female infanticide and early marriage (Bastagli et al. 2016, 212; Holmes and Jones 2013, 68). However, most programs have not altered the gendered division of labor. They "are not cognisant of women's dual roles as carers and productive workers, and do not consider the costs of having to collect transfers . . . , often at the expense of other income-generating activities" (Holmes and Jones 2013, 73). Literature review, primary document analysis, and qualitative analysis of interviews have built this argument. I performed about fifty interviews with policy makers and recipients of the Bonos in La Paz and El Alto between 2008 and 2010.[1] The use of discourse analysis for these interviews provides access to the perceptions and representations of the Bonos, as well as the gender relations and citizenship as constructed by policy makers and recipients.

THE STATE'S RESPONSIBILITY FOR SOCIAL INCLUSION AND SOCIAL CITIZENSHIP

Bolivia was one of the first testing grounds for structural adjustment policies imposed in the 1980s by international financial institutions, and one of the first Latin American countries to experiment with safety net policies in the 1990s. Strong anti-neoliberal social mobilizations in the 2000s brought the Movimiento al Socialismo (Movement Toward Socialism, MAS) to power in 2006 with the election of Evo Morales. Elected on a rhetoric of social inclusion and redistribution, Morales promised to change the Bolivian citizenship regime in two ways. First, the nationalization of hydrocarbons would bring the state back into social redistribution while guaranteeing social rights and social citizenship.[2] Indeed, "Morales's successful campaign for president in 2005 . . . included a call for 'health care for all'" (McGuire 2013, 20). Second, a new constitution would recognize and ensure collective rights for groups that had historically been excluded: peasants and Indigenous peoples. The Plurinational Constitution of Bolivia, approved by referendum in 2009, recognized a new political subject (Rice, this volume). In fact, article 30 of the Plurinational Constitution created a new category: "indigenous, native and peasant nation and people," who are a "whole human community that shares cultural identity, language, historical tradition, institutions, territoriality and worldview, whose existence predated the Spanish colonial invasion." Also, this constitution guarantees the right to education (arts. 77–90) and the right to health (arts. 35–39) (Estado Plurinacional de Bolivia 2009). It created "incentives to design programs like the Bono Juancito Pinto and the Bono Juana Azurduy in order to transform the rights into realities" (McGuire 2013, 25). In accordance with the main claims of the social movements that brought the MAS to power, the first reform adopted by Morales's government was the nationalization of the hydrocarbon industry. This reform ended the state's dependence on international aid and provided funding for new public policies, which strengthened the state, now explicitly responsible for social citizenship. Indeed, the "Plan nacional de desarrollo Bolivia digna, soberana productiva democrática y para Vivir Bien" (National Development Plan Bolivia Worthy, Sovereign and Productive, to Live Well, PND) of 2006 underlined that one of the first goals of the Morales administration was "to dismantle colonialism and neoliberalism in order to build a pluricultural and communitarian state" (Ministerio de Planificación del Desarrollo 2006, xv–2).[3] Under Evo Morales's government, the state has had a central role as the "promoter and agent of development through the industrialization of natural resources and increasing the added value of exports" (Ministerio de Planificación del Desarrollo 2006, 19). The new economic model of Andean-Amazonian capitalism developed by Bolivia's vice president, Garcia Linera, inspired the PND. This model aimed to decolonize the state by building "a strong state that regulates the expansion of the industrial economy, extracts its surpluses and transfers them to communities to make possible self-organization and mercantile development that is properly Andean and Amazonian" (García Linera 2005, 1). The driver of Andean-Amazonian capitalism was "no longer foreign investment but a productive state" (García Linera, in Natanson 2007, 163). Then the PND broke with its neoliberal citizenship regime insofar as the state increased its presence in key sectors of the Bolivian economy: hydrocarbon, mining, telecommunications, and electricity. During the neoliberal citizenship regime, private actors—and not public ones—played major roles in economic sectors. By contrast, under Morales's administration, the state became, according to Vice President García Linera, "the main collective entrepreneur" of the country (2010, 27). The following statistics confirm this. The public share in the economy rose from 13 percent to 22 percent in two and a half years (Svampa 2009, 57). Public investment also grew significantly: in 2002–5, it accounted for US$579 million a year, and in 2006–9 it was US$1,169 million a year; in 2009, it increased again, to US$1,439 million (Ministerio de Planificación del Desarrollo 2010). Public investment went from 6.3 percent of the gross domestic product (GDP) in 2005 to 10.5 percent in 2009 (Weisbrot, Ray, and Johnston 2009, 14). The trend continued; in 2010, it reached US$1527 million, of which close to a third was spent on social policies (Evia et al. 2011, 21). In 2014, the consolidated current public expenditures represented 46 percent of the GDP, whereas in 2005 it was 29 percent of the GDP. Public investment also increased in the past decade: in 2005, 63 percent of public investment came from external funding sources, compared to only 18 percent in 2013. By 2013, 40 percent of investment was spent on infrastructure, followed by 29 percent in the social sector, and 27 percent in the productive sector (IADB 2015, 4). These data show that the PND insistence on the "return of the state as an actor in the economy" was in fact taking place during the Morales administration. Moreover, the "return of the state" also concerned social policies. Since the nationalization of hydrocarbon, 91 percent of social spending was nationally funded

(Morales 2010, 6). The central government's social spending represented 17 percent of the GDP in 2013, an approximate increase of 5 percent compared to 2005 (IADB 2015, 15). The investment in public social spending in relation to the percentage of the total public expenditure increased significantly between 2006 and 2012, from 29.2 percent to 37.5 percent.[4] These numbers show that the state has increasingly taken on economic and social responsibilities. The shift in the role of the state made the Bolivian citizenship regime more inclusive, notably improving social policies. One of the main innovations in social policies were the Bonos. The BJP and BJA expedited the redistribution of resources resulting from the nationalization of hydrocarbons (Gray-Molina 2007). Bonos were also a response to pressures from many social groups for visible material gains (Canavire-Bacarreza and Mariscal 2010, 36). The BJP was established in October 2006 with three objectives: increase school enrollment, reduce the dropout rate, and diminish the intergenerational transmission of poverty (Estado Plurinacional de Bolivia 2006).[5] This program emerged hastily in response to a specific request from President Morales. Under the BJP, all children may receive 200 Bolivianos (around US$30) yearly upon meeting two conditions: enrollment in a public school and maintenance of a minimum of 80 percent rate of school attendance (Estado Plurinacional de Bolivia 2006, 1). Since 2006, the program has expanded to all grade levels of the public school system. Cecchini and Madariaga (2011) estimate that in 2010 this program reached 17.5 percent of Bolivia's total population, including 32.4 percent of its poor and 59.7 percent of the country's extreme poor. Therefore, "despite its universal character, . . . the BJP was one of the most progressive social programs in the country in terms of benefit and incidence" (McGuire 2013, 14). The BJA originated in other social policies proposed by the Evo Morales government that were never realized, such as the Plan de Erradicación de la Extrema Pobreza (PEEP) and the Plan Vida.[6] The majority of social policy projects developed under the PND included among their instruments a "mother-child" stipend, its objective being to reduce maternal and child mortality as well as child malnutrition. The BJA was the extension of a mother-child stipend, funded by the World Bank, that targeted the country's fifty-two poorest municipalities. The president decided to extend it to all pregnant women, those who were still breastfeeding, and those with children under two years of age who did not have another form of health care insurance. In order to receive the benefit (about US$260) over a period of thirty-three months, mothers were required (1) to have a formal form of identification for themselves and their children; (2) to attend prenatal health checkups; and (3) to commit to giving birth in a medical institution and follow through with postnatal checkups. They received different amounts of money for each condition fulfilled. In 2010, the BJA benefited 3.5 percent of Bolivia's total population, including 6.4 percent of the country's poor and 10 percent of its extreme poor (Cecchini and Madariaga 2011). Between 2009 and 2012, 33 percent of pregnant women who qualified for the BJA received it (Vidal Fuertes et al. 2015, 87). Both Bonos are CCTs. They share goals—to reduce poverty and to break the intergenerational cycle of poverty—and means—the conditions. However, the main difference between the Bonos and other CCTs in the region is their universalism. While almost all Latin American CCTs, and all CCTs implemented by rightist government (e.g., Mexico, Colombia, and Peru), are mean tested and targeted and address extreme poverty (Hunter and Sugiyama 2014), the selection of recipients for Bolivian Bonos is not based on income.[7] Indeed, all children enrolled in a public school and all mothers without health care insurance may benefit from the Bonos. For the government, this trend toward universalization of social policies has made the Bonos more in line with the processes of social justice, as highlighted by a BJA policy maker: "Being universal, the Bonos lead to a more equitable distribution of income ..., in line with certain concepts of universality and justice that the government wants to implement. Unlike others [CCTs] that are much more targeted" (quoted in Nagels 2013).

According to the Bonos' policy makers, the notions of social justice and the eradication of the causes of extreme poverty anchored in deep social inequalities are very strong in the Bonos. A PEEP policy maker explained this: "We are trying to put in place a structural change for the real eradication of extreme poverty, a level of social justice" (quoted in Nagels 2013).

The trend toward universalization of social assistance policies removed the controlling social function of the state and replaced it with the inclusion of previously excluded people. With the Bonos, the Bolivian state has guaranteed solidarity among all citizens belonging to the same country and the same political community. In this new citizenship regime, then, solidarity in terms of both state-society relations and relations among citizens has replaced individualism. Moreover, according to the Bonos' policy makers, the universality of the BJP and its having spread throughout Bolivian territory have improved social cohesion between the representatives of the state and recipients. The Bonos were perceived as intermediaries between public authorities and civil society, which brought the population closer to basic public services. According to a former director of the BJP, the Bonos have had a positive effect on access to all public institutions: "[Before the Bonos], no one was taking steps to get identity papers, because there was no obligation to do so. The peasant often thinks that censuses are done to impose taxes or something of the kind" (quoted in Nagels 2013).

Broadly speaking, one of main contributions of Evo Morales's government, as identified by our interlocutors, has been the recovery of the collective self-esteem of Indigenous and peasant people, resulting in their ability to exercise substantive citizenship. Under Morales's administration, all Bolivians know their rights and are able to claim them, for example, through massive mobilizations. The improvement in self-esteem of the lower strata of the population has contributed to greater social cohesion, as explained by a deputy minister of equality of opportunity:

> I believe that one of the most important impacts of this process of change is precisely the fact that we have succeeded in recovering the collective self-esteem of the Indigenous peoples and the popular sectors of our country, and also the substantive exercise of citizenship. . . . I believe that much has been done to recognize all Bolivians as citizens, with increasing opportunities in our country. (Quoted in Nagels 2013)

The integrating effects of the Bonos are very important at the symbolic level. They have demonstrated the government's commitment to the lower strata of the population and constitute an important break with former neoliberal antipoverty policies and citizenship regimes (Svampa 2009, 57). This commitment to improved social inclusion and the accompanying sense of belonging are essential to the citizenship regime. As highlighted by Hunter and Sugiyama in the Brazilian case,

"Governments that recognize all members of the national community as worthy enough to have their basic needs met and their life chances lifted can go far toward generating this sense [of belonging]" (2014, 830). The Bonos' universal design is then favorable to citizenship construction.

Nevertheless, this trend toward universalization has to be nuanced from a citizenship perspective. The Bonos have not sufficiently consolidated long-term social rights with assistance based on citizenship without depending on presidential or government preferences (Lautier and Ceballos 2007). Social rights based on citizenship should be universal in coverage, unconditional, and sustained by a progressive tax system (Lo Vuolo 2010). However, the Bonos are very much tied to the president, Evo Morales, as highlighted by a BJP recipient: "I thank Evo Morales, the president. He made it all possible. Because before, there was none of it! Nothing" (quoted in Nagels 2013). This quote shows that the recipients see the Bonos as a favor, a gift from the president, and not as a right based on citizenship.[8] Moreover, in a very unequal country such as Bolivia, the universalization of social protection requires major income tax reform, which requires societal compromise. This has not been reached in Bolivia where the core of the MAS—composed of peasants and workers in the informal sector—refused any tax reforms (Stefanoni 2010).

For the moment, coverage of the BJA and BJP has been universal, but the conditions have remained. The recipients' selection based on universalism has broken neoliberal means-testing targeting. However, the conditions linked to the Bonos—the obligation to attend school and undergo medical checkups—have made them more in line with neoliberalism, where such social policies function as tools for activating and controlling poor people. Besides, in order for the Bonos to be guaranteed as rights based on citizenship, universal social policies must "reach the entire population with similar generous transfers and high quality services, making the resort to markets strictly subject to preferences" (Martínez Franzoni and Sanchez-Ancochea 2014, 3–4). In Bolivia, public education and health services suffer from serious deficiencies in terms of quantity and quality. These deficiencies have encouraged families, even in low-income households, to use private services (McGuire 2013, 28). Even though the level of poverty is no longer the criterion for selecting Bonos recipients, the Bonos have not reduced dependence on the private sector because the quality of public health and education has not improved. The population covered by the Bonos has been too poor to access private education and health care insurance. "A large share of the population [benefiting from the Bonos] would pass a poverty means test if required to do so" (Hunter and Sugiyama 2014, 841). Therefore, the dichotomy between the poor—recipients of public social policies—and the others in society—those with access to private social protection systems—is maintained (Nagels 2018). To be considered universal rights based on citizenship, the entire population must be covered by these rights and social policies must not be only "social rights for the poor" (Nagels 2014, 124).

ENHANCING THE SENSE OF BELONGING WITHOUT IMPROVING WOMEN'S AUTONOMY

Postneoliberal social policies are often explicitly gender conscious (Macdonald and Ruckert 2009, 10). Established in the late 1990s, after the international conference on women in Beijing (1995), CCTs became concerned with the specific problems of "women in poverty" (Molyneux 2008, 22). They were based on the assumption that giving money to women empowered them by strengthening their bargaining power in intrahousehold decision making (Adato et al. 2000; Adato and Roopnaraine 2010). Recent studies have analyzed the gender characteristics of CCT programs in Latin America. By transferring income to women, these CCT programs have had positive effects on gender relations (e.g., Adato et al. 2000; Adato and Roopnaraine 2010; Bradshaw 2008; De Brauw et al. 2014; Escobar Latapí and González de la Rocha 2004; Holmes and Jones 2013; Hunter and Sugiyama 2014; Martínez Franzoni and Voorend 2012; Molyneux 2008). However, in most cases, these positive effects are felt largely at the individual and household levels. One exception may be found in the research of Hunter and Sugiyama (2014) on Bolsa Familia in Brazil. They demonstrated that this program enhanced the feeling of social inclusion and agency, hence improving poor Brazilian women's citizenship status. However, other studies have revealed that these programs have continued to be shaped by maternalism—even in Brazil (e.g., Gil-García 2015; Lavinas 2015; Molyneux 2007; Tabbush 2010). In other words, "women's unpaid care work continues to form the bedrock on which social protection is subsidised" (Hassim and Razavi 2006, 2). Throughout CCT programs, women are not seen as citizens or workers but rather as "mothers at the service of the state" (Molyneux 2007).[9]

Here we document the Bonos' positive effects on the recipients' sense of belonging as well as women's improved life conditions and argue that this sense of belonging is strictly linked to women's reproductive role, which reinforces maternalism. The design of the Bonos was not gendered and was not tied to Bolivian state institutions developed during the 1990s to reduce gender inequalities. Therefore, the Bonos reproduced maternalism and undermined female citizenship. First, women recipients of the Bonos appropriated them. As poor and Indigenous women, they have a greater sense of belonging to the national community. According to them, social policies such as the Bonos and more broadly the PND have served the interests of Indigenous peoples because these reflect their values and conceptions of development, as highlighted by a BJP recipient: "The Development Plan ... offers a different vision, a different conception from that of liberal individualism, a collective conception ... based on viable development models according to our new propositions of living well in Bolivia, which is our space" (quoted in Nagels 2013).

Therefore, poor and Indigenous women felt integrated in the political community, which shared their criteria, values, and representations. A delegate of the organization Bartolinas Sisas described this process:[10] "The Constitution was drafted based on suggestions from the community, and especially from social organizations. . . . The old Constitution before, no one knew how it had been made. . . . Now we have our Constitution drafted by ourselves. And above all there is a section dedicated to women who said that we must have a role in various secretariats and in more public positions (quoted in Nagels 2013).

These women sought inclusion in the political history of the country, from which they had always been excluded. Their citizenship in terms of belonging to the political community changed, as explained by a leader of the Coordinadora,[11] who emphasized how important it was to participate in the Constituent Assembly: "Before today, we, indigenous women, had not participated in the social pact for the formulation, elaboration, and promulgation of a Constitution recognizing us as women. . . . Now we are recognized. In addition, the new Constitution is for us the greatest qualitative leap at the political and strategic level in recent years (quoted in Nagels 2013).

The government's identification with Indigenous people and their values has improved the population's sense of belonging to the citizenship regime. For example, a female leader of the domestic workers expressed pride at the level of Indigenous representation in government: "From outside, we see us, because the government is indigenous and everything and this is the first time that indigenous people came to power, so we are very proud" (quoted in Nagels 2013). Indigenous peoples now find themselves with direct political representation. The government's representation of the MAS and especially of the president, Evo Morales, as both "Indigenous" and originating from the disadvantaged classes favored this identification between the "people" and the state.[12] Evo Morales wanted to embody, in the literal sense, the Bolivian people; he presents himself as the "savior" of the nation by continuing the long history of anticolonial struggles (De la Torre 2010, 57).

The second positive effect of the Bonos concerns the material gains for women. Recipients greatly appreciated the help that the subsidy represented in their daily lives, as expressed by one of the BJP recipients: "Wow, yes! It has changed a lot for us! It is a joy because we support our children. . . . This Bono Juana Azurduy is also a motivation for there to be more care in health centers. . . . It helps us a lot" (quoted in Nagels 2013). Recipients also underlined the positive shift in their circumstances since the Morales administration. One woman said, "Before there was nothing, like I told you. There was nothing of nothing. Without help, nothing . . . , before we had nothing. Here we were abandoned" (quoted in Nagels 2013). Although they highlighted the positive material gains, they linked them exclusively to their children's well-being. For example: "Now for babies, the Bono Juancito Pinto is something! For my children to go to school. [Before] how many patched sweaters I had to sell! Now all this has improved. Now schoolchildren can buy all the school supplies, clothes. . . . It is already something" (quoted in Nagels 2013).

These material gains enhanced Bonos recipients' sense of belonging and citizenship because they made it possible for them to live decent lives. Indeed, shoes and good clothing were seen as essential to a dignified existence (Hunter and Sugiyama 2014, 835). As Hunter and Sugiyama have written regarding the Brazilian case, "The daily fulfillment of basic needs is a precondition for feelings of social inclusion. Dignity is necessary for citizenship" (2014, 835). Similarly, the Morales administration's commitment to social integration improved the lower strata's sense of belonging. In Bolivia, this sense of belonging was also strengthened during the past decade by social and Indigenous movements and organizations that developed a vibrant sense of citizenship. With the "high level of social participation and community empowerment, ... Bolivians are more likely to have a sense of 'ownership'. These programs are no longer considered a temporary public benefit, but rather an acquired human right" (McGuire 2013, 23). In terms of gender relations, the Bonos allow for the relative economic empowerment of women. The direct transfer of subsidies to women strengthens their bargaining position within households for the allocation of these funds. Nevertheless, this improvement remains marginal because the subsidies are granted almost exclusively to meet primary needs such as food and clothes for children (Vidal Fuertes et al. 2015, 15) and are not sufficient for investing in income-generating activities (Molyneux and Thomson 2011, 208). Other positive effects for women are related to increased access to health services. For example, especially in rural areas, the BJA increased the monitoring of pregnancy, institutional birthing, and the postbirth process (Vidal Fuertes et al. 2015, 17). These positive changes are nevertheless very precarious and do not transform gender structures or the sexual division of labor. All the positive effects of the Bonos for women—the improvement of their maternal image in the home; the acquisition of an identity card; access to the bank, health care institutions, and public space; the increase in their self-esteem—are linked to their reproductive role. These changes did not lead to further structural changes in gender relations because the design of the Bonos relies largely on the unpaid care work of women in order to improve children's well-being. Indeed, two underlying conceptions of gender differences were used to justify the transfer of money exclusively to women, thus reinforcing the traditional gender roles. First, program managers and Bonos recipients assumed the existence of a clear difference between women and men as well as mothers and fathers in relation to children. The "cost-effectiveness" justifies paying the CCT to the mother, as illustrated by the following quote from the BJA operating chief: "Generally, in Bolivia ... the important person for health is the mother more than the father. The mother has more of a relationship with the child to go to health checkups; this is not the case with the father. And the aim is to strengthen this aspect, that is to say, the power that the mother has in [children's] health" (quoted in Nagels 2013).

Second, moral values are attributed to the sexes. In this strict and dichotomous view of men and women, vice is associated with the former and virtue with the latter. Men are described as likely to spend the subsidy for personal ends or on failings, such as alcohol. There was a clear justification for excluding men from CCT programs. A former male director of the BJA expressed this mistrust of men: "We were not able to be 100% sure that the fathers were not going to spend their money on drinks at the traditional bachelors' Friday night outings taking place all over the country" (quoted in Nagels 2013). The BJA coordinator for La Paz shared this view:

> If they [men] receive money for their children, they say "celebrate first": two small beers, then 4, 8, 10, 12 . . . and at 6:00 the next morning, there is no more money for the baby. . . . Because the idiosyncrasies of our people are that the man who receives the money will . . . squander it on alcoholic beverages. (Quoted in Nagels 2013)

Female recipients of the Bonos also shared these negative representations of men and depict themselves as mothers caring for their children. As seen above, recipients linked the material gains exclusively to their children. Moreover, they condemned men's behavior. For example, the director of an informal workers organization in La Paz spoke about men's tendency to party: "Some fathers who requested Juancito Pinto Friday reappeared on Tuesday penniless. . . . If it is the man who receives it, he goes to the bar and after 6 beers, he forgets Bono Juancito Pinto" (quoted in Nagels 2013). All actors involved in the Bonos, from policy makers to recipients, shared and never questioned this representation of men. What emerges is an overwhelming vision of men as irresponsible and selfish, focused on leisure and alcohol. While these representations have negative effects for men, most important, they reinforce social norms that assign women responsibility for maintaining the household, whether they have employment or not.

The Bonos rely largely on the unpaid care work of women to improve children's well-being. The programs therefore reinforce preexisting maternalism and the sexual division of labor. Because the Bonos discourage men from taking on the responsibility of care work and because of their conditional feature, they overburden women. Programs promoted women's role as the caregiver in the family and increased women's time poverty. The time invested in the fulfillment of conditions was time "stolen" from income-generating activities. The Bonos can therefore reduce the opportunities for women to graduate out of poverty (Holmes and Jones 2013, 73, 84). This extra work reinforces gender inequalities. As Molyneux highlighted, "Women's position within the social division of labor is not only reinforced by confirming their customary caregiving roles, but the programs depend to a significant degree upon their carrying out this work without any direct financial compensation for their time and, indeed, exist in tension with any income generating activities that they may undertake" (2007, 37).

Maternalism weakens the acquisition of social rights and thereby the citizenship regime. Maternalism hinders the process of individuation of women needed for the construction of full citizens holding rights and duties. This individuation involves the differentiation of the individual from social categories in order to be emancipated from all tutelage relationships—marital and paternal in the case of women—and to be able to integrate as subjects of law within a social group marked by power inequalities. In this dynamic, a wider identity, without reference to a social category in particular, is gradually built that generates links of responsibility and solidarity with other individual citizens (Jelin 1996, 267). The individuation process relates to the conditions of being and acting as a political subject, acquiring personal status without having to locate oneself as a member of a social category. For women, it therefore involves being recognized and recognizing themselves as subjects in themselvesand not being defined by their assigned roles as mothers and wives (Marques-Pereira and Santiso 2002, 77).

Maternalism is hegemonic insofar as women recipients have difficulties representing themselves as individuals, independent of their families. Because women identified their femininity primarily with maternity, their first responsibility being to sacrifice themselves for the needs of the home and their children, they did not position themselves as citizens entitled to their own rights with a sense of belonging to the community as individuals. For women, the process of individuation implies no longer perceiving themselves as constantly and exclusively based on others but recognizing and identifying the asymmetrical power relations that generate their subordination as women—and not only as poor and Indigenous mothers. This dynamic then leads to the politicization of gender relations through the representation of a collective identity of women rather than mothers. This would allow women to become equal individuals belonging to the political community who can influence public space (Marques-Pereira 1996, 21, 31).

However, as we have seen, far from being recognized as individuals and citizens, as equal in terms of rights and duties, the women recipients of the Bonos are seen more than ever as linked to the family. Maternalism has excluded women as subjects of law instead of including them as intermediaries in their roles as mothers. They are intermediaries between state actions and their children. This turns them into subject-subjected (to the private, the domestic) and not into equal and autonomous individual citizens (Marques-Pereira and Santiso 2002). The Bonos reinforce the maternalist stereotype associating motherhood with the moral virtues of self-sacrifice and altruism. As mothers, women, and not men, are seen as individually responsible for social well-being. Indeed, the Bonos' "reliance on female reproductive, care and domestic work is based on the hypothesis that women are naturally predisposed to serve their family and others" (Nagels 2016, 487). They instrumentalize and appropriate the voluntary work done by women, work that is naturalized and rendered invisible. Rather than question gender inequalities, the Bonos deepen them. Therefore, the citizenship regime of poor indigenous women weakens, as their individuation process is limited.

This chapter has argued that the Bolivian citizenship regime has shifted away from neoliberalism and that this shift has had consequences for gender relations. If the Bonos—the main social policies of the plurinational state of Bolivia—improved the state's commitment to those in the lower strata of society and their inclusion and sense of belonging, they did not address gender inequalities.

The Bonos are very similar to other CCT programs in Latin America implemented by both right- and left-wing governments but differ from them in their universality. The universal design of the Bonos proved the Morales administration's commitment to social inclusion and social citizenship. The citizenship regime shifted away from neoliberalism with the return of the state as an economic agent, as well as an agent in charge of social responsibility. The increase in public and social expenditures has demonstrated this. The inclusiveness of the Bonos improved the sense of belonging and the construction of social citizenship. The context of decades-long social mobilization and strong social movements is also essential in the appropriation process of the Bonos. Like Bolsa Familia, CCTs, "if designed . . . well, . . . can contribute to elevating a sense of belonging . . . in a setting where exclusion has rendered poor people effectively unable to even claim their citizenship rights" (Hunter and Sugiyama 2014, 841). However, the Bonos are insufficient to consolidate social rights to assistance based on citizenship because they are very strongly linked to President Evo Morales, because they do not limit the private/public dichotomy in the production of welfare, and because they do not improve the quality of public services.

The gender-related consequences of the Bonos are mixed. Women recipients appropriated the Bonos as Indigenous and poor people. In addition, the material gains enhanced their dignity, which is essential for citizenship. However, they strictly linked this sense of belonging to their Indigenous and social identity and not to their gender identity. Moreover, the maternalist design of the Bonos revealed the limitation of women's rights. Maternalism limits women's autonomy as "full citizens" and undermines social rights based on citizenship. Women are not full citizens but rather mothers at the service of others and the state. This undermines their individuation process and the possibility to claim rights as individuals—emancipated from marital or paternal tutelage relationships—with rights. Identified solely as mothers, women are subject to social rights only as mothers and acquire the rights of social citizenship only as "dependents." Therefore, social policies rely largely on the unpaid care work of women to improve children's well-being, reinforcing gender inequalities.

The gendered character of the new citizenship regime has not addressed the deep gender inequalities in Bolivia. In spite of the fact that Indigenous women have been more included in this citizenship regime, the gender agenda and the interests of women—subordinated to men—have not been taken sufficiently into account by the new administration. Thus gender inequalities are still very strong in Bolivia. For example, between 2009 and 2012, 64 percent of women who died were killed by femicide, and in 2014, 50 percent of Bolivian women had suffered from gendered psychological violence, 30 percent from physical violence, and 10 percent from sexual violence. These rates were some of the highest in Latin America (Coordinadora de la Mujer 2014, 102).

As a result, the Bolivian case provides insights for the analysis of other countries in the region. First, the Bonos are the only universal cash transfers in Latin America.[13] As McGuire has written, the case of Bolivia "shows that formally universalistic programs, at least within specific demographic domains, are affordable, as well as desirable, even in poor countries" (2013, 32). Universal social policies avoid the limitations of means-testing—the administrative costs, the stigmatization of recipients, and so on—and, overall, improve the sense of belonging and the construction of a citizenship regime based on social inclusion and solidarity. This sets an example for other leftist governments in the region that share those aims. However, universal social policies, without explicit gender equality objectives, fail to reduce gender inequalities (Jenson and Nagels 2016). They reproduce existing gender relations, in this case based on maternalism. Maternalism is a strong legacy of Latin American social policies (Ewig 2010), regardless of the government's ideological leanings. To break this legacy, leftist governments should articulate gender aims within their social justice objectives.

NOTES

1. All these interviews are analyzed in Nagels 2013.

2. Nationalization in this case was more of a negotiation on taxes with transnational corporations than expropriation (CEDLA 2006).

3. All translations are mine.

4. Website: http://dds.cepal.org/gasto/indicadores/ficha/2016#; consulted on November 4, 2016.

5. The BJP was promulgated in *Decreto Supremo* no. 28899, October 26, 2006.

6. The BJA was established in *Decreto Supremo* no. 0066, April 3, 2009. Interviews with policy makers of these programs and the BJA were conducted and analyzed.

7. In other leftist countries such as Argentina, the selection of CCT recipients is not based on income but on unemployment. In Brazil, even though

Bolsa Familia is means-testing targeted, its coverage is extensive—about 25 percent of the population (see Fenwick 2013 for a comparison of CCTs in Brazil and Argentina).

8. Molyneux and Thomson (2011, 49) also underlined this. In their interviews, husbands of women recipients perceived that the BJA children belonged to Evo Morales.

9. This paragraph is an adaptation of Nagels 2016.

10. Bartolinas Sisas was created in 1979 as the "female counterpart" to the Unique Confederation of Rural Laborers of Bolivia (CSUTCB).

11. The Coordinadora is an organization that brings together the main women's organizations in the country, such as Bartolina Sisa, informal workers, domestic workers, and women's ethnic organizations.

12. If President Morales presents himself and is represented on the international scene as "Indigenous," his ethnic Aymara or Quechua origin is debated. For more details, see esp. Canessa 2005, 2008; Lacroix 2007.

13. The only other universal CCT is in Mongolia (McGuire 2013, 27).

REFERENCES

Adato, Michelle, Benedicte De la Briere, Dubravka Mindek, and Agnes Quisumbing. 2000. *The Impact of PROGRESA on Women's Status and Intrahousehold Relations.* Washington, DC: International Food Policy Research Institute.

Adato, Michelle, and Terry Roopnaraine. 2010. "Women's Status, Gender Relations, and Conditional Cash Transfers." In Michelle Adato and J. Hoddinott, eds., *Conditional Cash Transfers in Latin America.* Baltimore, MD: Johns Hopkins University Press.

Barrientos, Armando. 2012. "Dilemas de las políticas sociales latinoamericanas: ¿Hacia una protección social fragmentada?" *Nueva Sociedad,* no. 239: 65–78.

Bastagli, Francesca, Jessica Hagen-Zanker, Luke Harman, Georgina Sturge, Valentina Barca, Tanja Schmidt, and Luca Pellerano. 2016. *Cash Transfers: What Does the Evidence Say? A Rigorous Review of Impacts and the Role of Design and Implementation Features.* London: Overseas Development Institute.

Bradshaw, Sarah. 2008. "From Structural Adjustment to Social Adjustment: A Gendered Analysis of Conditional Cash Transfer Programmes in Mexico and Nicaragua." *Global Social Policy* 8 (2): 188–207.

Canavire-Bacarreza, Gustavo, and Mirna Mariscal. 2010. *Políticas macroeconómicas, choques externos y protección social en Bolivia.* La Paz: CEPAL.

Canessa, Andrew. 2005. *Natives Making Nation: Gender, Indigeneity, and the State in the Andes.* Tucson: University of Arizona Press.

———. 2008. "The Past Is not Another Country: Exploring Indigenous Histories in Bolivia." *History and Anthropology* 19 (4): 353–69.

Cecchini, Simone, and Aldo Madariaga. 2011. *Programas de transferencias condicionadas: Balance de la experiencia reciente en América Latina y el Caribe.* Santiago de Chile: CEPAL.

Centro de Estudios para el Desarrollo Laboral y Agrario (CEDLA). 2006. *Legitimando el orden neoliberal: 100 días de gobierno de Evo Morales.* La Paz: CEDLA.

Coordinadora de la Mujer. 2014. *La situación de las mujeres en Bolivia: Encuesta nacional de discriminación y exclusión social.* La Paz: OXFAM International.

De Brauw, Alan, Daniel O Gilligan, John Hoddinott, and Shalini Roy. 2014. "The Impact of Bolsa Familia on Women's Decision-Making Power." *World Development* 59 (July): 487–504.

De la Torre, Carlos. 2010. *Populist Seduction in Latin America.* Athens: Ohio University Press.

Escobar Latapí, Agustín, and Mercedes González de la Rocha. 2004. *Evaluación cualitativa del programa Oportunidades.* Mexico: Centro de Investigación y Estudios Superiores en Antropología Social.

Estado Plurinacional de Bolivia. 2006. *Bono Juancito Pinto.* La Paz: Ministerio de Educación y de Cultura, Unidad Ejecutora del Bono Juancito Pinto.

———. 2009. *Constitución política del Estado Boliviano.* La Paz: Asamblea Constituyente and Honorable Congreso Nacional. http://pdba .georgetown.edu/constitutions/bolivia/bolivia.html.

Evia, José Louis, Rolando Jordán, Mauricio Medinaceli, and Mario Napoleón Pacheco. 2011. *Informe de Milenio sobre la economía: Gestión 2010.* La Paz: Konrad Adenauer Stiftung. https://fundacion-milenio.org/informe -economico/.

Ewig, Christina. 2010. *Second-Wave Neoliberalism: Gender, Race, and Health Sector Reform in Peru.* University Park: Pennsylvania State University Press.

Fenwick, Tracy Beck. 2013. "Stuck between the Past and the Future: Conditional Cash Transfer Programme Development and Policy Feedbacks in Brazil and Argentina." *Global Social Policy* 13 (2): 144–67.

García Linera, Alvaro. 2005. "Du 'capitalisme andino-amazonien.'" *El Diplo, édition du Cône Sud du Monde Diplomatique.* La Paz. www.eldiplo.org.

————. 2010. "El Estado en transición: Bloque de poder y punto de bifur-
cación." In Á. G. Linera, R. Prada, L. Tapia, and O. V. Camacho, eds., *El
Estado: Campo de la lucha*. La Paz: Muela del Diablo.

Gil-García, Óscar F. 2015. "Gender Equality, Community Divisions, and Autonomy: The Prospera Conditional Cash Transfer Program in Chiapas,
Mexico." *Current Sociology* 64 (3): 447–69.

Gray-Molina, George. 2007. "El reto posneoliberal de Bolivia." *Nueva Sociedad* 209 (May–June): 118–29.

Hassim, Shireen, and Shahra Razavi. 2006. "Gender and Social Policy in a
Global Context: Uncovering the Gendered Structure of 'The Social.'" In
Shireen Hassim and Shahra Razavi, eds., *Gender and Social Policy in a
Global Context*. New York: Palgrave.

Holmes, Rebecca, and Nicola Jones. 2013. *Gender and Social Protection in the
Developing World: Beyond Mothers and Safety Nets*. London: Zed Books.

Huber, Evelyne, and John D. Stephens. 2012. *Democracy and the Left: Social Policy
and Inequality in Latin America*. Chicago: University of Chicago Press.

Hunter, Wendy, and Natasha Borges Sugiyama. 2014. "Transforming Subjects
into Citizens: Insights from Brazil's Bolsa Família." *Perspectives on Politics* 12 (4): 829–45.

Inter-American Development Bank (IADB). 2015. *Bolivia 2011–2015: Evaluación del Programa País*. Washington, DC: IADB.

Jelin, Elizabeth. 1990. "Citizenship and Identity: Final Reflections." In Elizabeth Jelin, *Women and Social Change in Latin America*. London: Zed
Books.

————. 1996. "La construcción de la ciudadanía: Solidaridad, responsabilidad
y derechos." In N. Henríquez, ed., *Encrucijadas del saber: Los estudios de
género en las ciencias sociales*. Lima: Facultad de Ciencias Sociales, Pontifi-
cia Universidad Católica del Perú.

Jenson, Jane. 1997. "Fated to Live in Interesting Times: Canada's Changing
Citizenship Regimes." *Canadian Journal of Political Science / Revue canadienne de science politique* 30 (4): 627–44.

Jenson, Jane, and Nora Nagels. 2016. "Social Policy Instruments in Motion:
Conditional Cash Transfers from Mexico to Peru." *Social Policy and Administration* 52 (1): 323–42.

Lacroix, Laurent. 2007. "La gouvernance de l'ethnicité en Bolivie." *Outre-terre*
1 (18): 253–71.

Lautier, Bruno, and Marco Ceballos. 2007. "Les politiques sociales en Amé-
rique latine: 'Ciblage large' ou émergence d'un droit à l'assistance?" In
Georges Couffignal, ed., *Amérique latine: Les surprises de la démocratie*.
Paris: La Documentation Française.

Lavinas, Lena. 2015. "21st Century Welfare." *New Left Review* 84: 5–40.

Lo Vuolo, Rubén. 2010. *Las perspectivas de ingreso ciudadano en América Latina: Un análisis en base al "Programa Bolsa Familia" de Brasil ya la "Asignación Universal por Hijo para Protección Social" de Argentina.* Buenos Aires: Centro Interdisciplinario para el Estudio de Políticas Públicas.

Macdonald, Laura, and Anne Ruckert. 2009. "Post-Neoliberalism in the Americas: An Introduction." In Laura Macdonald and Anne Ruckert, eds., *Post-Neoliberalism in the Americas.* New York: Palgrave MacMillan.

Marques-Pereira, Bérengère. 1996. "Diversité des sens et perspectives de la citoyenneté sociale des femmes en Amérique latine et au Brésil." In B. Marques-Pereira and A. Carrier, eds., *La citoyenneté sociale des femmes au Brésil: Action collective, reproduction, informalité et domesticité, Paris, L'Harmattan.* Brussels: CELA-IS, L'Harmattan, UNESCO.

Marques-Pereira, Bérengère, and Javier Santiso. 2002. "Inclusion politique des femmes: Une démocratisation sans qualités?" In Javier Santiso, ed., *A la recherche de la démocratie: Mélanges offerts à Guy Hermet.* Paris: Karthala.

Martínez Franzoni, Juliana, and Diego Sanchez-Ancochea. 2014. "The Double Challenge of Market and Social Incorporation: Progress and Bottlenecks in Latin America." *Development Policy Review* 32 (3): 275–98.

Martínez Franzoni, Juliana, and Koen Voorend. 2012. "Blacks, Whites, or Grays? Conditional Transfers and Gender Equality in Latin America." *Social Politics* 19 (3): 383–407.

McGuire, James W. 2013. "Conditional Cash Transfers in Bolivia: Origins, Impact, and Universality." Paper delivered at the Annual Meeting of the International Studies Association, San Francisco.

Ministerio de Planificación del Desarrollo. 2006. *Plan nacional de desarrollo: Bolivia digna soberana, productiva y democratica para Vivir Bien.* La Paz: Ministerio de Planificación del Desarrollo. www.ademaf.gob.bo/normas /ds29272.pdf.

———. 2010. *Plan de desarrollo económico y social para el Vivir Bien.* La Paz: Ministerio de Planificación del Desarrollo. www.fndr.gob.bo/bundles /fndrdemo/downloads/pdes/pdes2016-2020.pdf.

Molyneux, Maxine. 2007. *Change and Continuity in Social Protection in Latin America.* Geneva: United Nations Research Institute for Social Development (UNRISD).

———. 2008. *Conditional Cash Transfers: A Pathway to Women's Empowerment?* Brighton: Institute of Development Studies, University of Sussex. http:// gsdrc.org/document-library/conditional-cash-transfers-a-pathway-to -womens-empowerment/.

Molyneux, Maxine, and Marilyn Thomson. 2011. "Cash Transfers, Gender Equity and Women's Empowerment in Peru, Ecuador and Bolivia." *Gender & Development* 19 (2): 195–212.

Morales, Natasha. 2010. *La política social en Bolivia: Un análisis de los Programas sociales (2006–2008)*. La Paz: Inter-American Development Bank. https://publications.iadb.org/bitstream/handle/11319/2763/lapoliticasocialenbolivia:unanalisisdelosprogramassociales(2006-2008).pdf?sequence=1.

Nagels, Nora. 2013. "Genre et politiques de lutte contre la pauvreté au Pérou et en Bolivie: Quels enjeux de citoyenneté?" PhD dissertation, Institut de hautes études internationales et du développement, Geneva.

————. 2014. "Programmes de transferts conditionnés au Pérou et en Bolivie: Entre ciblage et universalisation de l'assistance sociale." *Revue Internationale de Politique Comparée* 21 (1): 111–32.

————. 2016. "The Social Investment Perspective, Conditional Cash Transfer Programmes and the Welfare Mix: Peru and Bolivia." *Social Policy and Society* 15 (3): 479–93.

————. 2018. "Incomplete Universalization? Peruvian Social Policy Reform, Universalism, and Gendered Outcomes." *Social Politics: International Studies in Gender, State and Society* 25 (3): 410–31.

Natanson, José. 2007. "Las reformas pactadas: Entrevista a Álvaro García Linera." Buenos Aires. http://nuso.org/media/articles/downloads/3436_1.pdf.

Stefanoni, Pablo. 2010. "Bolivia después de las elecciones: ¿A dónde va el evismo?" *Nueva Sociedad* 225 (January–February): 4–18.

Svampa, Maristella. 2009. "Evo ou l'articulation du 'communautaire-indigène' au 'national-populaire.'" *Alternatives Sud* 16 (3): 45–61.

Tabbush, Constanza. 2010. "Latin American Women's Protection after Adjustment: A Feminist Critique of Conditional Cash Transfers in Chile and Argentina." *Oxford Development Studies* 38 (4): 437–59.

Tomazini, Carla. 2013. "Les conflits autour des politiques de transferts monétaires: Les coalitions de causes et le renforcement du paradigme 'capital humain' au Brésil et au Mexique." In Carla Tomazini and Melina Rocha Lukic, eds., *L'analyse des politiques publiques au Brésil*. Paris: Collection Logiques Politiques.

Vidal Fuertes, Cecilia, Sebastián Martínez, UDAPE, BID, Pablo Celhay, Sdenka Claros Gómez, and UDAPE. 2015. *Evaluación de impacto del Programa de Salud Materno Infantil "Bono Juana Azurduy."* La Paz: Unidad de Análisis de Politicas Sociales y Económicas (UDAPE).

Weisbrot, Mark, Rebecca Ray, and Jake Johnston. 2009. *Bolivia: The Economy during the Morales Administration.* Washington, DC: Center for Economic and Policy Research (CEPR).

NINE

Improvements at the Limits of Society

The Left Tide and Domestic Workers' Rights

MERIKE BLOFIELD

As the editors write in the introduction, the left "came into power with the promise of deepening and widening citizenship regimes" (Balán and Montambeault, this volume). The rights of paid domestic workers, that is, nannies and maids, is a particularly good case for examining whether the left has performed with regard to this promise, throughout society. Paid domestic workers suffer from multiple disadvantages as an occupational group: at about 15 percent of the urban female labor force in Latin America, they are overwhelmingly female, tend to be members of racial and ethnic minorities, and earn on average very low wages. Labor laws have explicitly discriminated against them, according them less rights and protections than other workers. Thus we can argue that the rights of paid domestic workers are a litmus test of the left's commitment to widening and deepening citizenship, both in terms of formal rules of citizenship and in terms of practices, as outlined in the introduction.

In this chapter, I examine whether Left turn governments, more than their nonleft predecessors and/or nonleft contemporary counterparts, have promoted domestic workers' rights. In 2000, only one country granted equal legal rights to domestic workers—Colombia—and this was through a 1998 Constitutional Court ruling rather than by the government. By 2016, however, much had changed: eleven of the eighteen countries in the region had reformed laws on domestic workers, and eight of these now grant domestic workers equal labor rights. Many have also strengthened efforts to enforce the laws and to formalize this sector. Drawing on Blofield (2012), I argue that stronger rights and protections were made possible by the interactive effects of domestic workers' organizing, more sympathetic left-wing governments, and the watershed International Labor Organization (ILO) 2011 Convention on Domestic Workers. First, I discuss the conceptual and empirical context of paid domestic workers in Latin America, then present my theoretical argument, and, in conclusion, discuss the changes in Latin America up to 2016.

THE DYNAMICS OF PAID DOMESTIC WORK IN LATIN AMERICA

Paid domestic work as an occupation has long remained invisible, both substantively among policy makers and theoretically among academics, the world over, including Latin America. Yet it is both substantively and theoretically relevant for many reasons, especially in Latin America. First, paid domestic work is a major source of employment for women in the region. The occupation employs about 15 percent of the economically active female population in Latin America and is hence the largest single source of employment for women (ILO 2010b). Concomitantly, about 15 percent of households in the region employ at least one full-time domestic worker; thus about 30 percent of all households in the region are intimately part of this economic exchange, either as employers or as workers. Second, given the high (even if slightly declining) socioeconomic inequalities in the region, the employment of nannies and maids is very much a domestic phenomenon in Latin American countries, unlike in many other parts of the world, especially in wealthier countries, where immigrants dominate in this occupation. Indeed, the prevalence of paid domestic work is a function of high socioeconomic inequalities, which have produced both the demand for the outsourcing of domestic activities and a ready supply of inexpensive labor in Latin America. Third, this domestic supply of relatively inexpensive labor has allowed for the massive increase in women's labor force participation in higher income quintiles, without putting as much pressure on renegotiating gender roles in family responsibilities. Fourth, this form of work embodies aspects characteristic of dependent wage labor; at the same time, it has some unique elements, as the household is the setting of employment. I return to this issue in the paragraph below. Fifth, this occupation crystallizes, perhaps more starkly than any other, class, gender, and race inequalities, as over 90 percent of domestic workers are women; they come from lower-income backgrounds and are often members of racial and ethnic minorities.[1]

A domestic worker is a person who provides cooking, cleaning, child care, or other prescribed services at an employer's private residence.[2] Sometimes the domestic worker also lives in the residence. Paid domestic work falls within the larger economy of care occupations, where women dominate the workforce. However, it also embodies some unique characteristics that differentiate it from other wage employment within the care occupations (such as early childhood education and care providers, nurses, and workers in retirement homes) as well as from other wage labor more generally. First, the realm of paid domestic work, as noted above, constitutes what is traditionally considered "women's work." Because of this, household work has historically not been viewed as "real" or productive work but is often considered unskilled and is not accorded the same status as paid work outside the home (Hondagneu-Sotelo 2001). Hence, even when such work is contracted out to a third party, it still tends to be viewed as less than "real work" by employers, in the law, and sometimes even by the employees themselves, who may see their jobs as "helping out" another family. Second, and relatedly, paid domestic work involves working within a household, in an otherwise nonpublic, nonbusiness setting. Many employers do not perceive themselves as employers in the way they do outside the home, nor do they view their homes as sites of employment (Hondagneu-Sotelo 2001, ch. 1). Hence the labor relation tends to be more informal. Contracts are often verbal, and boundaries regarding the rights and duties of employment are more fluid. In effect, the ILO characterizes the employee status of domestic workers as "invisible because they work inside the household" (2010a, 2). Third, in this work setting—and this characteristic applies to care occupations more broadly—human relations and affective ties are particularly important, especially when dealing with the care of children or the elderly. There is a widespread tendency among employers, across countries and continents, to claim that the employee is "like family" to the household (Bunster and Chaney 1985; Fish 2006; Gill 1994; Lan 2006, 19; Rollins 1985). These dynamics, combined with the perception that domestic workers do not do real work in a business setting, tend to obscure the labor relation. Yet, despite the informality and importance of affective ties, the relationship is fundamentally a labor relation, and a particularly unequal one at that.

In Latin America, domestic service has a legacy of deep inequalities, indentured servitude, and slavery. Until the late nineteenth and in many cases into the twentieth century, the domestic servant was "in a position of near absolute, unregulated subordination to the male head of household" (Kuznesof 1989, 28). Since then, governments have gradually established some protections but maintained explicit discrimination in labor codes. The deep socioeconomic inequalities, combined with outright racial and ethnic discrimination and notions of the appropriate status of "women's work," were reflected in the establishment of longer work hours and lower labor protections for this sector. In addition, enforcement of the rights that do exist has historically been virtually nonexistent, and domestic workers have been much more likely than other workers to labor informally, without written contracts or social security. This has left them without any labor protections when faced with employer abuse or social risks such as illness, disability, maternity, or old age and therefore, in the terms of the editors of this book, outside the practices of citizenship.

AN UNEQUAL SETTING: DOMESTIC WORKER ORGANIZING AND ELITE CULTURE

In this deeply unequal context, equal rights and respect have been longstanding demands of domestic workers' organizations (Chaney and Garcia Castro 1989). Yet the multiple intersectional disadvantages that characterize this workforce pose significant challenges for organizing among domestic workers. Unlike industrial workers and many service workers, by the nature of their work domestics are socially isolated and hard to reach. This is exacerbated if they live with their employer. They often work long hours, and they have few days off each month, as well as their own family responsibilities. In addition, in today's highly segregated Latin American urban centers, poor public transportation networks can add painfully long commutes to their days. Aside from these time constraints, lower socioeconomic status among domestic workers reduces resources for campaigns, and skills and social networks to access the political system are scarce (Blofield 2012). Consequently, organizational affiliations of any kind, even if technically allowed, have historically been extremely low among domestic workers (Chaney and Garcia Castro 1989; CONLACTRAHO 2004; Gill 1994; López, Soto, and Valiente 2005, 208; Valenzuela and Mora 2009). Despite these constraints, domestic workers have managed to organize in every country in the region, however minimally, to provide support for each other and to advocate for equal rights and respect (Chaney and Garcia Castro 1989). These organizations, aside from advocating for equal rights and respect, also often offer evening or weekend education classes, especially for adolescents who have dropped out of school to work as domestics. For live-in domestics, often migrants (internal or external), they offer spaces for women and girls to gather on their rare days off (Blofield 2012, 58). Politically, they have played a key role in making their cause visible. In 1988, leaders of national-level domestic workers' organizations founded a regional confederation of domestic workers. Given the time and resource constraints on domestic workers as a group, the vitality of these organizations has been highly dependent on pioneering leaders, who have sacrificed their personal lives to fully dedicate themselves to the cause of domestic workers' rights and to seek social and political allies. Such leaders played a key role in Bolivia, Chile, and Costa Rica, to name a few countries (Blofield 2012, 59).

Until the past decade, their demands have met with widespread rejection among elites, who had come to see a long historical legacy of servitude as natural. This resistance is not only economic; it is deeply cultural and intersects with class, gender, and racial/ethnic inequalities. Increasing the position and rights of domestic workers involves some form of redistribution, and such changes conflict with the interests of political elites themselves, most of whom have domestic workers at home, and their better-organized middle- and upper-class constituents. In addition, the traditional undervaluation of household and care work, performed by women, also plays a role, and, finally, racism among some elites may make them less likely to view domestic workers who are darker-skinned or from different ethnic groups as their social equals and deserving of the same rights (Blofield 2012, ch. 2). These views are reflected in arguments against equal rights. To defend the status quo, a male senator in Bolivia argued that domestic workers, unlike other workers such as miners, who really needed to rest, were not in need of legislated vacation time; in Costa Rica, a key female legislator argued that it was acceptable to retain a longer workday for domestic workers because they watched soap operas during the day. Another legislator in Peru remarked that employers' houses "are not hotels" (Blofield 2012, 51–52). Casanova's (2013) study of urban domestic workers in Ecuador recounts the dehumanizing behavior of employers toward them.

Even ostensible allies such as feminists and labor unions have tended to prioritize the interests of their more advantaged, organized members (Strolovitch 2006) and largely ignored or even acted against domestic workers. For example, according to a Mexico City government official, labor unions in Mexico have opposed any changes to the Labor Code regarding domestic workers, who have virtually no protections, as they fear that any reforms may open the door to a reduction of their extant rights (Blofield 2012). Feminist organizations have rarely made domestic workers' rights a priority; for example, none of the regional *encuentros feministas* (feminist encounters) have made this issue central to their demands.

BREAKING THROUGH THE STATUS QUO: EXPLAINING EQUAL RIGHTS REFORM, 2000–2016

Drawing on the theoretical framework developed earlier (Blofield 2012), I argue that domestic workers face a three-step struggle. First, they must make their cause visible and their demands heard. This organizing has been essential to progress toward the goal of equal rights, since few equal rights reforms have passed without substantial bottom-up pressure from the marginalized themselves. For this, they must organize and gain allies, which is a challenge, as discussed above. Second, to get equal rights on the political agenda, specifically, a plenary debate and a vote, they need executive backing (or an extraordinary confluence of unlikely political factors).[3] Presidents across Latin America have significant agenda-setting powers, and executive-initiated bills are more likely to be debated in and pass Congress (Siavelis 2000; Touchton, Sugiyama, and Wampler 2017). Legislative opponents have, very successfully until recently, focused on keeping reform off the political agenda, by burying bills in legislative committees and postponing debate, knowing that once a reform bill goes for a vote, it is uncomfortable for political elites to take a public stance against equal rights in the twenty-first century. Without presidential backing in heavily executive-dominated political regimes, advocates have in most countries been unable to overcome this resistance. Third, advocates need to maintain pressure on executive agencies tasked with implementation, including social security coverage. Here, executive support is as crucial as in step two, if not more (Blofield 2012).

The past decade has been a game changer for domestic workers' organizing and rights, for two reasons. The first factor, and crucially for the focus of this analysis, is an increase in executive support in the form of more sympathetic left-wing governments: between 1999 and 2016, eleven of the eighteen democratic Latin American countries elected (and often reelected) left-wing governments. Second, the passage of the 2011 ILO Domestic Workers Convention had an interactive effect. It was pushed for by labor advocates and, in turn, catalyzed more organizing and also provided an intergovernmental venue to promote equal rights. I discuss both in turn.

First, the political context shifted at the turn of the millennium, as an increasing number of countries elected left-wing governments that were more sympathetic to or even campaigned on redistributive demands (Campello 2015). This provided for a more open environment for domestic workers to organize and advocate for themselves and a more likely context in which to forge social and political allies, including, importantly, in the executive. This had potentially positive implications not just for legal reform, but for more effective implementation regarding written contracts, access to social security, and mechanisms for investigating labor violations. Still, at the turn of the millennium left platforms and programs paid no attention to this issue, as governments focused on delivering on campaign promises to their more vocal and organized constituents and on visible policies such as conditional cash transfer programs (Levitsky and Roberts 2011). However, over time, as domestic workers and their advocates organized and gained more visibility (discussed further below), left governments became more aware of and sensitized to the interests and rights of this group of workers. Advocates were also able to foster supportive relationships with specific left officials over time, made easier as left governments were often re-elected and stayed in power longer. Many left governments also focused on increasing formalization of the labor force (Martínez Franzoni and Sánchez-Ancochea 2016), which had direct and indirect benefits for domestic workers specifically.

Second, the interactive effect of domestic worker organizing and ILO support helped catalyze reform efforts. In the mid-2000s, domestic worker organizers in Latin America took their cause to the international level. They formed a network with skilled and sympathetic labor advocates in Europe, with whom they began to lobby the ILO to pick up the cause (IRENE and Agricultural IUF 2008).[4] The issue of domestic workers' rights had been present—though dormant—in the ILO for three quarters of a century, since 1936 (Valenzuela and Mora 2009, 290–94), but now for the first time it began to make headway. Heavy pressure by the network led to significant victories. After much awareness-building and lobbying by the advocate network, the ILO voted affirmatively in 2010 on whether to establish a convention (instead of a weaker recommendation), and in 2011, the convention was written and overwhelmingly approved by the ILO. The final vote in support was higher than expected (ILO 2011a, 2011b).[5]

The convention and ILO support more broadly, combined with domestic worker organizing, have had several positive effects. First, as the ILO has become more supportive, it has also provided more support to on-the-ground organizing, including financial and technical assistance to domestic worker organizations in Latin America. With such assistance, a regional federation of domestic workers, CONLACTRAHO, after being less active for many years, reconvened regional meetings in 2009. The leader of the regional federation during these years, Marcelina

Bautista, a Mexican domestic worker organizer, gained a high profile and quite a bit of press attention.

Second, the convention has had a crucial top-down effect as well. Convention 189, approved in 2011, includes clauses to ensure the freedom to form unions and elimination of discrimination in national laws, including work hours, protections for migrant workers, and employer responsibility for informing workers of the agreed-upon terms and conditions of work.[6] The convention has provided an important intergovernmental mechanism to push for legal reform in national contexts, by contributing visibility, by revitalizing domestic and regional advocates, and by engaging in government-level pressure to proceed with ratification and legal reforms (Blofield 2012).

The step following the convention approval is ratification by individual governments. Ratification makes the convention legally binding for governments, after which they are obligated to change their national laws to comply with the convention (if there are discrepancies). Ratification can thus be seen as a helpful (although not necessary) intermediate step toward national-level reform of labor codes. Indeed, some countries have reformed their laws following a convention without ratifying it, and vice versa.

Table 9.1 summarizes equal rights reforms across Latin America. The countries are grouped into three categories: those that have passed equal rights reforms, those that have passed partial reforms, and those that have passed minimal or no reforms between 1998 (the first equal rights reform) and 2016. A partial reform refers to a clear substantive reform, such as the application of the national minimum wage to domestic workers, but with a clear exclusion, such as the maintenance of higher daily work hours. A minimal reform is one that provides no clear reforms in work hours, minimum wage, or labor benefits such as severance pay, access to social security, or holidays. Within each group, the countries are listed in chronological order of reform. The columns indicate the year of reform (with year of ratification of Convention 189 in brackets), whether the reform was executive initiated, and whether it was passed under a left government.

The table indicates that eight countries had by 2016 passed equal rights reform. The first, Colombia, is special as its reform was passed by the Constitutional Court rather than by the government. In two of the earlier reformers, Bolivia in 2003 and Costa Rica in 2009, reform was

TABLE 9.1. Legal Reforms on Domestic Workers in Latin America, 1998–2016

	Year of Reform (year of ILO ratification)	Executive Initiated	Left Government
Equal rights reforms			
Colombia	1998* (2014)	No	No/court case
Bolivia	2003* (2013)	No	No
Uruguay	2006 (2012)	Yes	Yes
Costa Rica	2009 (2014)	No	No
Venezuela	2012	Yes	Yes
Brazil	2013	Yes	Yes
Argentina	2013 (2014)	Yes	Yes
Chile	2015* (2015)	Yes	Yes
Partial reforms			
Peru	2003	No	No
Ecuador	2012 (2013)	Yes	Yes
Paraguay	2015 (2013)	Check	No
Minimal or no legal reforms			
Nicaragua**	No reform (2013)	—	—
DR	No reform (2015)	—	—
Panama	No reform (2015)	—	—
El Salvador	No reform	—	—
Guatemala	No reform	—	—
Honduras**	No reform	—	—
Mexico	No reform	—	—

Source: Compilation by author.

*Labor codes retain longer work hours for live-in domestic workers but with limitations.
**Honduras and Nicaragua passed reforms in 2012 clarifying the labor code but without substantive changes to work hours or labor protections.

neither executive initiated nor under a left government. It came about as the result of legislative initiatives, after years of grassroots efforts by domestic worker organizations and their allies who managed to push through reform under circumstances driven by factors exogenous to domestic workers but helpful in providing legislative openings (Blofield 2012). In neither country has the executive made concerted efforts to implement the legal reforms and increase social security coverage. In the case of Bolivia, this is despite left governance since 2005.

The rest of the equal rights reformers—five in all—had both executive-initiated bills and left-wing governments: Uruguay, Argentina, Brazil, Chile, and Venezuela. The first one, Uruguay, preceded the ILO convention and in fact has been highlighted as a model reformer by the ILO.

Uruguay's trend-setting reform on domestic rights took place soon after the victory of the left-wing Frente Amplio (Broad Front, FA) government, which took an active role in encouraging collective organization among domestic workers, crafting and passing equal rights reform, and promoting social security coverage. With a left-wing majority in Congress, the bill was rapidly—and unanimously—approved. The Ministry of Labor included the newly revitalized domestic workers' union in salary negotiations, and the social security bank had a broad and effective campaign to register domestic workers for social security, including door-to-door campaigns with informational fliers and award-winning television ads (Blofield 2012, ch. 5). Social security coverage among domestic workers increased from 27 percent in 2004 to 50 percent in 2013 (Blofield and Jokela 2018).

The rest of the reformers followed the convention: Venezuela in 2012, Argentina in 2013, Brazil in 2013, and Chile in 2015. In all four countries, left executives introduced equal rights bills to Congress and ushered them through to reform. In the case of Venezuela, the reform was part of a broader labor reform.[7] In Argentina, Brazil, and Chile, the legislation pertained specifically to domestic workers. The passage of the ILO Convention factored into political debates on reform in these three countries and provided impetus for social advocates, government officials, and supportive legislators to push for speedy approval of government bills (CEMyT 2010; Ministerio de Justicia y Trabajo 2011). In Argentina, for example, government officials as well as the president of the Labor Commission in the Chamber of Deputies mentioned the importance of ILO attention in propelling political reform.[8] The executive bills faced obstacles, as some politicians were opposed to reform but hesitant to publicly declare their opposition. This led to delays as bills traveled through both houses of Congress; however, pressure from advocates and executive support broke through this resistance, culminating in near-unanimous votes in favor.

In Argentina, Brazil, and Chile, the executive also sought to increase formalization of this labor force, both before and after legal reform. In the Brazilian national household surveys, the share of domestic workers registered in social security increased from 32 percent to 42 percent between 2006 and 2013 (Blofield and Jokela 2018). Comparable data do not exist for Argentina and Chile; ILO data indicate that 43 percent of domestics in Chile and only 11 percent in Argentina had pension protections in 2008 (ILO 2010b). Left-wing executives in both Argentina (2005) and Brazil (2006) passed legal reforms allowing for employer tax deductions for registering domestic employees for social security.

The next group is the partial reformers: Ecuador, Peru, and Paraguay. In only one of the countries in this group did a left executive lead the reforms: Ecuador. It instituted by executive order in 2012 the national minimum wage to domestic workers and established that the work hours of live-out domestics should be equal to those of other workers. Live-in domestics, however, continued in 2016 to only be guaranteed one day off every two weeks. Given that the reforms are not enshrined in law and live-in domestics are excluded, Ecuador's reforms are classified as partial. Ecuador ratified the ILO convention in 2013 but has not to date reformed its labor code.

Peru's partial reform in 2003 was a result of legislative efforts. The reform equalized the work hours of live-in domestics but not live-out domestics and did not extend the national minimum wage to domestic workers. Also, the reform was not initiated by the executive, and as a result there has been little enforcement of the rights that do exist, or any attempts at formalization. Indeed, the proportion of domestic workers who possessed a written contract was 0.9 percent in 2004 and remained at 0.9 percent in 2013, while this proportion for the general workforce during the same time period improved from 43 percent to 53 percent (Blofield and Jokela 2018). Paraguay also passed a partial legal reform in 2015, according domestic workers equal work hours but establishing their minimum wage at 60 percent of the national minimum wage (up from 40 percent previously).

The remaining countries have passed minimal or no legal reforms. Nicaragua and Honduras in 2012 passed legal reforms more clearly specifying the statutes that apply to domestic workers, including restrictions on minors, but did not substantially change either work hours or salaries or benefits, and the reforms are therefore classified as minimal. Mexico, Panama, El Salvador, Guatemala, and the Dominican Republic have passed no reforms in the past fifteen years, maintaining the discriminatory statutes unchanged. While Nicaragua ratified the ILO Convention in 2013 and Panama and the Dominican Republic did so in 2015, their discriminatory labor codes to date remain unchanged.

The case of Mexico, with no federal left government during this period, stands out. Paid domestic work in Mexico is characterized by a complete lack of regulation, simply stipulating that workers must have enough time to rest and to eat, explicitly contradicting the Mexican Constitution of 1917, which grants all Mexicans an eight-hour workday. The share of domestic workers who have a written contract plummeted from 14.8 percent in 2004 to 1.2 percent by 2012 (Blofield and Jokela 2018). While domestic worker organizations have lobbied hard for equal rights reform and ILO ratification, they have to date been unsuccessful, as Mexican presidents and Congress have repeatedly ignored bills to reform the antiquated labor code. As mentioned, labor unions have not been allies either. Mexico is also almost alone in the region in not even legally requiring domestic workers to be registered for social security, explaining the dismal rates of coverage.

In sum, while having a left government in power has not been a necessary condition, it has clearly improved the chances of equal rights reform, especially after 2011. Moreover, left governments are more likely to put effort into implementation, including formalization of the workforce and enforcing labor rights. Here, however, there appears to be a distinction between the more institutionalized partisan left governments such as Uruguay, Chile, and Brazil and the more populist left governments (Blofield and Jokela 2018; Levitsky and Roberts 2011). At the same time, left governance since 2000 has not been a *sufficient* cause of equal rights reform. Nicaragua, under a left government, ratified the ILO Convention but has not passed legal reform. El Salvador, under a left-wing government, has neither ratified the convention nor passed legal reform. On the other hand, Panama and the Dominican Republic have recently ratified the convention under nonleft governments.

Domestic workers, constituting about 15 percent of the urban female labor force in Latin America, have been subject to discriminatory labor codes across the region and have faced significant difficulties in organizing, demanding equal rights, and gaining social and political allies.

In the most unequal region in the world, with a long legacy of deep class divisions, domestic workers' rights strike at the heart of a culture of privilege and servitude, masters and servants. It is thus perhaps not so surprising that at the turn of the millennium, well after the wave of democratic transitions and equal rights reforms in many other areas, labor codes on domestic workers remained in place across the region.

In the context of the regionwide shift to the left, the efforts of domestic workers have met with more success than before, especially following the ILO Convention. The partisan nature of equal rights reforms is clear: all executive-initiated equal rights reforms have taken place under left governments, and not a single nonleft executive has to date spearheaded equal rights reform. This said, not all left governments, especially more short-lived ones, have been active supporters of equal rights reform.

This analysis also highlights the important, interactive role that international organizations can play. Other analyses have evaluated the role played by international conventions in propelling legal reforms that establish or extend rights to vulnerable and marginalized groups, for example, laws on violence against women (Htun and Weldon 2012). The comparison of violence against women (VAW) laws with domestic workers' rights highlights how reforms that touch on socioeconomic privileges face a steeper uphill battle (Blofield and Haas 2011). The first wave of VAW reforms took place in the 1990s, with the strong support of women's movements, with international attention to the issue, and under nonleft governments (Htun and Weldon 2012). Both women's movements and governments ignored the issue of domestic workers at that time. It was under left-wing governments, and especially with ILO advocacy, that domestic workers' rights and protections—including enforcement—gained more traction. Given the clearly partisan nature of reform efforts, the current shift to nonleft governments in the region does not bode well for equal rights reform or for concerted efforts at implementation.

NOTES

This chapter draws on and updates my 2012 book, *Care Work and Class: Domestic Workers' Struggle for Equal Rights in Latin America.*
    1. See Blofield 2012, ch. 1, for further discussion of these points.

2. This paragraph is paraphrased from Blofield 2012, ch. 1.

3. Two such cases of rare equal rights victories without presidential backing were those in Bolivia and Costa Rica, the result of persistent efforts by advocates in the face of executive reticence, combined with almost unexpected and exogenous political "windows of opportunity" (Blofield 2012).

4. Karin Pape, coordinator of the International Domestic Workers' Network, 2009–11, interview by author, June 20, 2011 (over Skype). From Blofield 2012.

5. There were 396 votes in favor, 16 against, and 63 abstentions. International Labor Conference, 2011, Final Record Vote on the Adoption of the Convention Concerning Decent Work for Domestic Workers, Provisional Record, 100th session, Geneva; Pape, interview by author, from Blofield 2012.

6. International Labor Conference, Text of the Convention Concerning Decent Work for Domestic Workers, Provisional Record, 100th session, Geneva.

7. I have not been able to gain access to transcripts of this labor reform to determine any ILO influence.

8. Hector Recalde, president of the Labor Commission and legislator in the Chamber of Deputies, interview by author, Buenos Aires, March 29, 2011; official in the tripartite commission of the Ministry of Labor, interview by author, Buenos Aires, March 28, 2011.

REFERENCES

Blofield, Merike. 2012. *Care Work and Class: Domestic Workers' Struggle for Equal Rights in Latin America*. University Park: Pennsylvania State University Press.

Blofield, Merike, and Liesl Haas. 2011. "Gender Equality Policies in Latin America." In Merike Blofield, ed., *The Great Gap: Inequality and the Politics of Redistribution in Latin America*. University Park: Pennsylvania State University Press.

Blofield, Merike, and Merita Jokela. 2018. "Paid Domestic Work and the Struggles of Care Workers in Latin America." *Current Sociology* 66 (4): 531–46.

Bunster, Ximena, and Elsa M. Chaney. 1985. *Sellers and Servants: Working Women in Lima, Peru*. New York: Praeger.

Campello, Daniela. 2015. *The Politics of Market Discipline in Latin America: Globalization and Democracy*. New York: Cambridge University Press.

Casanova, Erynn Masi de. 2013. "Embodied Inequality: The Experience of Domestic Work in Urban Ecuador." *Gender & Society* 27 (4): 561–85.

Centro de Estudio de Mujeres y Trabajo de la Argentina (CEMyT). 2010. *Situación del trabajo en casas particulares: Hacia el reconocimiento de los derechos laborales.* Buenos Aires: Centro de Estudio de Mujeres y Trabajo de la Argentina. www.lavoz.com.ar/files/Informe_Trabajadoras_dom%C3%A9sticas_N%C2%BA2_CEMyT.pdf.

Chaney, Elsa M., and Mary Garcia Castro. 1989. *Muchachas No More: Household Workers in Latin America and the Caribbean.* Philadelphia: Temple University Press.

Confederación Latinoamericana y del Caribe de Trabajadoras del Hogar (CONLACTRAHO). 2004. *Humanizando el trabajo doméstico: Hacer visible lo invisible. la realidad de las trabajadoras del hogar en América Latina y el Caribe: Bolivia, Brasil, Costa Rica, Guatemala, México, Perú y República Dominicana.* Santiago de Chile: CONLACTRAHO.

Fish, Jennifer. 2006. *Domestic Democracy: At Home in South Africa.* New York: Routledge.

Gill, Lesley. 1994. *Precarious Dependencies: Gender, Class, and Domestic Service in Bolivia.* New York: Columbia University Press.

Hondagneu-Sotelo, Pierrette. 2001. *Domestica: Immigrant Workers Cleaning and Caring in the Shadows of Affluence.* Berkeley: University of California Press.

Htun, Mala, and S. Laurel Weldon. 2012. "Civic Origins of Progressive Policy Change: Combating Violence against Women in Global Perspective, 1975–2005." *American Political Science Review* 109 (1): 548–69.

International Labour Organization (ILO). 2010a. *Decent Work for Domestic Workers.* Geneva: International Labour Office. www.ilo.org/.

———. 2010b. *Panorama laboral 2010: América Latina y el Caribe.* Lima: International Labour Organization. www.ilo.org/.

———. 2011a. *Decent Work for Domestic Workers, Report IV (2a).* Geneva: International Labour Organization. www.ilo.org/.

———. 2011b. *Decent Work for Domestic Workers, Report IV (2b).* Geneva: International Labour Organization. www.ilo.org/.

IRENE (International Restructuring Education Network Europe) and Agricultural IUF (International Union of Food, Hotel, Restaurant, Catering, Tobacco and Allied Workers' Associations). 2008. *Respect and Rights: Protection for Domestic/Household Workers!* Amsterdam: IRENE and IUF. www.domesticworkerrights.org/sites/en.domesticworkerrights.org/files/ENGtextRaR.pdf.

Kuznesof, Elizabeth. 1989. "A History of Domestic Service in Spanish America, 1492–1980." In Elsa M. Chaney and Mary Garcia Castro, eds.,

Muchachas No More: Household Workers in Latin America and the Carib-bean. Philadelphia: Temple University Press.

Lan, Pei-Chia. 2006. *Global Cinderellas: Migrant Domestics and Newly Rich Employers in Taiwan*. Durham, NC: Duke University Press.

Levitsky, Steven, and Kenneth M. Roberts, eds. 2011. *The Resurgence of the Latin American Left*. Baltimore, MD: Johns Hopkins University Press.

López, Verónica, Lilian Soto, and Hugo Valiente. 2005. *Trabajo doméstico remunerado en Paraguay*. Lima: Oficina Internacional del Trabajo.

Martínez Franzoni, Juliana, and Diego Sánchez-Ancochea. 2016. *The Quest for Universal Social Policy in the South: Actors, Ideas and Architectures*. Cambridge: Cambridge University Press.

Ministerio de Justicia y Trabajo. 2011. *Viceministerio del Trabajo plantea ratificación del convenio de la OIT que protege a trabajadoras domésticas*. Asunción del Paraguay: Gobierno del Paraguay. www.mjt.gov.py/prensa/2011 /agosto/viceministerio-del-trabajo-plantea-ratificacion-del-convenio-de -la-oit-que-protege-a-trabajadoras-domesticas.

Rollins, Judith. 1985. *Between Women: Domestics and Their Employers*. Philadelphia: Temple University Press.

Siavelis, Peter. 2000. *The President and Congress in Post-Authoritarian Chile*. University Park: Pennsylvania State University Press.

Strolovitch, Dara Z. 2006. "Do Interest Groups Represent the Disadvantaged? Advocacy at the Intersections of Race, Class, and Gender." *Journal of Politics* 68 (4): 894–910.

Touchton, Michael, Natasha Borges Sugiyama, and Brian Wampler. 2017. "Democracy at Work: Moving beyond Elections to Improve Well-Being." *American Political Science Review* 111 (1): 68–82.

Valenzuela, María Elena, and Claudia Mora. 2009. *Esfuerzos concertados para la revaloración del trabajo doméstico remunerado en América Latina*. Santiago de Chile: Organización Internacional del Trabajo (ILO). www .ministeriodesarrollosocial.gob.cl/btca/txtcompleto/trabdomestico.pdf.

TEN

The Record of Latin America's Left on Sexual Citizenship

Jordi Díez

Latin America is at the forefront of the expansion of sexual rights. Sexual relations between consenting adults are legal in all of Hispanophone and Lusophone Latin America; several countries have introduced constitutional and legal protections of sexual minorities against discrimination; civil unions are a reality for millions of people in the region, and, perhaps more surprisingly, same-sex marriage is now accessible, through various means, to most citizens in the region. In effect, the right to marry irrespective of gender has been extended in countries in which more than 80 percent of Latin Americans live.[1] These formal advances have challenged some deeply, and rather widely, held stereotypes of the region as being very conservative and *machista*. Such unprecedented expansion of sexual rights, which Oscar Encarnación (2016) has appropriately termed a "gay rights revolution," has occurred during the region's so-called Pink Tide, a phenomenon that is usually traced to the election of Hugo Chávez in Venezuela in 1998. To the casual observer it would appear that there is a clear relationship between both phenomena.

Nevertheless, even though that relationship seems rather intuitive given that leftist parties tend to be more progressive on social issues, it is neither simple nor direct. Sexual rights as a category is too broad to be useful given that support for and opposition to them varies depending on the type of right one considers. Generally, opposition to same-sex marriage is a lot fiercer among socially conservative actors, such as the Catholic Church's leadership, making it more difficult for political leaders to expend political capital to pursue them. That partly explains why Michelle Bachelet's (2006–10, 2014–18) Partido Socialista de Chile (Socialist Party of Chile, PSCh) is the only major political party in Latin America to have explicitly supported same-sex marriage during an election campaign (2014). Other sexual rights, such as anti-discrimination legislation, tend to be less controversial, and most Latin American leftist parties tend to support some version of them. While some of the countries in which sexual rights have gone the furthest were indeed part of the Pink Tide, such as Argentina and Uruguay, others, such as Venezuela and Nicaragua, sit at the opposite end of that spectrum. Scholarship on the topic, once scant, suggests that the expansion, and stagnation, of sexual rights is a rather complex phenomenon and that the factors behind the "gay rights revolution" are multiple and cross-nationally varied (Corrales 2015b; Díez 2015; Encarnación 2016).

In this chapter, I address the question guiding this volume by looking at the Latin American left's record on the expansion of sexual citizenship. I attempt to demonstrate that this record is rather mixed given the heterogeneity that has characterized various leftist parties' positions not only on sexual rights generally, but on different types of rights. Building on previous work on the topic (Friedman 2010; Schulenberg 2013), I suggest that it simply is not possible to attribute the "gay rights revolution" to leftist parties alone. While their presence appears to have been an important condition in some countries for the expansion of some rights, it has not been sufficient, for otherwise we would see policy convergence across most of the region, which, as we shall see, is clearly not the case. I argue that agency is a key part of the story: in most cases, the expansion of rights has been driven by gay and lesbian activism. However, the success of this activism depends upon the type of rights that has been pursued and on broader political contexts. In some cases leftist governments have supported some rights, but in other cases they have rejected them altogether, while in others it has been the right that has supported their expansion. For example, Mexico's Vicente Fox (2000–2006), the most openly socially conservative president in recent memory, enacted the country's first national antidiscrimination legislation that includes the protection of sexual minorities, and Sebastián Piñera (2010–14), the first right-wing president to govern posttransition Chile, supported similar legislation during his term. In terms of antidiscrimination, some leftist governments have supported the inclusion of legal provisions that include the protection of sexual minorities when broader political opportunities have arisen, such as larger discussions on democratization, which in some cases have entailed a renegotiation of the terms of citizenship. These opportunities have allowed gay and lesbian activists to push for their demands, often very successfully. In terms of same-sex relationship recognition, activism has been successful in bringing about policy change when important alliances between non-state actors and state actors belonging to leftist parties have been forged, and where there were no parliamentary veto points to block reform. When these exist, activists have pursued their policy objectives through more receptive judiciaries. For the latter to occur, though, autonomous and active courts have been necessary.

This chapter is divided into three main sections. In the first section I give an overview of and classify the various types of sexual rights. In the second section, I develop a sexual citizenship score and give sixteen countries a score based on their record in sexual rights expansion. In the third section, I review the politics of sexual rights of the main Pink Tide leftist parties by looking at seven particular cases: Argentina, Bolivia, Brazil, Ecuador, Nicaragua, Venezuela, and Uruguay.

THE STATE OF SEXUAL RIGHTS IN LATIN AMERICA

What Are They?

Sexual rights are generally understood to be the rights that allow citizens to practice their sexuality freely and to enter into nonheteronormative social institutions sanctioned by the state.[2] Scholars place these rights in various categories. Diane Richardson (1998) divides them into three categories. The first, "practice" rights, refers to those rights that allow same-sex individuals to practice various forms of sexual activities. These generally refer to the right to practice nonheteronormative sexualities without state intervention. As former Canadian prime minister Pierre Trudeau famously declared when certain types of sexual practices were being decriminalized in 1968, the "state has no business in the bedrooms of the nation." The second category of rights, "expression," refers to those that allow individuals self-expression and the development of identities without discrimination. These are generally equated with antidiscrimination legislation. In the third category, called "relationship" rights, Richardson (1998) places those rights that allow for the legal recognition and inclusion in society of same-sex couples through social institutions such as marriage. Some scholars have argued that the acquisition of all these rights is important for the attainment of full citizenship.

As explained in chapter 1, conceptualizations of citizenship are relational and socially constructed, which inherently means fluid (Montambeault, Balán, and Oxhorn, this volume). In terms of sexual rights, debates have unfolded within larger debates, and some scholars and activists have also questioned liberal conceptions of citizenship not viewing individuals as sexless (Nussbaum 2002; Plummer 2003). For some, all citizenship is sexual because all citizens are sexed through political discourses of the family as heteronormative (Bell and Binnie 2000). New understandings of citizenship are therefore required to account for nontraditional sexualities given that notions of rights as a set of civil, political, and social rights, as well as common membership in a shared community, are closely associated with the institutionalization of heterosexuality (Richardson 1998). Because the institutionalization of heteronormativity has excluded those who engage or exhibit nontraditional sexual practices and behaviors, calls for the notion of "sexual citizenship" have emerged. However, there is little agreement on what sexual citizenship entails. As Diane Richardson has noted, "The idea of sexual citizenship is a work in progress" (2000, 86). For many theorists it encompasses claims for "sexual rights," and the expansion of these rights is seen as necessary for the attainment of full citizenship in contemporary democratic societies (Calhoun 2000; Kaplan 1997; Plummer 2003; Richardson 2000; Waites 1996; Weeks 1998; Weeks, Heaphy, and Donovan 2001). Sexual rights build on a long tradition of feminist scholarship that sees the private sphere as political (Pateman 1988). In what he calls "intimate citizenship," Ken Plummer, for example, reframes liberal democratic conceptions of citizenship based on public-private divisions to argue for a new definition of "rights, obligations, recognitions and respect around those most intimate spheres of life—who to live with, how to raise a child, how to handle one's body, how to relate as a gendered being, how to be an erotic person" (2001, 238). For these authors, democratic citizenship requires a robust conception of rights, which includes gay and lesbian rights.

Also establishing a strong connection between the personal and the political, Morris Kaplan argues that sexual desire is central to individual self-making and a fulfilled life, and, as such, the right to privacy is crucial in the development of the citizen: "The importance of personal liberty in shaping one's desires to determine the course of a life must be articulated in relation to the political freedom of citizens collectively to decide the forms of their common life" (1997, 3–4). For Kaplan, equal citizenship requires individual freedom to shape oneself through a variety of intimate associations. However, because our intimate associations extend to the social realm and shape our social identities, he argues that sexual justice and full democratic citizenship require more than simply the repeal of sodomy laws and the inclusion of sexual orientation in civil rights legislation; it requires the provision of social support and political possibilities through the extension of marital status to same-sex couples. Discussions of gay rights are thus necessarily embedded in larger ideas about morality. As Kaplan argues, contrary to the rights of other minority groups, the advancement of gay rights has been subjected to the moral principles of societies: "Lesbians and gays alone have been told that their freedom must be limited to accord with the moral standards of the community" (1997, 2). The acceptance of gay rights—and their relationship to larger notions of citizenship and democracy—inevitably depends on the extent to which nonheterosexual sexual expressions are viewed as ethical.

Richardson's categorization of sexual rights, within these larger discussions of sexual citizenship, is useful given that the politics surrounding each of them differs, sometimes quite significantly. While there is a growing consensus in Western Europe and the Americas, supported by regional international regimes, that individuals have the right not to be discriminated against on the basis of sexual orientation, relationship rights are highly contested. With some exceptions, the extension of sexual rights has tended to unfold in a linear manner, whereby practice rights are acquired first, followed by expression rights, and, in some cases, by relationship rights.

Regional Context

The expansion of sexual rights in Latin America has varied significantly. Historically, as elsewhere, homosexuality has been socially repressed and homophobia widely spread. During colonial times homosexuality was regarded as a sin and homosexuals were burned at the stake. However, it was not included as a crime in most legal systems of the new Latin American republics after independence. Indeed, the constitutions and subsequent legal frameworks drafted by liberal leaders, in their push to secularize states, reproduced Napoleonic codes of law, and, because the French Civil Code of 1804 did not criminalize homosexuality, most Latin American countries have never criminalized same-sex relations. With some clear exceptions, such as Chile (where the Belgian Civil Code was used as the model), and in stark contrast to Anglophone Caribbean nations, homosexuality has not been penalized by the region's criminal codes. This means that, contrary to what occurred in some countries, such as England, the United States, and Canada, most Latin Americans have historically enjoyed the first level of rights: the right to practice same-sex relations. Nevertheless, while intimate sexual relations between adults were decriminalized, provisions criminalizing "indecency" and "scandal" in the public sphere were included in penal codes. Homosexuality may have been decriminalized, but it continued to be socially unacceptable, and any public expression of "scandalous" homosexual activity was punishable. Generally these provisions have historically been invoked by security forces to harass, extort, repress, torture, and even kill gay individuals (Encarnación 2016; Green 1994). This legal situation fostered a certain degree of sexual freedom in the private sphere, all while cementing a restrictive one in the public sphere.

The landscape of expression rights is a great deal more mixed. These rights generally include two levels: the right to express one's identity without state oppression (i.e., holding a gay pride parade in public spaces) and the enactment of legislation that protects gays and lesbians from discrimination based on the expression of an identity (i.e., being denied employment) and/or hate crime legislation. In terms of the first, and unlike other parts of the world (Eastern European and Balkan countries), for the most part Latin American gays and lesbians are generally free to hold public events without fear of repression. In effect, gay pride parades are held annually in all Latin American capital cities without incidents of violence. However, in some countries municipal ordinances still penalize indecent behavior and security forces continue to invoke these legal provisions to harass citizens, especially the transgender population.

In terms of antidiscrimination legislation, the landscape is equally varied. The issue of discrimination and tolerance gained traction during the 1990s around the world, as debates regarding immigration, multiculturalism, and citizenship intensified, in what Michael Ignatieff termed the "rights revolution" (2002). Those debates partly led to the World Conference against Racism, Racial Discrimination, and Related Intolerance, held in 2001 in Durban, South Africa, by the United Nations. Signatories to the final declaration committed themselves to adopting policies that would prevent discrimination. The conference's final declaration did not include sexual orientation as a category to protect, mostly due to opposition from Middle Eastern countries, but it placed the issue atop the international agenda. In Latin America it assumed particular potency partly as a result of demands by Indigenous populations to renegotiate the terms of citizenship to allow for the official recognition of diversity. This context provided an opportunity for gay and lesbian activists to push for the inclusion of sexual orientation as a group needing protection, and in many cases they were successful. Legislation has been introduced in several subnational and national jurisdictions across the region and, in some cases, such as Ecuador and Mexico, enshrined in national constitutions. Nevertheless, out of the sixteen countries that I score in this chapter, four countries do not have national legislation protecting all citizens (Argentina, Brazil, Honduras, and Paraguay).[3] Technically, gender identity rights for transgender individuals are not generally considered a sexual right, but it could well be considered a sexual expression right given that it entails a person's right to express their chosen gender identity freely. Moreover, and as we have seen, historically in

Latin America legal provisions related to personal attire in public have been invoked by security forces to suppress both sexual and gender minorities. Gender identity rights are also included in several hate crimes laws in the region. Of the sixteen countries I look at in this chapter, nine have such legislation.

Variation also exists in regard to the expansion of sexual relationship rights. The demand for same-sex relationship recognition began in some countries, such as Argentina, in the mid-1990s as activists asked for the extension of public socioeconomic benefits, usually those provided to civil servants. It accelerated in the early 2000s in Argentina, Brazil, and Mexico, all federal states, at the subnational level, as well as in Colombia. In Argentina and Mexico, activists decided to push for non-gender-specific civil unions in Buenos Aires and Mexico City, cities that acquired significant policy-making independence as a result of constitutional reforms undertaken in 1994 in both countries. After heated debates, civil unions were approved in Buenos Aires (2002) and Mexico City (2006) (Díez 2013), placing the issue of same-sex relationship recognition in the region's national debates. In the case of Brazil, given that family law is administered by the states, gay and lesbian activists began to demand the enactment of civil unions at the subnational level, primarily looking for the extension of socioeconomic rights. Once activists were able to have civil unions enacted in Buenos Aires and Mexico City, they began to push for same-sex marriage recognition. The first jurisdiction was Mexico City in 2009, followed by Argentina in 2010, and Uruguay and Brazil in 2013.

At the risk of gross simplification, such multilevel variation is captured in table 10.1, which measures the degree to which countries have expanded sexual citizenship rights. Adapted from Javier Corrales's Lesbian, Gay, Transgender, and Bisexual Rights Index (2015a), countries are accorded a full point if the entire population enjoys full access to rights, half a point if some sectors of society do, and zero if the right does not exist. By looking at the total points scored by each country on the various categories, it becomes obvious that there is a great deal of variance, from countries such as Panama and Paraguay that score one point each to Uruguay, which has afforded all its citizens the expansion of all sexual rights.

TABLE 10.1. Sexual Citizenship Index

	Sexual Activity	Antidiscrimination Legislation	Hate Crimes Legislation	Gender Identity	Civil Unions	Marriage	Adoption	Total
Argentina	1	.5	0	1	.5	1	1	5
Brazil	1	.5	0	1	1	1	1	4.5
Bolivia	1	1	1	1	0	0	0	4
Chile	1	1	1	1	1	0	0	5
Colombia	1	1	1	1	1	0	1	6
Costa Rica	1	1	0	0	0	0	0	2
Ecuador	1	1	1	1	1	0	0	5
El Salvador	1	1	0	0	0	0	0	2
Guatemala	1	1	0	0	0	0	0	2
Honduras	1	0	1	0	0	0	0	2
Mexico	1	1	.5	1	.5	1	1	6
Nicaragua	1	1	1	0	0	0	0	3
Panama	1	0	0	0	0	0	0	1
Paraguay	1	0	0	0	0	0	0	1
Peru	1	1	0	1	0	0	0	2
Uruguay	1	1	1	1	1	1	1	7
Venezuela	1	.5	0	0	0	0	0	1.5

Source: Adapted from Corrales 2015a.

THE ROLE OF LEFTIST PARTIES IN THE EXPANSION
OF SEXUAL RIGHTS

The role the Left turn governments has played in the expansion of sexual rights in Latin America has varied significantly, making it exceedingly difficult to make any general statements. The support of leftist governments has been vital in some countries (Argentina, Uruguay), but in others they have in effect been the main obstacles to a discussion, let alone expansion, of sexual rights (Venezuela). Indeed, when referring to the relationship between the Pink Tide and the "gay rights revolution," a distinction ought to be made among the various governments depending on their levels of progressivism, which inevitably leads us to further categorization. I do so below.

Extant scholarship points to a variety of other factors that explain variance across the cases. For example, while early iterations of modernization theory may have been criticized on many fronts, levels of economic and social development matter. In effect, there exists a very clear association between levels of industrialization, urbanization, and education in a country and public support for sexual rights (Díez and Dion 2015; Lodola and Corral 2010). Higher support for sexual rights does not necessarily translate into sexual rights expansion, but it provides a more propitious environment in which government support is less politically costly, thereby increasing the likelihood of policy makers to support them. However, most scholars generally agree that agency has been a central factor in the process. Indeed, scholarship on the politics of sexual rights in Latin American shows that policy change has been primarily the result of social mobilization: non-state actors applying pressure on policy makers (Díez 2015; Encarnación 2016; Schulenberg 2012).

Central to these processes has been a certain degree of professionalization of gay and lesbian activism over the past decade. Since 2000, activists in the region have been able to obtain resources to establish professional nongovernmental organizations (NGOs), often staffed with well-trained individuals. An important share of this funding has been made available to Latin American activists to deal with the spread of HIV/AIDS: significant amounts of resources, both technical and financial, have been made available (Biagini 2009; Torres-Ruiz 2006).

Part of this phenomenon has involved what Sonia Álvarez (1999) has termed the "NGOization" of social mobilization, or the institutionalization of activism. Similar to what has occurred with other social movements, such as those advancing environmental and women's causes, gay and lesbian movements underwent a process of institutionalization. By the turn of the century, financial and technical support allowed activists throughout the region to acquire the necessary infrastructure to establish institutional operations and to recruit well-trained individuals to their organizations, many of whom were able to devote themselves fully to their causes (Sívori 2008; Torres-Ruiz 2011).

Nevertheless, scholarship on the topic also shows that the existence of pro–sexual rights movements is a necessary, but insufficient, condition for their advancement (Corrales 2015b). The ability of these movements to push successfully for policy change seems to be dependent upon two additional factors: the ability to forge alliances with actors in national-level politics and political opportunities that allow for a negotiation of the terms of citizenship. In most cases, gay and lesbian activists have been able to establish important relationships with leftist policy makers at the national level. Many of these parties elected to government emerged through grassroots mobilization and have strong links with civil society actors. Because they have in many cases recruited civil society individuals to government positions, relationships between state and non-state actors have developed.

In turn, these alliances seem to have been most successful where larger societal discussions have afforded opportunities for activists to push for sexual rights through a renegotiation of the terms of citizenship. In some cases, such as Argentina and Uruguay, discussions about citizenship rights have been intrinsically linked to broader national conversations on the meaning of democracy. Greater and sustained contestation over what constitutes democracy and citizenship has meant that there has been greater social and political receptiveness to demands made by activists. In both countries, discussions regarding human rights have been at the core of national debates, and democratization has been, at least discursively, largely equated with greater respect for human rights. Activists have successfully taken advantage of these political opportunities in order to push for policy change, arguing for the need to include sexual rights in debates over rights. In other cases, such as Bolivia and

Ecuador, constitutional reforms have also provided similar opportunities. In both countries, leftist governments undertook these processes in an attempt to redefine state-society relations, which inevitably involved discussions about citizenship rights.

A final factor that explains regional variance in sexual rights protections has been the extent to which socially conservative actors (both state and non-state) are able to act as veto players in policy making. For some of these mostly faith-based actors, discussions of sexual rights are not about human rights but morality. Driven by Natural Law ideas, these actors adhere to the historically dominant position that heterosexuality is the only legitimate sexuality and the heterosexual family the basic, and only, organizational unit of contemporary societies. Sexual rights necessarily challenge these heteronormative understandings, pitting them against arguments advanced by sexual rights advocates. For them, non-heterosexual sexualities should be sanctioned by the state, as there are legitimate bases upon which to demand state protection as well as the recognition of nontraditional family units. The expansion of sexual rights recognition necessarily provokes a clash between two very different worldviews and has ignited intense social and political struggles in Latin America over the past decade. The confrontation, which is, at its core, about the region's centuries-old struggle over the separation of church and state, has played out differently across the region. In some cases, socially conservative forces are able to express their opposition publicly, but they are unable to block change because of their lack of institutionalized political representation through the political party system. In Argentina and Uruguay, for example, none of the major national political parties is confessional, and opponents to the expansion of rights do not therefore possess a privileged and direct channel into the policy-making process. In other cases, such as Brazil, socially conservative groups, both Christian and evangelical, have political party representation in Congress, which makes them veto players and allows them to block reform.

The presence of parliamentary veto players has forced some sexual rights activists to turn to the judiciary to push for reform. In what is known as the "judicialization of politics," social movements have increasingly opted to seek the expansion of rights through the courts (Smulovitz 2012), and these have included sexual rights advocates. In Brazil and Colombia, high courts have been the main drivers of sexual rights expansion. However, the judiciary route is only available in countries that have active and independent judiciaries, which are but a handful (see Sandoval-Rojas and Brinks, this volume).

It should by now be clear that the politics of sexual regulation vary quite significantly in the region and that the role the Left has played in the expansion of sexual rights is complex at best. In the following section I look at some cases in more detail, by grouping several countries that share some characteristics, before drawing some general conclusions.

THE NEED FOR CATEGORIZATION: EXPLORING SOME CASES

Argentina and Uruguay

Argentina and Uruguay can be placed in a first group. In the two countries the left has played an important role in the expansion of sexual rights, and both score high on our Sexual Citizenship Index. Uruguay is the most progressive country in the Americas, with a score of 7 (see table 10.1). In terms of antidiscrimination legislation, in 2003 and 2004 the country undertook three legal reforms that resulted in the prohibition of discrimination on the grounds of sexual orientation in employment and the acquisition of goods and services. They also introduced provisions regarding hate speech. One of the results of these reforms was the establishment of the Honorary Commission against Racism, Xenophobia, and All Discrimination (Comisión Honoraria contra el Racismo, la Xenofobia y Toda Otra Forma de Discriminación). This intraministerial institution, while weak, has the mandate to eradicate discrimination in the country, which includes sexual orientation. Moreover, in 2009, it approved a "gender identity" law that allows individuals over the age of eighteen to change their name in all their legal documentation, reflecting the gender of their choice. Finally, after having been the first country in Latin America to have approved civil unions at the national level (2007), it enacted legislation that allows same-sex couples to marry, with full adoption rights (2013).

The passage of all these reforms in Uruguay, which has recently colloquially become known in Latin America as "our Holland," in such a short time is undeniably largely due to the role played by the Frente

Amplio (Broad Front, FA), which has governed uninterruptedly since 2004. All of these reforms where officially supported by successive FA governments and its parliamentary leaderships in both chambers. Indeed, the fact that the judiciary was not involved in any of them attests to the political receptiveness of the FA leadership. However, in all these cases, they followed a strong push by activists led by the leading gay rights organization, Ovejas Negras (Black Sheep). While Uruguay's activism has not been as strong and old as Argentina's, since its foundation in 2004 Ovejas Negras has assumed a very important public presence and has forced national discussions on gay rights. According to Deputy Washington Abdala, the founding of the organization marked a watershed moment in the discussions of gay rights (*un antes y un después*) in society and especially within the political class.[4] But beyond their public presence, they played an important role in bringing about the reforms. According to Senator Margarita Percovich, the main legislator behind civil union reform, "People usually identify me with the process [to bring about reform], but the organization [*colectivo*] Ovejas Negras was instrumental in bringing it about, and especially in pushing society and politicians forward."[5] Activism played a role in that reform, and it appears that it was crucial to the enactment of same-sex marriage legislation (Cariboni 2014).

Uruguayan activists acquired numerous allies within the governing Frente Amplio. Part of the reason relates to the grassroots origins of the political coalition: activists in favor of sexual rights had previously worked with state actors, before they were elected, in other movements such as women's and labor. According to Valeria Rubino, an Ovejas Negras activist and member of Congress during the passage of the same-sex marriage law, multiple militancy was important in gaining allies in the push for civil unions. The Frente Amplio, founded in the early 1970s, is a coalition of leftist parties that has strong links with grassroots social movements. Access to the policy process in Congress (Uruguay has a unitary system) by gay and lesbian activists was greatly facilitated by the election of a political coalition that has been sustained by progressive social movements.[6] Importantly, such access has not been obstructed by conservative social forces. In Uruguay, widely considered the most secular country in the Americas, the political representation of religious groups in Congress is minimal. Indeed, even within the main conservative party, the Partido Nacional (National Party), members of Congress do not expect to obtain support by appealing to religious arguments and in fact fear that, given the country's deeply entrenched secularism, attempts to do so may backfire.[7]

With a score of 5, Argentina has also gone far in sexual citizenship expansion, and, similar to Uruguay, the role leftist governments have played has been crucial, although some of them have not formed part of the Pink Tide. In regard to antidiscrimination legislation, only two cities, Buenos Aires and Rosario, have legislation that explicitly covers the protection of sexual minorities. In the case of the former, the devolution of power to the city of Buenos Aires after the 1994 constitutional reform (Pacto de los Olivos) opened a window of opportunity for activists to include these protections in the drafting of the city's first constitution in 1998. Such a reform was possible because of the presence of leftist *notables* in the Constituent Assembly (Encarnación 2016, 124–26). In Rosario, in the mid-1990s, when the by-law (*ordenanza*) was approved, activists found a very receptive political environment given that the city is the bastion of the country's socially progressive Partido Socialista (Socialist Party, PS).

At the national level, Argentina does not possess legislation that protects sexual minorities against discrimination. While it was the first country to have enacted a national antidiscrimination law (1988), sexual orientation is not included as a classification. However, the law established a national institute to combat discrimination (Instituto Nacional contra la Discriminación, la Xenophobia y el Racismo, INADI), which over the years has included sexual orientation as one of the groups that it attempts to protect in its programming, which has been strong. Indeed, partly as a result of the institute's active role in advancing sexual rights, a reform of the 1988 law to include sexual orientation has not been a top priority among activists.

In terms of expression and relationship rights, in 2010, Argentina undertook reforms to its civil code allowing same-sex marriage, making it the first country in the region, and tenth in the world, to have done so. Given that the code is national, that right was extended to its entire population. Moreover, in 2012, it enacted a gender identity law, which is widely considered one of the most progressive in the world given that it depathologizes transgenderism and does not require individuals to present legal or medical approval to submit a request: it is a mere administrative transaction. These reforms are part of a much larger, and very successful, trajectory of gay and lesbian activism in the country that dates to the late 1960s. In effect, Argentina possesses Latin America's oldest sexual rights movement, having seen the foundation of the first homosexual organization in Latin America in 1967, Our World (Nuestro Mundo). While the 1976–83 military dictatorship suppressed all types of social mobilization, which obviously included gay and lesbian activism, the return to electoral democracy soon allowed it to resurface and gain important national visibility. Since the mid-1980s sexual activism in Argentina has not only placed the issue of sexual regulation in national conversations, but has fought for, and achieved, numerous policy goals.

Nevertheless, activists' push for these reforms met a receptive leftist government that belonged to Latin America's Pink Tide: state actors (within the executive and both houses of Congress) belonging to the ruling (Peronist) Frente para la Victoria (Front for Victory, FPV) were central (Díez 2015). While noncommittal when the debate over gay marriage gained force in the lower house toward the end of 2009, both Néstor Kirchner (then a deputy) and Cristina Fernández de Kirchner (2007–15) pushed hard for the approval of reform as opposition stiffened in the Senate and the outcome of the vote became uncertain (it narrowly passed with thirty-one votes in favor and two against). However, as Fernández de Kirchner admitted when she promulgated the reforms of the civil code that allowed gay marriage in the Casa Rosada, surrounded by the lead activists, her government was reacting to a demand that had emanated from civil society: the main factor behind the attainment of gay marriage was activism. The Argentine case captures rather well the argument made by this book's editors that the expansion or retrenchment of citizenship is inherently linked to social mobilization.

Smaller and more socially progressive parties also played a role, such as the PS. When the debate over same-sex marriage accelerated, and as a vote became increasingly imminent, the FPV did not have a majority in the Chamber of Deputies. Collaboration with unaligned Peronist, Socialist, and other socially progressive legislators proved critical for activists to garner the needed votes from most represented parties. A similar process unfolded during the enactment of the gender identity law two years later, although with much weaker opposition: indeed, the law was approved by the Argentine Senate, which tends to be more conservative, with fifty-five votes in favor, one abstention, and *none* against (La Nación 2012). In both Argentina and Uruguay, the left's record on expanding sexual citizenship is evidently strong. However, in both cases, the pressure to expand sexual citizenship rights came from gay and lesbian social mobilization.

Ecuador and Bolivia

The expansion of sexual rights in both Ecuador and Bolivia has also gone far, and similarities between them warrant their placement in another category. Ecuador scores 5 on our index, like Argentina, and Bolivia scores 4. In both cases, the left has supported the extension of sexual citizenship, although that support has not been applied equally to the three levels of rights.

While they have not attracted much media or scholarly attention, sexual rights in Ecuador have been expanded in a very short time. Along with a handful of cases, such as Chile, same-sex sexual relations were illegal in Ecuador until the late twentieth century. In 1997, the country's Constitutional Court struck down an article (516) of the penal code that criminalized same-sex sexual activities. The following year, in an attempt to stabilize the country after political tumult (which witnessed the ousting of President Abdalá Bucaram in early 1997), the country's leadership decided to draft a new and more socially inclusive constitution, which emphasized social rights (Lind and Keating 2013, 521–22). In this context, activists found a propitious environment within which to push for the expansion of sexual rights. The push was successful: Ecuador's 1998 Constitution included a clause that protects sexual minorities from discrimination. It made the country the first in the region, and only third in the world, to enshrine such a right in its constitutional framework. The 1998 Constitution served as a basis for the constitutional reforms undertaken by the leftist president Rafael Correa (2007–17) in 2008, but the results were somewhat mixed in terms of sexual rights. The new constitution preserved the 1997 antidiscrimination provisions and included the recognition of transgender rights (which were subsequently used by activists to demand the enactment of a gender identity law, which passed in 2016). However, the new constitution also introduced a redefinition of the family that defines marriage explicitly between a man and a woman and adoption can only be undertaken by opposite-sex couples. Despite this constitutional ban, a provision in article 68 states that same-sex couples that enter a common-law relationship must enjoy the same rights and responsibilities as married couples. The clause provoked some ambiguity, which eventually led the country's Civil Registry to recognize officially common-law relationships as civil unions in 2014. Later that year, Correa signed an executive resolution formalizing civil unions and in early 2015 a reform of the civil code allowing same-sex couples to register their de facto unions. However, same-sex couples are still not able to adopt, and activists' attempts to reform the constitution to allow same-sex marriage have been rejected by Correa's administration.

Unlike Ecuador, in Bolivia sexual activities between two individuals of the same sex have not been illegal. Like Ecuador, the 2009 Constitution prohibits discrimination based on sexual orientation. Bolivia thus belongs to a small group of Latin American countries in which this sexual right is constitutionally enshrined. Further, in 2010, President Evo Morales (2006–) enacted a national antidiscrimination law that includes sexual orientation and gender identity as protected categories. In terms of transgender rights, in 2016 the Morales administration enacted a gender identity law that allows individuals over the age of eighteen to change their gender on official documentation. Unlike Argentina's progressive law, however, a psychological test is required. In regard to relationship rights, the 2009 Constitution explicitly limits marriage to a union between a man and a woman and common-law relationships (*uniones libres*). However, the interpretation of these constitutional provisions has varied and has not resulted in a de facto recognition of these relationships. Since the implementation of the constitution, several attempts at legalizing civil unions have been met with opposition by the Morales administration. In neither case are same-sex couples legally allowed to adopt or share parental rights and responsibilities.

Gay and lesbian activism in both countries has historically been weak and, until very recently, rather invisible. However, in both countries the recent constitutional reforms afforded activists rare political opportunities to push for the expansion of some sexual rights. Indeed, activists were central to the inclusion of sexual rights in the constitutions of both countries (Lind 2004). Despite their mobilizing weakness, the constitutional reforms specifically intended to redefine the concept of citizenship by recognizing the diverse social nature of the Bolivian and Ecuadorean societies within the overarching concept of plurinational states (see Rice, this volume). This broader social negotiation, which was primarily driven by the political elites, over the terms of citizenship allowed activists to insert sexuality and sexual rights into an expanded conception of individual, social, and cultural rights. Correa and Morales have explicitly supported the inclusion of antidiscrimination rights, despite some opposition.

It becomes clear, then, that the ideological orientation of these two administrations has been essential to the expansion of sexual citizenship. However, the support for relationship rights has been more mixed. During the Constituent Assembly deliberations in 2008, Correa openly declared his support for civil unions, citing the "intrinsic nature of human dignity," but, at the same time, he also supported defining marriage as between a man and a woman and preventing same-sex couples to adopt (Lind and Keating 2013). A constitutional ban on same-sex marriage makes it more difficult for activists to achieve it given that a higher parliamentary threshold is needed to approve a constitutional reform. Despite repeatedly having made overtly homophobic statements during his tenure, Morales's support for the inclusion of antidiscrimination provisions in the constitution, as well as the enactment of the antidiscrimination and gender identity laws, has been clear. However, his government has flatly rejected any attempt to introduce same-sex marriage (Página12 2015).

Nicaragua and Venezuela

Under another category one can place the leftist parties that have governed Nicaragua and Venezuela. Both countries score low on sexual citizenship, 3 and 1.5, respectively, and leftist governments have systematically rejected civil society demands to expand some sexual rights. Similar to most Latin American countries, same-sex sexual activities have never been illegal in postcolonial Venezuela. Antidiscrimination provisions protecting sexual minorities were introduced in the mid-1990s during the Rafael Caldera administration (1994–99) in labor legislation (hence the half point accorded to this country in table 10.1). Since the election of Hugo Chávez (1999–2013) in 1998, which is usually regarded as the onset of Latin America's Pink Tide, the country has enacted an antidiscrimination law and established an antidiscrimination institute (Instituto Nacional contra la Discriminación Racial). However, the law does not include sexual orientation as a category and the institute's mandate has been to eradicate racial discrimination, particularly against the Afro-Venezuelan population. Unlike in Argentina, the institute has not expanded its official mandate to include other vulnerable groups, such as sexual minorities. Activists advanced proposals to include antidiscrimination provisions during the drafting of the new constitution in 1999, but they were rejected and dropped from the final draft document. Proposals to include these provisions in the 2007 constitutional reforms were included in the referendum, but they were also rejected. In terms of relationship recognition, same-sex couples do not enjoy any legal recognition in Venezuela and have no joint maternal or parental adoption rights. A 2008 Supreme Court ruling declared that same-sex couples enjoy all the rights enshrined in the constitution, but since neither sexual orientation nor same-sex couples are mentioned in any clause, the puzzling ruling has not had any concrete implications. The Court also ruled that it is up to the National Assembly to legislate on the matter, essentially dodging the issue.

The sexual rights landscape in Nicaragua is very similar to Venezuela's. While same-sex activities were not criminalized after independence, the socially conservative administration of Violeta Chamorro (1990–97) undertook a reform of the Criminal Code that introduced "sodomy" as a sexual offense punishable by three years in prison. After strong mobilization, which included the support of international human rights organizations such as Amnesty International, article 204 of the Code, which contains sexual offenses, was reformed and the "sodomy" clause repealed. Nicaragua thus became the last country in Latin America to expand this basic practice right. Importantly, the same reforms resulted in the inclusion of various provisions that ban discrimination based on sexual orientation. It also makes such discrimination a crime (aggravating circumstances, or *circunstancias agravantes*, art. 36). Same-sex couples have no relationship rights, and reforms to the Family Code in 2014 defined marriage as exclusively between a man and a woman.

Despite Chávez's "Bolivarian Revolution," which was hailed discursively as ushering in a new chapter in Venezuela's political history through the inclusion of marginalized citizens and the broadening of conceptions of citizenships, sexual rights have not been supported by either the Chávez or the Nicolás Maduro (2013–) administrations. Unlike Bolivia and Ecuador, the renegotiation of citizenship rights through constitutional reforms, in Venezuela through the adoption of the new Bolivarian Constitution, has not included sexual rights. In this context, activists' demands have met categorical rejection from Venezuela's version of the Latin American left. While Venezuela's gay and lesbian movement has been weaker compared to their counterparts elsewhere, such as the Argentine and Mexican ones, they do have national visibility and have applied pressure on the state to expand sexual rights. Part of the reason appears to be the tightening of church-state relations that has characterized Bolivarian Venezuela. Gay and lesbian activists have found allies within Venezuela's governing Partido Socialista Unido de Venezuela (United Socialist Party of Venezuela, PSUV), but attempts to bring about reform have been blocked by Venezuela's left. For example, in 2009, after close collaboration with activists, a member of the National Assembly, Romelia Matute, attempted to introduce reforms to the Gender Equality Bill that would have recognized civil unions. But, as soon as the story broke in the news, the president of the Commission of Family, Women, and Youth, a PSUV member, under pressure from religious groups, rejected them. Given that the parliamentary route is clearly closed to the push for reform, activists have attempted to do so via the judiciary. However, in Bolivarian Venezuela the judiciary has lost significant autonomy (Brinks 2005) and the Supreme Court has rarely ruled against the general positions taken by the executive. The gay organization Unión Afirmativa (Affirmative Union) has submitted several constitutional challenges to the court, but they have not been successful.

In the case of Nicaragua, Daniel Ortega (2007–) promised to bring in a new era in citizenship rights through his "Second Sandinista Revolution." While expectations were high, given that the 1980 Sandinistas maintained fairly socially progressive positions on sexuality (openly gay individuals were senior government officials), sexual citizenship has only advanced in practice and expression rights. Nicaragua's version of Latin America's left has therefore not been a full supporter of sexual rights. Stagnation in the relationship rights front could be partly attributed to Nicaragua's comparatively weak gay and lesbian rights movement, a weakness that is to a certain extent explained by the introduction of article 204 of in 1992: it forbade the public advocacy of sexual rights. However, with the support of the women's movement, there has been gay and lesbian organizing in Nicaragua for at least twenty years (Babb 2003; Kampwirth 2014). Lack of progress on relationship rights appears to be more the result of the socially conservative position adopted by Ortega, as the reforms of the Family Code shows, than of weak activism. Activists have simply not found a receptive government. Ortega's administrations have attempted to forge a collaborative relationship with gay and lesbian activists, through the adoption of a friendly discourse as well the distribution of financial resources to some gay organizations. However, the real objective seems to have been an attempt to weaken women's groups—with which they have been allies and against which Ortega has launched an aggressive delegitimation campaign (Kampwirth 2014, 323–24, 327–29)—rather than a genuine desire to expand sexual citizenship: because women's movements have been some of the most critical of the regime's undemocratic practices, the redirection of financial resources to gay and lesbian movements has had political objectives other than sexual rights expansion.

Brazil

The politics of sexual citizenship in Brazil are a veritable puzzle, and the country can therefore be safely placed in a category of its own. Brazil has one of Latin America's oldest gay rights movements in Latin America, and its Partido dos Trabalhadores (Workers' Party, PT), which formed government from 2003 to 2015, historically held a fairly progressive position on the regulation of sexuality. Yet it only scores 4.5 on our Sexual Citizenship Index. The answer to that puzzle seems to be related to the country's type of federalism as well as the institutional veto conservative religious groups wield. In terms of practice rights, same-sex sexual activities have not been criminalized in Brazil since 1830, when Emperor Dom Pedro adopted the country's Imperial Civil Code. Brazil's postmilitary constitution, enacted in 1988, guarantees strong individual freedoms and explicitly forbids any of the states to enact legislation that undermines personal freedoms. While it does not explicitly include sexual orientation or gender identity, its meaning has over the years been more expansively interpreted by subnational governments and the judiciary to include both sexual orientation and gender identity. This interpretation has been the basis for the enactment of antidiscrimination legislation in many states (hence the .5 score accorded on this front in table 10.1) and a slew of judicial rulings that have expanded a variety of rights at the state and national levels on all three levels of rights.

In terms of same-sex relationship recognition, and unlike in Argentina, Brazil's family law is administered by the states. Similar to the United States, there has been a great deal of variance at the subnational level: some state governments and courts have expanded numerous socioeconomic rights to same-sex couples, and some states have legalized them (Marsiaj 2012). Such variance came to an end with two important High Court rulings. In May 2011, the country's Supreme Federal Court ruled, based on the fact that some subnational courts had ruled positively on the matter, that civil unions be recognized throughout the country. The ruling argued that denial of this right violated the rights-based principles enshrined in the 1988 Constitution. Two years later, in May 2013, the National Council of Justice ordered all notary publics to register same-sex civil unions as marriages upon request. With the stroke of a pen, then, same-sex marriage was expanded universally in a country of two hundred million inhabitants.

Much of the advance in sexual citizenship in Brazil is the result of strong activism at the subnational level, but the PT has also played a significant role. Similar to Uruguay's Frente Amplio, Brazil's main leftist party emerged from social mobilization in the late 1970s and adopted fairly progressive social positions as it became a serious political contender for national office. Given its roots, gay and lesbian activists have been able to forge important alliances with numerous state and nonstate actors affiliated with the PT. However, the ability of the PT to help push for sexual rights has not been as strong as other leftist parties in Latin America. Very different from the Argentine and Uruguayan cases, socially conservative religious groups wield significant policy-making influence. Because of Brazil's highly fractured party system, the executive requires the support of a variety of smaller parties and factions to get legislation through the National Congress. Conservative groupings representing Brazil's large socially conservative evangelical community are as a result able to wield significant influence, which amounts to a veto power over moral policy reform. Nothing illustrates this better than

President Dilma Rousseff's (2011–15) need to meet with religious leaders during the runoff to her presidential election in late 2010. After that
meeting she was forced to sign an open letter in which she promised to
respect the family and committed herself not to pursue reform in the
moral policy area (Marsiaj 2012).

After two decades of economic crises and market-friendly structural adjustment, Latin Americans exchanged neoliberals for social democrats
at the ballot box, and, invariably, the new leaders spoke of the dawn
of a more promising era in Latin America that would finally eradicate
poverty, reduce the world's worst wealth distribution, and include the
historically marginalized through more inclusive citizenship. As Latin
America's Pink Tide ebbs with the defeat or weakening of these leaders,
one can start looking at the record left by the left on the drying sand. In
some areas, this record has been undeniably solid: poverty and inequality
have been reduced in most countries (with the exception of Mexico and
some Central American countries), and Latin America's middle class
has expanded to its largest size in history. Nevertheless, as the editors of
this volume argue, optimism was also expressed by state and non-state
actors who hoped that, under the Pink Tide, the improvement of people's lives would not be limited to socioeconomic conditions but would
also encompass an expansion of a variety of citizenship rights.

    In terms of sexual rights, the record, as I have tried to show in this
chapter, has been decidedly mixed. Having availed the reader of the
Sexual Citizenship Index to guide our assessment of the left's record on
sexual rights expansion, it is clear that there exists wide regional variance.
In some cases, such as Argentina, Bolivia, and Uruguay, the expansion
of sexual rights under leftist governments has been nothing short of remarkable. In a relatively short time, these governments have for the most
part supported most efforts to expand all three levels of sexual rights:
practice, expression, and relationship. This support has pushed these
countries closer to the attainment of fuller sexual citizenship. The record
looks a lot weaker in other cases, such as Nicaragua and Venezuela. In
these cases, which sit at the opposite end of the sexual citizenship spectrum, and despite grandiose promises to expand citizenship rights to all,
the leftists leaders' support for sexual rights expansion has been selective at best. As we have seen, for a variety of reasons, Venezuela's Hugo

Chávez and Nicolás Maduro and Nicaragua's Daniel Ortega showed tepid support for some rights and outright rejection of others. However, a careful analysis of the politics of sexual rights during the Pink Tide reveals that even in those cases in which leftist governments have lent support for the expansion of some sexual rights, the expansion of sexual citizenship has come as a result of organized efforts by gay and lesbian activists who have made their demands on the state. In this story, then, the main actors have been activists themselves, with *some* leftist leaders playing a supporting role.

NOTES

1. It is now a legal right in Argentina, Brazil, Mexico, Colombia, and Uruguay.

2. "Heteronormativity" refers to a "set of institutionalized norms and practices that supports and compels private heterosexuality, marriage, family, monogamous dyadic commitment and traditional gender roles" (Green 2002, 542 n. 4).

3. Some states in Brazil and some cities and provinces in Argentina have this type of legislation. In Brazil a national law was passed in the lower house but has stalled in the Senate due to opposition from religious senators. Argentina has had a national law since 1988, but it does not include sexual orientation. Reforms to the bill have been passed in the lower house of Congress as well but have also stalled in the Senate.

4. Interview with Deputy Washington Abdala, Montevideo, October 29, 2010.

5. Interview with Senator Margarita Percovich, Montevideo, October 25, 2010.

6. Interview with Senator Mónica Xavier (2005–10), Frente Amplio, Montevideo, October 29, 2010.

7. Interview with Deputy Alvaro Lorenzo, Partido Nacional, Montevideo, November 3, 2010.

REFERENCES

Álvarez, Sonia E. 1999. "Advocating Feminism: The Latin American Feminist NGO 'Boom.'" *International Feminist Journal of Politics* 1 (2): 181–209.

Babb, Florence E. 2003. "Out in Nicaragua: Local and Transnational Desires after the Revolution." *Cultural Anthropology* 18 (3): 304–28.

Bell, David, and Jon Binnie. 2000. *The Sexual Citizen: Queer Politics and Beyond.* Cambridge: Polity Press.

Biagini, Graciela. 2009. *Sociedad civil y VIH-SIDA: ¿De la acción colectiva a la fragmentación de intereses?* Buenos Aires: Paidós.

Brinks, Daniel M. 2005. *The Judicial Response to Police Killings in Latin America: Inequality and the Rule of Law.* New York: Cambridge University Press.

Calhoun, Cheshire. 2000. *Feminism, the Family, and the Politics of the Closet: Lesbian and Gay Displacement.* Oxford: Oxford University Press.

Cariboni, Diana. 2014. "The LGBT, Feminist and Student Voices Behind Uruguay's Radical Reforms." *The Guardian.* Montevideo. www.theguardian .com/global-development/2014/aug/01/uruguay-lgbt-feminist-student -protest-liberal-reforms.

Corrales, Javier. 2015a. *LGBT Rights and Representation in Latin America and the Caribbean: The Influence of Structure, Movements, Institutions, and Culture.* Chapel Hill: University of North Carolina Press.

———. 2015b. "The Politics of LGBT Rights in Latin America and the Caribbean: Research Agendas." *European Review of Latin American and Caribbean Studies. 50th Anniversary Special Issue: New Directions in Latin American and Caribbean Studies* (100): 53–62.

Díez, Jordi. 2013. "Explaining Policy Outcomes: The Adoption of Same-Sex Unions in Buenos Aires and Mexico City." *Comparative Political Studies* 46 (2): 212–35.

———. 2015. *The Politics of Gay Marriage in Latin America: Argentina, Chile, and Mexico.* New York: Cambridge University Press.

Díez, Jordi, and Michelle L. Dion. 2015. "Support for Same-Sex Marriage in Latin America." Paper delivered at the Annual Meeting of the International Political Science Association, Montreal, July 20–24.

Encarnación, Omar. 2016. *Out in the Periphery: Latin America's Gay Rights Revolution.* New York: Oxford University Press.

Friedman, Elisabeth Jay. 2010. "Seeking Rights from the Left: Gender and Sexuality in Latin America." In Amrita Basu, ed., *Women's Movements in the Global Era: The Power of Local Feminisms.* Boulder, CO: Westview Press.

Green, Adam Isaiah. 2002. "Gay but not Queer: Toward a Post-Queer Study of Sexuality." *Theory and Society* 31 (4): 521–45.

Green, James N. 1994. *Beyond Carnival: Male Homosexuality in Twentieth-Century Brazil.* Chicago: University of Chicago Press.

Ignatieff, Michael. 2002. *The Rights Revolution.* Toronto: House of Anansi.

Kampwirth, Karen. 2014. "Organising the Hombre Nuevo Gay: LGBT Poli-
   tics and the Second Sandinista Revolution." *Bulletin of Latin American
   Research* 33 (3): 319–33.
Kaplan, Morris B. 1997. *Sexual Justice: Democratic Citizenship and the Politics of
   Desire.* New York: Routledge.
Lind, Amy. 2004. "Legislating the Family: Heterosexual Bias in Social Wel-
   fare Policy Frameworks." *Journal of Sociology and Social Welfare* 31 (4): 21.
Lind, Amy, and Christine Keating. 2013. "Navigating the Left Turn: Sexual
   Justice and the Citizen Revolution in Ecuador." *International Feminist
   Journal of Politics* 15 (4): 515–33.
Lodola, Germán, and Margarita Corral. 2010. *Support for Same-Sex Mar-
   riage in Latin America.* Nashville, TN: Latin American Public Opinion
   Project, Vanderbilt University. www.vanderbilt.edu/lapop/insights/I0844
   .enrevised.pdf.
Marsiaj, Juan. 2012. "Federalism, Advocacy Networks, and Sexual Diversity
   Politics in Brazil." In Jordi Díez and Susan Franceschet, eds., *Compara-
   tive Public Policy in Latin America.* Toronto: University of Toronto Press.
La Nación. 2012. "El Senado dio luz verde a la ley de identidad de género." *La
   Nación.* Buenos Aires. www.lanacion.com.ar/1471886-el-senado-dio-luz
   -verde-a-la-ley-de-identidad-de-genero.
Nussbaum, Martha. 2002. "Education for Citizenship in an Era of Global
   Connection." *Studies in Philosophy and Education* 21 (4): 289–303.
Página12. 2015. "Tenemos un gran colchón financiero." *Página12.* Buenos
   Aires. www.pagina12.com.ar/diario/elmundo/subnotas/279517-73990
   -2015-08-17.html.
Pateman, Carole. 1988. "The Patriarchal Welfare State." In Amy Gutmann,
   ed., *Democracy and the Welfare State.* Princeton, NJ: Princeton University
   Press.
Plummer, Ken. 2001. "The Square of Intimate Citizenship: Some Preliminary
   Proposals." *Citizenship Studies* 5 (3): 237–53.
———. 2003. *Intimate Citizenship: Private Decisions and Public Dialogues.*
   Montreal: McGill-Queen's University Press.
República de Nicaragua. 2002. *Código Procesal Penal de la República de Nicara-
   gua.* Managua: Asamblea Nacional.
Richardson, Diane. 1998. "Sexuality and Citizenship." *Sociology* 32 (1): 83–100.
———. 2000. "Constructing Sexual Citizenship: Theorizing Sexual Rights."
   Critical Social Policy 20 (1): 105–35.
Schulenberg, Shawn. 2012. "The Construction and Enactment of Same-Sex
   Marriage in Argentina." *Journal of Human Rights* 11 (1): 106–25.

———. 2013. "The Lavender Tide? LGTB Rights and the Latin American Left Today." In María Gracia Andía, Daniel Bonilla, Margarita Corral, Germán Lodola, Genaro Lozano, and Diego Sempol, eds., *Same-Sex Marriage in Latin America: Promise and Resistance*. Lanham, MD: Lexington Books.

Sívori, Horacio Federico. 2008. "LGTB y otros HSH: Ciencia y política de la identidad sexual en la prevención del Sida." In Jason Pierceson, Adriana Piatti-Crocker, and Shawn Schulenberg, eds., *Same-Sex Marriage in the Americas*. Lanham, MD: Lexington Press.

Smulovitz, Catalina. 2012. "Public Policy by Other Means: Playing the Judicial Arena." In Jordi Díez and Susan Franceschet, eds., *Comparative Public Policy in Latin America*. Toronto: University of Toronto Press.

Torres-Ruiz, Antonio. 2006. "An Elusive Quest for Democracy and Development in a Globalized World: The Political Economy of HIV/AIDS in Mexico." PhD dissertation, University of Toronto.

———. 2011. "HIV/AIDS and Sexual Minorities in Mexico: A Globalized Struggle for the Protection of Human Rights." *Latin American Research Review* 46 (1): 30–53.

Waites, Matthew. 1996. "Lesbian and Gay Theory, Sexuality and Citizenship." *Contemporary Politics* 2 (3): 139–49.

Weeks, Jeffrey. 1998. "The Sexual Citizen." *Theory, Culture & Society* 15 (3): 35–52.

Weeks, Jeffrey, Brian Heaphy, and Catherine Donovan. 2001. *Same Sex Intimacies: Families of Choice and Other Life Experiments*. London: Routledge.

ELEVEN

Sustainable Development Reconsidered

The Left Turn's Legacies in the Amazon

Eve Bratman

As leftist leadership gained political power in the early 2000s in Latin America, environmental protection—and nature itself—became a more prominent regional political issue than ever before. The Ecuadorean and Bolivian constitutions embraced the rights to nature, and atop Machu Picchu, Peru's newly inaugurated President Alejandro Toledo symbolically gave an offering to Pachamama, the Andean divinity of Mother Earth. El Salvador issued a ban on gold mining, confronting the mining giant Pacific Rim corporation's interests. In Brazil, the environmentalist turn involved a measured but positive prognosis, with President Luiz Inácio Lula da Silva of the Partido dos Trabalhadores (Workers' Party, PT) appointing a former rubber tapper, Marina Silva, minister of the environment. These moves all suggested to observers that conservation, Indigenous rights, and forest people's concerns would be championed as priorities.

At the same time, however, the new developmentalist economic orientation embraced by these same governments led to positioning environmental needs as subservient to national and international imperatives for industry-led economic growth and commodity production based largely on resource extraction (Haarstad 2011). Under the left's leadership in many parts of Latin America, this revived developmentalist approach reinvigorated an emphasis on energy and infrastructure while still actively engaging in the global economy (Amado and Mollo 2015; Baletti 2012; Ban 2012; Bresser-Pereira 2011; Hochstetler and Kostka 2015; Klein 2015; Morais and Saad-Filho 2012; Sikkink 1991; Zhouri 2010). Was sacrificing ecosystem health the inevitable cost of these economic growth models? Contradictions generally marked the Left turn's environmental politics, despite the conceptual appeal offered through the three-pillared model of sustainable development, wherein economic, social, and environmental factors would be harmonized for mutual benefit.

This chapter focuses on the environmental legacy of the left in the Amazon basin by examining a few key issue areas and interrogating the ways in which environmental policies varied over time. I specifically give attention to divergences in practice from governmentally articulated environmental discourses of sustainable development. Given that two-thirds of the Amazon basin is within Brazilian territory, this chapter primarily focuses on that country's track record on environmental issues while also offering some comparative analysis of Brazil with Ecuador and Bolivia. I interrogate how the Left turn governments approached deforestation, mining, and energy production in the Amazon region. Many of these issues intersect with human rights, justice, and land rights issues rather than a more narrow understanding of environmental policies and impacts per se. Other pertinent environmental issues, including climate change policies, water, soil, and air quality, are beyond the scope of this chapter.

A central theme of this book concerns how the New Left in Latin America expanded its reach by granting rights and empowering some groups that had previously not been a mainstay of the traditional left—environmental activists being a key constituency. As citizenship claims and expressions of rights became more central to social movement activism and mobilization in Latin America in the 1990s, claims to citizenship expanded into the more pluralistic identity-based groupings of gender, religion, sexual orientation, and Indigeneity, among many increasingly active groups (Montambault, Balán, and Oxhorn, this volume). An even more expansive approach to the notion of citizenship was the push by some leftist leaders to expand the sphere of rights beyond humans and their identity groups to nature itself. This, among other multiscalar and intersectional dimensions of citizenship regimes, figures prominently in the legacy of the leftist governments on environmental issues. The environmental legacy of the left should be assessed not only by evaluating how expansions of rights took shape, but also how, in practice, legal and political norms relating to environmental issues transformed social and ecological relationships.

The field of environmental citizenship begins with an ethical starting point that concentrates on the types of responsibilities that people have as stewards of the earth and in relation to whole communities of life on the planet (Hargove 1989; Rozzi et al. 2012). Environmental citizenship theorization focuses on the relationships between democracy, space, place, and the kinds of rights and responsibilities involved in contesting and upholding environmental values (Dobson 2006). While the citizens of any liberal democratic state can exercise basic political rights, including voting, freedom of expression, free association, and legal procedural pursuits, green movement actors may be left at a disadvantage because ecological concerns are often ignored. Environmental well-being frequently involves externalized costs and foci of concern that are beyond the scope of civil and political rights. Ecological welfare concerns are also often traded off against the immediate demands that are better represented in politics through capital and labor (Eckersley 1996). This strengthening of ecological concerns may be bolstered by the adoption of an environmental rights framework and an understanding of environmental rights as consistent with a co-constituted relationship between ecological and social beings (Benton 1993; Eckersley 1992; Sagoff 2008). Ecological and democratic concerns can be connected through this line of thinking but are not necessarily intuitive allies; some green political theorists looked to eco-authoritarian solutions (Hardin 1972; Heilbroner [1974] 1991; Ophuls and Boyan 1992), but by the late 1970s, green political theory tended to embrace fuller participatory engagement as a central part of its approach (Eckersley 1996).

This chapter especially concerns the environmental politics of the Brazilian Amazon, which comprises around 70 percent of the region, although examples are also drawn from neighboring countries in the region. I begin by noting several important contextual and theoretical dimensions regarding environmental issues and the environmental movement in the Amazon as a whole. Subsequently, an empirically grounded discussion of the legacy of environmental policies of leftist governments is presented, followed by analysis and some general conclusions about the meanings of environmental citizenship and environmental policies in present-day Amazonia.

BACKGROUND: AMAZONIAN SOCIO-ENVIRONMENTALISM AND LEFTIST POLITICS

The Amazon is arguably the world's most symbolically charged landscape for environmental conservation issues. Since the time of colonization and early explorations by people of European descent, the Amazon has alternately been represented by explorers, writers, conservationists, politicians, and the media as a fragile rainforest ecosystem in need of protection or as a wild jungle, which, if tamed, promised wealth and a civilizational triumph (Slater 2002, 2015). These competing visions were navigated most prominently through the discourse of sustainable development. In the late 1980s and early 1990s, sustainable development was a concept that involved the tandem aim to protect the earth for future generations without compromising on the economic and social aspirations embodied in the shorter-term development agenda. Brazil's role as host to the Rio Earth Summit in 1992 and the Rio+20 Summit in 2012 shed a spotlight on Amazonian forest protection in the arena of global environmental politics and cast the region as playing a central role in political debates over how best to manage the challenges of biodiversity losses, deforestation, and climate change.

Beyond the symbolic level, the Amazon's role as an ecosystem of global importance is physically and materially significant. As the world's largest tropical rainforest, the carbon captured by Amazonian forests could significantly mitigate global warming by being a carbon sink. Research estimates that if the Amazonian mature forest biomass was increased by just 0.3 percent, the absorption of greenhouse gases would be equal to the entire yearly fossil fuel emissions of Western Europe (Phillips and Lewis 2014). Deforestation in the Amazon, meanwhile, can also have significant effects in terms of global climate change, because significant amounts of greenhouse gases are released through the burning and decomposition of vegetation in rainforest ecosystems. The Amazon River accounts for one-fifth of the world's freshwater, and Amazonian precipitation patterns are linked to precipitation patterns as far away as Argentina and California (Medvigy et al. 2013).

Historically, environmental issues have not been an especially strong current of leftist politics in Latin America. While there is affinity with the left's agenda for environmental issues in Latin American contexts, the left is dominated by labor and class analysis more than anything else. Labor groups often express a sympathetic concern for environmental issues, but the relationship between class analysis and environmental politics is generally undertheorized in the literature (Bull and Aguilar-Støen 2015; Terhorst, Olivera, and Dwinell 2013; Veiga and Martin 2012). A "traditional" environmentalism embodies a conservationist orientation, which tends to view the protection of parks for the purposes of plant, soil, and wildlife protection as a priority, regardless of social concerns. Most common in the Amazon region among "greens" is a more integrative analysis of the relationship between issues of social justice and environmental protection, which tends to fall into the domain of environmental justice and socio-environmentalism. These approaches begin with the idea that people's issues are inextricably linked with nature itself. Socio-environmentalism focuses on the interconnections of human needs and livelihoods with environmental concerns, while environmental justice tends to center on the fair treatment of all people with regard to facing the burdens of negative environmental consequences.

Given the robustness of socio-environmentalism in the Amazon region, the traditionally "red" leftists showing an alliance with the "green" environmentalists is relatively unsurprising, particularly on issues of social accountability and the coupling of forest people's movements with conservation goals (Hochstetler and Keck 2007). Using a socio-environmental framework, critiques of capitalism were leveraged to draw affinity and broad bases of mobilization among environmental groups, land reform activists, union leaders, and a wide range of human rights issues. Illustrative of this is that the Movimento dos Trabalhadores Rurais Sem Terra (Landless Workers' Movement, MST) and the larger peasant movement, La Via Campesina, positioned itself against genetically modified organisms and pesticide use in the late 1990s, linking land reform and inequality directly to critiques of agribusiness and environmental protection. Another example derives from the Movimento dos Atingidos por Barragens (Movement of People Affected by Dams, MAB), which took aim at hydroelectric projects and their associated human displacements as part of a broader critique of industrial capital and privatization of energy. As neoliberal democracies established in Latin America after authoritarian regimes lost their hold, social rights and reduced access to the inclusive rights of citizenship tended to take shape in the form of market-based incentives, consumption, and access to personal resources (Oxhorn 2011). In response to the confines of market-led and export-oriented growth strategies of the postneoliberal period, the argument that citizenship should not be confined to one's consumption and wealth was strengthened across Latin American social movements. As a result, social movements were able to articulate broader messaging on equality, inclusion, and cultural recognition, and the array of social movement actors became more heterogeneous and engaged in identity-based politics (Grugel and Riggirozzi 2012; Ruckert, Macdonald, and Proulx 2016).

These broader tensions with neoliberalism notwithstanding, a certain irony prevailed during the Latin American Pink Tide with regard to environmental issues. Socio-environmental groups coalesced around their common opposition to neoliberal economic reforms, agribusiness, and privatization of natural resources, but the respect for Indigeneity and nature that were prevalent in the postneoliberal order became problematically intertwined with liberal concepts of citizenship that had assimilationist tendencies (Ettlinger and Hartmann 2015). In what some scholars refer to as the "not-quite-neoliberal natures" approach, a mix of heavy state spending channeled wealth from extractive activities into social spending (Brannstrom 2009; De Freitas, Marston, and Bakker 2015; Ettlinger and Hartmann 2015; Nel 2015; Sawyer 2005). Driving such spending, resource extraction became paired with dispossessions of land and resources, in the name of economic growth. The consequences especially affected Indigenous communities, who were displaced and frequently lost possession and control of their lands (De Freitas, Marston, and Bakker 2015). Land grabbing has problematic environmental consequences, including increases in fossil fuel drilling, deforestation, and land conversions. Simultaneously, "green grabs," illustrated by attempts to privatize and commodify nature while private or state investors frequently expropriate land and resources from smallholders, commonly leads to an increase in pipelines, highways, plantations, and tourist developments (Hall et al. 2015).

Illustrative of how state spending came at the expense of environmental concerns is the case of Bolivia under Evo Morales and the Movimiento al Socialismo (Movement toward Socialism, MAS), which used oil and gas programs to fund the bulk of its social redistribution programs, despite the direct conflicts that arose with Indigenous, environmental, and other civil society organizations. Notably, Brazil's contributions to funding the highway that would run through Bolivia's Territorio Indígena y Parque Nacional Isiboro Sécure (Indigenous Territory and Isiboro Sécure National Park, TIPNIS) is also illustrative of this tension, manifested as a broader geopolitical prioritization of infrastructure development over environmental conservation throughout the region. Despite the gains for Indigenous consultation that were won in the Bolivian 2009 Constitution, the protests against the highway construction in 2011 suggested that the approach was neither distinctively one of dispossession-through-neoliberalism nor one of postneoliberal inclusion and social welfare policies. It also revealed the complexity of social movement alliances and dynamics, given that Indigenous groups did not have a unanimous position in relation to extractivism but rather, a complex and long history with regard to the use of their natural resources and the economic gains that could be made from extractive activities (De Freitas, Marston, and Bakker 2015; McNeish 2013). As far as social movement dynamics were concerned, some friction with the more industrial base of workers that centrally worked to defend workers' rights and other social concerns diverged from Indigenous groups and conservationists over these issues. While "red" and "green" alliances may have been present and social movements more heterogeneous under the left's leadership in Brazil and Bolivia, such affinities were easily fractured.

It is worth noting briefly the linkage of environmental and rule-of-law issues more broadly in the Amazonian context. Environmental human rights defenders are easily more threatened in Latin America than any other part of the world at present (Article 19, CIEL, and Vermont Law School 2016), and this was also the case under the Left turn governments. The struggle to defend environmental defenders' rights often conflicts with national extractive sector projects, which, on the whole, were increasing in the Amazon under the Left turn governments. A report coauthored by the Center for International Environmental Law notes:

> In Colombia, coal extraction between 2000 and 2010 nearly doubled and the number of mining concessions has similarly maintained an accelerated pace. This has resulted in a substantial increase in attacks across the region. According to the Guatemalan Human Rights Commission/USA, in the decade between 2000 and 2010, 118 environmental human rights defenders in Guatemala were murdered and over 2,000 assaults occurred against groups of protesters. . . . [T]he majority of environmental killings in Peru were being perpetrated by the State and private security forces, and most were related to extractive sector projects. (Article 19, CIEL, and Vermont Law School 2016)

In addition to the statistics above, environmental rights defenders were subject to worrisome levels of violence, including assassinations, disappearances, torture, and violent attacks. In the 2003–13 period, nearly 2,500 rural workers received death threats in Brazil (Human Rights Watch 2014). The year 2015 was the worst on record for environmental and land defenders around the world, with Brazil ranked as the worst (Global Witness 2016).[1]

The interlinked notions of labor rights, forest preservation, and economic opportunity for forest peoples were most prominently articulated by the Amazonian rubber tapper Chico Mendes, who reflected in 1988 on the alliances that the rubber tappers formed with international environmental lobby groups, the Brazilian PT, Indigenous groups, and urban students as key contributors to their broader success (Mendes 1989). In no small measure, these sorts of intersectional alliances and approaches to forest conservation and economic development influenced the formation of Amazonian socio-environmental activism. The debate—especially among the international environmental community—largely shifted after Chico Mendes's assassination in December 1988. The stance that was skeptical of forest peoples as viable allies in rainforest protection that was largely held by traditional conservationists became more marginal, and the perspective that forest peoples' abilities to live and work within the region was compatible with ecological balance became increasingly mainstreamed. The shift was not instantaneous or directly linked to Chico Mendes's martyrdom, but the connections between Indigenous groups, anti–hydroelectric dam activism, rubber tappers, riverine peasants, and land reform did become more proximate during the late 1980s and early 1990s. These groups remained a strong part of the left's political base, and many of Brazil's socio-environmental activists were affiliated with the PT nearly from the time of the party's inception.

The Pink Tide did notably involve stepping into leadership on environmental issues in other Amazonian nations, actively embracing a more expansive notion of environmental citizenship through participatory politics and granting rights for nature in the Ecuadorean and Bolivian constitutions. The rights for nature idea considerably extends the notion of rights and protections beyond environmental defenders and beyond socio-environmentalism into a broader conception of nonhuman rights and ontological relationships (Youatt 2017). Ecuador and Bolivia are the most prominent Latin American nations to support the idea of environmental human rights and the rights of nature and have engaged this idea within the United Nations and other international forums (Conca 2015). Ecuador's Indigenous communities, in fact, largely led the global governance reforms that pushed the notion of *sumak kawsay* into globally institutionalized watershed management regimes (Kauffman 2017; Kauffman and Martin 2014).[2] The incorporation of rights of nature in practice, however, suggests that while a robust discourse of sustainable development is being reimagined, it is being done in such a way that the initiatives look like "cheap talk" because of a lack of enforcement, at least until the norms and jurisprudence associated with them become strengthened (Kauffman and Martin 2017).

DEFORESTATION, CONSERVATION AREAS, AND REFORESTATION

The Pink Tide governments were under considerable scrutiny in terms of their environmental policies, especially in the beginning years of the leftist leadership and particularly in the Amazon, as a region that holds long-standing global symbolic and ecological importance. Squaring environmental conservation with the need to secure and strengthen the economic goals that Latin America's Left turn articulated was a formidable challenge, particularly given the diversity and complex histories of Amazonian populations. In Brazil, environmental attention—and a desire to be recognized as a leader in global environmental politics especially because of its share of Amazonian rainforest lands—predated the rise of the Left turn governments by over a decade (Ferreira et al. 2014; Loyola 2014).

From the time of the country's new democratic constitution in 1988 until 2003, the Brazilian government became increasingly friendly toward and more proactive about environmental issues. Under the centrist leadership of Fernando Henrique Cardoso (president of Brazil, 1995–2002), a federal environmental agency was established, along with a host of new environmental policies and a national system for parks and conservation areas. Brazil hosted the 1992 Earth Summit and that same year gained US$428 million in funding to launch the PPG7, or Pilot Program to Conserve the Amazon Rainforest, which funded and promoted the creation of new conservation areas and demonstration projects for community-based agroecological and agroforestry production.

During Brazilian president Lula's first term, from 2003 to 2006, the outlook for strong environmental policies seemed to some observers to offer game-changing prospects for rainforest protection. Deforestation rates precipitously declined in this period, as shown in figure 11.1. The reductions in deforestation were so significant that President Lula committed in December 2008 to cutting the rate of gross Amazonian deforestation by 80 percent from historical levels (1996–2005) by 2020 as part of its national climate change action policy (Federative Republic of Brazil 2010). In the Bolivian, Colombian, and Peruvian Amazon, in contrast, deforestation increased from 2000 to 2011 (Song et al. 2015). In Brazil, the scientific community's deforestation models predicted that

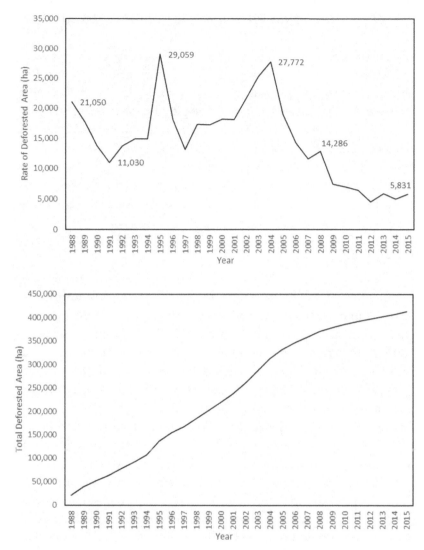

FIGURE 11.1. Deforestation in the Brazilian Amazon, 1988–2015. *Source*: Ministério do Meio Ambiente (Ministry of the Environment, MMA).

significant amounts of rainforest (30 percent and more in some Brazilian states) would be lost by 2050 if major policy changes were not undertaken (Nepstad et al. 2008; Soares-Filho et al. 2005). The aforementioned red-green alliances exerted political pressure, while a series of environmental governance proposals that blended market-based approaches for conservation, such as payment for ecosystem services and carbon credits, offered economic incentives for rainforest protection.

The antideforestation gains of Latin America's Pink Tide were achieved largely by setting aside significant amounts of Amazonian lands for conservation purposes during the 2003–8 interval. Marina Silva, who oversaw and spurred many of these areas as the Brazilian minister of the environment from 2003 to 2008, was a former rubber tapper, friend of and collaborator with Chico Mendes in the state of Acre, and a founder of the local rural workers' union. With the creation of a variety of new extractive reserves, national parks, and national forests, among other types of conservation areas, the Brazilian Amazon saw a 35 percent increase in conservation areas (MMA 2007). The basis of such policies was that regularizing landholdings and achieving forest protection could be achieved in tandem with improved livelihoods for small-scale farmers, rubber tappers, fishermen, and other Amazonian peasants (Duchelle et al. 1995; Wunder 2007).

Yet contradictions marked the sustainable development politics of the day, more than coherency. Even as deforestation rates dropped substantially during this time, infrastructure plans of the Initiative for the Integration of the Regional Infrastructure of South America (IIRSA) and Brazil's Plans for Accelerated Growth (PAC), along with the commodities boom, raised concern among many observers that infrastructure and export-centered development strategies would lead to further forest losses (Baletti 2014; Hecht 2005; Lilley 2004; Nepstad et al. 2014). The strong correlation that scientists observed between road projects and forest losses (Barber et al. 2014; Fearnside 2008; Godar, Tizado, and Pokorny 2012; Goodland and Irwin 1975; Walker and Arima 2011) therefore raised concerns that the Lula administration was essentially updating the national integration plans and developmental logics that characterized the 1970s and 1980s strategy for Amazonian development, with similarly concerning environmental ramifications. Ultimately, the environment and development politics was one of trying to have it both ways, with national economic modernization and small-scale livelihood and land protection happening in tandem within the Amazon region.

The results of such policies were highly uneven and somewhat schizophrenic. Rates of deforestation remained low even as significant safety issues remained for environmental defenders; socio-environmental activists continued to be persecuted and assassinated for defending the standing forest, including, most prominently, the assassination of Dorothy Stang in 2005 and Jose Claudio Ribeiro and his wife, Maria do Espirito Santo.[3] Such killings received high-profile media attention, thrusting Brazil into an embarrassing spotlight. They were sometimes met with gains for conservation, such as the creation of a mega-corridor mosaic of conservation areas that followed Dorothy Stang's assassination (Bratman 2011), but at other times, Brazil was more oriented toward accounting for deforestation than taking strong policy steps to counteract it, illustrated by the DETER real-time deforestation monitoring system that was installed in 2007. Meanwhile, high commodity prices and deforestation were strongly correlated and went relatively unchecked by policy measures aiming to quell the spread of soybean or cattle-related agriculture into Amazonian rainforests. An emergency decree, Federal Decree 6321/07, did block access to credit and land speculation for landowners in the thirty-six rural counties that were the hot spot locations for deforestation. The measure helped to attenuate the commodity price–deforestation link, even if it did not break it entirely (EDF 2009). Several NGO–private sector initiatives, including the Roundtable for Responsible Soy and the Roundtable for Sustainable Livestock, also helped industry players such as McDonald's, Walmart, and Cargill engage in Amazonian business with greater environmental commitments. Additional measures, such as the establishment of a rural lands registry, aimed to control illegal land-grabbing. Yet these supply-chain voluntary measures faced leakage and challenges of broadening participation in practice (Meijer 2015), and environmental and human rights norms showed some regressions during this same period (Bratman 2014).

The idea that forest protection is compatible with Brazil's commodity-oriented growth strategy was belied by the middle of President Dilma Rousseff's administration, in 2011, as deforestation reached new highs. Several factors were at work, contributing to the increases. First, President Rousseff, who in 2002 was minister for energy under President Lula, was deeply committed to bolstering national infrastructure plans, especially in the form of Amazonian hydroelectric dam construction and encouraging mining investments. The second Plan for Accelerated Growth (PAC II, 2010–14) was a R$1.59 trillion plan (around US$485 billion), up nearly threefold from PAC I. Second, the political power of the rural agribusiness lobby (*ruralistas*) had by that point increased in the Brazilian Senate and Congress, overshadowing environmental conservation drastically in terms of political influence. The Chamber of Deputies and the Senate passed a bill that revised the federal Forest Code in 2012. While Rousseff vetoed many of the most problematic components of the new law, Greenpeace bemoaned the dilution of Brazil's formerly robust Forest Code, calling it "another instrument for farmers to turn on their chainsaws" (Greenpeace 2011). The law, even in its stronger earlier iteration, was not much enforced. Nearly half of Brazil's greenhouse gas emissions stem from Amazonian deforestation, and very few of the fines and penalties for illegal deforestation were ever actually paid (Soares-Filho et al. 2014). Kátia Abreu, a ruralista strongly opposed to agricultural subsidies and the main proponent of the Forest Code revisions, was appointed minister of agriculture in 2014. Generally, the Rousseff administration favored commodity-driven agricultural development and major infrastructure improvements, with environmental protection as a tertiary concern.

Amazonian protection measures did, notably, also involve some significant market-based mechanisms that sought to pair forest protection with income-generating livelihoods for Amazonian residents, including Indigenous populations and small-scale farmers. While the nascent Proambiente program, originally proposed to introduce payment for ecosystem services for smallholders, was adopted into President Lula's Ministry of the Environment in 2004, the program was frequently plagued by inconsistent financing, administrative challenges, and legal hurdles (Hall 2008). An important UN-based program of financing known as Reduced Gas Emissions from Deforestation and Forest Degradation (REDD and REDD+) channeled incentives to landholders through the Amazon Fund, established in 2008. The fund, to which the government of Norway was committed to contributing around US$1 billion between 2008 and 2015, was established to help reduce deforestation and thereby further global climate change emissions reduction goals.

While these funding programs do suggest substantial possibilities for antideforestation efforts in the Amazon, it is important to observe that their approach to forest protection involves little by way of direct domestic financial commitments and policy actions. The assumption embedded in these approaches is fundamentally that economic incentives are an adequate means of generating rainforest protection. These market mechanisms frequently lack adequate local participation (Cromberg, Duchelle, and Oliveira Rocha 2014) and also tend to ignore the causes of deforestation in the first place. The economist Alain Karsenty has noted that REDD financing also can be gamed to steer funding based on baseline scenarios: "Despite its very low deforestation rates to date, Guyana presented a baseline scenario in August 2009 that anticipated the conversion of 90% of its forests into industrial crops over the next 25 years; this was in order to maximize its chances of being paid for any deforestation rate below this figure" (2009, 4). Another potential perverse effect is known as environmental blackmailing, whereby farmers with intact forests may let their forests be destroyed unless they are paid (Wunder 2007). Still, funding to address the issue is a positive start, and certainly preferable to inaction.

Even when these shortcomings are considered, there is strong potential for these programs to notably mitigate the effects of climate change and to shift the long-standing legacy of perverse incentives for deforestation in the Amazon into positive incentives for forest protection. The actual implementation of these programs and their longer-term reliance on neoliberal approaches ultimately also indicates that to a large extent the Latin American left's legacy on deforestation issues is that of a decentralized, market-led reliance, coupled with heavy state investments. These dynamics ultimately led to the triumph of extraction-oriented developmental strategies over the more small-scale, livelihoods-based approaches that had appeared more viable as models for the region's development in the earlier years of the Pink Tide.

RESOURCE EXTRACTION OVER SUSTAINABLE USE AND *BUEN VIVIR* DEVELOPMENT

The new developmental economic strategy embraced by Latin America's leftist governments was one of the most distinctive features of their leadership, and one of its most distinctive features was commodity-driven growth and natural resource extraction. Paradoxically, this traditional growth and development model was championed at the same time as alternatives to the modern paradigm of economic development, articulated by social movements and embraced in Ecuadorean and Bolivian constitutions that were rewritten under the Left turn governments through the idea of *buen vivir*, that is, living well in community (Gudynas 2011).

In Ecuador, the 2007–8 decision to grant rights to nature in its highly participatory process of constitutional rewriting established nature's legal *right to exist, persist, maintain, and regenerate its vital cycles*. The people were granted legal authority to enforce these rights on behalf of ecosystems, with ecosystem(s) able to be named as a defendant in cases brought to the courts. Granting nature rights illustrates an expanding notion of citizenship insofar as nature becomes a rights-bearing subject. It also involves considerably more participatory processes, though it is arguable whether the basis of expanding rights to nature encodes a variety of progressive liberalism in governance (Nash 1989; Stone 1974) or whether it entrenches a paradigm of market-based environmental governance, in which nature is commodified and controlled instrumentally according to human desires (Arsel and Büscher 2012). In empirical practice, neither view has entirely triumphed. In any case, there are significant ramifications for legal and sociological theory as nature is granted increasing personhood status (Akchurin 2015; Colon-Rios 2015; Youatt 2017). It is also important to remember that despite the possibilities for more widespread public participation as defenders of rights to nature, the most successful rights to nature lawsuits are not those led by civil society (Kauffman and Martin 2017).

Ecuador's contradictions in terms of environment and development conflicts are especially illustrative of these challenges. By the late 1990s, half of Ecuador's national budget was made up from oil revenues, and this continued into the early 2000s. As the anthropologist Suzanna Sawyer explains, the strong presence of multinational oil companies and liberal logics that resulted "intruded ever more intensely into local people's lives and shifted the terms of debate around identity, rights, and representation" (2005, 9). An economic irony also marked the nation's crude oil dependency; Ecuador's reliance on export markets and foreign financial and technological investments were accentuated instead of achieving their national social and economic developmental aspirations (Kimerling 2013).

Moreover, as protests emerged over oil development in the Yasuní National Park, President Correa's response was rooted in a hard-nosed economic deal, known as Yasuní-ITT: if the international community could muster half of the sum of the expected oil revenues from the region (a whopping US$3.6 billion) through voluntary contributions, then operations for the Ishpingo-Tambococha-Tiputini (ITT) oil project would be suspended indefinitely. Within three years of being proposed, however, the initiative had gained only US$200 million, or 0.37 percent of the target, in funding commitments, and so by 2013 the government decided to turn the two hundred thousand hectares of the Yasuní territory into oil concessions (Davidsen and Kiff 2013).[4] The disjuncture between natural resource exploitation and the language of alternative development and Indigenous knowledge sought to articulate a commitment to alternative development trajectories while simultaneously masking strong priorities for short-term economic gain.

Mineral mining activities also grew considerably during the left's leadership in Peru, as a boom in gold in the Madre de Dios region made the country the Amazonian leader in mining and the world's sixth leading producer of gold. As in the Peruvian Andes, this boom led to significant cultural shifts and environmental justice concerns. The ramifications involved mercury poisonings and malaria increases (Sanchez et al. 2017; Yard et al. 2012), in addition to changes in the cultural rituals that grant permission and legitimacy for extracting value out of certain forms of land uses amid transformations of local economies into mining towns that seek to balance local entrepreneurship with the temporal and spatial pressures of massive state and private enterprise investments in mining activities (Hirsch 2017). In the Upper Beni region of the Bolivian Amazon, serious environmental health consequences of small-scale gold mining took a measurable toll on communities living directly near the mines and in their vicinity; environmental effects extend as far as 150 kilometers downstream from the mining activities (Sponsel 2016). Moreover, Evo Morales drastically expanded oil and gas operations in Bolivia between 2007 and 2012, increasing oil concessions from 7.2 million acres to 59.3 million (Achtenberg 2015). Conflicts between small-scale gold miners and Indigenous groups in isolated parts of the entire Amazon basin continue to cause concern that mercury contamination and human encroachments are threatening the very survival of several tribes and causing severe environmental destruction (Cremers, Kolen, and Theije 2013).

Even in countries more moderate in their embrace of alternative development models, such as Brazil, the discourse of sustainable development was pervasive even as extraction-oriented developmental economies were championed. The social movements that once were the base of leftist support tried to offer an Amazonian development alternative, in the form of renewable resource–based activities (rubber tapping, nut gathering, fishing, agroforestry, for example) as the basis for economic and development policies in the Amazon. This entailed channeling funding for rural credits for smallholders and expansion of the extractivist reserve model as a means of creating viable livelihoods for rubber tappers, nut gatherers, and riverine fishing communities and creating strong environmental enforcement policies (Bebbington and Bebbington 2012; Campos and Nepstad 2006; Hall 2004; Hecht 2007; Pokorny 2013). Put succinctly, despite laudable international commitments on environmental issues, "in terms of national policy, the Brazilian government is consistently making decisions that go against the global policies it ratifies" (Loyola 2014, 1365). While there were a few successes in terms of new conservation areas being created, as earlier noted, by the end of 2014, the pressure on existing conservation areas increased at the same time that the government began downsizing and diminishing the size of other protected areas (Bernard, Penna, and Araújo 2014). Brazil's general approach to curbing deforestation in the Amazon relies on a command-and-control model, while the economic basis for Amazonian land uses continues to privilege export-oriented commodities such as soybeans, cattle, and timber over protecting the standing forest (Nobre et al. 2016).

Heavy investments in mining activities in the Brazilian Amazon are also important for understanding how the Amazon landscapes were reshaped while the Left turn governments were in power. Between 2000 and 2011, mining grew from 1.6 percent of Brazil's gross domestic product (GDP) to 4.1 percent, and production is expected to at least triple that amount again by 2030 (Ferreira et al. 2014). Brazil's increased greenhouse gas emissions, highway paving, and mining in the Brazilian Amazon are specifically linked to the paving of the Interoceanic Highway, new timber concessions, and gold mining (Monteiro, Seixas, and Vieira 2014). A case in point is the Volta Grande gold mine near the

Xingu River; run by a Canadian company called the Belo Sun Mining Corporation, the open-pit mine will be located in the area between two Indigenous reserves, where the Xingu River ran before its course was altered by the Belo Monte hydroelectric dam project, which was built between 2011 and 2016. The project is slated to become Brazil's largest gold mine, and would have an active life span of twelve years. It would yield a post-tax net present value of US$665 million per year for the company, or US$7.98 billion, over the course of the mine's active life (Belo Sun Mining Corporation 2016). Brazil would accrue US$270 million (R$850 million) over the course of the mine's installation and operation through state and federal taxes and royalties.[5] As with the case of the nearby Belo Monte hydroelectric dam, the lack of Indigenous free, prior, and informed consent and governmental coordination problems have plagued the licensing process for the mine, yet it continues to proceed through the bureaucratically complicated processes of licensing at a relatively swift pace (Bratman and Dias 2018; Dias 2017). The recent growth of the mining industry corresponds with policies that expanded allowances for mining within protected areas, including Indigenous reserves and national parks. The "multiple and severe" consequences include loss of forests and native habitat and species extinctions, as well as a host of indirect consequences (Ferreira et al. 2014). The ramifications for environmental citizenship suggest a tendency to limit rather than expand the protections and Indigenous rights framework.

Coupled with the risks of expanded mining activities, the lack of oversight for existing environmental protection infrastructures is deeply concerning from both human welfare and ecological perspectives. A non-Amazonian example compellingly portrays the reason for consternation. On November 5, 2015, as President Dilma Rousseff was in the last months of her corruption-worn second term, the bucolic town of Bento Rodrigues in Minas Gerais was inundated by a monumental tidal wave of mud—the sludge of iron ore mine tailings—from the Fundão dam. The dam was run by a company called Samarco—a joint venture of Brazil's Vale and Australia's BHP Bilton. The Fundão dam burst was Brazil's largest environmental disaster ever, and an entirely man-made tragedy. Nineteen people died, and countless livelihoods were ruined as the toxic sludge covered homes in their entirety, washed away local farms, and stirred up mercury deposits that had long settled in the Rio

Doce and some five thousand nearby streams, ruining fishing and agricultural productivity for the 500 kilometers of river downstream of the dam. Despite the legal frameworks that establish environmental licensing for these tailings dams and other infrastructure projects, monitoring and enforcement continue to be a major challenge in Brazil. This is also the case with other mine tailings dams around the world, where more accidents are predicted to occur, especially as the commodity prices of metals drop (Keirnan 2015). Brazilian proposals to reform environmental licensing procedures and the mining laws notwithstanding, few close observers have confidence that the reforms will ultimately strengthen environmental governance and enforcement, while others are concerned that the existing frameworks will become further diluted (Fearnside 2016).

INFRASTRUCTURE AND ENERGY

In the Brazilian Amazon, the drive for economic growth was most clearly specified in infrastructure plans for the region, many of which had been in place prior to the PT's leadership of the country. Under Avança Brazil (Forward Brazil), established in 2000, transportation networks were planned to span across environmental corridors, leaving many observers skeptical as to whether the environmental protection policies would be undermined (Carvalho 2006; De Sartre and Taravella 2009; Kanai and da Silva Oliveira 2014; Monteiro, Seixas, and Vieira 2014; Zimmerer 2011). Coupled with the domestic strategy, PAC I and PAC II (2007–10 and 2011–14, respectively) proposed considerable investments by the Brazilian state in projects that ultimately spur economic growth through major civil construction projects for highways, energy infrastructure, and support of industrial zones. IIRSA, was also established that year, with commitments of over US$69 billion in road building, hydroelectric dams, and other major infrastructure projects throughout South America, including in the Amazon region.[6] There are 348 projects that are being contemplated as part of this massive continental infrastructure strategy.

Illustrative of the Amazonian infrastructure-based strategy for growth was a plan to pave the BR-163 highway (Cuiabá-Santarém). The highway paving was spurred in the early 2000s by the boom in soybean production, largely driven by massive agribusiness operations in the *cerrado* region in the state of Mato Grosso. Soybean production increased steadily, and in the 2005–7 period Brazil began rivaling the United States as the global export leader of the commodity (Masuda and Goldsmith 2009). Instead of transporting agricultural products south to ports near São Paulo, a paved BR-163 would provide a reliable northern route, with eventual export out of the new US$20 million port on the Amazon River built by the Cargill corporation in Santarém. Other roads, too, including BR-319, BR-230, and AM-174, were slated for paving, both through IIRSA and Brazil's domestic program for infrastructure development, Avança Brasil. The prospect of the paving was highly symbolically charged, given that when Amazonian highways were first cut under the military dictatorship, deforestation followed, and the roads led to new settlers, land speculation, and unregulated ranching and logging activities. The Amazonian researcher Philip Fearnside (2002) estimated that of the US$43 billion in projects over the eight-year period of Avança Brasil, some US$20 billion were allocated to projects causing environmental damage. By emphatically continuing the IIRSA programs through national plans for accelerated growth and direct investments, the PT gave primacy to modernization-oriented development priorities as a matter of policy while making Amazonian lands more vulnerable to uncontrolled development. Simultaneously, the cerrado began being transformed from a biodiversity hot spot into a region largely consisting of soybean monocultures.[7] Still, the discourse behind IIRSA planning was distinctively couched in the language of sustainable development.

> IIRSA's comprehensive approach to projects places a priority on environmental protection and is responsive to a growing awareness of its importance by the people of the region. . . . The IIRSA approach of applying the concept of hubs helps address environmental issues in a structured way and offers planners and other stakeholders a vision of development opportunities, alternatives and needs to ensure effective and balanced regional integration. (IDB, October 2006, 17, quoted in Van Dijck 2008, 101)

The environment-development conflict was attenuated through emphasis on road building and integration that fundamentally was oriented around the economic opportunities in each hub of IIRSA infrastructure development projects.[8] The proposed highway through Bolivia's Isiboro Sécure National Park and Indigenous Territory (TIPNIS), is a prominent example of this tension. The TIPNIS highway would connect the Amazon to the Andes, and it is motivated largely by the possibility of transporting Brazilian soybeans, which would be shipped from the Pacific ports to China. Oil exploration rights near the TIPNIS park are also held by the Brazilian oil giant Petrobras (Friedman-Rudovsky 2012). The result was an exacerbated pattern of uneven development and a system of investments that indicated priority to benefits to multinational firms, well above environmental protection and social equity considerations (Castro 2012; Kanai 2016).

The political doubling down on infrastructure in the name of "sustainable development" priorities was also significant in the case of hydroelectric dams. Brazilian energy planners forecasted that the country would need to substantially increase energy production in order to keep pace with economic growth rates (Empresa de Pesquisa Energética 2012; Ministério de Minas e Energia 2011). These studies, coupled with President Lula's Luz para Todos (Energy for All) program and major energy crises in 2001, 2002, and 2010, established a clear governmental priority for dam building to strengthen energy infrastructure and combat energy poverty (Giannini Pereira, Vasconcelos Freitas, and Fidelis da Silva 2011). The plans ultimately hinged on new hydroelectric dam construction in the Amazon, with major Chinese investments in building the electrical grid to stabilize and strengthen transmission. Around 80 percent of Brazilian energy comes from the renewable energy source of hydroelectric dams. While technically considered a viable mode of clean energy development, Amazonian dams present substantial environmental challenges, most notably because they are historically and even at present known for involving serious social and environmental consequences. There are over four hundred dams planned for the Amazon basin, making the region subject to massive ecological changes and social problems if these mega-projects are carried forward (Little 2014).

Perhaps the most symbolically important, if not also the most ecologically significant, project of Brazilian hydroelectric development in the past thirty years is the case of the Belo Monte dam. Located on the

Xingu River, Belo Monte is a run-of-river-type dam that is the world's third-largest hydroelectric project in terms of its energetic potential. The dam, a project that totaled some US$16 billion in construction costs, was promoted as a cornerstone of Brazilian "green energy" development and was emphatically promoted by President Rousseff as a signature project. It was a source of diplomatic insistence even at the Rio+20 Earth Summit that the dam represented an exemplar of Brazilian green development (Bratman 2014). The concerns about the dam, which have been well documented by scholars,[9] included doubts about its true costs and energetic yields, irregularities in environmental licensing, social impacts for Indigenous groups, urban dislocations and displacements, Indigenous human rights abuses, substantial losses to biodiversity, and a whole host of related environmental concerns. Much of the energy from Belo Monte was slated to be bought for the explicit use of the bauxite and iron ore mines present in the state of Pará, and the rerouting of the Xingu River also literally laid the ground bare for the aforementioned Belo Sun gold mining operation to become feasible.

As if damming the river in order to capitalize on natural resources was not environmental harm enough, the social and political implications of the Belo Monte dam involved substantial corruption. Just as the dam's final turbines were being installed (and despite court orders that repeatedly suspended the dam's operating license due to unfulfilled obligations), Operation Car Wash (Lava Jato) corruption investigations pointed to a host of bribes associated with the dam's construction consortium and campaign kickbacks to politicians; plea bargain testimonies released from the investigations suggest that the construction companies contributed around 1 percent of contract values to the PT and the Partido do Movimento Democrático Brasileiro (Brazilian Democratic Movement Party, PMDB) in 2010, 2012, and 2014 (Haidar and Gorczeski 2016). The twenty-two legal actions filed by the Ministério Público were never acted on due to judicial system delays and conflicts of interest and are now irrelevant (Da Fonseca and Bourgoignie 2011). The dam is operable, but the damage is already done, and its energetic yields are not likely to be as bountiful as originally anticipated by governmental planners due to increased droughts and deforestation affecting the region (Stickler et al. 2013).

LEFT BEHIND: THE ENVIRONMENTAL LEGACY OF THE LEFT

Taken as a whole, the left's legacy on environmental issues in Latin America is fraught with contradictions between a discursive emphasis on sustainable development and rights to nature and practices that are largely environmentally destructive. Despite emphasis on "clean" and "renewable" energy and environmental protection, simultaneous forest policy dilutions, gold and oil mining, and hydroelectric dam construction projects in the Amazon directly conflicted with environmental goals. These projects, in Brazil as well as in Bolivia and Ecuador, were the basis of significantly more financial investments and monumental landscape changes relative to conservation-oriented policies and projects. Such interventions brought about significant human consequences, which included violence against activists and displacement of local communities, in addition to deforestation, biodiversity losses, and other ecological harms. In the context of the Amazon, the disjuncture between sustainable development discourses and practice is profound.

Deforestation in the Amazon declined but then began rising significantly during the latter part of Latin America's Pink Tide, largely because of a lack of deeper political commitments and failures to embed policies with consistent enforcement in practice. Throughout the region social and environmental considerations were sidelined to larger logics of extractivism and economic growth, bolstered by the global boom in commodities prices. Brazilian infrastructure investments in other Amazonian countries fueled such infrastructure developments, as did electrification and mining investments from Chinese, Canadian, and other foreign powers throughout the region. Energy investments based on oil production ramped up, as did a new emphasis on developing energy infrastructure, roads, and massive hydroelectric projects.

In their mutual embrace of participatory approaches, green politics and the participation-oriented, inclusionary social agenda of the leftist governments in Latin America found an affinity, but this was more an ideational convergence than one manifested in political practice. In large part, the variation over time is attributable to the different backgrounds and political and economic opportunity structures that Lula and Dilma faced. In other parts, however, it is also important to recognize that sustainable development discourses always embodied a conflict, involving the contradiction between conservation and economic growth. In the broader context of Bolivia and Ecuadorean Indigenous politics and environmental policies, moreover, the tension of balancing a strongly environmentalist, indigenously oriented, and rights to nature approach markedly contrasted with the desire to fund social programs and maintain economic growth through the extraction of natural resources. As a result, the legacy of selective and uneven attempts to incorporate environmental issues in the Amazon under the left governments involved significant reconfigurations of societal actors and ecological phenomena, with generally deteriorating—and at times catastrophically disappointing—results in terms of socio-environmental outcomes. While strengthened on some counts, overall, the legal frameworks for environmental protection were stronger on paper and symbolically than in practice. The materialist explanations of neoliberal economic integration, neodevelopmental state investments, and short-term resource extractive motives go a long way toward explaining why this mismatch ruled the day.

Ultimately, the Left turn governments managed to signal left but then turned right on environmental issues in the Amazon. This took activists somewhat by surprise, and undermined what might otherwise have been stronger civil society resistance to specific policies that ultimately hitched the left's legacy to the power of corporate influence and export-oriented economic approaches through the new developmental strategies they adopted. For the most part, a mutually beneficial relationship between socio-environmental and development interests was a fleeting feature of the Left turn governments, instrumentally leveraged in combating deforestation or creating new conservation areas, and conveniently ignored when substantially more financial gain could be achieved, even at high environmental costs.

Despite the promise of expanding environmental rights and progressive discourses that challenge the typical growth narrative of development, the legacy of Latin America's Left turn evokes new understandings of what environmental citizenship looks like. Articulations of the environment as having a different legal stature accorded nicely with most Indigenous traditions and brought many more stakeholders into the political process, but close empirical study indicates the risk of undermining those interests as they become encoded in policy and weak practice. Subsumed within the state-led discourses of green development, little legal traction was given to the more revolutionary concepts of *buen vivir* and rights to nature, while their utility as discourses of opposition and resistance lost some power. Instead, strong "green states" emerged for a time, that is, states aiming to govern markets, land, people, and global political relations in new and sometimes authoritarian ways (Death 2015). Yet there was a transformation during the Left turn decade and a half, as "deep green" policies turned into lighter green approaches to environmental protection and the Left regimes weakened politically and economically, becoming less able to govern as the strong states they once were.

While the left-leaning social movements of Latin America were once at the forefront of articulating that development and conservation goals were ostensibly not in contradiction with each other, by the end of the "left" period, the debate between conservation and development was ultimately reignited. This was exemplified as Bolivia, Ecuador, and Brazil approved mining, road building, oil drilling, and hydroelectric projects throughout the region. The neodevelopmental models ruled the day, encoding a sustainable development paradigm rooted in older, modernization-oriented economic models. Skeptical though this view may be, the question of what's next does not leave much room for optimism about greater environmental protection in the region. As the decade's progress and environmental issues become ever more pressing, the imperative to adopt new logics of political governance and economic models is ever more urgent. At present, however, the political turn to the right that marks the end of the Pink Tide in Latin America appears to have little interest in managing present-day environmental challenges, let alone investing in ecological restoration.

NOTES

1. The situation of rural land conflict is gravest in the Amazon, and worst specifically in the state of Pará. In the aforementioned 2003–13 statistic, 692 took place in the state of Pará. The Pastoral Land Commission, which collects data on these death threats as well as related slave labor conditions, also reported in 2011 that twelve of twenty-nine assassinations in the country occurred in Pará. The International Labor Organization estimates that there

are over twenty-five thousand people experiencing slavery at any given time in Brazil, although no one has been jailed for perpetrating such oppression (Bevins 2012; Human Rights Watch 2014).

2. *Sumak kawsay* is a variant of Living Well, or *buen vivir*, and is the traditionally used term of Andean communities to describe an alternative model for development.

3. These are just the most high-profile cases. Between 2010 and 2015, Brazil ranked worst in the world in its cumulative number of assassinations of land and environmental defenders, at over two hundred killings.

4. While Ecuadorean officials blamed the lackluster funding on the international community, some close observers also noted that Ecuador's commitment did not indefinitely leave the oil in the ground for subsequent administrations and was disingenuous because the government was continuously preparing for the eleventh round of oil negotiations. See, e.g., www.pachamama .org/news/a-deeper-perspective-on-the-end-of-the-yasuni-itt-initiative.

5. The royalties estimates are R$5 million per year, totaling around R$60 million over the twelve years of operation. An estimated R$130 in national, state, and local taxes will be collected during installation and thereafter R$55 million per year. Based on my own calculations from corporate presentations, over twelve years, the Brazilian government (state and federal) would thus receive US$270 million in taxes in royalties from the Belo Sun project. For the Canadian Belo Sun company, the estimates are a twelve-year yield of US$7.98 billion, based on earnings of US$665 million per year in net present value (NPV), after taxes, with an internal rate of return (IRR) of between 20 percent and 32 percent. Some employment benefits are also notable, totaling 2,100 construction jobs and 526 longer-term positions. See Belo Sun Mining Corporation 2016; Melo 2017.

6. The US$69 billion figure is for the thirty-one IIRSA projects completed by 2010. For more on IIRSA, see www.iirsa.org/ and www.bankinfor mationcenter.org/regions/latin-america/biceca/.

7. Associated with the increased power of Brazilian agribusiness but wary of the long-standing legacy of agrarian inequality in Brazil, the modernization in the Brazilian agricultural sector has spurred land grabbing and a transplanting of Brazilian firms and technical expertise to Mozambique. See, for more, Clements and Fernandes 2013.

8. Three quarters of the IIRSA Consensus Agenda was devoted to road infrastructure from 2005 to 2010.

9. See, e.g., Berchin et al. 2015; Bingham 2010; Bratman 2015; Da Fonseca and Bourgoignie 2011; Experts Panel 2009; Haidar and Gorczeski 2016; Hall and Branford 2012; Randell 2016.

REFERENCES

Achtenberg, Emily. 2015. "Morales Greenlights TIPNIS Road, Oil and Gas Extraction in Bolivia's National Parks." North American Congress on Latin America (NACLA). Washington, DC. http://nacla.org/blog/2015/06/15/morales-greenlights-tipnis-road-oil-and-gas-extraction-bolivia%E2%80%99s-national-parks.

Akchurin, Maria. 2015. "Constructing the Rights of Nature: Constitutional Reform, Mobilization, and Environmental Protection in Ecuador." *Law & Social Inquiry* 40 (4): 937–68.

Amado, Adriana Moreira, and Maria de Lourdes Rollemberg Mollo. 2015. "The 'Developmentalism' Debate in Brazil: Some Economic and Political Issues." *Review of Keynesian Economics* 3 (1): 77–89.

Arsel, Murat, and Bram Büscher. 2012. "'Nature' Inc.: Changes and Continuities in Neoliberal Conservation and Market-Based Environmental Policy." *Development and Change* 43 (1): 53–78.

Article 19, CIEL, and Vermont Law School. 2016. *A Deadly Shade of Green: Threats to Environmental Human Rights Defenders in Latin America.* London: CEIL, Vermont Law School, SIDA. www.ciel.org/wp-content/uploads/2016/08/Deadly_shade_of_green_English_Aug2016.pdf.

Baletti, Brenda. 2012. "Ordenamento Territorial: Neo-Developmentalism and the Struggle for Territory in the Lower Brazilian Amazon." *Journal of Peasant Studies* 39 (2): 573–98.

———. 2014. "Saving the Amazon? Sustainable Soy and the New Extractivism." *Environment and Planning A* 46 (1): 5–25.

Ban, Cornel. 2012. "Brazil's Liberal Neo-Developmentalism: New Paradigm or Edited Orthodoxy?" *Review of International Political Economy* 20 (2): 298–331.

Barber, Christopher, Mark A. Cochrane, Carlos M. Souza Jr., and William F. Laurance. 2014. "Roads, Deforestation, and the Mitigating Effect of Protected Areas in the Amazon." *Biological Conservation* 147: 203–9.

Bebbington, Denise Humphreys, and Anthony Bebbington. 2012. "Post-What? Extractive Industries, Narratives of Development, and the Socio-Environmental Disputes across the (Ostensibly Changing) Andean Region." In Håvard Haarstad, ed., *New Political Spaces in Latin American Natural Resource Governance.* New York: Palgrave Macmillan.

Belo Sun Mining Corporation. 2016. "Presentation to Investors." Belo Sun Mining Corp., Toronto. www.belosun.com/investor_center/presentations/.

Benton, Ted. 1993. *Natural Relations: Ecology, Animal Rights and Social Justice.* London: Verso.

Berchin, Issa Ibrahim, Jéssica Garcia, Mauri Luiz Heerdt, Angélica de Que-
vedo Moreira, Ana Clara Medeiros Silveira, and José Baltazar Sal-
gueirinho Osório de Andrade Guerra. 2015. "Energy Production and
Sustainability: A Study of Belo Monte Hydroelectric Power Plant."
Natural Resources Forum 39 (3-4): 224–37.

Bernard, Enrico, Lao Penna, and E Araújo. 2014. "Downgrading, Downsizing,
Degazettement, and Reclassification of Protected Areas in Brazil." *Conservation Biology* 28 (4): 939–50.

Bevins, Vincente. 2012. "Brazil Workers Exploited as Modern-Day Slaves."
Los Angeles Times. http://articles.latimes.com/2012/jun/07/world/la-fg
-brazil-slave-labor-20120607.

Bingham, Alexa. 2010. "Discourse of the Dammed: A Study of the Impacts of
Sustainable Development Discourse on Indigenous Peoples in the Bra-
zilian Amazon in the Context of the Proposed Belo Monte Hydroelectric
Dam." *Polis Journal* (University of Leeds) 4: 1–47.

Brannstrom, Christian. 2009. "South America's Neoliberal Agricultural Fron-
tiers: Places of Environmental Sacrifice or Conservation Opportunity?"
Ambio 38 (3): 141–49.

Bratman, Eve Z. 2011. "Villains, Victims, and Conservationists? Representational Frameworks and Sustainable Development on the Transamazon
Highway." *Human Ecology* 39 (4): 441–53.

———. 2014. "Contradictions of Green Development: Human Rights and
Environmental Norms in Light of Belo Monte Dam Activism." *Journal
of Latin American Studies* 46 (02): 261–89.

———. 2015. "Passive Revolution in the Green Economy: Activism and the
Belo Monte Dam." *International Environmental Agreements: Politics, Law
and Economics* 15 (1): 1–17.

Bratman, Eve, and Cristiane Bená Dias. 2018. "Development Blind Spots in
Environmental Impact Assessment: Tensions between Policy, Law and
Practice in Brazil's Xingu River Basin." *Environmental Impact Assessment
Review* 70: 1–10.

Bresser-Pereira, Luiz Carlos. 2011. "An Account of New Developmentalism
and the Structuralist Macroeconomics." *Revista de Economia Política* 31
(3): 493–502.

Bull, Benedicte, and Mariel Aguilar-Støen. 2015. *Environmental Politics in
Latin America: Elite Dynamics, the Left Tide and Sustainable Development.*
London: Routledge.

Campos, Marina T., and Daniel C. Nepstad. 2006. "Smallholders, the Amazon's New Conservationists." *Conservation Biology* 20 (5): 1553–56.

Carvalho, Georgia O. 2006. "Environmental Resistance and the Politics of Energy Development in the Brazilian Amazon." *Journal of Environment & Development* 15 (3): 245–68.

Castro, Edna. 2012. "Expansão da fronteira: Megaprojetos de infraestrutura e integração Sul-Americana." *Caderno CRH* 25 (64): 45–61.

Clements, Elizabeth Alice, and Bernardo Mançano Fernandes. 2013. "Land Grabbing, Agribusiness and the Peasantry in Brazil and Mozambique." *Agrarian South: Journal of Political Economy* 2 (1): 41–69.

Colon-Rios, Joel I. 2015. "The Rights of Nature and the New Latin American Constitutionalism." *New Zealand Journal of Public and International Law* 13 (1): 107.

Conca, Ken. 2015. *An Unfinished Foundation: The United Nations and Global Environmental Governance.* New York: Oxford University Press.

Cremers, Leitien, Judith Kolen, and Marjo de Thieje. 2013. *Small-Scale Gold Mining in the Amazon: The Cases of Bolivia, Brazil, Colombia, Peru, and Suriname.* Amsterdam: Centre for Latin American Studies and Documentation.

Cromberg, Marina, Amy E. Duchelle, and Isa de Oliveira Rocha. 2014. "Local Participation in REDD+: Lessons from the Eastern Brazilian Amazon." *Forests* 5 (4): 579–98.

Da Fonseca, Patricia Galindo, and Antoine Bourgoignie. 2011. "The Belo Monte Dam Case." *Environmental Policy and Law* 41 (2): 104–7.

Davidsen, Conny, and Laura Kiff. 2013. "Global Carbon-and-Conservation Models, Global Eco-States? Ecuador's Yasuní-ITT Initiative and Governance Implications." *Journal of International & Global Studies* 4 (2): 1.

Death, Carl. 2015. "Four Discourses of the Green Economy in the Global South." *Third World Quarterly* 36 (12): 2207–24.

De Freitas, Corin, Andrea J. Marston, and Karen Bakker. 2015. "Not-Quite-Neoliberal Natures in Latin America: An Introduction." *Geoforum* 64: 239–45.

De Sartre, Xavier Arnauld, and Romain Taravella. 2009. "National Sovereignty vs. Sustainable Development Lessons from the Narrative on the Internationalization of the Brazilian Amazon." *Political Geography* 28 (7): 406–15.

Dias, Cristiane Bená. 2017. "Communities' Engagement in Environmental Impact Assessment (EIA) in Brazil: A Legal Proposal to Amplify the Voices of Those Who Are Most Affected and Hardly Listened to." PhD dissertation, American University, Washington, DC.

Dobson, Andrew. 2006. "Citizenship." In Andrew Dobson and Robyn Eckersley, eds., *Political Theory and the Ecological Challenge.* Cambridge: Cambridge University Press.

Duchelle, Amy E., Marina Cromberg, Maria Fernanda Gebara, Raissa Guerra, Tadeu Melo, Anne Larson, Peter Cronkleton, Jan Börner, Erin Sills, Sven Wunder, Simone Bauch, Peter May, Galia Selaya, and William D. Sunderlin. 2014. "Linking Forest Tenure Reform, Environmental Compliance, and Incentives: Lessons from REDD+ Initiatives in the Brazilian Amazon." *World Development* 55: 53–67.

Eckersley, Robyn. 1992. *Environmentalism and Political Theory: Toward an Ecocentric Approach.* Albany: State University of New York Press.

———. 1996. "Greening Liberal Democracy: The Rights Discourse Revisited." In Brian Doherty and Marius de Geus ed., *Democracy and Green Political Thought.* London: Routledge.

Empresa de Pesquisa Energética. 2012. *Avaliação socioambiental de usinas hidrelétricas.* Brasilia: Ministério de Minas e Energia. www.epe.gov.br /MeioAmbiente/Documents/Estudos%20PDE%202021/20121227_1 .pdf.

Environmental Defense Fund (EDF). 2009. "Brazilian National and State REDD." EDF. Washington, DC. www.edf.org/sites/default/files/10438 _Brazil_national_and_state_REDD_report.pdf.

Ettlinger, Nancy, and Christopher D. Hartmann. 2015. "Post/Neo/Liberalism in Relational Perspective." *Political Geography* 48: 37–48.

Experts Panel. 2009. "A Critical Analysis of the Environmental Impact Studies for the Belo Monte Hydroelectric Dam." Ibama, Belém.

Fearnside, Philip M. 2002. "Avança Brasil: Environmental and Social Consequences of Brazil's Planned Infrastructure in Amazonia." *Environmental Management* 30 (6): 735–47.

———. 2008. "The Roles and Movements of Actors in the Deforestation of Brazilian Amazonia." *Ecology and Society* 13 (1): 23.

———. 2016. "Brazilian Politics Threaten Environmental Policies." *Science* 353 (6301): 746–48.

Federative Republic of Brazil. 2010. *Decreto nº 7.390, de 9 de dezembro de 2010.* Brasilia: Casa Civil Subchefia para Assuntos Jurídicos Presidência da República. www.planalto.gov.br/ccivil_03/_Ato2007-2010/2010 /Decreto/D7390.htm.

Ferreira, Joice, L. E. O. C. Aragão, J. Barlow, P. Barreto, E. Berenguer, M. Bustamante, T. A. Gardner, A. C. Lees, A. Lima, J. Louzada, R. Pardini, L. Parry, C. A. Peres, P. S. Pompeu, M. Tabarelli, and J. Zuanon. 2014. "Brazil's Environmental Leadership at Risk." *Science* 346 (6210): 706–7.

Friedman-Rudovsky, Jean. 2012. "In Bolivia, a Battle over a Highway and a Way of Life." *Yale Environment* 360. New Haven. https://e360.yale.edu /features/in_bolivia_a_battle_over_a_highway_and_a_way_of_life.

Giannini Pereira, Marcio, Marcos Aurélio Vasconcelos Freitas, and Neilton Fidelis da Silva. 2011. "The Challenge of Energy Poverty: Brazilian Case Study." *Energy Policy* 39 (1): 167–75.

Global Witness. 2016. *On Dangerous Ground*. London: Global Witness.

Godar, Javier, Emilio Jorge Tizado, and Benno Pokorny. 2012. "Who Is Responsible for Deforestation in the Amazon? A Spatially Explicit Analysis along the Transamazon Highway in Brazil." *Forest Ecology and Management* 267: 58–73.

Goodland, Robert J. A., and Howard S. Irwin. 1975. *Amazon Jungle: Green Hell to Red Desert? An Ecological Discussion of the Environmental Impact of the Highway Construction Program in the Amazon Basin*. Amsterdam: Elsevier Scientific.

Greenpeace. 2011. *"Dia de Vergonha Brasília."* Greenpeace Brasil. www .greenpeace.org/brasil/pt/Noticias/Dia-de-vergonha/.

Grugel, Jean, and Pía Riggirozzi. 2012. "Post-Neoliberalism in Latin America: Rebuilding and Reclaiming the State after Crisis." *Development and Change* 43 (1): 1–21.

Gudynas, Eduardo. 2011. "Buen Vivir: Today's Tomorrow." *Development* 54 (4): 441–47.

Haarstad, Hv. 2011. *New Political Spaces in Latin American Natural Resource Governance*. New York: Palgrave Macmillan.

Haidar, D., and V. Gorczeski. 2016. "Delação da Andrade Gutierrez mostra um belo monte de propinas." *Época*. http://epoca.globo.com/tempo /noticia/2016/04/delacao-da-andrade-gutierrez-mostra-um-belo-monte -de-propinas.html.

Hall, Anthony L. 2004. "Extractive Reserves: Building Natural Assets in the Brazilian Amazon." Working Paper. Amherst. www.peri.umass.edu /publication/item/94-extractive-reserves-building-natural-assets-in-the -brazilian-amazon.

———. 2008. "Better RED than Dead: Paying the People for Environmental Services in Amazonia." *Philosophical Transactions of the Royal Society of London B: Biological Sciences* 363 (1498): 1925–32.

Hall, Anthony, and Sue Branford. 2012. "Development, Dams and Dilma: The Saga of Belo Monte." *Critical Sociology* 38 (6): 851–62.

Hall, Ruth, Marc Edelman, Saturnino M. Borras, Ian Scoones, Ben White, and Wendy Wolford. 2015. "Resistance, Acquiescence or Incorporation? An Introduction to Land Grabbing and Political Reactions 'from Below.'" *Journal of Peasant Studies* 42 (3-4): 467–88.

Hardin, Garrett. 1972. *Exploring New Ethics for Survival: The Voyage of the Spaceship Beagle*. New York: Viking.

Hargrove, Eugene C. 1989. *Foundations of Environmental Ethics*. New York: Prentice Hall.

Hecht, Susanna B. 2005. "Soybeans, Development and Conservation on the Amazon Frontier." *Development and Change* 36 (2): 375–404.

———. 2007. "Factories, Forests, Fields and Family: Gender and Neoliberalism in Extractive Reserves." *Journal of Agrarian Change* 7 (3): 316–47.

Heilbroner, Robert L. [1974] 1991. *An Inquiry into the Human Prospect*. New York: Norton.

Hirsch, Eric. 2017. "Investment's Rituals: 'Grassroots' Extractivism and the Making of an Indigenous Gold Mine in the Peruvian Andes." *Geoforum* 82: 259–67.

Hochstetler, Kathryn, and Margaret E. Keck. 2007. *Greening Brazil*. Durham, NC: Duke University Press.

Hochstetler, Kathryn, and Genia Kostka. 2015. "Wind and Solar Power in Brazil and China: Interests, State-Business Relations, and Policy Outcomes." *Global Environmental Politics* 15 (3): 74–94.

Human Rights Watch. 2014. *World Report 2014: Events of 2013*. New York: Human Rights Watch. www.hrw.org/report/2014/01/21/world-report-2014/events-2013.

Kanai, J. Miguel. 2016. "The Pervasiveness of Neoliberal Territorial Design: Cross-Border Infrastructure Planning in South America since the Introduction of IIRSA." *Geoforum* 69: 160–70.

Kanai, J. Miguel, and Rafael da Silva Oliveira. 2014. "Paving (through) Amazonia: Neoliberal Urbanism and the Reperipheralization of Roraima." *Environment and Planning A* 46 (1): 62–77.

Karsenty, Alain. 2009. "What the (Carbon) Market Cannot Do." *CIRAD-Perspectives* 1 (November). Online. www.cirad.fr/en/content/download/3837/31548/version/31543/file/Persp31501_Karsenty_eng.pdf.

Kauffman, Craig M. 2017. *Grassroots Global Governance: Local Watershed Management Experiments and the Evolution of Sustainable Development*. New York: Oxford University Press.

Kauffman, Craig M., and Pamela L. Martin. 2014. "Scaling up Buen Vivir: Globalizing Local Environmental Governance from Ecuador." *Global Environmental Politics* 14 (1): 40–58.

———. 2017. "Can Rights of Nature Make Development More Sustainable? Why Some Ecuadorian Lawsuits Succeed and Others Fail." *World Development* 92 (April): 130–42.

Keirnan, Paul. 2015. "Mining Dams Grow to Colossal Heights, and So Do the Risks." *Wall Street Journal*. New York. http://www.wsj.com/articles

/brazils-samarco-disaster-mining-dams-grow-to-colossal-heights-and
-so-do-the-risks-1459782411.

Kimerling, Judith. 2013. "Oil, Contact, and Conservation in the Amazon: Indigenous Huaorani, Chevron, and Yasuni." *Colorado Journal of International Environmental Law and Policy* 24 (1): 43–115.

Klein, Peter Taylor. 2015. "Engaging the Brazilian State: The Belo Monte Dam and the Struggle for Political Voice." *Journal of Peasant Studies* 42 (6): 1137–56.

Lilley, Sasha. 2004. "Paving the Amazon with Soy." Corp Watch. https://corpwatch.org/article/paving-amazon-soy.

Little, Paul. 2014. "Mega-Development Projects in Amazonia: A Geopolitical and Socioenvironmental Primer." *Derecho, Ambiente y Recursos Naturales* 145.

Loyola, Rafael. 2014. "Brazil Cannot Risk Its Environmental Leadership." *Diversity and Distributions* 20 (12): 1365–67.

Masuda, Tadayoshi, and Peter D. Goldsmith. 2009. "World Soybean Production: Area Harvested, Yield, and Long-Term Projections." *International Food and Agribusiness Management Review* 12 (4): 143–62.

McNeish, John-Andrew. 2013. "Extraction, Protest and Indigeneity in Bolivia: The TIPNIS Effect." *Latin American and Caribbean Ethnic Studies* 8 (2): 221–42.

Medvigy, David, Robert L. Walko, Martin J. Otte, and Roni Avissar. 2013. "Simulated Changes in Northwest US Climate in Response to Amazon Deforestation." *Journal of Climate* 26 (22): 9115–36.

Meijer, Karen S. 2015. "A Comparative Analysis of the Effectiveness of Four Supply Chain Initiatives to Reduce Deforestation." *Tropical Conservation Science* 8 (2): 583–97.

Melo, Licio. 2017. "Belo Sun Investirá US $5 milhões no Pará em 2017." *BVMI*. São Paulo. www.bvmi.com.br/belo-sun-investira-us-5-milhoes-no-para-em-2017/.

Mendes, Chico. 1989. *Fight for the Forest: Chico Mendes in His Own Words*. London: Latin America Bureau.

Ministério de Minas e Energia. 2011. "Projeto da Usina de Belo Monte: Perguntas mais frequentes." Webpage. Governo do Brasil, Brasilia. www.mme.gov.br/mme/galerias/arquivos/belomonte/BELO_MONTE_-_Perguntas_mais_Frequentes.pdf.

Ministério do Meio Ambiente (MMA). 2007. "Relatório sobre desmatamento na Amazônia. Brasília: Ministério do Meio Ambiente, Grupo Permanente de Trabalho Interministerial Sobre Desmatamento na Amazônia." www.mma.gov.br/estruturas/ascom_boletins/_arquivos/gt.pdf.

Monteiro, Marko, SA, Sonia Regina da Cal Seixas, and Simone Aparecida Vieira. 2014. "The Politics of Amazonian Deforestation: Environmental Policy and Climate Change Knowledge." *Wiley Interdisciplinary Reviews: Climate Change* 5 (5): 689–701.

Morais, Lecio, and Alfredo Saad-Filho. 2012. "Neo-Developmentalism and the Challenges of Economic Policy-Making under Dilma Rousseff." *Critical Sociology* 38 (6): 789–98.

Nash, Roderick. 1989. *The Rights of Nature: A History of Environmental Ethics*. Madison: University of Wisconsin Press.

Nel, Adrian. 2015. "The Neoliberalisation of Forestry Governance, Market Environmentalism and Re-Territorialisation in Uganda." *Third World Quarterly* 36 (12): 2294–2315.

Nepstad, Daniel, David McGrath, Claudia Stickler, Ane Alencar, Andrea Azevedo, Briana Swette, Tathiana Bezerra, Maria DiGiano, João Shimada, Ronaldo Seroa da Motta, Eric Armijo, Leandro Castello, Paulo Brando, Matt C. Hansen, Max McGrath-Horn, Oswaldo Carvalho, and Laura Hess. 2014. "Slowing Amazon Deforestation through Public Policy and Interventions in Beef and Soy Supply Chains." *Science* 344 (6188): 1118–23.

Nepstad, Daniel C., Claudia M. Stickler, Britaldo Soares-Filho, and Frank Merry. 2008. "Interactions among Amazon Land Use, Forests and Climate: Prospects for a Near-Term Forest Tipping Point." *Philosophical Transactions of the Royal Society of London B: Biological Sciences* 363 (1498): 1737–46.

Nobre, Carlos A., Gilvan Sampaio, Laura S. Borma, Juan Carlos Castilla-Rubio, José S. Silva, and Manoel Cardoso. 2016. "Land-Use and Climate Change Risks in the Amazon and the Need of a Novel Sustainable Development Paradigm." *Proceedings of the National Academy of Sciences* 113 (39): 10759–68.

Ophuls, William, and A. Stephen Boyan. 1992. *Ecology and the Politics of Scarcity Revisited: The Unraveling of the American Dream*. New York: W. H. Freeman.

Oxhorn, Philip. 2011. *Sustaining Civil Society: Economic Change, Democracy, and the Social Construction of Citizenship in Latin America*. University Park: Pennsylvania State University Press.

Phillips, O., and S. L. Lewis. 2014. "Recent Changes in Tropical Forest Biomass and Dynamics." In D. A. Coomes, D. F. R. P. Burslem, and W. D. Simonson, eds., *Forests and Global Change*. Cambridge: Cambridge University Press.

Pokorny, Benno. 2013. *Smallholders, Forest Management and Rural Development in the Amazon.* New York: Earthscan.

Randell, Heather. 2016. "Structure and Agency in Development-Induced Forced Migration: The Case of Brazil's Belo Monte Dam." *Population and Environment* 37 (3): 265–87.

Rozzi, Ricardo, Juan J. Armesto, Julio R. Gutiérrez, Francisca Massardo, Gene E. Likens, Christopher B. Anderson, Alexandria Poole, Kelli P. Moses, Eugene Hargrove, Andres O. Mansilla, James H. Kennedy, Mary Willson, Kurt Jax, Clive G. Jones, J. Baird Callicott, and Mary T. K. Arroyo. 2012. "Integrating Ecology and Environmental Ethics: Earth Stewardship in the Southern End of the Americas." *BioScience* 62 (3): 226–36.

Ruckert, Arne, Laura Macdonald, and Kristina R. Proulx. 2017. "Post-Neoliberalism in Latin America: A Conceptual Review." *Third World Quarterly* 38 (7): 1583–1602.

Sagoff, Mark. 2008. *The Economy of the Earth: Philosophy, Law, and the Environment.* New York: Cambridge University Press.

Sanchez, Juan F., Andres M. Carnero, Esteban Rivera, Luis A. Rosales, G. Christian Baldeviano, Jorge L. Asencios, Kimberly A. Edgel, Joseph M. Vinetz, and Andres G. Lescano. 2017. "Unstable Malaria Transmission in the Southern Peruvian Amazon and Its Association with Gold Mining, Madre de Dios, 2001–2012." *American Journal of Tropical Medicine Hygiene* 96 (2): 304–11.

Sawyer, Suzanna. 2005. *Crude Chronicles: Indigenous Politics, Multinational Oil, and Neoliberalism in Ecuador.* Durham, NC: Duke University Press.

Sikkink, Kathryn. 1991. *Ideas and Institutions: Developmentalism in Brazil and Argentina.* Ithaca, NY: Cornell University Press.

Slater, Candace. 2002. *Entangled Edens: Visions of the Amazon.* Berkeley: University of California Press.

———. 2015. "Visions of the Amazon: What Has Shifted, What Persists, and Why This Matters." *Latin American Research Review* 50 (3): 3–23.

Soares-Filho, Britaldo Silveira, Daniel Curtis Nepstad, Lisa Curran, Gustavo Coutinho Cerqueira, Ricardo Alexandrino Garcia, Claudia Azevedo Ramos, Eliane Voll, Alice McDonald, Paul Lefebvre, Peter Schlesinger, and David McGrath. 2005. "Cenários de desmatamento para a Amazônia." *Estudos Avançados* 19 (54): 137–52.

Soares-Filho, Britaldo Silveira, Raoni Rajão, Marcia Macedo, Arnaldo Carneiro, William Costa, Michael Coe, Hermann Rodrigues, and Ane Alencar. 2014. "Cracking Brazil's Forest Code." *Science* 344: 363–64.

Song, Xiao-Peng, C. Huang, S. S. Saatchi, M. C. Hansen, and J. R. Townshend. 2015. "Annual Carbon Emissions from Deforestation in the Amazon Basin between 2000 and 2010." *PloS One* 10 (5): e0126754.

Sponsel, Leslie E. 2016. "The Master Thief: Gold Mining and Mercury Contamination in the Amazon." In Barbara Rose Johnston, ed., *Life and Death Matters*. 2nd ed. New York: Routledge.

Stickler, Claudia M., Michael T. Coe, Marcos H. Costa, Daniel C. Nepstad, David G. McGrath, Livia C. P. Dias, Hermann O. Rodrigues, and Britaldo S. Soares-Filho. 2013. "Dependence of Hydropower Energy Generation on Forests in the Amazon Basin at Local and Regional Scales." *Proceedings of the National Academy of Sciences of the United States of America* 110 (23): 9601–6.

Stone, Christopher D. 1974. *Should Trees Have Standing? Toward Legal Rights for Natural Objects*. Los Altos, CA: W. Kaufmann.

Terhorst, Philipp, Marcela Olivera, and Alexander Dwinell. 2013. "Social Movements, Left Governments, and the Limits of Water Sector Reform in Latin America's Left Turn." *Latin American Perspectives* 40 (4): 55–69.

Van Dijck, Pitou. 2008. "Troublesome Construction: The Rationale and Risks of IIRSA." *European Review of Latin American and Caribbean Studies / Revista Europea de Estudios Latinoamericanos y del Caribe* 85 (October): 101–20.

Veiga, João Paulo Cândia, and Scott B. Martin. 2012. "Climate Change, Trade Unions and Rural Workers in Labour: Environmental Alliances in the Amazon Rainforest." In Nora Räthzel and David Uzzell, eds., *Trade Unions in the Green Economy: Working for the Environment*. London: Routledge.

Walker, Robert, and Eugenio Arima. 2011. "Smallholder Timber Sales along the Transamazon Highway: A Comment." *Ecological Economics* 70 (9): 1565–67.

Wunder, Sven. 2007. "The Efficiency of Payments for Environmental Services in Tropical Conservation." *Conservation Biology* 21 (1): 48–58.

Yard, E. E., J. Horton, J. G. Schier, K. Caldwell, L. Lewis, C. Sanchez, and C. Gastanaga. 2012. "Mercury Exposure among Artisanal Gold Miners in Madre de Dios, Peru: A Cross-Sectional Study." *Journal of Medical Toxicology* 8 (4): 441–48.

Youatt, Rafi. 2017. "Personhood and the Rights of Nature: The New Subjects of Contemporary Earth Politics." *International Political Sociology* 11 (1): 39–54.

Zhouri, Andréa. 2010. "'Adverse Forces' in the Brazilian Amazon: Developmentalism versus Environmentalism and Indigenous Rights." *Journal of Environment & Development* 19 (3): 252–73.

Zimmerer, Karl S. 2011. "'Conservation Booms' with Agricultural Growth? Sustainability and Shifting Environmental Governance in Latin America, 1985–2008 (Mexico, Costa Rica, Brazil, Peru, Bolivia)." *Latin American Research Review* 46 (4): 82–114.

TWELVE

Changes in Urban Crime

From the "Neoliberal Period" to the "Left Turn"

GABRIEL KESSLER

During the "neoliberal period" in Latin America, urban crime rose in tandem with the increase in poverty, unemployment, and inequality (PNUD 2013).[1] Certainly, other variables like drug trafficking also figured significantly in countries such as Colombia and Brazil (Bagley 2013; CAF 2015; Thoumi 2012). At that time the connection between social issues and crime seemed so significant that it led to tacit consensus that on the improvement of the social situation, crime would decrease (Kessler 2014). Yet, even though social indicators improved during the "Left turn," crime increased in most countries (or did not decrease as expected) (see Bergman 2018; Jaitman 2017).[2] In fact, this occurred both in those countries experiencing the Left turn, such as Argentina, Uruguay, Bolivia, Brazil, Venezuela, Ecuador, and El Salvador, and in those that were not part of the Left turn, such as Mexico, Peru, and some Central American nations.

To delve into this issue, we should first answer the question, is it possible to speak about a "common" Latin American "crime problem"?[3] If we were to rely solely on homicide rates, the answer would be no. Differences among Latin American countries are broader than in any other region: they range on a scale from the most violent countries in the world (Venezuela, El Salvador) to countries in middle-high positions to countries whose rates are near or below the global average (UNODC 2014). Yet other indicators suggest otherwise. First, all Latin American countries have high rates of victimization by theft. The distance between them in terms of theft is lower than that in terms of homicides (Latinobarómetro 2015). Second, crime has long been the primary or secondary major concern in every single country in the region. However, such proximity tells us nothing about the intensity, the way in which this concern bears on everyday life and politics in very different countries. But it is clear that the issue is at the center of public debate in every country in Latin America, without exception (see Dammert and Lagos 2012). And third, there is widespread reference to crime as a common problem in the region among both scholars and local politicians. This can be seen in Latin American conferences on the subject as well as in studies that focus on the transnationalization of organized crime or, more recently, the *diaspora criminal* (Garzón Vergara et al. 2013). Scholars have also crafted intimidating categories such as "mexicanization" or "colombianization," employed to define a country on the basis of a particular and prevailing sort of violence. All in all, these indicators point to the existence of a common Latin American reference to a shared problem.

In line with the above concerns, a question that emerges is whether there has been a Left turn in security policies. In general, the answer is no (see Sozzo 2015), although the countries that make up the Left turn have dealt with the problem in not so different ways. They have at least five common features: they show no major innovations in terms of security policies, their focus remains "police centered," they saw militarization processes in most cases, their prison populations increased,[4] and there were no significant changes in terms of rehabilitation policies. Even if it is true that these administrations launched social and comprehensive prevention programs, these were generally underbudgeted, had limited territorial scope, and lacked sustainability over time. Notwithstanding, "star plans" spread throughout the region as role models: Rio's

Unidade de Polícia Pacificadora (Pacifying Police Unit, UPP) and Fica Vivo, its now more progressive counterpart in Belo Horizonte, as well as some specific municipal policies in Colombia and innovations in policing in Chile. Nevertheless, it would be difficult to argue that there was a Left turn on safety issues (see PNUD 2013).

Why were these administrations not reformist in terms of safety issues? Because they were confronted with at least three problems. First, the classic challenge left-wing agendas are compelled to deal with is security. Second, the growing social concern, largely embodied by an increasingly punitive public, did not act as an incentive for governments to implement progressive measures. The third problem, why the reduction in inequality does not imply a reduction in crime, is the focus of my chapter and part of a self-critical process. Latin American sociology and anthropology have greatly contributed to the belief that an improvement in the social situation and in particular inequality would bring about a decrease in crime. This belief arose both from our work and from our political stance. The increase in crime was one of neoliberalism's most dire consequences, and thus we rightly advocated for more social policies instead of more repression. I do not think our descriptions or explanations of the phenomena were wrong, or misleading; but we mulled over future scenarios too little (strictly speaking and honestly, we are not used to doing so). For example, our dire predictions about neoliberalism did not conceive of a Left turn (and to this day not everyone in our field agrees that it actually existed; see Dabène, this volume).

The present work is based on my own research, which was carried out in Argentina during the past decade and a half, among young people who committed property crimes involving violence (Kessler 2004, 2013). For heuristic purposes, I define its aims as a comparison of the neoliberal (1990–2003) and postneoliberal periods (2003 on). Based on the life trajectory and history of more than a hundred youths, it seeks to assess the changes and continuities from one period to another. Finally, this chapter delves into a matter of particular concern among colleagues from different countries in the region: namely, why did the reduction in inequality not result in a decrease in crime? I argue that the changes in the forms of crime are largely shaped by two sets of events. On the one hand, there have been mutations in the labor market (in addition to the variable availability of jobs, changes in their quality, and the relationship youths establish with work in each period). On the other hand, in every period crime is influenced by the way in which a number of societal factors such as deprivation, consumption, stigma, youth identities, peer groups, and police relations are experienced.

This work drifts away from those criminological theories that seek to unveil the keys to "criminal conduct." Conversely, it puts the question of crime at the core of sociological theory to connect what happened in terms of crime to what happened in other dimensions of social life. Based on the Argentine case, it aims to serve as a comparison for other national cases. The chapter is organized in three parts: first it presents the main features of crime during the neoliberal period, then it delves into crime during postneoliberalism, and finally it draws a comparison between both periods.

CRIME, YOUTH, AND EMPLOYMENT IN ARGENTINA

According to official government statistics, the number of crimes committed in Argentina doubled during the 1990s, from 560,240 in 1990 to 1,062,241 in 1999; over 70 percent of all crimes committed in Argentina were property crimes (DNPC 2010). The corresponding figures for the country's capital city, Buenos Aires, were even higher: 2,046 per 100,000 in 1990 and 6,301 per 100,000 in 1999. The latter are often particularly associated with youths; over 90 percent of those charged with a property crime in Buenos Aires were young men under the age of twenty-five. Not surprisingly, perhaps, the average age of the Argentine prison population dropped from thirty-one in 1984 to twenty-one in 1994 (Citara 1995). This has occurred during a period of unprecedented economic hardship, marked in particular by high levels of unemployment and rising inequality. Thus many researchers have made the case that there is likely to be a relationship between these two trends. Navarro (1997), for example, suggests that rising unemployment can be directly correlated with rising criminality, while Cerro and Meloni (1999) contend that inequality in income distribution is the determining factor, the latter even going so far as to suggest that every 10 percent increase in inequality can be correlated with a 3 percent rise in the crime rate.

Contrary to Western European labor markets, unemployment in 1990s Argentina tended to be short term.[5] What changed was the underlying nature of the labor market, as jobs became increasingly low paid and precarious, offering minimal salaries and no benefits, and often lasting only a few months at a time. This labor market transformation led to a fundamental change in employment patterns, with new entrants into the labor market, in particular, developing unstable job trajectories characterized by frequent changes from one low-paid, short-term precarious job to another, with short periods of unemployment in between. The kinds of employment associated with the young people interviewed for this research were jobs such as office or delivery boys, cleaning and maintenance workers, salespersons in small shops, short-haul truck loaders, babysitters, and car washers, among others. The length of time on the job declined from twenty months for the first job, compared to ten months for the second and third. It is this new type of employment pattern rather than unemployment per se that has had particular consequences for crime in Argentina.

Crime, Employment, and the "Procurer Rationale"

The changing nature of the labor market has had critical ramifications for the way in which work is conceived by contemporary Argentine youths, particularly in low-income communities. Unlike their parents (in some cases, their grandparents because their parents' work was too unstable), who entered the labor market with expectations of stable, long-term employment, they assume that they will inevitably experience job insecurity. This normalization of labor instability has had critical sociopsychological consequences. Upward mobility in a "meaningful occupation" has become difficult to imagine, and the notion that a job is a source of status, values, and a living wage has been superseded by the idea that a job is simply a means of obtaining money. I define this change as a transition from a "worker rationale" to a "procurer rationale" (see Kessler 2013), with the key difference between the two perspectives being the way that the source of income is legitimized. In the worker rationale, legitimacy resides in the *origin* of income: it is the fruit of "honest" labor in a socially recognized, respectable occupation. The procurer's source of legitimacy, however, is to be found, not in the origin of the money, but in its *utilization* to satisfy needs. In a word, any source of money, regardless of means, is regarded as legitimate so long as it is used to satisfy a need. The range of legitimate needs goes far beyond basic ones such as food, for example, but includes anything considered a need by the individuals themselves: paying a utility bill; buying clothes, beer, or marijuana; celebrating a friend's birthday; or even going to see the Iguazú Falls (a major tourist attraction in Argentina).

This transformation in the way work is perceived has led to low-income youths in Argentina increasingly regularly combining—both simultaneously and consecutively—legal and illegal income-generating activities. Certainly, the youths interviewed for this research all combined legal employment with criminal activities. In some cases they resorted to crime whenever they were out of work, but in most cases legal and illegal income-generation occurred concurrently. Most earned low incomes in precarious legal jobs, which they supplemented by begging, demanding a "toll" (obstructing foot traffic on a neighborhood street and demanding money to pass), mugging, or engaging in petty robbery. The distinction between legal and illegal income generation largely faded away as a result, with the choice of resorting to one or the other largely dependent on the opportunities that presented themselves at any given point in time. Indeed, the procurer rationale can be said to be intricately linked to an informal Argentinean cultural code known as *ventajeo*, that is, trying to "take advantage" of people and situations, by any means possible. This is a modus operandi that requires quick thinking and anticipating the moves of others—an analogy can perhaps be made here with duels in cowboy movies; the first one to draw wins—and is therefore underpinned by a sense of immediacy.

The procurer rationale is to this extent very different from the economic analysis of crime famously put forward by Gary Becker (1968). This theory supposes the existence of rational actors, *homo economicus* who carry out cost-benefit analyses before deciding whether or not to commit a crime. In other words, they will consider factors such as unemployment or low income—both of which are seen as increasing the likelihood of committing a crime—against the chances of being caught and the nature of potential punishment—increased policing and longer sentences are both thought to reduce the attractions of crime—in order to come to a logical decision. In order to rationally weigh the costs and benefits of an eventual criminal act, the potential delinquent must be able to see beyond the act itself and have a sense of the potential consequences that might be suffered, however. This was clearly not something that came to the minds of the youths interviewed for this research, whose intention was very obviously to fulfill an immediate need, explaining their crime in terms such as, "I needed money and went out to look for it" or "I had a job and needed money to get to it, so I went out to steal the money for the bus." Indeed, much of the criminal activity carried out by the youths interviewed for this research was highly contingent.

This is not to say that delinquent youths were not subject to certain codes. This was especially evident in relation to the money obtained from crime. Money is not neutral; when these youths combined legal and illegal activities, a "two-money" system tended to emerge in which the "hard" earned money on the legal job was used for important expenses like helping out at home or commuting to and from work while the "easy" money acquired through crime was used for nonessential expenses such as a night on the town, beer, name-brand shoes, or gifts. This two-money system was a sign that the blurring of the boundary between legal and illegal activities was not complete; certain distinctions persisted, in this case, the dual system for spending money according to its origin that clearly differentiated legal activities from illegal ones.

There also existed widespread difference in the value accorded to different types of income generation. Formal work was normatively considered "better" than crime, for example; there was thus no evidence of a subcultural construction diametrically opposed to the mainstream. Beyond this normative discourse, however, the young people's relationship to work emerged as highly instrumental. Job insecurity and instability offered no chance for learning a trade or acquiring specific job skills and furthermore made constructing any kind of workplace identity—whether based on a particular trade, trade union, or company—difficult. In the absence of the skill-generating and socializing aspects traditionally associated with the world of work, employment became merely instrumental to the youths we interviewed, a way to procure money among many others, including crime.

The Fading Away of the Law

The blurring of the boundary between legal and illegal economic activity has had ramifications beyond the world of work. In the not so distant past, the workplace was terrain in which social and labor rights were experienced (Jelin 1996). Part of the social training provided by a job consisted in learning about and having recourse to laws governing the relationship between employer and employee, limiting exploitation, and mediating conflicts and distribution disputes involving wages and benefits. Argentina has also long had laws determining compensation in the case of hardship, such as an accident or sickness. These laws clearly were not applied to the overwhelming majority of youths interviewed, who reported being fired without being paid or even being told why they were fired, being sent back home without medical attention after work-related accidents, and so on. Some even took a job and worked without knowing how much they were to earn, and many stressed the highly informal nature of their—generally unwritten—work arrangements. The world of work as a place governed by the rule of law had in other words been replaced by a workplace that appeared to be governed exclusively by the will of the employer, unchecked by any sort of predictable rules and regulations.

Perhaps not surprisingly, as a result many of these youths clearly failed to perceive the law as a mediating factor that could legitimately intervene in private conflicts. One youth, for example, could not understand why he was charged with robbery after he had said he was sorry and had returned to his victim what he had stolen. He was even more indignant when talking about the neighbor who had denounced him and his fellow thieves: "I don't understand, if I didn't steal from him, why did he have to get involved?" Certainly, the possibility of an external agent intervening in private conflicts was seen as so unlikely that any reference to the state as a party to their destiny was incomprehensible to these youths. When, after being asked to describe their—generally harsh—economic situation, they were asked what they saw as the state's potential role in solving their problems, the youths often didn't grasp what was meant. "The state of what?," they would reply, as if I had asked them a completely nonsensical question. More generally, it was striking how none of the state institutions that routinely affected the lives of these youths, such as school or the police, emerged as representing a legitimate source of authority for them.[6]

The police, in particular, were simply seen as an(other) armed group, albeit better armed and trained than the others occupying their local space, which is why they were greatly feared, although more because of the possibility of being killed or hurt if one fell into the hands of the policethan because they would be charged and sent to trial. In addition, the youths viewed the police as corrupt, and because they were petty thieves, burglars, whose ill-gotten goods were of little value, they were not perceived as interesting partners to negotiate with, either to buy their freedom if they were arrested or to be forced to share with the police what they obtained. At the same time, however, police officers were not strangers to the youths we interviewed; often they were neighbors or came from the same neighborhoods, and occasionally they were even family members. Indeed, some of the youths I interviewed actually stated that in the future they would stop robbing and become policemen, perceiving that the skills and behavior required were quite similar to the ones that they were acquiring through crime.

The effect of peer groups was particularly salient. Our interviewees passed from childhood to adolescence in the early and mid-1990s. During that time, their parents faced increasing difficulties securing a stable income given the growing unemployment and job insecurity in the country. Thus these youths moved into their teen years in families with declining income. They have teenage consumer demands without the opportunity to satisfy them. Many of the youths in the same situation share the same territory. Even if there were no gangs, bands, or groups with strong cohesion and a defined identity, peer groups' person-to-person effect was significant. This is evident in their stories of early crime experiences: one asks a neighborhood friend or a friend asks him if he wants to "try," another said he's got a gun, someone else says he knew about someone he went to school with who is stealing and did alright, and so on.

When I conducted the first phase of the research I was struck by the extreme pragmatism and fatalism of the stories the interviewees told. They did not express a counterculture: for example, they did not boast about what they had done, nor did they see a "deviant career" as a project of life antagonistic to the procurer as described by Becker (1968). Rather, they described very specific spatial and temporally defined situations that gave them no other possible choice than the one they chose—sort of a dead-end juncture. So, for instance, if money was needed, they seized the option that appeared to be more available, whether work or theft. At that time I thought that such a spatial and temporal assessment of each action was a trait of adolescence, but in the next phase of research spatiotemporal fragmentation was much less, and the new respondents could indeed imagine the future and different possible courses of action.

In this second phase, inequality was growing, but no one spoke about it; these youths did not think of it as a possible category, nor was there any sort of political critique of social injustice. The experience they reported put more emphasis on the idea of "need." They were able to criticize how little they earned for their work, yet failed to come to a broader assessment of the situation. In several cases there were allegations of police brutality but not in terms of human rights violations or discrimination, as we shall see in the next phase. During the 1990s, the discourse about rights and discrimination was absent from the state. Social movements such as *piquetero* (street picketer) organizations had not yet reached these youths. But in just a matter of years some of them would experience a social reinsertion through political engagement with these groups. Today, we assess that period, the end of the 1990s, as a stage of proliferation of the procurer rationale, yet still without the politicization or availability of a cultural script in which to inscribe their own experience. The period that follows will mark changes.

CRIME IN THE LEFT TURN

In 2003 the cycle of economic and social recovery with reduction of poverty, unemployment, and inequality began in Argentina. By 2002, the country had reached its highest peak in crime since the 1980s. The next couple of years saw an insignificant decrease (i.e., not below 1990s levels), and in 2008 the incidence of crime grew once again (Kessler 2013; Kessler and Bruno 2018). Victimization surveys carried out in large and medium-size urban centers indicated that about one-third of the population had been victims of crime over the course of a year—a significant percentage of the total population. In short, improvement in the social situation was not followed by an equally significant drop in crime. Homicide rates remained around 5 to 7 persons in 100,000, among the lowest in Latin America. At the same time, as worries over the economy calmed, the feeling of insecurity peaked. In 2003, for the first time concerns about crime exceeded those of fear of unemployment and economic crisis: about 80 percent of the population considered it a major problem and believed that it would continue thus.

I conducted fieldwork in 2007 with Pablo Seman and again in 2010 in a project area in the suburbs of greater Buenos Aires. The community was built in the early 1970s and had a population of about twenty thousand; it is heavily stigmatized by both the media and the public as a dangerous place. Violation of the law is a central stigma for the public, but the neighborhood is ruled by other values. Local categories weigh the breakdown of law with another locally cherished value: the contribution to local peace and order. Residents' assessment of any sort of crime goes hand in hand with whether the offense undermines the peace or is neutral or, conversely, if criminals contribute to the order of the community. This led to a fairly sophisticated hierarchical moral rating of criminals that I did not see in the previous decade. It is certainly a by-product of the social experience of more than two decades of high crime rates. What are the changes and continuities from one period to another? I want to shed light on some of the paradoxes of the improvement inf the social situation and its impact on crime.

Work, Stigma, and Fun

After 2003 the economy and employment rates recovered. In 2007 the unemployment rates for young men from fifteen to twenty-four years old was about 21.5 percent, 2.5 times the rate of the overall population (ILO 2007). Yet numbers from the community point to a 12 percent general rate of unemployment, which if we were to include young people could climb to almost 30 percent. The stigma attached to the neighborhood was such that it led young people to use addresses outside the neighborhood or otherwise lie about where they lived when trying to get jobs.

One young man reported, "When in an interview they realize that you come from here, they say they're going to call, but you know for a fact that they won't, as soon as you leave they'll throw your application away." Some informants pointed to that kind of discrimination as being a large part of the explanation for local crime rates. A change with regard to the previous phase of research is discontent with an employment horizon that offers more, yet less attractive, opportunities. The biggest employer in the area is one of the private concessionaires for garbage collection in the city of Buenos Aires whose wages are deemed acceptable (a risky job with a strong union) but whose work is very difficult ("You poke that shit then," said one respondent). Thus, I identified a critique of the world of work that was missing in the previous period and that, to some extent, had led to an idealization (on the part of both researchers and some sectors of society) of the "wage society," disregarding earlier critiques of exploitation and alienation.

Contrary to the outside stigma, there is a strong community identity linked to positive values, solidarity, geographic proximity to urban centers, and, above all, fun. During the 1990s, life in the community was gray, dull, and sad. People rarely left the neighborhood because public transportation was expensive; in addition, with no resources for consumption, going to town seemed pointless. That changed. The neighborhood is now an attractive place for young people; in addition, there is much better access to different areas of the city. However, the young people complained that they were denied their right "to free movement, to go wherever they want." They were talking about how policemen and private security guards stop them or deny them access to places such as shopping malls.

A change linked with the above is the development of a popular culture that has taken on these youths' everyday life images and significances. The first paradigmatic example was *cumbia villera* ("slum music"). Martín (2008) argues that it re-creates narratives present in their universe: the value of leisure time, theft, and nonregulated time, as opposed to work and traditional ways of building their masculinity. Its lyrics, he adds, question discrimination, vindicating being *negro*, which in Argentina is less of an ethno-phenotypic designation than a pejorative moral attribute. A striking fact is that CDs of this music, at its moment of greatest popularity, represented between 25 percent and 50 percent of the market.

This casts light on the ambiguous relationship that the hegemonic culture and the market have always established with both violence and crime: rejection and condemnation, on the one hand, but commodification and commercial movement of that which they scorn, on the other.

What is interesting to note is that this music expresses an aesthetic and some meanings that drift away from the simple story of deprivation and exclusion, almost hegemonic in sociological discourses about the lives of these youths. Throughout the decade, a second process took place. Movies, TV, fiction, and nonfiction portraying the lives of youths living in the periphery proliferated.

Finally, we should take note of the growing cultural production that took place within the periphery carried out by middle sector and popular sector youth. It was not just music, but visual arts, film, and literature (Cueto and Ferraudi Curto 2015). This challenged the historic trend in which the city produces culture, which then moves to the periphery. Many Latin American cities have beene witnessing their peripheries becoming very dynamic places of cultural production. Why should we include this variable in a study about crime? Because it is an indicator of the availability of cultural scripts that confer meanings and contribute to making sense of the experience of poor youths. This experience comprises all conflictive situations, police brutality, crime, leisure, and fun, as well as a freer sexuality, for both men and women. Thus it drifts away from the "miserabilism" in terms of which periphery cultural productions have often been discussed.

Consumption and Relative Deprivation

For some years now, different countries in the region have defined poor sectors' increased access to goods because of the improved economic situation and the lowering of the prices of certain goods—for example, mobile phones and personal computers—as consumption democratization (see Dewey 2015). This community is not alien to such phenomena and the overall general upswing. Together with the perpetuation of housing and health shortages—to name a few—one can see within the community name-brand shoes, fitness equipment, cell phones, MP3s, and motorcycles, among other goods. Products can be legitimate, fakes of varying quality, and others whose source is indecipherable. Thus there are more objects circulating, but above all, there is a discourse that is much more widespread than in the preceding period that centers on consumption as a form of individual pleasure, on the "envy" that new goods can trigger, on the need to wear specific brands to "get approved" by one's peers. Boys also complain that popular girls are more attracted to the guy who has a bike irrespective of his physical appeal and attractiveness.

Concurrently, it would seem that at times of economic recovery and a renewed promise of consumption, there is a reconfiguration in terms of relative and absolute deprivation. On the one hand, there are more goods circulating, which would reduce such absolute deprivation; and the largest local consumption results in a continuous comparison with one's peers' access to certain goods. On the other hand, this seems to multiply juvenile distinction strategies tied to these goods. In addition, consumption triggered a rise in popular sectors' indebtedness, especially among its youth. But what should be noted is that consumption appears as a form of pleasure and even implicitly as a right, as the following testimony shows.

> Being broke brings you down. If I steal, then I spend my own bucks as I want, why do they fuck with me? That's discrimination, as long as I'm not hurting anybody they should keep their noses out of my business.

Another change from the 1990s is that the distinction between easy and hard-earned money (which actually comes from the 1950s and 1960s) is less apparent. Since the moment of extreme family hardship is now over, there is less of a need to "help the mother" or pay household expenses, primary uses for hard-earned money. In other cases, family relations are strained, because parents know about and disapprove of the actions of their sons. Instead of contributing to the family budget, youths use their money for their own consumption, in which the distinction between "easy" and "hard-earned" is blurry. New forms of distinction, thus, have changed how expenditures are gauged; for example, brand-name garments, which used to be an item for easy money, is no longer perceived as a luxury expenditure but as a necessity in order to avoid being seen as "less than others."

Crime in the Field of Experiences

In the previous phase of research, crime was described as the only option when confronted with a specific situation of need. Now, for some crime appears as an option within the field of experiences. The youths described a variety of options among which crime is just one more. They highlight agency, as the following exchange illustrates.

> *And what do you do about the economic issue?*
> I always manage one way or another to get some money, I do OK with just a couple of bucks. I'm twenty-eight years old, and I have never worked. I spent four years in prison. I never worked, until now, I had never worked. I just started a few months ago at that factory.

> *And what are the alternatives?*
> The Plan (cash transfers) when it came out they gave it to everyone, but then they cut it down and no one else got one.

> *So what are the alternatives?*
> Stealing. I see kids who don't even have a peso to spare to buy you a coke, . . . and when I don't have cash I'm out of my mind. I can't ask my mom because I can't, she won't give; she works for her, to eat and to help my sister and her children. So far, since I got out, I was never out of cash. One way or another you manage to get it, and being around here makes it easier to get into that shit with someone else. If you're out there thinking, "Should I do it or not," you will always find someone who will come along and nudge you in. I don't do it, but if I had to, I will. I mean, if I have nothing to eat, I will do it. But I wish to avoid it.

A range of options, though limited, keeps the procurer rationale in play, but it is portrayed with less fatalism than in the earlier stage. Why is crime part of the range of experiences? I think that crime is now very present in the experiences of older cohorts—who are still very young—who have stolen. Age differences are minor—between three and five years—and in the community they are referred to as *camadas*.[7] In other words, unlike the previous stage when there was no presence of older generations, now everybody knows other youths around their age who have committed crimes at some point, either directly or by reputation. The logic of ventajeo was less present, for there is more thought put into whether to use violence, possibly because of recent years' experiences.

Another change is connected to peer groups. During postneoliberalism, I identified the combined effect of the multiplication and interaction of youths in similar situations of need concentrated in the same areas, where explicit peer group pressure is one of the issues of greatest tension between parents and children. It is as if, at least from the perspective of adults, early on there was a struggle between parents trying to prevent children from "deviating" because of their friends' influence and friends who criticize the children for being too much under the control of their families. Different strategies are employed. For example, parents may ban children from any local contact. These children are then stigmatized as the "locked downs" and faced with retaliation by their peers. But parents evaluate their children in terms of how many "did well and how many did badly."

Early Death in the Community

In contrast to what happened in past decades, the death of other youths of the same "class," or camada, or just a bit older, is now a recurring theme: killed by the police, by other youths, but also by traffic accidents, HIV-AIDS, or other less clear reasons. The community's stories are full of young people who died during the past fifteen years. Often a mother tells us, "From the friends of my son, only a few are left," pointing in a photo of a group of smiling youths to those who died. Death is not a taboo even for some children or pubescent youths: parents, to prevent them from "deviating," usually warn their kids about the possibility of being killed if they turn to crime and give them examples of those they know who "have fallen." Thus there is daily management of life and death meant to avoid the possibility that fate will strike a loved one, especially a child.

For residents, young death or the idea of great misfortune is also not taboo. The death of a young man does not elicit a unique sort of emotion or unanimous condemnation. In some interviews, certain deaths were accepted or even celebrated, for example, the deaths of those who were involved in less desirable categories of crime (referred to in dehumanizing terms, such as epidemic, garbage, insects), or the deaths are legitimized. One young man said, "Now almost everyone is dead and some are in jail; many bands are in prison, but they always come back, like cockroaches you kill them and they manage to come back."

What I want to stress is that death appears to young people as a repeated event in the recent past and in the present, as well as a future possibility. Neighbors also see youth death as a regular event. Theories of rational choice would tell us that the omnipresence of death would be a key deterrent, as the highest "cost"; yet the situation is much more complex. Certainly in some cases the possibility of death may be a deterrent to crime; but in others, recurrence leads to death being part of the horizon of possible experiences. It's not that life doesn't matter or that a short life filled with pleasures is most highly valued, as work on Colombia's *sicariatos* proposes (Salazar 1990). Death is thought of as a hazard of the "rule of theft." A remarkable change has been how to honor youths killed by the police; friends build shrines, arguing that "the family goes to the cemetery, but we build our shrines." They also have rituals when someone dies (e.g., parading the body through the soccer field and having a barbecue). There is a kind of reflection about death that was absent in the earlier period: it is an option in the course of life they have chosen.

Confrontation with the Police

As one might expect, the opinions of this community about the police, especially its youth and even more particularly of those in conflict with the law, was extremely negative. Yet in almost every interview people seem to have information about the different forms in which the police regulate local crime. On the other hand, there are countless cases of institutional violence, from homicide to everyday forms of hostility. Growing up in the neighborhood is getting used to being stopped over and over, searched, and delayed by the police with varying degrees of abuse: being young and from the community means you are a suspect. Findings of a 2011 study (Kessler and Dimarco 2013), not only in this district, but in almost all popular areas, show that in recent years there has been an increased presence of security forces in the streets as a response to society's demand for more security, which in turn implied an increased frequency in all sorts of controls over young men and women as soon as they enter their teenage years.

In terms of politicization, I was able to identify broader use of the notion of rights together with a critique of what youths see as discrimination on the part of the police. Young people see a contradiction: they find one kind of discourse about rights in the media, public life, and at school, yet that discourse clashes with what they endure where they live and in their daily lives. Demands for "the right to free movement" and not being "discriminated" against, because "they too have human rights," were constant when critiquing police action. In fact, it was during this period when human rights organizations' actions strengthened in popular communities (e.g., projects, slums) to educate youths about their rights vis-à-vis police brutality.

I also noted differences with regard to the role played by the police in the regulation of crime. In the previous period, so-called amateur criminals' small booty meant they had little or nothing to bargain with. At this stage, I once again found in the stories an obligatory and complex bargaining process with the police that took various forms. The following exchange is illustrative.

> *All those who make it their business need to get involved with the police?*
> Whether you like it or not, you must always engage with the police. Because if you get caught, then the commissioner tells you give me five grand. No, I have three. Well, give me the three. Now beat it. He opens the door, and you go out the back door.

> *However, there are plenty of kids who get locked down . . .*
> That's because they do not want to settle things right, or don't work with them, or already have long criminal records . . . many things, or hurt or killed someone, that's another thing, much more money, maybe even there's not enough money to fix things.

> *Everything has a price?*
> I think that freedom is priceless, but everything has its tag. You do something, you have to work it out. If you stole 100, you must keep 20 no matter what, you have to save 20. You get caught, those 20 will be of use. Be it for an attorney or for the police who caught you. Say that you stole 12 grand, 7,000 pesos are yours and the police get 5,000.

The degree of complexity in the interactions between police and criminals that is told in the interviews is shocking. They render information about alleged values and freedom rates that increase depending on the severity of the crime and the number of years in prison one could get. One interviewee told me, "What you are asked for depends on how long you might be getting down for, and on what sort of goods you are stealing, they know everything."

CRIME, NEOLIBERALISM, AND THE LEFT TURN

What are the continuities and differences between the two periods? How much of this helps us understand the persistence of high crime rates despite improvement in the social situation? During the first period, work becomes rarified, and then it becomes unstable; it does not disappear from the horizon but becomes a means among others, equated to other forms of provision. Thus the boundaries between what is legal and what is illegal fade but do not disappear. A moral assessment especially embodied by the "two-money system" remained. In the second period, work once again becomes part of the social landscape, though unstable by definition; yet stigma and distrust of young people impair their access to it, and, in turn, there is a growing appreciation for a sensual life beyond the work routine that turns labor into a less desirable prospect.

As for the world of goods, in the first stage, the consumer society is already present but access is hard. Youths fluctuate between relative and absolute deprivation; given the context of family hardship, little or no money is left for their needs. During the second stage, the procurer logic persists, and greater possible access to goods overlaps with the growing importance of consumption in the construction of their own subjectivity and the relationship with others. So the demand for goods and money is higher than in the previous period. Paradoxically, the experience of relative deprivation, while objectively less severe than in the first period, is subjectively higher, since it operates according to youth acceptance and distinction strategies.

The city, of course, also changes, especially in the way youths experience it. During the first stage, youths seem more confined to their neighborhoods, with little opportunity to leave. Both downtown and the city in general are not present in their day-to-day cartography, but that is not surprising: policemen, neighbors, and private security guards regard them with contempt, suspicion, and hostility as they see them pass by. Nor do they have money to spend on consumption. Public control and policing units remain widespread; in fact, the community I studied is surrounded by security forces. At the same time, life in the 'hood is perceived as more sensual and fun than in the previous stage. Youths manage, not without opposition from their parents and the police, to use and enjoy local public spaces. Mobility increases: the city is once again an appealing place, and conflict over their presence in middle- and upper-class areas heightens.

The weight of peer groups and networks changes. In the first stage, I found many youths in the same situation sharing the same territories. This enhanced the weight of peer groups in everyday interactions, although this did not lead to the formation of bands or gangs. The weight of peer groups is more intense during the second stage. Pressure is not only horizontal and contextual: while in the first stage youths speak as if they were the first "class" linked to crime, in the second there is a strong presence of reoffenders from different generations that reinforce the weight of peer groups.

A result is that crime does not appear in the accounts as the only possible option. Now work, social programs, and crime are options that can coexist at any one moment; the novelty is that crime falls within the field of experiences as one of the possibilities. This is evidenced in youths often explaining not only why they choose to do crimes but also why they choose not to take that "road." Another of the implications of more than a decade of high crime rates is that young death is omnipresent. As a matter of fact, death enters the field of possibilities for young people not only because of crime, since conditions such as HIV-AIDS or strange accidents also play a part. In addition, there are different types of relationships with youth deaths, that is, the anticipation of rituals and desirable forms of remembrance, which until this time had not been part of local popular culture.

The relationship with the police, during both moments, shares some features depending on the criminal hierarchy. Throughout time the most professional criminals are those who know about the forms of negotiation and the buying of freedom. In both periods, our "amateur" crime cases do not point to any sort of relationship of negotiation, since they had nothing to offer and to contour the law with; disposable as bargain *partenaires*, they were often objects of extreme violence or of outright murder on the part of security forces.

The above-mentioned differences and continuities allow us to advance two hypotheses. First, there are changes in crime linked to the particularities of each era. Second, nearly two decades of high crime rates have had profound implications for the experiences, the repertoire of action, and the resources of subsequent generations. Those two decades resulted in social sedimentation, which is not necessarily affected by changes in social conditions.

Finally, I would like to return to one of my initial questions: why does the reduction of inequality not imply a reduction in crime? This question is valid for every Left turn country. On this issue I can only lay out some ideas and hypotheses for future research. First, it is necessary to clarify the causal links (beyond statistical correlations) between both problems. Second, it is possible that some of the same consequences of the decline in inequality are implicated in maintaining or even increasing the rates of certain crimes. As for the first issue, it is necessary to think about the links between these processes: while it is probable that these processes are causally linked in its expansion phase, even if the independent variable (in this case, inequality) begins to recede, the dependent variable (crime) may have gained autonomy as a social phenomenon and therefore no longer responds to the downward course of the independent variable, explaining its upward cycle. In the same vein, there might be some sort of autonomy vis-à-vis long-run social phenomena; I am thinking about crime dynamics and markets that could emerge and linger throughout time. Strictly speaking, this assumption applies to some processes and not others. For example, you should not think of a stable contingent of groups that began to engage in crime in the 1990s and continued to the present. Generational turnover has been fast. A vast majority of juveniles who commit crimes drop out at the beginning of adulthood, and more crimes are committed by new cohorts who in the 1990s were young children. Hence the hypothesis of a generation of criminals that began in the late 1990s and continues to this day does not seem plausible.

Conversely, one could find continuity and some sort of autonomy in terms of crime markets, which, once established, while experiencing some sort of turnover in its agents, continue to exist as illegal markets. An example is car theft and its dismantling circuits and illegally exported cars. Even if there are other cohorts actually stealing cars, the circuits, chop shops, and retail networks are already established. Something similar can be said about other illegal markets, such as drug dealing, mobile phones, metals, drugs, and trafficking of women for sexual exploitation, to name a few. In short, although I am not inclined to the idea of a continuum of the same generation, almost two decades of high crime have left their mark on younger cohorts. One of its consequences is that crime began to be inscribed in the field of possible experiences; even when youths chose not to engage in it, many regarded it as one possible choice to deal with a specific situation.

There are other lines to investigate the relationship between inequality and crime. Even if I established general explanations, and at the level of communities or neighborhoods I have proposed and proven hypotheses about the impact of the general decline in job opportunities as well as the effects of residential segregation and impoverishment of social capital to explain different areas' different crime rates, it is less clear how these variables operate at the level of individual experience. We know little about inequality's persistent effects throughout generations; that is, what has been the impact of these poor conditions in their early years and if they have operated thereafter despite the fact that social conditions have changed.

In addition, the idea of a homogeneous reduction of inequality should be relativized. Available data do not allow us to account for the density of inequality in a given neighborhood, or the effects of stigma and the accumulation of disadvantages in neglected areas. We should also consider other aspects of the economic recovery that might be playing a role in maintaining high crime rates. A staple case is the high-tech theft that occurs in almost every developed country in the world; it seems to be a by-product of the influx of netbooks, iPhones, iPads, tablets, and other high-value, low-volume, and lightweight technology devices. In Argentina and particularly in the city of Buenos Aires in recent years, economic growth has led to the increased circulation of technological goods, and automobiles and tourism saw exponential development. In this context, crime opportunities became greater, thus resulting in the high rates of street robbery and theft. A consequence of increasing car sales, for example, is the flourishing of spare parts markets, which in turn, given the high cost of new parts, created a demand for stolen parts.

These are some of the differences and similarities relative to the two periods. Beyond the question about the decrease or increase in crime, we must look into the changes endured by those who commit crimes. Such changes, I have tried to show, are linked to some of the transformations from one period to another. An assessment of how policies sought to deal with the issue of crime in each period would be useful for better characterizing new and long-run forms of crime. These policies have not necessarily been reformist, as other dimensions of the Left turn have been. Would a more precise characterization of the actors, their motivations, be useful? I believe that it would, for every attempt to challenge the "strong identity" images of those who commit a crime, which seem to be totally different from the personalities or mentalities of those who do not break the law, can and will be useful.

Montambeault and Balán state in the introduction to this book that after neoliberalism "Left turn governments . . . came to power with the promise of deepening and widening citizenship regimes, for which a renewed relationship with traditionally excluded actors and civil society organizations was key." They consider citizenship a nonlinear social construction with circumstantial contradictions and tensions between social groups and the state. Following the works of Yashar and Oxhorn, they add that citizenship should be defined by "who is included, who is excluded, and why." I share this view, and this chapter shows one of the limits encountered by the Left turn inclusion process. In fact, although popular sectors were symbolically included in Left turn citizenship, some were excluded from it when some law was violated. Mass incarceration increased during the Pink Tide (Sozzo 2015), and security policies were not different from those of the neoliberal past. Why were postneoliberal countries incapable of showing more creativity in this field? Future research should ponder factors such as the historical weight of the law as a limit, the conception of the lumpen proletariat as an enemy of the working class, the lack of a social movement criticizing prison conditions, and the increasing security demands across Latin America. The point is that something like a Left turn in criminal law and security policy never happened. It was in these fields that an opportunity was missed. The current

"Right turn" thus assures even more pain for those among the already marginal who are most marginalized.

NOTES

1. There are big differences among countries in the rate of victimization, but for the entire region it increased from 29 percent in 1995 to 44 percent in 2015 (Latinobarómetro 2015).

2. According to sources such as Latinobarómetro, Barometros de las Américas, and national surveys, victimization rates increased from 2003 to 2013 in Argentina, Brazil, Bolivia, Uruguay, Ecuador, and Venezuela.

3. Consider, for example, the differences in the homicide rates in Caracas (123 homicides per 100,000 inhabitants), Guatemala (118) and Montevideo (4), and Buenos Aires (5) (UNODC 2014).

4. For a general appraisal of security policies in different "postneoliberal" administrations, see the special issue of *Cuestiones de Sociologia*, available at www.cuestionessociologia.fahce.unlp.edu.ar/issue/view/240.

5. Certainly, of the seventy youths interviewed for this research who had committed a crime, only 37 percent were unemployed, while 45 percent said that they were working part-time or irregularly and 16 percent were working full-time.

6. Obviously, Argentina's history of dictatorship can also be seen as having contributed to this discrediting of the state within wider society.

7. *Camadas* is the Spanish word referring to graduation classes, e.g., camada 2010. But in the community this concept refers to age groups, spanning differences of two to five years approximately. Thus there are groups within generations.

REFERENCES

Bagley, Bruce. 2013. "The Evolution of Drug Trafficking and Organized Crime in Latin America." *Sociologia, Problemas e Práticas* (71): 99–123.

Becker, Gary S. 1968. "Crime and Punishment: An Economic Approach." In N. G. Fielding, A. Clarke, and R. Witt, eds., *The Economic Dimensions of Crime*. London: Palgrave Macmillan.

Bergman, Marcelo. 2018. *More Money, More Crime: Prosperity and Rising Crime in Latin America*. Oxford: Oxford University Press.

Cerro, Ana María, and Osvaldo Meloni. 1999. *Análisis económico de las políticas de prevención y represión del delito en la Argentina.* Córdoba: Ediciones Eudecor.

Citara, Rodolfo. 1995. "El plan penitenciario Bonaerense." *Revista del Servicio Penitenciario Bonaerense* 8: 56–69.

Corporación Andina de Fomento (CAF). 2015. "The Criminal Justice System." In Pablo Sanguinetti, Daniel Ortega, Lucila Berniell, Fernando Álvarez, Daniel Mejía, Juan Camilo Castillo, and Pablo Brassiolo, eds., *Towards a Safer Latin America: A New Perspective to Prevent and Control Crime.* Bogotá: CAF.

Cueto, C., and C. Ferraudi Curto. 2015. "Made in conurbano: La cultura en el Gran Buenos Aires." In Gabriel Kessler, ed., *El Gran Buenos Aires.* Buenos Aires: UNIPE/Edhasa.

Dammert, Lucía, and Marta Lagos. 2012. *La seguridad ciudadana: El problema principal de América Latina.* Providencia: Latinobarómetro. www.latinobarometro.org/documentos/LATBD_La_seguridad_ciudadana.pdf.

Dewey, Matías. 2015. *El orden clandestino: Política, fuerzas de seguridad y mercados ilegales en la Argentina.* Buenos Aires: Katz Editores.

Dirección Nacional de Política Criminal (DNPC). 2010. *Informe Anual de Estadísticas Policiales.* Buenos Aires: Ministerio de Justicia, Seguridad y Derechos Humanos. www.argentina.gob.ar/justicia/institucional/subsecretaria-politica-criminal.

Garzón Vergara, Juan Carlos, Marianna Olinger, Daniel M. Rico, and Gema Santamaría. 2013. *La diáspora criminal: La difusión transnacional del Crimen Organizado y cómo contener su expansión.* Washington, DC: Wilson Center.

International Labor Organization (ILO). 2007. *Trabajo decente y juventud en Argentina.* Lima: ILO. www.ilo.org/.

Jaitman, Laura. 2017. *Los costos del crimen y de la violencia: Nueva evidencia y hallazgos en América Latina y el Caribe.* New York: Banco Internacional de Desarrollo.

Jelin, Elizabeth. 1996. *Vida cotidiana y control institucional en la Argentina de los 90.* Buenos Aires: Grupo Editor Latinoamericano.

Kessler, Gabriel. 2004. *Sociología del delito amateur.* Buenos Aires: Paidós.

———. 2013. "Ilegalismos en tres tiempos." In Robert Castel, Gabriel Kessler, Denis Merklen, and Numa Murad, eds., *Individuación, precariedad y riesgo: ¿Desinstitucionalización del presente?* Buenos Aires: Paídos.

———. 2014. "¿Responsables del temor? Medios y sentimiento de inseguridad en América Latina." *Nueva Sociedad* (249): 137–48.

Kessler, Gabriel, and Matías Bruno. 2018. "Inseguridad y vulnerabilidad al delito." In J. I. Piovani and A. Salvia, eds., *La Argentina del siglo XXI*. Buenos Aires: Siglo Veintiuno.

Kessler, G., and S. Dimarco. 2013. "Violencia, jóvenes e interacción con la policía en Buenos Aires." In Arturo Alvarado Mendoza, ed., *Acceso a la justicia y violencia en América Latina*. Mexico City: Ediciones del Colegio de México.

Latinobarómetro. 2015. *Informe 2015*. Santiago de Chile: Latinobarómetro. http://www.latinobarometro.org/latContents.jsp.

Martín, Eloísa. 2008. "La cumbia villera y el fin de la cultura del trabajo en la Argentina de los 90." *Revista Transcultural de Música 2008* (12). Online. www.redalyc.org/html/822/82201205/.

Navarro, Lucas. 1997. "En Argentina el crimen paga." *Novedades Económicas* 19 (196): 17–28.

Programa de las Naciones Unidas para el Desarrollo (PNUD). 2013. *Informe regional de desarrollo humano 2013–2014. Seguridad ciudadana con rostro humano: Diagnóstico y propuestas para América Latina*. New York: PNUD.

Salazar, Alonso. 1990. *No nacimos pa semilla*. Medellín: Cinep.

Sozzo, Máximo. 2015. "¿Más allá del neoliberalismo? Cambio político y penalidad en América del Sur." *Cuadernos del Pensamiento Crítico* 23 (May 2015): 1–4.

Thoumi, Francisco E. 2012. "Vulnerable Societies: Why Antidrug Policies Fail, Why There Is a Need for Reforms and Why They Are Unlikely to Be Implemented." *Substance Use & Misuse* 47 (13–14): 1628–32.

United Nations Office on Drugs Crime (UNODC). 2014. *Global Study on Homicide 2013: Trends, Contexts, Data*. New York: UNODC. www.unodc.org /documents/data-and-analysis/statistics/GSH2013/2014_GLOBAL _HOMICIDE_BOOK_web.pdf.

PART 4

Conclusions

THIRTEEN

Uses and Misuses of the "Left" Category in Latin America

Olivier Dabène

Leftist ideas and organizations have a long history in Latin America. Starting at the beginning of the twentieth century, they inspired social movements from Argentina and Chile up to Central America and Mexico. This long journey has been marked by pervasive violence. Events such as the Santa Maria de Iquique massacre (Chile, 1907), the "tragic week" in Buenos Aires (January 1919), or the great strike in Costa Rica's banana plantations (1934) will forever remain imprinted in the labor movement's collective memory. This history was also accompanied by an intellectual effort to adapt European ideologies (notably Marxism) to local realities. José Carlos Mariátegui's *Seven Interpretative Essays on Peruvian Reality* (1971) epitomizes such an attempt. Later during the Cold War, leftist movements were systematically and brutally repressed. Some turned to armed resistance, others to forced exile. All redeemed hope when the military started to plan returning to their barracks at the end of the 1970s. They would strengthen the "resurrection of civil society" theorized by transition analysts (O'Donnell and Schmitter 1986). During the "long night of neoliberalism," a term coined by Ecuadorean president Rafael Correa in the 1990s, the left envisioned alternative policies that finally convinced voters during the 2000s. Slightly deviating from its traditional agenda, centered on democratization and agrarian reform since the Mexican and Cuban Revolutions, the left emphasized poverty and inequality reduction. Social and political inclusion became the top priority for all leftist governments, moderate or radical (Montambeault, Balán, and Oxhorn, this volume).

Referring to this period covering much of the twentieth century, historians could easily define the left as being first influenced by the Bolshevik Revolution and then by the Cuban one (Angell 1995). In the absence of shared policies, and confronted with growing new social movements in the 1980s, the left diversified. Yet, for much of the twentieth century, the left embodied a claim for social justice and political empowerment. The opposition right/left made sense for the analysts simply because the political debates were shaped along these lines.

That dramatically changed with the so-called Left turn. Prior to the 2000s, except for some rare occasions following revolutionary victories (Cuba, 1959; Nicaragua, 1979), or close electoral success (Chile, 1970), the left had never been in a position to actually govern for a fairly long period of time and implement its inclusionary program. During the 2000s, the left not only achieved power through elections in a majority of countries, but it also proved remarkably resilient. In some countries, leftist governments' domination extended for well over a decade. That spurred a completely new political setting, providing a unique opportunity to observe the left "in action" over the long run. As a result, and quite paradoxically, many observers grew increasingly confused as to how they should characterize the left. The left/right divide suddenly appeared excessively simplistic, unable to capture the complexity of ideological and political components. Many contributors to this volume acknowledge the variety of leftist experiments, referring to "multiple lefts" and to a wide range of dichotomies and adjectives, such as old/new, liberal/illiberal, social democratic/populist, functional/dysfunctional, or outward/inward looking. Even though all agreed to deny any value to the binary conception of a good left and a bad left that was so popular in the media (Young 2013), they had to think of infinite nuances to tell their story.

The contrast between presidents rhetorically self-proclaiming themselves as "leftists" and acting like any of their "rightist" colleagues is also puzzling and should prompt us to make a distinction between notions commonly used by the actors and a more robust analytical category.

A full literature review would further confirm these hesitations. Suffice it to mention some telling examples. In the introduction to his 2010 edited volume, Max Cameron took issue with the overly simple dichotomy between a populist and a social democratic left (Cameron and Hershberg 2010). He emphasized the diversity of experiences and systematically referred to the Left turns (plural). Juan Pablo Luna (2010), in the same volume, suggested paying attention to endogenous constraints (potential conflicts within the partisan organizations and social base of leftist governments) as well as exogenous ones (state institutions and global economy). Depending on the level of constraints, he distinguished between several types of left.

Steven Levitsky and Kenneth M. Roberts (2011) defined the left as all partisan organizations placing redistribution and social equality at the top of their agendas and consistently pursuing that objective while in office. They elaborated a typology based on parties' organizational features (level of institutionalization and locus of political authority).

Olivier Dabène (2012) and his collaborators explained the diversity of the left in power by referring to the different challenges it had to meet. They put the emphasis on three types of constraints: the legacy of neoliberal reforms, the internationalization of economies, and the domestic political game (such as party systems or divided governments). The overlapping of these constraints could severely limit the margins of maneuver of some leftist governments more than others, helping to explain cross-country differences.

In the quest to build typologies or ideal-types, some observers went as far as pointing out that there had been more differences within the leftist family than between the moderate social democratic left and the progressive right, especially when assessing policy performance. Using a survey of country experts, Wiesehomeier (2010) showed that on a left-right axis, there is less distance between Néstor Kirchner (left, Argentina) and Omar Torrijos (right, Panama) than between Néstor Kirchner and Hugo Chávez (left, Venezuela).

This type of conclusion has spurred considerable confusion regarding the use of the Left-Right categories and calls for prudence. In this concluding chapter, I treat these vacillations seriously, questioning the categories we have been using in the past fifteen years.

As everyone minimally aware of Latin America's political evolutions knows, the Left turn began with a series of electoral victories, following Chávez's in 1998 in Venezuela. A dozen newly elected presidents claimed they belonged to the leftist family, in opposition to the rightist neoliberal one. They built a narrative based on new hope after a tragically long neoliberal night. And they proved convincing in heralding a new era of a more active state fighting poverty and inequality. "The Left" became a label for winning elections against the neoliberal and pro-U.S. conservative forces. Reacting swiftly, the academic community enthusiastically endorsed the idea that the left was finally in power and ready to act. The left quite abusively became a descriptive and even an analytical category. Although, as we saw, there were many efforts to distinguish between several lefts, each with a specific adjective, the Pink Tide sequence was overwhelmingly described as a new era of postneoliberalism. And although many scholars of comparative politics had reflected on the European left/right dichotomy's application to the rest of the world, in the past decade this type of epistemological vigilance was forgotten. The "break with pre-notions," recommended long ago by the French sociologist Émile Durkheim, was discarded.

Without doubt, there have been many changes in Latin America in the past fifteen years. The region grew less unequal, and poverty was massively reduced. Those changes were brought about by newly elected politicians displacing the ones who proceeded to adjust the economies in the 1990s. They all introduced more or less radical policy shifts in the region. Yet there is scope to doubt that the use of the "Left" as a descriptive or analytical category allows for an accurate understanding of these recent evolutions.

This chapter confirms those doubts, providing somewhat negative answers to three distinct but related questions: Did the Left turn change the political offer? Does the left/right divide make sense for the Latin American voter? And did the leftist governments' policy outcomes differ from the rightist ones? The answers are not all negative but sufficiently so to justify some skepticism regarding the left-right divide.

The chapter is divided into three sections. The first assesses the way the left altered the political offer, introducing new ideas and new political personnel. The second section considers whether the left/right dichotomy makes sense for voters and helps them make their choice. The third section interrogates the policies implemented during the leftist domination period and considers if they substantially differed from the "rightist" ones.

The chapter concludes that the left introduced a paradigmatic change in the region and triggered a modest circulation of elites that slightly oxygenated democracy. Yet in many countries the left/right dichotomy makes no sense for voters, and there are very few policy areas where the left has actually made a lasting impact. Hence, the chapter closes on a note of distrust and calls for a very careful use of the "Left" category in Latin America. It argues that there has been a wave of leftist governments in the region, provided we accept the restrictive lines defined in the following sections. Likewise, the observers already heralding a turn to the right in Latin America, following Macri's victory in the 2015 Argentine presidential election and the PT's misfortune in Brazil in 2016, would be well advised to think twice before they make the same unsubstantiated generalizations evoked in this chapter regarding the left.

DID THE LEFT CHANGE THE POLITICAL OFFER IN LATIN AMERICA?

In this section, I consider the political offer as composed of ideas and actors, or programs and partisan organizations and their leaders and candidates. Many analysts of the Left turn have used an ideational approach to show that the "New" Left introduced a paradigm change (Barrett, Chavez, and Rodríguez-Garavito 2008). A new leadership emerged, conveying an alternative to neoliberalism that was designed and ultimately implemented. Politicians with different social or ethnic and professional backgrounds replaced the typical white male Chicago or Harvard boys.

Looking first at discourse and ideas, there has definitively been a change that can parallel previous important path-defining moments in Latin American history. Not all of them were left/right swings, though. Paradigm shifts have always been crisis-induced, starting with the 1929 depression being followed by half a century of import substitution industrialization (ISI). After World War II, the ISI model was diffused in Latin America by the *técnicos* of the Economic Commission for Latin America and the Caribbean (ECLAC). Dependency theory was by then dominant. During the 1980s, the debt crisis precipitated another swing. The new ideas, first applied in authoritarian Chile during the second half of the 1970s, emphasized the imperative of international economic insertion. The notorious Washington Consensus, imposed on Latin America by International Monetary Fund (IMF) loans' attached conditionality, introduced market-friendly reforms in the region. The neoliberal climax came to an abrupt end in the late 1990s, with an amazing proliferation of financial crises around the globe. In Latin America, it prompted a massive repudiation of its founding principles. A new narrative emerged, blaming the "markets" for the social backwardness of the region. This new conjuncture opened up new opportunities for the left to win elections.

How useful is the left-right divide for understanding this series of paradigm shifts? The ISI model could hardly be labeled leftist or rightist. Many politicians in the region embraced it, in the name of developmentalism and nationalism. One of its major supporters, ECLAC's first secretary-general, Raúl Prebisch, was surely not a leftist, although he was suspected by some to be a neo-Marxist in the context of the Cold War (Dosman 2008). There was a polarized debate, but it was not structured along the left/right divide. The opponents of ISI were traditional neoclassical economists who could be labeled "conservatives." One of their prominent figures was the Brazilian Antônio Delfim Netto, finance minister between 1967 and 1973, during the military dictatorship. But the left was also critical of some aspects of the model. The first steps of the regional integration process, the 1960 Latin American Free Trade Association (LAFTA), led to an impressive penetration of foreign capital and North American multinationals in the region. Consequently, important leaders of the left, such as Eduardo Galeano, or exposers of the dependency theory, such as André Gunther Frank and Fernando Henrique Cardoso, lamented the "development of under-development" the model of regionalism entailed.[1] Conservatives attacked ISI's protectionism, while the left denounced its imperialism. There was no clear-cut left-right cleavage regarding the ISI model.

In a way, the polarization became simpler with the neoliberal model. The Latin American left opposed vigorously its main tenets, echoing a global resistance, while the right defended it on an ideological basis or in the name of pragmatism and necessary adaptation to globalization. The elaboration of an alternative model started at the beginning of the 1990s. The objective was to bring social issues back to the top of the political agenda. And the method consisted in resuscitating a state-led strategy of development. The ambition was to craft redistributive policies that could efficiently reduce poverty and inequality. The São Paulo Forum (SPF) was a fascinating incubator for this new doctrine. Starting in 1990, the yearly gathering of all leftist Latin American organizations never produced a coherent set of beliefs or a blueprint for a government program. The final declarations read like long lists of critiques of the dominant neoliberal order, with some suggestions to reverse it with policy shifts. Yet, even if there was no clear leftist equivalent to the Washington Consensus and Marxism was not replaced, the SPF helped build a network of organizations that, over the years, managed to do some brainstorming and elaborate many sectorial proposals. When the left started to win elections at the turn of the millennium, the early birds experimented with solutions and later shared their best practices.[2] The SPF was also instrumental in solidifying networks of solidarity that would later be activated to rebuild regionalism on a different, post-trade, basis (Tussie and Riggirozzi 2012).

A genuine leftist identity emerged from these meetings. However, from the beginning, the left was also very diversified. Forty-eight organizations attended the first meeting in São Paulo on July 4, 1990, with dissimilar ideological references. They all shared an aversion to neoliberalism and to the United States as its main exporter, but they disagreed on a lot of economic, political, environmental, cultural, and international issues. There was no consensus regarding the magnitude of the liquidation of the neoliberal legacy, for instance. When the commodity export boom erupted, all leftist governments took advantage of the extractivist model of development and welcomed foreign investors to develop mining activities, at the expense of the environment and traditional culture conservation. In some cases, like the Belo Monte dam in Brazil, the PT managed to garner support from some social movements against environment activists. In other Andean cases, leftist governments unevenly asked for the Indigenous populations' previous consent, even when their country had ratified the International Labor Organization's (ILO's) Convention 169.[3] That generated divisions between the "green" left and the "developmentalist" one, with the latter a clear winner (Bratman, this volume).

Over the years, the Latin American left grew further polarized, both within and across countries, to a point that the dichotomies mentioned earlier did capture part of the reality. There were three main contentious issues: political, economic, and international. Without going into details, there were discrepancies regarding the way to build a "popular" democracy. The increase of state intervention in the economy was also discussed. And finally, anti-imperialism was more or less popular among leftist leaders. Based on rhetoric (the policy outcomes are examined in the last section), there was definitively an ambitious "revolutionary" left, as opposed to a more "reformist" one. Or as Weyland (2010) put it, there was a "contestatory" and a "moderate" left. The former Bolivarian one was a source of inspiration for a lot of movements worldwide (especially in southern Europe), while the latter hardly differentiated itself from moderate conservative governments. In a nutshell, however gradual and diversified it has been, the paradigmatic change introduced by the left is difficult to deny.

Moving on to the leaders side of the political offer, there was also a change. As compared to other historical periods, a summit of Latin American presidents during the 2000–2009 decade offered an original photo opportunity. There were fewer formal suits and ties, not only because there were more women, but also because some presidents like Evo Morales (Bolivia) or Rafael Correa (Ecuador) wore traditional Indigenous-inspired shirts. Fashion always carries symbols, in that case, a diversification and a rupture with white males who had dominated politics for centuries. Much has been said about the new profiles of the leftist leaders who won elections: women, Indigenous leaders, trade union members, workers, and so on. Too often, the conclusions reached are based on the examination of very few cases, namely, the presidents. There is no doubt that the elections of Lula in Brazil and Morales in Bolivia were important symbols. They reshuffled the cards, proving that representative democracy is not a closed game for popular sectors. Yet, did the Left turn entail a broader change of politicians?

A study of Brazil, where Lula and Dilma Rousseff have personified the accession to power of new categories, shows that the change was superficial but not negligible (Louault 2012). There were more women in Lula's first government than in all combined governments since the return of democracy in 1985, and even more during Dilma's first term. The feminization reached the top of the administrative staff within the ministries. The number of trade union members or activists turned ministers also exploded with Lula's presidency, at the expense of the private sector. Dilma, however, was surrounded by economists and lawyers, going back to the more traditional pattern of elite recruitment. Looking at the parliament, the conclusions are straightforward. The left was not able to curb the domination of traditional elites, mainly because the incumbents are frequently reelected in Brazil. The specificity of the Brazilian political system, known as coalitional presidentialism, probably makes this country a least-likely case regarding elite circulation. As such, and in the absence of comparative empirical evidence, it is difficult to offer broader conclusions for other countries in Latin America. Bolivia comes to mind as a potential case of more important renewal of its political class that would deserve close scrutiny.

However, it is fair to say that the left only modestly opened the playing field. Over time, this limited political circulation may undermine the whole legitimacy of the equalitarian leftist project. The left supporters may end up considering that a "citizen revolution" (Ecuador) not translating into opportunities to actually be part of the decision-making process is just another example of politicians lying in their faces.

DOES THE LEFT/RIGHT DIVIDE MAKE SENSE FOR THE LATIN AMERICAN VOTER?

The Left turn is usually associated with a series of electoral victories of new self-proclaimed leftist leaders. Does this mean that Latin American voters expressed a preference for the left? There is room to doubt it. Different surveys showed that the left was the beneficiary of a vote against neoliberalism triggered by an economic crisis more than a vote in favor of its projects. There was no evolution of public opinion in favor of the left, according to Latinobarómetro's self-placement index, or electoral realignment (Arnold and Samuels 2011). There was, as Baker and Greene (2011) put it, a declining enthusiasm for market reforms.

In the 1990s, "outsiders"[4] initially harnessed the frustration of the middle class over their loss of purchasing power and anger at "traditional" political parties. These outsiders soon lost their credibility by implementing the same neoliberal policies they had criticized during their campaigns (Stokes 2001). This opened the way for the left, which appeared free of all compromise with the corrupt political classes and could not be blamed for the social impact of structural adjustment. In other words, the turn to the left in Latin America was first and foremost a swing of the pendulum back toward the center brought about by the economic crisis of the years 1998–2002. The explanation for the many victories of the left in the years 2006–9 is different. It was a vote of appreciation for the performance of the leftist incumbents, in a most favorable economic climate (commodity boom).

In both cases, however, we are dealing with a rational vote, punishing or supporting the incumbents for their policy records. That should not come as a surprise, if we agree with Elizabeth Zechmeister when she claims that "the political significance of the left-right semantics in Latin America is comparatively quite low" (2015, 196). Results from surveys (LAPOP 2008) show that the left/right notions have no meaning for 20 percent of the respondents (a nonresponse rate similar to the one in Eastern Europe), ranging from 8 percent in Uruguay to 32 percent in Ecuador. In 2012, the average nonresponse was 18.6 percent, with a minimum of 9.3 percent in Uruguay to 38.1 percent in Costa Rica. For the rest, the notions have a meaning mainly related to economic policy preferences: support for free trade or a market economy (as opposed to an active state role in the economy) is a good predictor of rightist inclination, at least in some countries and for the respondents with high political knowledge. In Brazil and Venezuela, it does not work at all (Zechmeister and Corral 2010).

There are significant differences across countries, though. In Brazil, Ames and Smith found that "while the levels of left-right self-identification are fairly high, many Brazilians able to identify their own position on the left-right spectrum do not have a clear understanding of an ideological content behind it" (2010, 28). Comparing Mexico to Argentina, Zechmeister found that in the former, "left-right ideological labels show an ability to orient individuals with respect to relevant policy divides and with respect to political choices (PRD vs. PAN)," while "left-right semantics are clearly less politically useful in Argentina" (2006, 165).

In addition, the Latin American Public Opinion Project (LAPOP 2008) shows a large number of respondents with a centrist self-placement: 38.2 percent in Colombia, 41.4 percent in Ecuador, 46.3 percent in Bolivia, 46.2 percent in Peru, 48.4 percent in Paraguay, 51.8 percent in Chile, 34.4 percent in Uruguay, 41.3 percent in Brazil, 42.4 percent in Venezuela, and 46.8 percent in Argentina. That too could reveal confusion vis-à-vis the left/right categories. We can assume that another way to refuse the left/right scale consists in declaring neutrality, a dimension that has not received sufficient attention in the literature. When voters do accept the left/right scale, Zechmeister found, "self-placements are minimally or not at all connected to voter choice in many Latin American countries" (2015, 209). Two factors seriously hinder the greater relevance of self-placement to predict the vote: fragmentation (the higher the effective number of parties, the lower the clarity for the voter) and clientelism. More important still, Zechmeister found "no evidence that the pink tide significantly altered the nature and political relevance of left-right leanings in Latin America" (2015, 215). This result clearly runs counter to the belief that the turn to the left has had a polarizing effect among voters. Zechmeister has an important point. Party-voter linkages in Latin America are not only characterized by clientelism. There are ideological components of voting behavior, but there is no coherent set of preferences that coalesce to form an ideology. Again, this finding contradicts the idea that the radical left managed to elaborate a sort of postneoliberal ideology (Cameron, this volume).

Even if a preference for a market economy is a predictor of a rightist vote, the question remains, are there any other shared beliefs? Nina Wiesehomeier and David Doyle found that there are coherent ideological groups "which share common convictions regarding the responsibility of the state to level the playing field and its role in the national economy" (2012, 25). Again, is there more to it? Following Bobbio (1996), it could be argued that the crucial issue for defining the left lies in the way inequality is addressed. However, we lack empirical evidence to prove that voters have a preference for the left on those grounds.

Zechmeister's conclusion could very well summarize the point made in this chapter: "A healthy dose of skepticism with respect to the heuristic value of the Left-Right semantics is warranted when considering the Latin American voter" (2015, 216).

Indeed, the last section of this chapter adds further justifications to this call for prudence.

DID THE LEFTIST GOVERNMENTS' POLICY OUTCOMES DIFFER FROM THE RIGHTIST ONES IN LATIN AMERICA?

Answering this question obviously far exceeds the purpose of this chapter. However, some contributors to this volume have already provided valuable elements. This section relies on them and adds some remarks on the left's signature policy shifts.

This volume's chapters show that, for different reasons, the so-called leftist policies did not differ much from the more rightist ones. In addition, some found that the left did not make much of a difference in addressing certain issues such as violence (Kessler),[5] Indigenous-state relations (Rice),[6] sexual rights (Díez),[7] domestic workers (Blofield),[8] or sustainable development (Bratman).[9]

If we turn to the left's signature policies, like the ones designed to reduce poverty and inequality or to expand social protection coverage and benefits, there is ample evidence that the policy instruments were convergent between the left and the right (see Nagels, this volume). The outcomes were also very comparable. And when the outcomes were dissimilar, the left/right divide did not appear to be the most accurate explanation.

According to ECLAC experts, "The region's countries clearly differ in the progress they have made towards strengthening their social protection systems and in their preferences with regard to policy instruments." More precisely:

> The greatest advances have been in countries whose welfare gaps were smallest to begin with, namely Argentina, Brazil, Chile, Uruguay and, to a lesser extent, Panama. Four cases are exceptions to this generalization: Ecuador, El Salvador, the Plurinational State of

Bolivia and, to a lesser extent, Mexico have made progress despite having wide (or, in the case of Mexico, moderate) welfare gaps. Colombia and Peru, whose welfare gaps are moderate, have made progress, although initiatives there have not always been sound. The Dominican Republic and Paraguay have some interesting policies and programs, but their level of fiscal commitment is still very low. Progress has been most modest in Guatemala, Honduras and Nicaragua, where welfare gaps are large. (Cecchini et al. 2015, 26)

There is no clear pattern of the left being more efficient than the right if we consider this ECLAC evaluation.

More than the political orientation of a given government, what really seems to matter is the ability to reach an overarching agreement, a "compact," such as in Mexico, Chile, and Uruguay (Maldonado 2015). Consensus building beyond the left/right divide is the key, much more than the dominant position of the left allowing a government to freely implement its program.

Mexico epitomized the importance of consensus building. The first poverty alleviation program, offering conditional cash transfers, was launched in 1997, at a time when the Partido Revolucionario Institucional (Institutional Revolutionary Party, or PRI; center right) held the presidency. The program was later expanded even though the PRI lost the elections in 2000 to the Partido Acción Nacional (National Action Party, or PAN; right). In 2004, the Mexican congress unanimously passed an ambitious social development act.

In addition to social pacts, comparing Argentina, Chile, Uruguay, and Venezuela, Jennifer Pribble (2013) found that policy legacy, electoral competition, and the ideology and organization of political parties shaped social reforms.

If we focus on the crucial issues of poverty and inequality reduction, the same conclusion can be reached. The left/right divide is not relevant for explaining policy performances. The most efficient countries regarding poverty alleviation between 2010 and 2014 were leftist Uruguay and rightist Peru (ECLAC 2016). Moreover, there was substantial inequality reduction in left-leaning countries such as Brazil and Bolivia, but Mexico and Colombia with rightist governments were efficient as well. True, there is always a debate about the metrics used to gauge inequalities. The Gini index, based on the top 10 percent as compared to the next 40 percent, might not account for some extreme concentration of wealth, as Piketty (2013) convincingly showed looking at France and the United States. As the Piketty "top 1 percent" methodology becomes influential around the world, there is now plenty of empirical evidence about the golden years (2003–8) that saw an impressive increase in the number of millionaires in the region. Studying inequalities in Brazil over the long run, Souza and Medeiros (2015) showed that "the apparent decline in the Gini coefficient recorded by surveys in 2006–2012 vanishes once we correct for the underestimation of top incomes." In some countries governed by the left, a category of nouveaux riches emerged. Popular common sense, prompt to mock the contradictions of the left, coined the terms *boliburgesía* (bourgeoisie linked to the Bolivarian Revolution in Venezuela), *burgesía chola* (Indigenous bourgeoisie in Bolivia under Morales), and *empresarios K* (businessmen with political ties to the Kirchner family in Argentina) to describe this new hyperconcentration of wealth. These social evolutions were made possible because the left increased state intervention in the economy, especially in Brazil, where it was broader than in any other Latin America countries (Schneider 2016).

On a more political note, the left consistently put the emphasis on the need to "democratize democracy," adding some participatory components to representative practices. Participatory budgeting, as popularized by Porto Alegre (Brazil), became another signature policy of the left (Goldfrank, this volume). Yet, for two reasons, there is room to nuance that statement. First, the early generation of constitutional reforms introducing participatory devices dates to the end of the 1980s, in a Latin America still under the influence of neoliberalism. The Brazilian (1988) and Colombian (1991) constitutions were much-praised examples. And so was the 1994 Bolivian Law of Popular Participation, enacted by the neoliberal president Gonzalo Sánchez de Lozada. After the turn to the left swept the continent, many conservative mayors also allowed the citizens to oversee public expenditures and somehow be part of the decision-making process. And second, even if participatory budgeting was widely adopted by PT-run municipalities in Brazil in 2000, it was not always for the assumed "good" reasons. The party leaders were undoubtedly sincere believers in the virtues of participation, but they also submitted part of the budget to local assemblies' deliberation because they were looking for ways to strategically circumvent municipal assemblies where they could not rely on a majority of votes. In a way, they developed participatory democracy against representative democracy (Ribeiro Dias 2002).

In the same vein, some leaders like Hugo Chávez, Rafael Correa, and Evo Morales spent much of their first mandate refounding a political order with a new constitution that entailed a modified balance of power favoring the "people." The citizen revolution in Ecuador sought to expand the scope of participation to all of the policy-making process. In Venezuela, article 70 of the 1999 Constitution included a long list of forms of political participation: voting to fill public offices; referendums; recall referendums; legislative, constitutional, and constituent initiatives; the open town hall; and the Citizens' Assembly, whose decisions are binding. In addition, at the local level, the communal councils (*consejos comunales*) were supposed to empower popular organizations, allowing the communities to plan their own development.

This effort of participation promotion had unexpected consequences. All the leaders faced the dilemma of decentralizing and disseminating power while keeping a firm grip on the revolutionary processes. They all sought to secure electoral victories at all costs. In Venezuela, more than anywhere else with the exception of Nicaragua, electoral campaigns were not fair and balanced (IACHR 2009). The most radical of the leftist experiments ran the risk of falling into the category of competitive authoritarianism (Levitsky and Way 2002). Yet this regression could hardly be considered a specificity of the left. Fujimori in Peru and Mexico for decades were landmark antecedents, not to mention the way some military regimes used to organize elections "without choice" (Hermet, Rouquié, and Rose 1978). All in all, some leaders may have undermined representative democracy; yet it would be excessive to throw out the baby with the bathwater. Some real progress was made regarding participatory democracy and empowerment of until then disenfranchised categories, and the left can legitimately claim credit for it. As the literature on subnational politics has clearly showed, different qualities of democracy can coexist in a given country. There can be more participatory democracy at the local level and less representative democracy at the national level (Giraudy 2010).

A final remark concerns policy instruments. We know how crucial they are to convert intentions and policies into desirable outcomes. For reasons that would deserve a systematic exploration, it might be that the left neglected them. In his chapter in this volume, Max Cameron makes an interesting point when he asserts:

> The transformative potential of progressive policies has often gone unfulfilled due to the manner in which they have been implemented. Recent "Left turn" governments in Latin America have implemented redistributive and participatory policies without reinforcing civil liberties, the rule of law, and restraints on the abuses of power, thereby threatening to turn well-meaning policies and institutions into instruments of clientelistic control, partisan co-optation, and bureaucratic domination.

Yet, again, is that specific to the left? When it comes to assessing the "transformative potential of progressive policies," what really matters are state capacities. Leftist and rightist governments in Latin America are equally concerned with potential governability deficits (Brassiolo et al. 2016). Probably the only leftist government that made a substantial effort to improve state capacities was Ecuador. It remained an exception.

It could be argued that any transformative intention has to be supported by an extra effort regarding the consolidation of institutions. In the 1970s, Albert Hirschman (1973) already convincingly highlighted that point. The left probably paid a lot more attention to the global architecture (new constitutions) than to the construction materials (institutions). Worse, it did not dismantle the web of independent agencies created by neoliberals and used to operate with neoliberal software (Maillet and Mayaux 2012).

In that sense, the left did not invent a type of governance of its own. In Brazil, the once-publicized *modo PT de governar* (PT way of governing), a mix of political opening, fiscal responsibility, and resistance to traditional clientelism and corruption, is now bitterly mocked by Brazilians.

Scholarly common sense considers that without institutionalization and state capacity improvement, the policies are not resilient and can be easily reversed. These policy-making features are not defined by the political inclination of the governments, left or right.

Let me add three distinctions that help account for the policy-making processes better than the left/right one. Two have to do with the way decisions are made, one with the content of the decisions. They partially overlap with the left/right dimension, but they are more specific.

1) Participatory/centralist. As mentioned above, the left tried to improve the quality of democracy, adding a participatory dimension. Yet it was not exclusive of leftist governments. Latin American governments are constantly trying to strike a balance between top-down and bottom-up decision making. And both neoliberal- and leftist-sponsored participatory democracies face the same dilemma of sustainability in the face of participation fatigue and politicization.

2) Responsive/programmatic or reactive/planning. The issue here is how to respond to demonstrators taking to the streets. How to deal with social movements, especially in times of changing economic conditions? Does democracy give the elected governments a mandate to implement their planned programs, or are they supposed to adapt and meet new demands? Those are important issues that transcend the left/right divide.

3) Progressive/conservative. The question that arises is whether Latin American governments have granted new rights. The responses partially overlap with the left/right divide but with exceptions. The emblematic Uruguayan president Pepe Mujica used to criticize same-sex marriage, abortion, and marijuana legalization as bourgeois rights. Although he did not block the reforms, he was more interested in social rights than in so-called postmodern ones.

If we take same-sex marriage as a yardstick, there is no clear pattern between left and right (Díez, this volume). Among the six countries that legalized marriage or other types of partnership in South America, five were leftists when they passed legislation (Argentina, Brazil, Uruguay, Chile, and Ecuador, with Colombia being the exception). Yet we also have three leftist countries among the list of seven where it is not recognized or banned (Venezuela, Ecuador, Bolivia, along with Peru, Guyana, Suriname, and Paraguay).

Hirschman (1973) pointed out some characteristic features of policy making in Latin America, such as the poor selection of problems to tackle or the motivation to act without proper understanding of the problems. The first two distinctions suggested here, participatory/centralist and responsive/programmatic, follow the same logic of describing a "Latin American style" beyond partisan cleavages. The third one sets the record straight regarding the amalgam left-progressive as opposed to right-conservative. All three would evidently deserve further exploration.

Where does this series of skeptical remarks lead us? I'm not arguing that the left/right distinction is useless. I showed in this chapter that the left partially changed the political offer, introducing an alternative program to break away from neoliberalism and new elites with a different profile. This conclusion is compatible with Kenneth Roberts's point regarding the way the Left turn revived a programmatic competition in the region (Roberts, this volume). However, I tend to consider that the contrast with ancient times' ideologically undifferentiated patronage machines should not be overrated. Some parties in the past were programmatic, and many leftist parties today, such as the PT in Brazil, have turned into efficient patronage machines.

I also contend that the left had a meaning for some voters in some countries and helped them define their vote. Finally, in some policy areas, the left managed to introduce some reforms. My point is to call for cautious use of the left/right dichotomy.

With the exception of Venezuela, Latin America is a better place to live today compared to fifteen or twenty years ago, and in many countries, the left can legitimately claim some credit for it. This improved well-being is particularly important for lower social categories who benefited from citizenship extension. Yet, regarding the three dimensions of citizenship suggested by the editors of this volume, the progress has been modest. As Abbott and Levistky (this volume) argue, the left made a difference for social and participatory rights, much more than for liberal-democratic ones.

The left has been very lucky to govern during an exceptional half decade. The real test of its resilience is its capacity to muddle through harsh times. In 2015–16, the picture for the left seemed gloomy, from Brazil to Venezuela or even in Chile. But is it really? In the vein of this chapter, I would argue that the fact that the left is in trouble now has nothing to do with the left being the left. It owes more to the mechanical effect of time and adverse economic conditions eroding the governments' approval rates. Incumbents are in trouble, and if many of them happened to be leftists, it is simply because there were many leftist governments on the map of Latin America during the past decade.

NOTES

José Solares, University of California, Irvine, senior student, provided efficient research assistantship for this piece while doing an internship at Sciences Po's Political Observatory for Latin America and the Caribbean (OPALC) in June 2016.

1. I surveyed the "leftist" conceptions of regional integration in chapter 11 of Dabène 2012 (titled "Au-delà du régionalisme ouvert: La gauche face au piège de la souveraineté et de la flexibilité").

2. Participatory budgeting is an emblematic example of such policy diffusion.

3. All but a few Latin American countries have ratified the Indigenous and Tribal Convention, including the Andean ones developing devastating mining activities on Indigenous lands.

4. This notion was developed to describe politicians who did not come from the political class and whose campaign theme was "antipolitics." Alberto Fujimori, president of Peru from 1990 to 2000, is one such outsider.

5. See also Kessler 2016.

6. See also Rice 2016.

7. See also Díez 2016. Regarding sexual rights, the scoreboard presented by Díez was emblematic of the confusion: Uruguay (left) was first, but Colombia and Mexico (right) were second, and Venezuela (left) was last.

8. See also Blofield 2016. The author found that "programmatic left-wing governments have tended to be less maternalist than nonleft governments and more likely to increase public services rather than cash transfers and subsidies."

9. See also Bratman 2016.

REFERENCES

Ames, Barry, and Amy Erica Smith. 2010. "Knowing Left from Right: Ideological Identification in Brazil, 2002–2006." *Journal of Politics in Latin America* 2 (3): 3–38.

Angell, Alan. 1995. "The Left in Latin America since c. 1920." In Leslie Bethell, ed., *The Cambridge History of Latin America*. Cambridge: Cambridge University Press.

Arnold, Jason Ross, and David Samuels. 2011. "Evidence from Public Opinion." In Steven Levitsky and Kenneth M. Roberts, eds., *The Resurgence of the Latin American Left*. Baltimore, MD: Johns Hopkins University Press.

Baker, Andy, and Kenneth F. Greene. 2011. "The Latin American Left's Mandate: Free-Market Policies and Issue Voting in New Democracies." *World Politics* 63 (1): 43–77.

Barrett, Patrick, Daniel Chavez, and César Rodríguez-Garavito. 2008. *The New Latin American Left: Utopia Reborn*. London: Pluto Press.

Blofield, Merike. 2016. "Moving Away from Maternalism? Policies on Work and the Family in Latin America in the Past Decade." Paper presented at RÉLAM conference, "What's Left? The Left Turn in Latin America, 15 Years After," Montreal, March 23–25.

Bobbio, Norberto. 1996. *Left and Right: The Significance of a Political Distinction*. Chicago: University of Chicago Press.

Brassiolo, Palbo, Pablo Sanguinetti, Fernando Álvarez, Luis Quintero, Lucila Berniell, Dolores de la Mata, Lesbia Maris, and Daniel Ortega. 2016. *A More Effective State: Capacities for Designing, Implementing, and Evaluating Public Policies*. Bogotá: RED 2015.

Bratman, Eve. 2016. "The Leftist Politics of Sustainable Development in the Amazon." Paper presented at RÉLAM conference, "What's Left? The Left Turn in Latin America, 15 Years After," Montreal, March 23–25 .

Cameron, Maxwell A., and Eric Hershberg, eds. 2010. *Latin America's Left Turns: Politics, Policies, and Trajectories of Change*. Boulder, CO: Lynne Rienner.

Cecchini, Simone, Fernando Filgueira, Rodrigo Martínez, and Cecilia Rossel. 2015. *Towards Universal Social Protection: Latin American Pathways and Policy Tools*. Santiago de Chile: ECLAC.

Dabène, Olivier. 2012. *La gauche en Amérique latine, 1998–2012*. Paris: Presses de Sciences Po.

Díez, Jordi. 2016. "How Velvet Was the Pink Tide?" Paper presented at RÉLAM conference, "What's Left? The Left Turn in Latin America, 15 Years After," Montreal, March 23–25.

Dosman, Edgar. 2008. *The Life and Times of Raúl Prebisch, 1901–1986*. Montreal: McGill-Queen's Press-MQUP.

Giraudy, Agustina. 2010. "The Politics of Subnational Undemocratic Regime Reproduction in Argentina and Mexico." *Journal of Politics in Latin America* 2 (2): 53–84.

Hermet, Guy, Alain Rouquié, and Richard Rose. 1978. *Elections without Choice*. London: Wiley.

Hirschman, Albert O. 1973. *Journeys toward Progress: Studies of Economic Policy-Making in Latin America*. Boulder, CO: Westview Press.

Inter-American Commission on Human Rights (IACHR). 2009. *Democracy and Human Rights in Venezuela*. Washington, DC: Organization of American States (OAS).

Kessler, Gabriel. 2016. "Changes in Urban Crime in Argentina: From the 'Neoliberal Period' to 'the Left Turn.'" Paper presented at RÉLAM conference, "What's Left? The Left Turn in Latin America, 15 Years After," Montreal, March 23–25.

Latin American Public Opinion Project (LAPOP). 2008. "The AmericasBarometer by the Latin American Public Opinion Project (LAPOP)." www.vanderbilt.edu/lapop/about-americasbarometer.php.

Levitsky, Steven, and Kenneth M. Roberts. 2011. "Conclusion: Democracy, Development, and the Left." In Steven Levitsky and Kenneth M. Roberts, eds., *The Resurgence of the Latin American Left*. Baltimore, MD: Johns Hopkins University Press.

Levitsky, Steven, and Lucan Way. 2002. "The Rise of Competitive Authoritarianism." *Journal of Democracy* 13 (2): 51–65.

Louault, Frédéric. 2012. "Un renouvellement brésilien en trompe-l'oeil?" In Olivier Dabène, ed., *La Gauche en Amérique Latine*. Paris: Presses de Sciences Po.

Luna, Juan Pablo. 2010. "The Left Turns: Why They Happened and How They Compare." In Max Cameron, ed., *Latin America's Left Turns: Politics, Policies and Trajectories of Change*. Boulder, CO: Lynne Rienner.

Maillet, Antoine, and Pierre-Louis Mayaux. 2012. "Gérer l'héritage de l'état neoliberal: Les gauches Latino-américaines face aux régulateurs indépendants." In Olivier Dabène, ed., *La Gauche en Amérique Latine, 1998–2012*. Paris: Presses de Sciences Po.

Maldonado, Carlos. 2015. "Building Compacts for Social Protection." In Simone Cecchini, Fernando Filgueira, Rodrigo Martínez, and Cecilia Rossel, eds., *Towards Universal Social Protection: Latin American Pathways and Policy Tools*. Santiago de Chile: ECLAC.

Mariátegui, José Carlos. 1971. *Seven Interpretive Essays on Peruvian Reality*. Austin: University of Texas Press.

O'Donnell, Guillermo, and Philippe C. Schmitter. 1986. *Transitions from Authoritarian Rule: Tentative Conclusions about Uncertain Democracies*. Baltimore, MD: Johns Hopkins University Press.

Piketty, Thomas. 2013. *Le capital au XXIe siècle*. Paris: Le Seuil.

Pribble, Jennifer. 2013. *Welfare and Party Politics in Latin America*. New York: Cambridge University Press.

Ribeiro Dias, Marcia. 2002. *Sob o signo da vontade popular: O orçamento participativo e o dilema da Câmara Municipal de Porto Alegre*. Belo Horizonte: Editora UFMG.

Rice, Roberta. 2016. "Indigenous-State Relations and the New Left: Challenges and Opportunities." Paper presented at RÉLAM conference, "What's Left? The Left Turn in Latin America, 15 Years After," Montreal, March 23–25.

Schneider, Ben Ross. 2016. *New Order and Progress: Development and Democracy in Brazil*. Oxford: Oxford University Press.

Souza, Pedro, and Marcelo Medeiros. 2015. "Top Income Shares and Inequality in Brazil, 1928–2012." *Journal of the Brazilian Sociological Society* 1 (1): 119–32.

Stokes, Susan C. 2001. *Mandates and Democracy: Neoliberalism by Surprise in Latin America*. New York: Cambridge University Press.

Tussie, Diana, and Pia Riggirozzi. 2012. *The Rise of Post-Hegemonic Regionalism: The Case of Latin America*. London: Springer.

United Nations Economic Commission for Latin America and the Caribbean (ECLAC). 2016. *Social Panorama of Latin America 2015*. Santiago de Chile: ECLAC. www.cepal.org/en/publications/39964-social-panorama -latin-america-2015.

Weyland, Kurt. 2010. "The Performance of Leftist Governments in Latin America." In Kurt Weyland, Raúl Madrid, and Wendy Hunter, eds., *Leftist Governments in Latin America: Successes and Shortcomings*. Cambridge: Cambridge University Press.

Wiesehomeier, Nina. 2010. "The Meaning of Left-Right in Latin America: A Comparative View." Kellog Institute Working Paper. https://kellogg.nd .edu/documents/1686.

Wiesehomeier, Nina, and David Doyle. 2012. "Attitudes, Ideological Associations and the Left-Right Divide in Latin America." *Journal of Politics in Latin America* 4 (1): 3–33.

Young, Kevin. 2013. "The Good, the Bad, and the Benevolent Interventionist: US Press and Intellectual Distortions of the Latin American Left." *Latin American Perspectives* 40 (3): 207–25.

Zechmeister, Elizabeth. 2006. "What's Left and Who's Right? A Q-Method Study of Individual and Contextual Influences on the Meaning of Ideological Labels." *Political Behavior* 28 (2): 151–73.

———. 2015. "Left-Right Identifications and the Latin American Voter." In Ryan Carly, Matthew Singer, and Elizabeth Zechmeister, eds., *The Latin*

American Voter: Pursuing Representation and Accountability in Challenging Contexts. Ann Arbor: University of Michigan Press.

Zechmeister, Elizabeth, and Margarita Corral. 2010. "The Varying Economic Meaning of 'Left' and 'Right' in Latin America." *AmericasBarometer Insights Series* 38: 1–10.

FOURTEEN

The Left Turn and Citizenship

How Much Has Changed?

JARED ABBOTT AND STEVEN LEVITSKY

The aim of this concluding chapter is to more systematically examine the relationship between left government and citizenship expansion during the Left turn. What general claims can we make about the extent of citizenship extension, or about the left's impact on citizenship extension, over the past two decades? We address these questions by taking up the editors' call to answer the following questions: (1) Do citizenship regimes now reach traditionally excluded sectors to a greater extent than they did prior to the Left turn? And (2) what are the legacies of the Left turn in Latin America?

In answering the first question, we provide a framework for assessing citizenship extension by disaggregating citizenship into three dimensions: (1) liberal democratic rights, which combine Marshall's (1950) civil and political rights; (2) social rights, and (3) active citizenship, or participatory rights. For each dimension we develop a set of indicators that can be measured to yield yearly country-level scores assessing the extent to which the extension of each set of rights has occurred across Latin America during the Left turn. We find a marked expansion of citizenship rights along all three dimensions during the Left turn. On two dimensions—social and participatory rights—the degree of rights extension was greater in countries led by left-of-center governments than under those governed by the right (though only slightly greater in the case of participatory rights). In the aggregate, however, we find no significant difference in rights extension between countries governed by the left and those governed by the right. Radical left-driven rights expansion on the social and participatory dimensions is effectively canceled out by the erosion of liberal democratic rights.

Like those of Olivier Dabène (this volume), then, our findings are modest. Although partisan ideology is indeed an important factor in determining the extent of rights extensions, its role should not be overstated. As various contributions to this volume show, other factors—such as state (in)capacity and the incentives and constraints imposed by capitalist economies and democratic institutions—weigh heavily in shaping both policy change and policy implementation. Social democratic governments often yielded to these economic and institutional constraints, resulting in more modest rights expansion; radical left governments challenged (and sometimes overcame) these constraints in the pursuit of more far-reaching social and participatory rights expansion, but these efforts often came at the cost of violating liberal democratic rights. Further, as Goldfrank's chapter makes clear, the sustainability of advances made by radical left governments in these areas is in doubt. Finally, in examining the legacies of the Left turn, we argue that although the Left turn has contributed to several longer-term changes in Latin American societies and polities, including increasing the political efficacy of traditionally marginalized groups and laying a foundation for the development of more inclusive welfare states, an analysis of public opinion data on citizenship extensions raises questions about their sustainability.

MEASURING CITIZENSHIP EXTENSIONS

To take stock of the extent of citizenship extension during the Left turn, we begin by offering a basic framework for measuring citizenship rights. We do this by disaggregating citizenship into the three classic Marshallian categories of civil, political, and social rights (Marshall 1950) and by adding the dimension of participatory rights. We define participatory rights as mechanisms of political participation that allow citizens to engage actively in shaping political or policy outcomes, either through new forms of participatory democracy or through enhanced engagement in civil society organizations. We then combine Marshall's civil and political rights into a single dimension, which we call liberal democratic rights. That leaves us with three dimensions—liberal democratic, social, and participatory rights—that, taken together, yield a reasonable measure of citizenship in a given country. The indicators of each dimension are presented in appendix 14.1.[1] With this framework in place, we now proceed to examine changes along each dimension during the Left turn.

Liberal Democratic Rights

To capture liberal democratic rights, we use the Liberal Democracy Index of Varieties of Democracy (VDEM) (2017). This measure includes a range of indicators that capture the combination of civil and political rights described in appendix 14.1.[2] In figures 14.1 and 14.2 below, we report VDEM scores for left and right governments, as well as for radical and social democratic left governments (see appendix 14.2 for coding), for the 1999–2015 period.[3] We compare the average VDEM score for each type of government at the beginning and end of their period in office. Figures 14.1 and 14.2 show a slight overall increase in the exercise of liberal democratic rights in countries with right-leaning governments and a slight decrease in the exercise of these rights in left-governed countries. The real difference, however, lies between radical and social democratic left governments: whereas the social democratic cases experienced no change in liberal democracy scores, the radical left cases suffered a sharp decline. Thus, the overall difference between left and right governments is driven by three radical left cases: Venezuela, Bolivia, and Ecuador. Given the widely documented limitations of radical left governments with respect to political and especially civil liberties (Cameron and Hershberg 2010; Castañeda 2006; Handlin 2015; Levitsky and Roberts 2011; Weyland, Madrid,

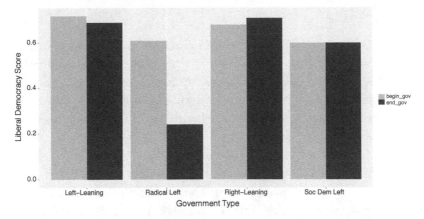

FIGURE 14.1. Change in Liberal Democracy Scores. *Source*: Coppedge et al. 2017.

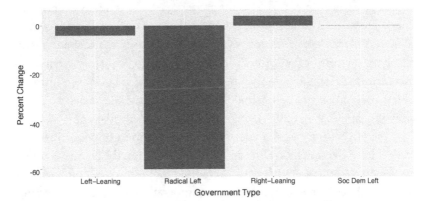

FIGURE 14.2. Percent Change in Liberal Democracy Scores during the Left Turn (VDEM). *Source*: Coppedge et al. 2017.

and Hunter 2010), this is not a surprising finding. The slight increase in liberal democracy scores in countries with right-leaning governments can be attributed largely to Peru's democratization in 2000, a decline in violence in Colombia, and modest steps toward democratic consolidation and human rights protection in postconflict Central American countries. Thus, beyond radical left governments in Bolivia, Ecuador, and Venezuela, which challenged some of the core tenets of liberal democracy (Cameron and Hershberg 2010), there is little evidence that partisanship or ideology shaped liberal democratic rights extension during the Left turn.

Social Rights

We turn now to the extension of social rights. To measure social rights, we draw on data from the United Nations Commission on Latin America and the Caribbean (ECLAC) that offers government spending figures (as a share of GDP) for education, housing, pensions, unemployment insurance, antipoverty programs, and health care for all Latin American countries during the Left turn (ECLAC 2017). There is some variation across ideological type on each of these dimensions, but since our objective is to broadly summarize rights extension during the Left turn, we sum them up for each country-year to generate a single number for social spending as a percentage of GDP. We then take the average level of social spending for each government type measured at the beginning and the end of each government. The results are reported in figures 14.3 and 14.4 below. Here we see a substantial difference between left and right governments. Whereas left-of-center governments increased social spending by nearly 20 percent in the 1999–2015 period, right-of-center governments increased social spending only 3 percent. Given the explicit commitment of left governments to addressing poverty, inequality, and social exclusion (Levitsky and Roberts 2011), these results are not surprising.

The largest increases in social spending occurred in countries with radical left governments, although it should be noted that these countries (Bolivia, Ecuador, Venezuela) benefited more from the commodities boom of the 2000s than either social democratic left or right-of-center governments (Campello 2013; Weyland 2009). Thus, it was not only radical left governance per se but also the fiscal flexibility afforded these governments by resource rents that explains the particularly large increase in social spending in countries like Bolivia, Ecuador, and Venezuela. That said, when we control for level of resource dependence (as a percentage of GDP) in a statistical analysis of the relationship between partisan ideology and social spending, we still find a substantial positive and statistically significant relationship between the presence of a radical left government and levels of social spending.

While our findings clearly suggest that radical left governments have performed the strongest with respect to the expansion of social rights, it is important to view these results with some circumspection. First, given

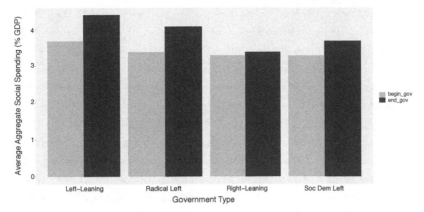

FIGURE 14.3. Change in Social Spending during the Left Turn (% GDP). *Source*: ECLAC 2017.

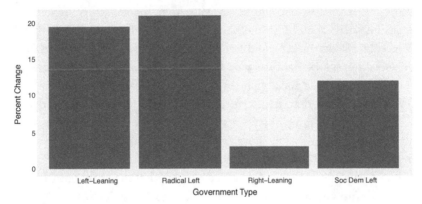

FIGURE 14.4. Percent Increase in Social Spending during the Left Turn. *Source*: ECLAC 2017.

the fact that radical left governments were led by relatively new and weakly institutionalized parties in countries with comparatively weak democratic institutions, the quality and sustainability of their projects are likely to be lower than those of social democratic governments, which were led by more institutionalized parties in more established democracies (e.g., Chile, Uruguay) (Huber and Stephens 2012; Pribble 2008). As Huber and Stephens (2012) have shown, weak party institutionalization and limited experience with democracy are associated with more dramatic but poorly designed policy innovations that tend to be less efficient or sustainable (e.g., Venezuela's Misiones). They also tend to give rise to strong partisan identification with radical left parties (Handlin 2017). Strong partisan identification of social programs with radical left parties has at least two negative consequences. First, it increases the likelihood of attempts to overturn these policies when opposition parties take power. Second, it can increase resistance to these programs from within the existing state bureaucracy, leading to the creation of unnecessary parallel institutions that carry out the same tasks as existing state agencies and/or to the incomplete implementation of programs (as bureaucrats simply choose not to implement aspects of a given program) (Abbott, Soifer, and Vom Hau 2017).

Given that social spending by radical left governments may be less efficiently allocated than government spending by social democratic governments, it could be the case that the relatively higher increase in social spending we observe by radical left compared to social democratic governments does not translate into greater positive effects on social outcomes. Scholars who have examined the impact of left-of-center governments' social policies on inequality and poverty reduction, for instance, find that after controlling for country-level fixed effects, social democratic governments actually have a more substantial impact on income inequality and poverty reduction than radical left governments (Cornia 2010; McLeod and Lustig 2011). This suggests that higher levels of social spending among radical left governments did not translate into commensurate effects on key social indicators, likely due to the inefficiency-producing mechanisms described above. Whether or not the impact of social spending by radical left governments will ultimately be less sustainable than that of social democratic governments is still an open question, though if recent backsliding on poverty and other key social outcomes in Venezuela (Universidad Católica de Venezuela 2017) is any indication,[4] they likely will be.

Participatory Rights

Finally, we turn to participatory rights, or channels through which traditionally excluded groups can increase their role in democratic decision making. This dimension includes (1) participatory-democratic mechanisms including (but not limited to) participatory budgeting, prior consultation, and policy councils; (2) direct-democratic mechanisms such as referendums and plebiscites; and (3) participation in associational life, either in political organizations (such as political parties) or in civil society organizations. To capture these dimensions, we construct aggregate scores based on the following:

(1) The density of participatory institutions in each country, as reported by the LATINNO dataset (LATINNO 2018).

(2) A modified version of VDEM's Participatory Democracy Index, which includes measures of direct democracy as well as the autonomy of civil society organizations from the state (a critical factor in determining whether civil society participation is genuinely rights enhancing or whether it simply reinforces existing hierarchical client-patron relationships).[5]

(3) A per country-year average of participation rates across a wide range of associational activities, as reported by LAPOP for 2006 and 2014. Specifically, we average participation rates in religious meetings, parent-teacher association meetings, city council meetings, community association meetings, meetings of political parties, rates at which individuals contact municipal officials, and rates at which individuals participate in protests. This set of indicators provides a representative summary of both directly political forms of associational activity (such as involvement with political parties) and indirectly political forms of associational activity (from community associations to parent-teacher associations).

Each variable is scaled from 0 to 1, so we simply take the average of the three to generate per-year participatory citizenship scores. Figures 14.5 and 14.6 present a summary of these scores by government type. Interestingly, despite the near-universal identification of left-leaning governments with efforts to expand political participation (Cameron and Sharpe 2012; Cannon and Kirby 2012; Levitsky and Roberts 2011; Philip and Panizza 2011), we find an across-the-board expansion of participatory rights, which suggests that government partisanship may not be the best predictor of expanded opportunities for participation.

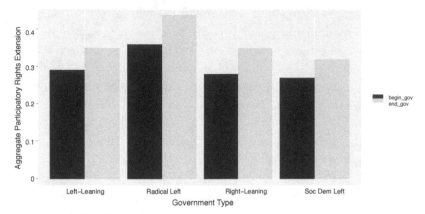

FIGURE 14.5. Change in Aggregate Participatory Rights Extension during the Left Turn. *Source*: Coppedge et al. 2017; LATINNO 2018; LAPOP 2018; Latinobarómetro 2017.

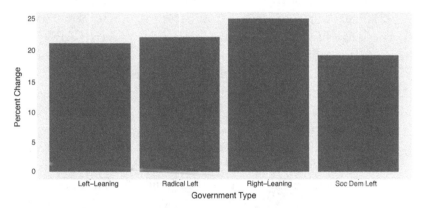

FIGURE 14.6. Percent Change in Participatory Rights Extension during the Left Turn. *Source*: Coppedge et al. 2017; LATINNO 2018; LAPOP 2018; Latinobarómetro 2017.

Indeed, the magnitude of participatory rights extension in countries with right-of-center governments was slightly higher than that in countries with left-of-center governments. This outcome may be the product of a diffusion process, in which participatory rights and institutions are first designed by left-of-center governments and are later imported by nonleft governments. This appears to have been the case with participatory budgeting in many instances (Goldfrank 2012).

It may also be the case that electoral threats from the left induce right-of-center governments to pursue participatory reforms. Indeed, regression analysis reveals a positive and statistically significant relationship between left party vote share in the most recent presidential elections and yearly aggregate participatory rights scores for countries governed by the right. Moving from a left vote share of 0 percent to a left vote share of 100 percent is associated with a more than 1 standard deviation increase in participatory rights scores in these countries. This finding suggests that the Left turn's impact on participatory rights is not only based on the policies of the Left in power, but also on the broader strength of left-leaning parties.

We also find variation among left-of-center governments. As figure 14.6 shows, participatory rights expansion was considerably greater in radical left countries than in social democratic ones. This difference holds even when we control for natural resources wealth in our statistical analysis, suggesting that radical left governments' actions had some impact on participatory rights independent of their fiscal largesse from resource rents. The difference between radical and social democratic left governments may be driven by ideology, but it also may be rooted in different historical trajectories. Whereas radical left governments in Bolivia, Ecuador, and Venezuela were led by new parties that were born during periods of popular mobilization, social democratic governments were led by older, more institutionalized parties whose previous experience with democratic breakdown and repressive military rule led them to adopt more cautious strategies with respect to popular mobilization (Levitsky and Roberts 2011).

Despite the real advances made by radical left governments in terms of participatory rights, however, there are reasons to question both the quality and the sustainability of participation in these cases (see Goldfrank, this volume). Although we include VDEM's participatory democracy scores in our analysis to capture the possibility that popular participation may be controlled or manipulated by the state, our indicators cannot fully assess whether participation is empowering communities in a sustainable way. As Goldfrank (this volume) argues, in countries with radical left governments (particularly Venezuela), there is considerable evidence suggesting that despite an overall expansion of participation, participatory institutions are often highly politicized, which can lead to self-selection out of participation by individuals who do not support the systematic exclusion of government critics from participation. That said, there is also considerable evidence to suggest that despite the politicization of participation in countries with radical left governments, these experiences have been genuinely empowering for many citizens (Hawkins 2010; Machado 2009; Rhodes-Purdy 2015).

Aggregating Rights Extension

We now aggregate our three dimensions to provide a summary rights extension score for each country-year. Figure 14.7 summarizes these data, sorting them by ideological orientation. Our findings suggest that governments' ideological orientation had little overall effect on rights extension during the Left turn. Indeed, overall rights expanded to roughly the same degree under right-of-center and left-of-center governments. This finding obviously obscures important differences across ideological types: as noted above, left-of-center (and especially radical left) governments oversaw social rights expansions that greatly exceeded those that occurred under right governments. At the same time, however, radical left governments were associated with an erosion of liberal democratic rights unlike anything that occurred elsewhere.

Some scholars may view the aggregation of liberal democratic, social, and participatory dimensions as unfairly obscuring important advances made by radical left governments, particularly in the area of social rights. By weighing left governments' performance with respect to liberal democratic rights against their performance with respect to social rights, it could be argued, we apply an inappropriate standard. In this alternative view, liberal institutions inhibit badly needed democratizing and redistributive efforts; thus, citizenship extension requires a political model that moves beyond liberalism (Beasley-Murray, Cameron, and Hershberg 2010; Cameron and Hershberg 2010). As Beasley-Murray, Cameron, and Hershberg (2009, 329) put it, "Taking liberalism as the normative standpoint from which to begin the debate, the options are reduced to: either reject liberalism and be denounced as a populist, or accept liberalism and promote social change within it like 'good' social democrats." From this perspective, aggregating liberal democratic

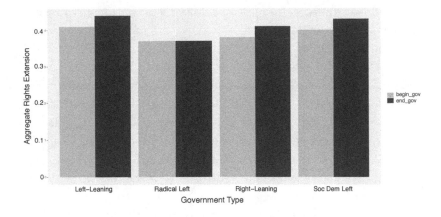

FIGURE 14.7. Change in Aggregate Rights Extension during the Left Turn

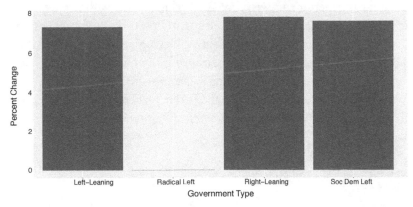

FIGURE 14.8. Percent Change in Aggregate Rights Extension during the Left Turn

with social and participatory rights, such that backsliding on one dimension can effectively cancel out advances in the others, obscures crucial advances secured by radical left governments that are fundamental to longer-term projects of citizenship extension.

We argue, to the contrary, that civil and political rights are an essential component of any citizenship regime. Freedom of expression and association and the basic rights to organize, protest, compete for public office, and vote are necessary conditions for the exercise of citizenship under all governments. They are especially important for the poor and other historically excluded groups, because the mobilization of numbers—on the streets and at the ballot box—is often the most potent tool available to them in the struggle for social rights. Indeed, as Marshall and others have argued, civil and political rights are an essential foundation for the achievement of social rights. Logically, then, restrictions on liberal democratic rights should be understood as limiting effective citizenship. This does not mean that advances in social rights should be ignored (indeed, we highlight these advances above) but rather that in the absence of liberal democratic rights, claims of an overall extension of citizenship may be misleading.

Overall, then, as this volume's case studies of policy areas in different countries of the region have illustrated qualitatively, the Left turn generated real but modest steps toward the extension of citizenship. Although left governments were, predictably, associated with greater social and (in the case of radical left governments) participatory rights extension, the overall effect of partisanship or ideology was less marked than many observers expected (or hoped) during the heady days of the Left turn. Here we agree with the initial hypothesis formulated by the editors and support the conclusions of Olivier Dabène (this volume): left government mattered during the Left turn, but its impact should not be overstated.

Why Such Modest Advances?

The relatively modest achievements of left governments over the past two decades should not be overly surprising. Governments do not operate in a vacuum. In all states, but especially in poorer and more peripheral ones, they are constrained by a range of structural forces. One of these—long highlighted by dependency theorists—is the global capitalist economy (Campello 2013; Wibbels 2006). With the partial exception of Venezuela, contemporary left-of-center governments in Latin America remained both predominantly capitalist and integrated into the global economy. Nearly all of them—including Venezuela—remained dependent on international trade and, to varying degrees, private investment. Even during an extraordinary commodities boom such as that of 2002–13, the constraints imposed by domestic and international markets raised the cost of radical redistributive measures aimed at advancing social citizenship (Campello 2013). Governments may ignore those constraints, but the costs of such action—in terms of capital flight, disinvestment, and, ultimately, low growth and declining revenue—will likely undermine any intended advances toward social citizenship in the medium term.

A second structural constraint is state weakness (Dabène, this volume; Handlin 2017; O'Donnell 1993). In much of Latin America, state capacity—the ability of state agencies to enforce the law and implement policy—is at best modest. In the Andes, where the most ambitious left projects emerged during the early twenty-first century, state capacity is quite low (Handlin 2017; Mainwaring 2006). State weakness undermines efforts to extend citizenship in several important ways. First, as Guillermo O'Donnell argued (1993, 1999), weak states cannot systematically enforce the rule of law, which limits governments' ability to uphold civil and other basic rights that are essential to citizenship. In the context of widespread unrule of law, the citizenship rights of the poor invariably go unprotected (O'Donnell 1999). Second, state weakness limits governments' ability to advance social citizenship through wealth redistribution. Weak states tend to have limited tax capacity, which inhibits redistribution and reduces the revenue available for social policy (Fukuyama 2004; Ravallion 2009). Moreover, because weak states tend to have ineffective—that is, markedly non-Weberian—bureaucracies, social policies tend to be marred by inefficiency, corruption, and clientelism. In such a context, ambitious social programs tend to fall well short of their goals. Finally, state weakness limits the effectiveness of participatory institutions. In a context of the unrule of law, ineffective bureaucracies, and scarce tax revenue, institutions designed to provide new channels of popular participation are more likely to politicized and used for clientelistic ends, corrupted by powerful actors, or simply neglected (Abers and Keck 2009; McNulty 2011).

A third structural constraint is imposed by democracy itself. Although elections and free association provide essential channels through which poor and historically marginalized groups may participate in politics, democratic institutions also constrain. Liberal democratic institutions protect minority rights and constrain executive power. As Michael

Albertus (2015) argues, wealthy elites frequently use the courts, legislatures, and other representative democratic institutions to water down or block measures aimed at radical redistribution or otherwise empowering the poor.[6] Left-leaning presidents may find their agendas stymied by nonleft majorities in Congress, as in Brazil, Chile, El Salvador, and Paraguay, or by courts defending property rights. And ultimately, of course, democratic presidencies confront term limits. Under liberal democracy, then, reforms aimed at extending citizenship tend to be incremental, piecemeal, and subject to reversal following turnover in power. Democracy thus opens the door to rights expansion, but at the same time, it creates multiple opportunities for opponents of rights expansion to water down and even derail such initiatives.

In sum, although the relatively modest nature of the gains made by left governments in early twenty-first-century Latin America disappointed many observers, these outcomes should not surprise us. Latin American leftists ascended to power in peripheral states with relatively open market economies. They were, to varying degrees, constrained by ineffective state bureaucracies and the very rules and procedures of liberal democracy. The mix of institutional constraints varied: where states were stronger, as in Brazil, Chile, and Uruguay, democratic institutions tended to be more constraining; where democratic institutions could be bent or broken, as in Bolivia, Ecuador, and Venezuela, state deficiencies were more severe. But for all the talk of revolution, refoundation, and twenty-first-century Socialism, the constraints could not be wished away. Finally, given the importance of these constraints in determining variation in citizenship extensions during the Left turn, we agree with Dabène (this volume) and others (Maldonado 2015; Pribble 2013) that these and other structural factors better predict variation in citizenship expansion than a government's location on the left-right spectrum.

LEGACIES OF THE LEFT TURN

Although the legacy of Latin America's Left turn may appear underwhelming in terms of the extension of citizenship overall, there is some reason to believe that it may have a substantial long-term impact on citizenship in the region. First, countries with left-of-center governments have seen greater increases in the exercise of participatory rights among traditionally excluded sectors than countries with right-of-center governments. This is a critical development, as increased participation among these groups provides a foundation for further reducing inequalities in political representation across class, gender, racial, ethnic, and other demographic lines. Further, we argue that, especially in countries with social democratic governments, the Left turn laid an institutional foundation for the expansion of universalistic social policies. We address each of these issues in turn.

Changes in Participation among Traditionally Excluded Groups

What effect (if any) have citizenship extensions had on the propensity of traditionally excluded groups to actually *exercise* their rights? To answer this question, we examine public opinion data on seven forms of political and civil society participation to assess whether participation has indeed increased among traditionally excluded sectors (specifically, women, the poor, blacks, and Indigenous people).[7] Figures 14.9 and 14.10 provide a summary of our findings, reported by government type. Participation rates of traditionally excluded groups increased nearly across the board, with the exception of Indigenous peoples, for whom there was no statistically significant change in participation. Thus, it appears that the overall citizenship extension discussed above was, in fact, associated with an increase in active citizenship among traditionally excluded populations, particularly blacks and the poor. Given that inequalities in participation tend to generate inequalities in political representation (Bartels 2008; Key and Heard 1949; Lijphart 1997), we argue that these increases in participation among traditionally excluded groups have laid a foundation for further decreases in inequalities of political representation across demographic groups. In turn, as traditionally excluded groups exercise more influence in political decision making, the likelihood of public policies being enacted that will have a positive impact on their participation propensities also increases, generating a virtuous cycle of increased participation, more equal political representation, and more equity-enhancing public policies.

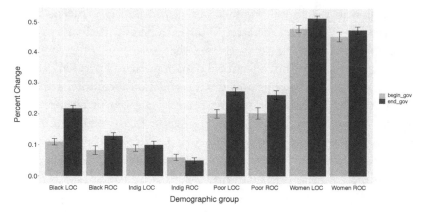

FIGURE 14.9. Change in Aggregate Participation during the Left Turn. *Source*: LAPOP 2018.
Note: ROC = right-of-center government; LOC = left-of-center government.

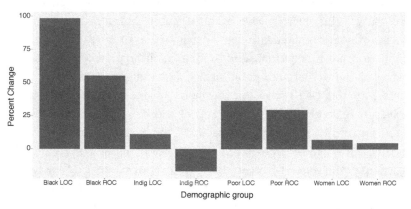

FIGURE 14.10. Percent Change in Aggregate Participation during the Left Turn. *Source*: LAPOP 2018.

We also find important differences in participation rates across government type that suggest the Left turn itself played a role in generating increases in participation among traditionally excluded groups. Although we observe an across-the-board increase in participation in countries with right-of-center governments, the increase is substantially higher (among the poor, among women, and particularly among blacks) in countries with left-of-center governments. This divergence is likely a consequence of three principal. First, greater emphasis on the importance of representing traditionally excluded groups in the political rhetoric and public policy of left-of-center governments has produced a stronger sense of political efficacy among excluded groups (Fernandes 2010; Hunter and Borges Sugiyama 2014; Perlman 2010). Given that extensive scholarship has shown that political efficacy is positively associated with political and civil society participation (Almond and Verba 1965; Reichert 2016; Seligson 1980; Verba and Nie 1972), it is likely that increased feelings of political efficacy among traditionally excluded groups have contributed to higher rates of political and civil society participation. Second, given that countries with left-of-center governments saw larger increases in social spending than those with right-of-center governments, that traditionally marginalized groups are disproportionately represented among the beneficiaries of left-of-center governments' social policies, and that participation in government programs has been shown to increase individuals' incentives to participate in politics (often in order to ensure the programs' continuation) (Ortega-Nieto 2014), it is plausible that increased social spending increased political and civil society participation among these groups. Finally, since participatory institutions are disproportionately composed of individuals from traditionally excluded groups, particularly the poor (Avritzer 2009; Machado 2009; Wampler and Touchton 2014), and since left governments (particularly radical left governments) are associated with higher increases in the density of participation in these institutions, it is likely that radical left governments' policies with respect to participatory institutions have played a role in increasing participation among traditionally excluded groups.

Interestingly, the only demographic group for which we find no statistically significant increase in participation among either left-of-center or right-of-center governments is Indigenous people. This finding may appear surprising, given the rhetorical emphasis that many left-led governments—particularly in the Andean region—placed on Indigenous empowerment during this period (Anria 2016; Becker 2010; Postero 2010). Given that our data only capture 2006 and after, however, we should not read too much into the limited increases in Indigenous participation, since Indigenous groups, particularly in the Andes, were highly mobilized in the years prior to 2006 (Van Cott 2005; Yashar

2005). It is hardly surprising that when governments came to power in large part as a result of this mobilization (e.g., Morales, Correa) and began to implement changes demanded by those movements, levels of mobilization would decrease. Indigenous movements saw that they had sympathetic interlocutors in power and that their interests were finally being reflected, at least to some degree, in government policies, so they no longer needed to maintain high levels of mobilization (Davies and Falleti 2017).

Institutionalizing Universalistic Social Policies

Left-of-center governments (particularly social democratic left governments) have also laid an institutional foundation for longer-term welfare state development (Garay 2016; Huber and Stephens 2012). As Candelaria Garay (2016) has shown, governments across Latin America took major steps toward universalizing social policy during the early 2000s. Not only were health insurance, pension, family allowance, and other social policies expanded to include the informal and rural poor, but in many cases, they included measures to ensure universal—as opposed to clientelist—access to these policies (Garay 2016). According to Huber and Stephens (2012), the turn toward universalistic social policies was most strongly associated with social democratic governments such as those in Brazil, Chile, and Uruguay. Although most of these policy measures were modest in scope, they were built on a relatively broad political consensus and a relatively sound fiscal and institutional foundation. Thus, they are likely to be sustainable. This is crucial. Social democratic welfare states are not built in a day—or even a decade. Even in Scandinavia, welfare state development began slowly and took half a century (Baldwin 1990; Esping Andersen 1990). But once the building blocks of universalistic social policies are in place, their removal becomes politically difficult (Pierson 1996); indeed, it often generates a ratchet effect that gradually fuels welfare state expansion over time. Thus, although comparisons between postwar European welfare states and those in contemporary Latin America should not be overdrawn, there is at least some reason to think that Latin America's Left turn may have left behind the foundations for a fairer and more generous welfare state.

PUBLIC OPINION AND THE SUSTAINABILITY
OF CITIZENSHIP EXPANSION

How sustainable are Latin America's newly expanded citizenship regimes? A critical factor in ensuring the durability of public policies is public support, which, if sufficiently broad, can dramatically increase the electoral costs of retrenchment (Huber and Stephens 2001; Pierson 1996). Consequently, policies that are only supported by a minority of the population are more vulnerable to attack than those that have acquired broad-based societal consensus. With this insight in mind, we ask whether it is the case that the extension of citizenship during Latin America's Left turn has generated this kind of consensus or whether these policies have generally outpaced prevailing public sentiment.

To answer this question, we turn to public opinion data from Latinobarómetro and LAPOP, and examine changes in average survey responses during the Left turn to questions related to public attitudes regarding rights extensions. We choose multiple proxies for each of our three dimensions and present average changes in public opinion for each, broken down by government type. Our findings are mixed: while we do not find evidence that support for liberal democratic or participatory rights has increased (indeed, support for participatory rights has *decreased* significantly across all government types), we find consistent evidence that support for social rights has increased across all government types.

With respect to changes in support for liberal democratic rights, we look at support for freedom of expression and freedom of association, two of the most critical dimensions of liberal democratic rights.[8] We include a direct measure of support for freedom of expression (fig. 14.11) and two proxies to capture support for freedom of association, one with respect to political association (fig. 14.12) and one with respect to civil society association (fig. 14.13). Our findings show slight increases—though not statistically significant—in support for freedom of expression, virtually no change in support for the right to political association, and significant decreases in support for the right to civil society association. The decline in support for the right to civil society association is observed across government types but is of a significantly larger

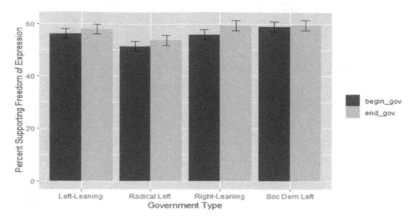

FIGURE 14.11. Change in Support for Liberal Democratic Rights: Freedom of Expression. *Source*: Latinobarómetro 2017.

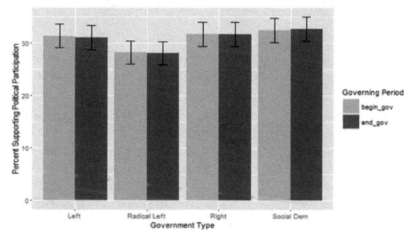

FIGURE 14.12. Change in Support for Liberal Democratic Rights: Freedom of Association (Political Participation). *Source*: Latinobarómetro 2017.

magnitude among countries with left-of-center governments (particularly radical left governments).

Turning to changes in public opinion on social policy, we look at three measures that capture whether respondents are more likely to support social policies that would extend additional social rights to the poor: solidarity with the poor (which is likely correlated with support for social policies aimed at reducing poverty) (fig. 14.14), support for a more

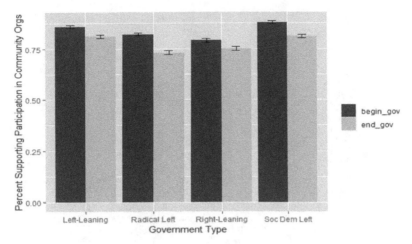

FIGURE 14.13. Change in Support for Liberal Democratic Rights: Freedom of Association (Community Organization). *Source*: Latinobarómetro 2017.

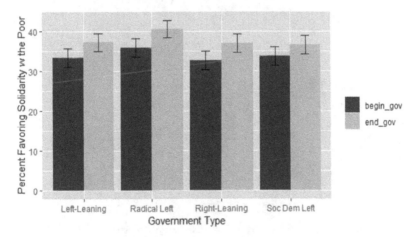

FIGURE 14.14. Change in Support for Social Rights: Solidarity with the Poor. *Source*: Latinobarómetro 2017.

just distribution of wealth (a reasonable proxy for willingness to redistribute government revenues from the wealthy to the poor) (fig. 14.15), and support for social security (a direct measure of support for social insurance) (fig. 14.16).[9] We find across-the-board increases in support for each measure. Specifically, Latin Americans living under both left and right governments demonstrated increased solidarity with the poor,

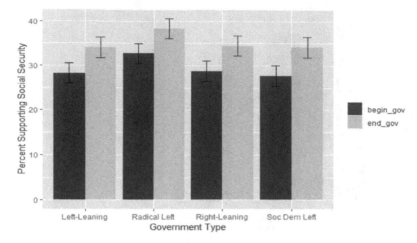

FIGURE 14.15. Change in Support for Social Rights: Support for Social Security. *Source*: Latinobarómetro 2017.

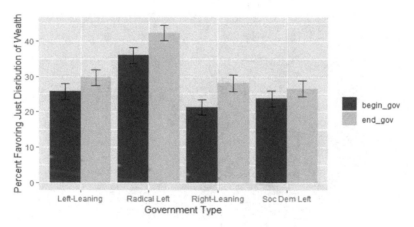

FIGURE 14.16. Change in Support for Social Rights: Just Distribution of Wealth. *Source*: Latinobarómetro 2017.

although this increase is only statistically significant in the radical left cases. We also observe statistically significant increases—among respondents across all government types—in support for social security and a more just distribution of wealth (although on the latter question the increase is not statistically significant for the social democratic cases). Contra earlier studies (Arnold and Samuels 2011), then, we observe a significant leftward shift in public opinion in Latin America with respect to social policy preferences, which augers well for the possibility of sustaining political coalitions in support of increased social rights for the poor across the region in the coming years.

Finally, we examine changes in support for participatory rights. Although no ideal measures were available, we look at two measures that capture whether respondents believe participatory rights are important enough to be considered a basic dimension of citizenship, one measuring whether respondents believe participating in social (civil society) organizations should be considered a basic element of citizenship (fig. 14.17) and the other doing the same for political organizations (fig. 14.18).[10] If it is the case that citizens view participatory rights as a fundamental component of citizenship, it is reasonable to assume they will be more likely to support expanded access to these rights through mechanisms such as participatory budgeting and prior consultation. We find an across-the-board decline in support for participatory rights with respect to the duty to participate in social organizations, as well as a decline in support for the duty to participate in political organizations across all government types except for radical left, where we see a slight (statistically insignificant) increase. This suggests Latin Americans may be experiencing a degree of participatory fatigue that may limit their future interest in participatory experimentation.

In sum, the broad constituency needed to sustain expanded citizenship rights appears to exist with respect to social rights but less so with

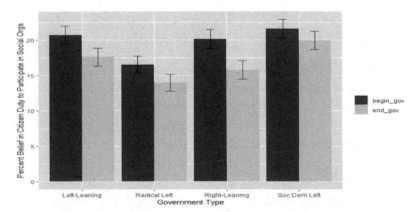

FIGURE 14.17. Change in Support for Participatory Rights: Duty to Participate in Social Organizations. *Source*: Latinobarómetro 2017.

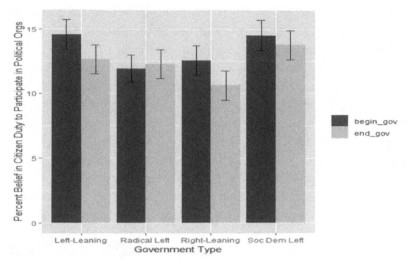

FIGURE 14.18. Change in Support for Participatory Rights: Duty to Participate in Political Organizations. *Source*: Latinobarómetro 2017.

respect to liberal democratic or participatory rights. This is a potentially troubling finding, for it suggests that respondents may be willing to sacrifice liberal democratic and participatory rights for social rights. Given the importance of democracy to sustain pro-poor social policies (Huber and Stephens 2012; Rueschemeyer, Stephens, and Stephens 1992), however, it is likely that in the medium-term such a tradeoff will undermine the sustainability of social rights as well.

Have Latin Americans Moved Left?

Another potential predictor of the sustainability of social and participatory rights (though not necessarily of liberal democratic rights) is whether Latin American electorates have moved ideologically to the left. Since support for the left is generally associated with increased support for both redistributive and socially inclusionary public policy, we expect that increased support for the left will be associated with increased support for social and participatory rights. Figure 14.19 shows significant increases in left partisan identification among countries under both right-of-center and radical left governments, suggesting that the constituencies for redistributive and socially inclusionary public policies may be larger today

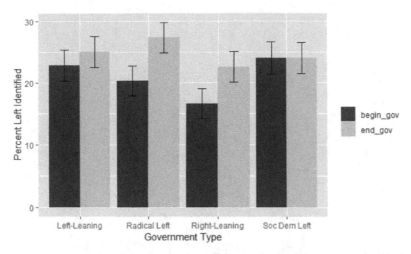

FIGURE 14.19. Change in Partisan Identification. *Source*: Latinobarómetro 2017.

than they were before the Left turn. Interestingly, however, among respondents in countries with social democratic left governments, we see no overall change in left identification.[11] There are a few possible explanations for this outcome. One, put forth by Handlin (2013), is that whereas social democratic governments tended to pursue technocratic social policies, which earned them little partisan credit, radical left governments deployed politicized social programs, which enabled them to build up partisan support. A second possible explanation, following Lupu (2016), is that social democratic governments' policy moderation diluted left party brands, which weakened partisan identities as voters no longer viewed these parties as "standing for" something. By contrast, radical left governments more clearly stood for something, which, if Lupu's theory is correct, should reinforce partisan brands and strengthen partisan identities. A third possible explanation is that the difference we observe is driven by a significant decline in left partisan identification in social democratic countries (most notably, Brazil) between 2013 and 2015 (see fig. 14.20).

In this chapter, we have attempted to take stock of changes in citizenship in Latin America during the Left turn. We first examined levels of citizenship expansion and contraction across dimensions and in the aggregate, comparing changes across governments of the left and right. We

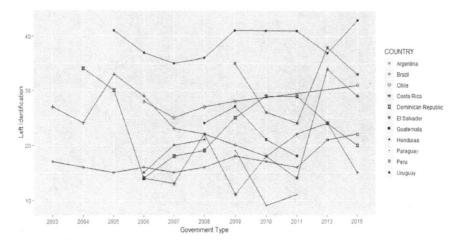

FIGURE 14.20. Change in Partisan Identification in Countries with Social Democratic Governments. *Source*: Latinobarómetro 2017.

then examined two likely legacies of the Left turn: greater political and civil society participation among traditionally excluded groups and the institutionalization of universalistic social policies. Finally, we examined changes in public support for social policies associated with expansions in citizenship rights.

This assessment yielded four main findings: First, citizenship rights *have* been extended in Latin America over the past twenty years, both in the aggregate and across each of our three dimensions. Second, however, the impact of the Left turn on this extension has been limited mainly to social and participatory rights. In terms of aggregate rights extension, left-of-center governments performed only marginally better than right-of-center governments, and radical left governments performed worse (due to regressions in the area of liberal democratic rights). Third, despite similar levels of citizenship extension observed between right- and left-of-center governments, the exercise of participatory rights among traditionally excluded groups increased more markedly under left-of-center governments. Finally, although the Left turn generated clear positive legacies with respect to equalizing active citizenship and laying the institutional bases for universal social policies, public support for expanded citizenship rights has not grown sufficiently to ensure their sustainability.

In sum, the Left turn produced uneven gains with respect to citizenship extension. These gains fell well short of many observers' expectations, but given the constraints imposed by capitalist economies, weak states, and liberal democratic institutions, such an outcome should not surprise us. A key question looking forward is how sustainable newly expanded citizenship rights will be. Although the institutional and public opinion bases of social rights expansion appear solid, the foundations for liberal democratic and participatory rights are weaker. This is a cause for concern, for without open and active citizen participation, the sustainability of the socioeconomic gains made during the Left turn remains uncertain.

APPENDIX 14.1

Measuring Political, Civil, Social, and Active Citizenship Rights

1. Liberal Democratic Rights
   A. Civil Rights (assessed by examining cross-national civil rights indices, particularly V-Dem's Liberal Democracy Index
      i. Freedom of Expression and Beliefs
      ii. Freedom of Association
      iii. Personal Autonomy
   B. Political Rights
      a. Formal Extension of Rights (assessed by examining constitutional and other formal changes in the extension of these rights)
         i. Head of government elected through free and fair elections
         ii. National legislature elected through free and fair elections
         iii. Universal adult suffrage
      b. Exercise of Rights (assessed by examining cross-national political rights indices, particularly V-Dem's Liberal Democracy Index)
         i. Head of government elected through free and fair elections
         ii. National legislature elected through free and fair elections

2. **Social Rights**
    a. Formal Extension of Rights (assessed by examining constitutional and other formal changes in the extension of these rights)
        i. Right to education
        ii. Right to housing
        iii. Right to old-age security
        iv. Right to unemployment insurance
        v. Freedom from poverty
        vi. Right to medical services
    b. Exercise of Rights (assessed by examining government spending in each of these areas)[12]
        i. Education spending as % of GDP
        ii. Housing spending as % of GDP
        iii. Pension spending as % of GDP
        iv. Unemployment Insurance spending as % of GDP
        v. Antipoverty program spending as % of GDP
        vi. Health spending as % of GDP
3. **Participatory Rights**
    a. Formal Extension of Rights (assessed by examining constitutional and other formal changes in the extension of these rights)
        i. National-level participatory institutions
        ii. Regional/local-level participatory institutions
            1. Binding participatory institutions
        iii. Referendums/Plebiscites
    b. Exercise of Rights (assessed by examining number of instances of each institution in a given country as well as the estimated number of participants in each institution. The LATINNO dataset and LAPOP datasets will be the primary data sources for these indicators, as well as David Altman's Direct Democracy Index for referendums/plebiscites.)
        i. National-level participatory institutions
        ii. Regional/local-level participatory institutions
        iii. Referendums/plebiscites
        iv. Associational life
            1. Nonvoting political participation
            2. Civil society organization participation

APPENDIX 14.2

Classifying Government Ideological Orientation

Given the ideology inconsistency of many Latin American political parties, and the fact that key political cleavages often do not fall neatly on the traditional right-left scale (Coppedge et al. 1997), it is not easy to characterize the ideology of governments in the region. However, following Coppedge et al. (1997), we argue that even when governments' ideologies are somewhat unclear given factors such as clientelism, populism, regionalism, and so on, they tend to be more or less classifiable in left-right terms. Our classification scheme involves two steps: first, using criteria from Coppedge et al. (1997), whose classificatory system has the benefit of being precise and tailored to the particularities of Latin America, we make a first distinction between left-of-center and right-of-center governments. This system is based on (1) the classes to which parties appeal and (2) parties' social/economic policies/platforms.

Left-of-center governments are those that target voters from the middle and/or popular classes and whose platforms and policies stress justice, equality, redistribution, and the inclusion of excluded groups. By contrast, right-of-center governments are those that target voters both from the elite classes and from the middle and lower classes and stress the importance of the private sector, public order, and the priority of growth over redistribution.

In step 2, we distinguish between types of left-of-center governments. Following Weyland, Madrid, and Hunter (2010), Panizza (2005), and others, we classify left-of-center governments as either "radical" or "social democratic." This distinction is drawn primarily in terms of economic policy. While both radical and social democratic governments prioritize (at least rhetorically) policies aimed at decreasing inequality and increasing social inclusion, radical left governments are characterized by relatively statist economic policies, whereas social democratic governments are characterized market-oriented economic policies, and their social policies are constrained by the demands of macroeconomic stability. Following Levitsky and Roberts (2011), we do not include populist characteristics in this classification, since populism is a phenomenon common to governments of all ideological orientations.

TABLE 14.1. Latin American Governments during the Left Turn by Ideology

Country	Year	Center Left	Radical	Soc Dem	Center Right
Argentina	1998	0	0	0	1
Argentina	2003	1	0	1	0
Argentina	2015	0	0	0	1
Bolivia	1998	0	0	0	1
Bolivia	2006	1	1	0	0
Brazil	1998	0	0	0	1
Brazil	2003	1	0	1	0
Chile	1998	1	0	1	0
Chile	2010	0	0	0	1
Chile	2014	1	0	1	0
Colombia	1998	0	0	0	1
Colombia	2015	0	0	0	1
Costa Rica	1998	0	0	0	1
Costa Rica	2006	1	0	1	0
Cuba	1998	1	1	0	0
Dominican Republic	1998	1	0	1	1
Dominican Republic	2001	1	0	1	0
Dominican Republic	2005	0	0	0	1
Ecuador	1998	0	0	0	1
Ecuador	2007	1	1	0	0
El Salvador	1998	0	0	0	1
El Salvador	2009	1	0	1	0
Guatemala	1998	0	0	0	1
Guatemala	2008	1	0	1	0
Guatemala	2012	0	0	0	1
Honduras	1998	0	0	0	1
Honduras	2006	1	0	1	0
Honduras	2009	0	0	0	1
Mexico	1998	0	0	0	1
Nicaragua	1998	0	0	0	1
Panama	1998	0	0	0	1
Paraguay	1998	0	0	0	1
Paraguay	2009	1	0	1	0
Paraguay	2012	0	0	0	1
Peru	1998	0	0	0	1
Peru	2012	1	0	1	0
Uruguay	1998	0	0	0	1
Uruguay	2005	1	0	1	0
Venezuela	1998	0	0	0	1
Venezuela	1999	1	1	0	0

Based on these criteria, below we present a table of our classifications of government ideologies for each country during the Left turn. We include the country-year of each change in government ideology, so, for instance, Argentina 1998 indicates the beginning of the period (in our dataset) when Argentina had a right-of-center government, and 2003 indicates the beginning of the period when Argentina had a left-of-center government. In the table, 0 = No and 1 = Yes.

NOTES

1. For the purposes of this chapter, we focus only on the exercise of rights, rather than the formal extension of rights, since it is the exercise, rather than the parchment existence of rights, that is relevant if we seek to isolate substantive changes in rights extensions.

2. VDEM's Liberal Democracy Index (v2x_libdem) is an aggregation of variables (scaled 0–1) capturing protection of individual liberties, including those capturing personal autonomy (property rights, freedom from torture, freedom of movement, access to justice), freedom of association and expression, as well as protection of political liberties through free and fair elections and universal suffrage.

3. This framework draws on the categorization offered by Levitsky and Roberts (2011). For a full description of our country/government coding choices, see appendix 14.2.

4. According to *Encuesta sobre Condiciones de Vida en Venezuela* (UCAB 2017), despite significant decreases in poverty between 2003 and 2012, as of 2016 poverty had skyrocketed to well above pre-2003 levels, reaching an astounding 80 percent by 2016.

5. While VDEM provides a comprehensive participatory democracy index, it includes a number of components that lie outside the range of our conceptualization of participatory democracy, including modes of candidate selection by political parties, whether local-regional governments exist, and whether their leadership is elected, etc. As a result, we construct our own measure of participatory democracy that takes the average of VDEM variables that capture two critical components of participatory democracy not addressed by the LATINNO and LAPOP measures we employ: (1) the frequency extent and success of direct democracy mechanisms (referendums, plebiscites), for which we use VDEM's "Plebiscite Credible Threat" variable (v2ddthrepl, scale of 0–1); and (2) the independence of civil society organizations from the state,

for which we use VDEM's "CSO Participatory Environment" variable, (v2c-sprtcpt, originally scaled 0–3, normalized here to 0–1). VDEM's participatory environment variable also captures the relationship between the density of civil society organizations and levels of popular involvement in civil society organizations (CSOs), so, for instance, a country that has many CSOs but very limited public participation in CSOs would receive a lower score than a country that has many CSOs and widespread public participation in CSOs.

6. Indeed, as Albertus (2015) shows, nearly all of the most radical land reform projects in Latin America occurred under dictatorship.

7. LAPOP asks respondents to report whether they attend meetings of their local city council, a political party, parent-teacher associations, religious organizations, or community organizations; if they have participated in a protest over the past twelve months; or if they have made a request to a municipal official over the past twelve months. Figures 14.9 and 14.10 report the difference in country-year averages of the participation rates of respondents in these seven activities. For this analysis, data are only available for the years between 2006 and 2014, meaning that we have censored the early years of the Left turn. Nonetheless, this period encompasses the central years that the commodities boom affected government spending across the region, as well as the vast majority of country-years that experienced left-of-center governments between 1998 and 2014.

8. Data for the freedom of expression and political participation variables are from Latinobarómetro surveys conducted in 2007, 2008, 2009, 2011, and 2015; and data for the community participation variable are from LAPOP surveys conducted in 2006, 2008, 2010, 2012, and 2014 (LAPOP question E8).

9. Data for each of these questions is from Latinobarómetro surveys conducted in 2007, 2008, 2009, 2011, and 2015.

10. Data for each of these questions are from Latinobarómetro surveys conducted in 2007, 2008, 2009, 2011, and 2015.

11. It is important to note that partisan self-identification has divergent meanings across countries and that in many Latin American countries it does not strongly predict voters' preferences with respect to public policy orientations traditionally associated with the left, such as the role of the state in society (Zechmeister and Corral 2010).

12. Government spending is preferable to outcomes for these indicators because the effects of government actions can only be traced to actions taken by a particular government, not larger societal factors that may have affected these indicators. Not at all sure about this decision.

REFERENCES

Abbott, Jared A., Hillel David Soifer, and Matthias Vom Hau. 2017. "Transforming the Nation? The Bolivarian Education Reform in Venezuela." *Journal of Latin American Studies* 49 (4): 885–916.

Abers, Rebecca Neaera, and Margaret E Keck. 2009. "Mobilizing the State: The Erratic Partner in Brazil's Participatory Water Policy." *Politics & Society* 37 (2): 289-314.

Albertus, Michael. 2015. *Autocracy and Redistribution: The Politics of Land Reform.* New York: Cambridge University Press.

Almond, Gabriel A., and Sidney Verba. 1965. *The Civic Culture.* Boston: Little Brown.

Anria, Santiago. 2016. "Delegative Democracy Revisited: More Inclusion, Less Liberalism in Bolivia." *Journal of Democracy* 27 (3): 99–108.

Arnold, Jason, and David Samuels. 2011. "Latin America's Left Turn? Evidence from Public Opinion: A Conceptual and Theoretical Overview." In Steven Levitsky and Kenneth M. Roberts, eds., *The Resurgence of the Latin American Left.* Baltimore, MD: Johns Hopkins University Press.

Avritzer, Leonardo. 2009. *Participatory Institutions in Democratic Brazil.* Baltimore, MD: Johns Hopkins University Press.

Baldwin, Peter. 1990. *The Politics of Social Solidarity: Class Bases of the European Welfare State, 1875–1975.* New York: Cambridge University Press.

Bartels, Larry M. 2008. *Unequal Democracy: The Political Economy of the New Gilded Age.* Princeton, NJ: Russell Sage Foundation, Princeton University Press.

Beasley-Murray, Jon, Maxwell A. Cameron, and Eric Hershberg. 2009. "Latin America's Left Turns: An Introduction." *Third World Quarterly* 30 (2): 319–30.

———. 2010. "Latin America's Left Turns: A Tour d'Horizon." In Maxwell A. Cameron and Eric Hershberg, eds., *Latin American Left Turns: Politics, Policies, and Trajectories of Change.* Boulder, CO: Lynne Rienner.

Becker, Marc. 2010. "Correa, Indigenous Movements, and the Writing of a New Constitution in Ecuador." *Latin American Perspectives* 38 (1): 47–62.

Cameron, Maxwell A., and Eric Hershberg, eds. 2010. *Latin America's Left Turns: Politics, Policies, and Trajectories of Change.* Boulder, CO: Lynne Rienner.

Cameron, Maxwell A., and Kenneth E. Sharpe. 2012. "Institutionalized Voice in Latin American Democracies." In Maxwell A. Cameron, Eric Hershberg, and Kenneth E. Sharpe, eds., *New Institutions for Participatory*

Democracy in Latin America: Voice and Consequence. New York: Palgrave Macmillan.

Campello, Daniela. 2013. "The Politics of Financial Booms and Crises: Evidence from Latin America." *Comparative Political Studies* 47 (2): 260–86.

Cannon, Barry, and Peadar Kirby. 2012. *Civil Society and the State in Left-Led Latin America: Challenges and Limitations to Democratization.* London: Zed Books.

Castañeda, Jorge G. 2006. "Latin America's Left Turn." *Foreign Affairs* 85. 28 pp.

Coppedge, Michael, Steffan I. Lindberg, John Gerring, Svend-Erik Skaaning, Jan Teorell, David Altman, Michael Bernhard, M. Steven Fish, Adam Glynn, Allen Hicken, Carl Henrik Knutsen, Joshua Krusell, Anna Lührmann, Kyle L. Marquardt, Kelly McMann, Valeriya Mechkova, Moa Olin, Pamela Paxton, Daniel Pemstein, Josefine Pernes, Constanza Sanhueza Petrarca, Johannes von Römer, Laura Saxer, Brigitte Seim, Rachel Sigman, Jeffrey Staton, Natalia Stepanova, and Steven Wilson. 2017. "V-Dem [Country-Year/Country-Date] Dataset v7.1." www.v-dem.net /en/data/data-version-7-1/.

Cornia, Giovanni Andrea. 2010. "Income Distribution under Latin America's New Left Regimes." *Journal of Human Development and Capabilities* 11 (1): 85–114.

Davies, Emmerich, and Tulia G. Falleti. 2017. "Poor People's Participation: Neoliberal Institutions or Left Turn?" *Comparative Political Studies* 50 (12): 1699–1731.

Esping Andersen, Gøsta. 1990. *The Three Worlds of Welfare Capitalism.* Princeton, NJ: Princeton University Press.

Fernandes, Sujatha. 2010. *Who Can Stop the Drums? Urban Social Movements in Chávez's Venezuela.* Durham, NC: Duke University Press.

Fukuyama, Francis. 2004. "The Imperative of State-Building." *Journal of Democracy* 15 (2): 17–31.

Garay, Candelaria. 2016. *Social Policy Expansion in Latin America.* New York: Cambridge University Press.

Goldfrank, Benjamin. 2012. "The World Bank and the Globalization of Participatory Budgeting." *Journal of Public Deliberation* 8 (2): 18 pp.

Handlin, Samuel. 2013. "Social Protection and the Politicization of Class Cleavages during Latin America's Left Turn." *Comparative Political Studies* 46 (12): 1582–1609.

———. 2015. "How to Keep the Playing Field Tilted: Mass Organization and the Durability of Competitive Authoritarianism." Social Science

Research Network Working Paper. https://papers.ssrn.com/sol3/papers
.cfm?abstract_id=2546196.

———. 2017. *State Crisis in Fragile Democracies: Polarization and Political Regimes in South America*. New York: Cambridge University Press.

Hawkins, Kirk A. 2010. "Who Mobilizes? Participatory Democracy in Chávez's Bolivarian Revolution." *Latin American Politics and Society* 52 (3): 31–66.

Huber, Evelyne, and John D. Stephens. 2001. "Welfare State and Production Regimes in the Era of Retrenchment." Princeton, NJ: Institute for Advanced Study, School of Social Science. Occasional Papers. www.sss.ias .edu/files/papers/paperone.pdf.

———. 2012. *Democracy and the Left: Social Policy and Inequality in Latin America*. Chicago: University of Chicago Press.

Hunter, Wendy, and Natasha Borges Sugiyama. 2014. "Transforming Subjects into Citizens: Insights from Brazil's Bolsa Família." *Perspectives on Politics* 12 (4): 829–45.

Innovations for Democracy in Latin America (LATINNO). 2018. "Innovations." www.latinno.net/en/innovations.

Key, Valdimer Orlando, and Alexander Heard. 1949. *Southern Politics in State and Nation*. New York: Alfred A. Knopf.

Latin American Public Opinion Project (LAPOP). 2018. "The Americas Barometer by the Latin American Public Opinion Project (LAPOP)." www .LapopSurveys.org.

Latinobarómetro. 2017. "Latinobarómetro: Banco de datos." www.latino barometro.org/latContents.jsp.

Levitsky, Steven, and Kenneth M. Roberts. 2011. "Introduction: Latin America's 'Left Turn': A Framework for Analysis. In Steven Levitsky and Kenneth M. Roberts, eds., *The Resurgence of the Latin American Left*. Baltimore, MD: Johns Hopkins University Press.

Lijphart, Arend. 1997. "Unequal Participation: Democracy's Unresolved Dilemma, Presidential Address, American Political Science Association, 1996." *American Political Science Review* 91 (1): 1–14.

Lupu, Noam. 2016. *Party Brands in Crisis: Partisanship, Brand Dilution, and the Breakdown of Political Parties in Latin America*. New York: Cambridge University Press.

Machado, Jesús. 2009. "Participación social y consejos comunales en Venezuela." *Revista Venezolana de Economía y Ciencias Sociales* 15 (1): 173–85.

Mainwaring, Scott. 2006. "The Crisis of Representation in the Andes." *Journal of Democracy* 17 (3): 13–27.

Maldonado, Carlos. 2015. "Building Compacts for Social Protection." In Simone Cecchini, Fernando Filgueira, Rodrigo Martínez, and Cecilia Rossel, eds., *Towards Universal Social Protection: Latin American Pathways and Policy Tools.* Santiago de Chile: ECLAC.

Marshall, Thomas H. 1950. *Citizenship and Social Class: Citizenship and Social Class and Other Essays.* New York: Cambridge University Press.

McLeod, Darryl, and Nora Lustig. 2011. "Inequality and Poverty under Latin America's New Left Regimes." Tulane Economics Working Paper Series. Working Paper 1117.

McNulty, Sarah. 2011. *Voice and Vote: Decentralization and Participation in Post-Fujimori Peru.* Palo Alto, CA: Stanford University Press.

O'Donnell, Guillermo. 1993. "On the State, Democratization and Some Conceptual Problems: A Latin American View with Glances at Some Postcommunist Countries." *World Development* 21 (8): 1355–69.

———. 1999. "Polyarchies and the (Un)Rule of Law in Latin America: A Partial Conclusion." In Juan Méndez, Guillermo O'Donnell, and Paulo Sérgio Pinheiro, eds., *The (Un)Rule of Law and the Underprivileged in Latin America.* South Bend, IN: University of Notre Dame Press.

Ortega-Nieto, David. 2014. "The Politics of Urban Poverty: Participation and Welfare." PhD dissertation, Georgetown University.

Perlman, Janice. 2010. *Favela: Four Decades of Living on the Edge in Rio de Janeiro.* Oxford: Oxford University Press.

Philip, George, and Francisco Panizza. 2011. *The Triumph of Politics: The Return of the Left in Venezuela, Bolivia and Ecuador.* Cambridge: Polity Press.

Pierson, Paul. 1996. "The New Politics of the Welfare State." *World Politics* 48 (1): 143–79.

Postero, Nancy 2010. "Morales's MAS Government: Building Indigenous Popular Hegemony in Bolivia." *Latin American Perspectives* 37 (3): 18–34.

Pribble, Jennifer. 2008. "Protecting the Poor: Welfare Politics in Latin America's Free Market Era." PhD dissertation, University of North Carolina at Chapel Hill.

———. 2013. *Welfare and Party Politics in Latin America.* New York: Cambridge University Press.

Ravallion, Martin. 2009. "Do Poorer Countries Have Less Capacity for Redistribution?" World Bank Policy Research. Working Paper 5046. https://elibrary.worldbank.org/doi/abs/10.1596/1813-9450-5046.

Reichert, Frank. 2016. "How Internal Political Efficacy Translates Political Knowledge into Political Participation: Evidence from Germany." *European Journal of Psychology* 12 (2): 221–44.

Rhodes-Purdy, Matthew. 2015. "Participatory Populism: Theory and Evidence from Bolivarian Venezuela." *Political Research Quarterly* 68 (3): 415–27.

Rueschemeyer, Dietrch, Evelyne Huber Stephens, and John Stephens. 1992. *Capitalist Development and Democracy.* Chicago: University of Chicago Press.

Seligson, Mitchell. 1980. "Trust, Efficacy and Modes of Political Participation: A Study of Costa Rican Peasants." *British Journal of Political Science* 10 (1): 75–98.

United Nations Economic Commission on Latin America (ECLAC). 2017. "CEPALSTAT." http://estadisticas.cepal.org/cepalstat/portada.html ?idioma=english.

Universidad Católica de Venezuela. 2017. "Encuesta sobre condiciones de vida en Venezuela." www.fundacionbengoa.org/encovi/encovi-2016.asp.

Van Cott, Donna Lee. 2005. *From Movements to Parties in Latin America: The Evolution of Ethnic Politics.* New York: Cambridge University Press.

Verba, Sidney, and Norman H. Nie. 1972. *Participation in America.* New York: Harper & Row.

Wampler, Brian, and Michael Touchton. 2014. "Improving Social Well-Being through New Democratic Institutions." *Comparative Political Studies* 20 (10): 1–28.

Weyland, Kurt. 2009. "The Rise of Latin America's Two Lefts: Insights from Rentier State Theory." *Comparative Politics* 41 (2): 145–64.

Weyland, Kurt, Raúl Madrid, and Wendy Hunter. 2010. *Leftist Governments in Latin America: Successes and Shortcomings.* New York: Cambridge University Press.

Wibbels, Eric. 2006. "Dependency Revisited: International Markets, Business Cycles, and Social Spending in the Developing World." *International Organization* 60 (2): 433–68.

Yashar, Deborah. 2005. *Contesting Citizenship in Latin America: The Rise of Indigenous Movements and the Postliberal Challenge.* New York: Cambridge University Press.

Zechmeister, Elizabeth, and Margarita Corral. 2010. "The Varying Economic Meaning of 'Left' and 'Right' in Latin America." *AmericasBarometer Insights Series* 38: 1–0.

CONTRIBUTORS

Manuel Balán is associate professor of political science and international development at McGill University and founding member of the Réseau d'études latino-américaines de Montréal (RELAM). His work centers on the study of corruption, corruption scandals, political competition, and media and politics in Latin America, with a focus on the Southern Cone (Argentina, Brazil, Chile). His ongoing research projects relate to two main issues: the changing patterns of corruption practices and judicial responses to corruption in Latin America; and the study of patterns of media polarization—through the analysis of images—and its political consequences. He has an upcoming book, *Today's Allies, Tomorrow's Enemies? The Political Dynamics of Corruption Scandals in Latin America*, to be published by the University of Notre Dame Press. His work has also been published in several journals, including *Comparative Politics, Desarrollo Económico*, and the *Journal of Politics in Latin America*.

Françoise Montambeault is associate professor of political science at the Université de Montréal and codirector of the Réseau d'études latino-américaines de Montréal (RELAM). Her work has focused on participatory democracy and the construction of citizenship in Latin America, with a particular interest in Brazil and Mexico. Her most recent projects are developed along two main questions: first, informal participation and the transformation of citizens' engagement practices in the urban space, and second, the translation and appropriation of the free, prior, and informed consent (FPIC) norms as participatory rights by Indigenous peoples and state actors at the domestic level in the Americas. Her book, *The Politics of Participatory Democracy in Latin America: Institutions, Actors and Interactions*, was published by Stanford University Press in 2016, and her work has been published in several journals, including *Politics and Society*, *Latin American Politics and Society*, *Journal of Civil Society*, and *Participation*.

Jared Abbott is a PhD candidate in government at Harvard University. His work is situated at the intersection of political parties, social movements, and participatory democracy, particularly in Latin America.

Merike Blofield is associate professor of political science and director of women's and gender studies at the University of Miami. Blofield's research focuses on gender and socioeconomic inequalities, politics, and policy, with a focus on Latin America. Her books include *Care Work and Class: Domestic Workers' Struggle for Equal Rights in Latin America*, *The Politics of Moral Sin: Abortion and Divorce in Spain, Chile and Argentina*, and the edited volume, *The Great Gap: Inequality and the Politics of Redistribution in Latin America*. Her articles have appeared in *Comparative Politics*, *Latin American Research Review*, *Current Sociology*, and *Social Politics*, among other journals, and she has received grants from the Ford Foundation and Fundação de Amparo à Pesquisa do São Paulo. Blofield was also coordinating lead author of the chapter on families for the *International Panel on Social Progress*.

Eve Bratman (PhD, American University, 2009) is assistant professor in environmental studies at Franklin & Marshall College. Her research concerns sustainable development politics and environmental governance and focuses on the links between environmental policy, infrastructure, agriculture, and human rights in the Brazilian Amazon. Her publications include *Governing the Rainforest: Sustainable Development Politics in the Brazilian Amazon* (Oxford University Press, 2019) and articles in the *Journal of Latin American Studies*, *Antipode*, *Human Ecology*, *International Environmental Agreements*, and *Third World Quarterly*, among other journals.

Daniel A. Brinks is associate professor of government and of law in the fields of comparative politics and public law. His research focuses on the role of the law and courts in supporting or extending human rights and many of the basic rights associated with democracy, with a primary regional interest in Latin America. He has published four books: *The DNA of Constitutional Justice in Latin America: Politics, Governance and Judicial Design* (with Abby Blass), *Reflections on Uneven Democracies* (co-edited with Scott Mainwaring and Marcelo Leiras), *Courting Social Justice: The Judicial Enforcement of Social and Economic Rights in the Developing World* (co-edited with Varun Gauri), and *The Judicial Response to Police Violence in Latin America: Inequality and the Rule of Law*—as well as numerous articles and book chapters.

Maxwell A. Cameron is professor of political science and director of the Centre for the Study of Democratic Institutions at the University of British Columbia (UBC), in which capacity he runs the annual Summer Institute for Future Legislators. His research focuses on comparative democratization (especially in Latin America), constitutions, and ethics in politics. His publications include *Strong Constitutions* (Oxford University Press, 2013) and *Political Institutions and Practical Wisdom* (Oxford University Press, 2018). As part of a research cluster on the "Global Challenges to Democracy," funded by the Vice President for Research and Innovation at UBC, Cameron is currently preparing an edited book titled *The Survival of Defective Democracies in the Andes*.

Olivier Dabène is professor of political science at the Paris Institute of Political Studies (Sciences Po) and senior researcher at the Center for International Studies and Research (CERI, Sciences Po). He is also president of the Political Observatory of Latin America and the Caribbean (www.sciencespo.fr/opalc) and visiting professor at many Latin American universities. His latest books include *The Politics of Regional Integration in Latin America* (Palgrave Macmillan, 2009), *La gauche en Amérique latine, 1998–2012* (Presses de Sciences Po, 2012) and *Summits and Regional Governance: The Americas in Comparative Perspective* (with Gordon Mace, Jean-Philippe Terrien, and Diana Tussie) (Routledge, 2016).

Jordi Díez is professor of political science at the University of Guelph, Canada. He has published extensively on Latin American politics in the areas of environmental policy and politics, comparative public policy, civil-military relations, social movements, the politics of sexual and reproductive rights, and public opinion formation. His most recent book,

The Politics of Gay Marriage in Latin America: Argentina, Chile and Mexico, published by Cambridge University Press, was published in Spanish by the Fondo de Cultura Económica in 2018. He held the 2014–15 Peggy Rockefeller Visiting Scholarship at Harvard University.

Benjamin Goldfrank is associate professor and department chair at Seton Hall University's School of Diplomacy and International Relations. He received a PhD in political science at the University of California, Berkeley, in 2002. His research interests focus on the comparative analysis of Latin American politics, especially democratic experiments such as participatory budgeting. He teaches classes on Latin American politics, society, and economic development, as well as U.S. foreign policy on the region. He is the author of *Deepening Local Democracy in Latin America: Participation, Decentralization, and the Left* and co-editor of *The Left in the City: Participatory Local Governments in Latin America*.

Gabriel Kessler is professor of sociology at the Universidad Nacional de La Plata (UNLP) and the Universidad Nacional de San Martin, Argentina, and head researcher at CONICET (National Council of Science and Technology) in Buenos Aires. His research focuses on inequality, violence, and Latin America's social structure. His latest books include *Controversias sobre la desigualdad*, *La sociedad Argentina hoy* (editor), and *Muertes que importan* (with S. Gayol).

Elizabeth Jelin is an Argentine sociologist engaged in research in the areas of human and citizenship rights, social inequalities, gender and the family, social movements, and memories of political repression. She is a senior researcher at the National Council of Scientific and Technical Research (CONICET) in Buenos Aires and professor in the Doctoral Program in the Social Sciences, IDES-UNGS (Universidad Nacional de General Sarmiento). She is the author of numerous books and articles, among them, *State Repression and the Labors of Memory* (2003) and *La lucha por el pasado: Cómo construimos la memoria social* (2017). In 2013, she was awarded the highest prize for scientific achievement in Argentina, the Bernardo Houssay National Prize for her Research Trajectory in the Social Sciences. In 2014, she received a Doctorate Honoris Causa at Université Paris Ouest, Nanterre–La Defense.

Steven Levitsky is professor of government at Harvard University. His research interests include political parties, authoritarianism, and democratization and weak and informal institutions, with a focus on Latin America. He is the author of *Transforming Labor-Based Parties in Latin America: Argentine Peronism in Comparative Perspective* (2003), co-author (with Lucan Way) of *Competitive Authoritarianism: Hybrid Regimes after the Cold War* (2010), and co-editor of *Argentine Democracy: The Politics of Institutional Weakness* (2005), *Informal Institutions and Democracy: Lessons from Latin America* (2006), and *The Resurgence of the Left in Latin America* (2011). He is currently engaged in research on the durability of revolutionary regimes, the relationship between populism and competitive authoritarianism, problems of party building in contemporary Latin America, and party collapse and its consequences for democracy in Peru.

Nora Nagels is assistant professor of political science at the Université de Québec à Montréal (UQAM). Her research is concerned with gender, citizenship, and social policies in Latin America. Nagels has recently published on comparative politics, conditional cash transfers, development, citizenship, and gender in leading journals such as *Social Politics, Social Policy & Administration, Social Policy & Society, Revue internationale de politique comparée*, and *Lien social et Politiques*.

Philip Oxhorn (PhD, Harvard) is professor of political science at McGill University and Founding Director of the Institute for the Study of International Development. He is a recognized expert on democratic development, civil society, international indigenous issues, human rights, and governance. Oxhorn has worked extensively in Latin America, North America, and Africa, and has also worked as a consultant to the Inter-American Development Bank; the United Nations Development Programme; the United Nations Population Fund; the Canadian International Development Agency; the International Development Research Centre; the Department of Foreign Affairs and International Trade, Canada; Department for Aboriginal Affairs and Northern Development, Canada; the Ford Foundation; the Carter Center; the Woodrow Wilson Center for International Scholars; and the Mining Association of Canada.

Roberta Rice is associate professor of Indigenous politics in the Department of Political Science at the University of Calgary, Canada. Her book *The New Politics of Protest: Indigenous Mobilization in Latin America's Neoliberal Era* (University of Arizona Press, 2012) was nominated for the 2014 Comparative Politics prize by the Canadian Political Science Association. Her work has appeared in the *Canadian Journal of Latin American and Caribbean Studies*, *Latin America Research Review*, *Comparative Political Studies*, and *Party Politics*. Rice is currently working on a comparative project on Indigenous rights and representation in Canada and Latin America funded by the Social Sciences and Humanities Research Council of Canada. Her cases include Yukon and Nunavut alongside Ecuador and Bolivia.

Kenneth M. Roberts is Richard J. Schwartz Professor of Government and director of Latin American studies at Cornell University. His research explores the politics of inequality in Latin America, working at the intersection of political parties, populism, and social movements. His most recent work, *Changing Course in Latin America: Party Systems in the Neoliberal Era* (Cambridge University Press, 2014), studies the transformation of party systems and political representation during the critical juncture of market liberalization in the 1980s and 1990s. He is also the author of *Deepening Democracy? The Modern Left and Social Movements in Chile and Peru* (Stanford University Press, 1998), and the co-editor of *The Resurgence of the Latin American Left* (Johns Hopkins University Press, 2011), *The Diffusion of Social Movements* (Cambridge University Press, 2010), and *Beyond Neoliberalism in Latin America: Societies and Politics at the Crossroads* (Palgrave Macmillan, 2009).

Nathalia Sandoval Rojas is a PhD candidate in the Department of Government at the University of Texas at Austin. She graduated in law at the Universidad Nacional in Colombia and has a master's degree in political science from the Universidad de Los Andes. Her work focuses on the impact of judicial decisions on institutions and on citizens' lives, as well as on the relationship between human rights rulings and inequalities.

Celina Van Dembroucke is a PhD candidate in communication studies at McGill University. She received a master's degree in Latin American

Studies at the University of Texas at Austin, where she worked extensively on issues of representation on photographs of people kidnapped by the Argentine military dictatorship in the 1970s. Prior to coming to North America, she studied communication at the Universidad Nacional de Entre Ríos, in Argentina, and worked for several years in human rights NGOs. Her current research deals with media, photography, temporalities of the digital, and the impact of mobile technology in photographic practice, particularly in the Latin American region.

INDEX

CPSIA information can be obtained
at www.ICGtesting.com
Printed in the USA
LVHW082142130120
643535LV00009B/152/P